With Snow on Their Boots

With Snow on Their Boots

The Tragic Odyssey
of the Russian Expeditionary Force
in France during World War I

Jamie H. Cockfield

St. Martin's Press
New York

ISBN 0-312-17356-3

Library of Congress Cataloging-in-Publication Data
Cockfield, Jamie H.
      With snow on their boots : the tragic odyssey of the Russian
  Expeditionary Force in France during World War I / Jamie H. Cockfield.
          p.   cm.
      Includes bibliographical references and index.
      ISBN 0-312-17356-3
      1. Russia.   Armiia. Ekspeditsionnyi korpus vo Frantsii — History
    2. World War, 1914-1918 — Regimental histories — Russia.   I. Title.
    1914-1918 — Regimental histories — Russia.   I. Title.
    D550.C62   1997
    940.4'147 — dc21   97-21440
                                                                          CIP

Design by Acme Art, Inc.
First edition: January 1998

10 9 8 7 6 5 4 3 2 1

To the Memory of

THOMAS TAYLOR HAMMOND

My Teacher, Mentor, and Friend

Contents

Eight pages of photos appear between pages 200 and 201.

Preface

THE GREAT WAR OF 1914 TO 1918, fought in Europe by countries from all over the world, saw the creation of a number of "expeditionary" armies that left their homelands to fight on the Western Front. The British army in the West went by that name, as did the American. Australia and Canada as well had armies in Europe with that appellation. The least known, however, and the one whose history can only be described as a saga, was the Russian Expeditionary Force (REF), two brigades that fought as a unit in France from 1916 until Russia had its own distinctive revolution in 1917. Even after the mutiny of the force in May of that year, fragments of the REF remained in the struggle until the armistice in November 1918. Some of the men even continued to fight in other theaters after the war's end. Unrecognized at the time, the story of these two brigades, known simply as the First and the Third, foretold in a large measure the events to come in their homeland, from the great revolution of 1917 through the civil war that followed. Only the final outcome did not mirror the result of the greater turbulence in Russia itself.

By 1915 the French came to see the teeming Russian masses as a possible antidote for their own hemorrhage of manpower in the trenches. To lure Russian troops there, the French proffered arms to a Russia starved for war matériel on her own front against Germany and Austria. Those Russians who finally went to bolster the Western Front had thus been quite literally "sold for shells," as one memoirist described it. When the revolution occurred in Russia, in their bitterness these soldiers held their own revolution in France.

The social composition of the two brigades differed markedly. Whereas both units revolted, their respective collapse of discipline took dissimilar turns. The first regiment of the First Brigade had been recruited largely from the working-class sections of Moscow, where the men had been exposed to Marxist rhetoric and from where many had at least childhood recollections of the Bolshevik uprising there in December 1905. In time this regiment became quite radical and dictated the actions of the First Brigade. The Third Brigade was, however, taken from rural, peasant elements in western Siberia and was to be much more conservative. The fact that its radicalism was so short-lived prevented a catastrophe of major proportions and provides a contrasting study of revolutionary fever in urban and rural elements. The contradiction in social composition proved decisive when in time these two brigades went to war with each other in the south of France, fighting what was in reality one of the first battles of the Russian Civil War.

It would be practically impossible to acknowledge personally everyone who helped me in this endeavor. For the most part I must anonymously thank the overworked and underpaid librarians and archivists of the numerous institutions in which I did my research: the Archives Nationals in Paris, the Bibliothèque Slave de Paris, the Bibliothèque Tourgenev in Paris, the Bibliothèque Nationale de Paris, the British Library in London, the British Public Record Office, the Russian archive of the Hoover Institution at Stanford University, the Lenin Library in Moscow and the Saltykov-Shchedrin Library in St. Petersburg, the National Archives and the Library of Congress in Washington, D.C., the Duke University Library in Durham, North Carolina, the Woodruff Library at Emory University, and last but not least the Mercer University library on my own campus. I must especially note Ms. Ellen Scruffi of the Bakhmetev Archive in the Butler Library of Columbia University, who so often went way beyond the call of duty, making my work both easier and possible.

To those who read a chapter or two and gave me great advice and guidance, I owe a great debt of gratitude. The length of the work prevented my asking my busy colleagues from reading too much of it, so I never asked anyone to examine more than two chapters. They are the late Carlos Flick, John Dunaway, Robert Good, Wayne Mixon, Tom Scott, Doug Steeples, Dale Steiner, and May McMillan, the latter of whom at great inconvenience read two chapters while she was preparing for very serious surgery. Without their help and guidance, this work would never have been completed. In the same vein, I must thank Michael Flamini, my editor at St. Martin's Press, who provided help, guidance, and encouragement in the work and whose enthusiasm for the project affected even me.

I owe much to Inna Cantou and Igor Simorov of Paris, France, who often had me into their home, fed me, and treated me like a member of their own family, behavior one typically expects of Russians. They continue even now to introduce me to numerous members of the Russian community. I count them as lifelong friends. The late Mr. Mikhail Kolomitsev, a Russian veteran of the Great War who lived in Meudon, France, had me to his home and shared with me his experiences and memories. The former caretaker of the Russian Church and cemetery at Mourmelon-le-Grand, Mr. Dmitri Varenov of St. Nazaire, France, spent an afternoon with me in his apartment, giving me background and guidance. He also answered several questions of mine by mail. Princess Zinaida Shakhovskaia likewise entertained me often when tracing down for me obscure sources and answering many questions that only a leader of the Paris émigré community might know. Dean William Baskin of the American College in Paris gave me much practical advice on how to survive in the French capital.

Especially to be singled out for their help, however, are my good friends Denise and Vladimir Volkoff, now of Bordeilles, France, whose assistance was as catholic as it was extensive: They gave me free of charge their apartment in Paris for many months, they introduced me to the Parisian émigré community, they untiringly advised me on the shades of meaning of both Russian and French words and idioms that only a native speaker might know, and Vladimir assisted me countless times to understand Russian and French military terms and jargon. Without their help, this work might never have been finished. Of course, I assume all responsibility for any errors in meaning and translation.

Two people who must be thanked for a different type of help are Jim Griffin and Tonyia Andrews. Both charted me through the shoals of cyberspace: They cheerfully took my calls (sometimes at home at night) to bail me out when my PC was playing tricks on me, they often came to my office to give me lessons in how to use it, and they went beyond the call of duty to print out the many drafts of the manuscript. In short, they performed countless tasks enabling me to wean myself emotionally from the typewriter and utilize the modern computer.

Finally, I would like to dedicate this work to the memory of Professor Thomas Taylor Hammond, my dissertation director at the University of Virginia. His recent death prevented his ever seeing any part of the manuscript, although I talked with him about it on several occasions. Tom guided and directed my graduate education, often believing in me more than I believed in myself. He was that rare person in one's life who could be described at once as being a teacher, mentor, and friend.

ONE

A Deal Is Struck

December 1915

*The art of war is of vital importance to the state. It is a matter of
life and death, a road either to safety or to ruin. Hence under no
circumstances can it be neglected.*

—Sun Tzu[1]

*The ebb and flow of the Russian armies has the appearance of an
irresistible phenomenon . . . . The wave recedes only to advance.*

—*L'Homme Enchaîné*
February 21, 1915

*The formation of the [Franco-Russian] alliance aroused in me at
first a feeling of amusement, then perplexity, then indignation . . . .*

—Leo Tolstoy[2]

IN THE CHAOTIC DAYS OF EARLY AUGUST 1914, when all across Europe
millions of men rushed off eagerly to war for what would be the last time
in history, a rumor swept Great Britain that troops of their Russian ally
had landed in Scotland on their way to the Western Front. The whole
operation was, of course, a secret, so no one telling of it had actually seen
these Russians; they had only talked to someone who had, or someone
who knew someone who had. These stories manufactured mysterious
trains passing through English villages carrying hordes of Russians
"incognito" to join their British and French comrades to fight the Germans on the Western Front. There were always those who knew of

someone who had seen Russians being fed in Colchester. Others knew of Russians landing in Yorkshire. One person noted that no fewer than 80,000 had passed by rail through Oxford in a single day, making civilian travel difficult. From her bedroom window one enterprising old servant in rural England watched "train after train" full of Russians pass her house at night in the direction of Bristol. Despite the pitch-black dark windows of the carriages, this clever lady had recognized that they were Russians because their cigars and cigarettes provided just enough light for her to see their black beards, an ever-present stereotypical appendage to every Russian in the English imagination of 1914. As the weeks passed the stories fed on themselves, and there continued to be Russian sightings well into October, each one became more fantastic than the last. The most ridiculous account of all, however, was the one in which the first Russians had been identified early in August. Russian soldiers had been "seen" standing on the railroad platform in Edinburgh waiting to entrain for the south. The "person" who had always "seen" these men in those sultry August days had known them to be Russians, the story went, because these soldiers all had had "snow on their boots."[3] Beyond the normal hysteria, the reason for this story is unknown, but a few Russian officers had appeared in Scotland to take up staff positions and buy munitions. Their arrival coincided with the general secret movement of troops, and in this combination the myth was probably born.[4] Yet within less than two years, the myth would become a reality and would give birth to one of the most fantastic episodes of the Great War.

Russia had entered the First World War with the enthusiasm and dedication of a fanatic for the Allied cause. The Russians' attitude in 1914, however, was no different from that of any of the allies on either side. The German soldier fought for what he believed to be the very existence of his national state, forged by the legendary Otto von Bismarck with Emperor Wilhelm I, called "the Great" by everyone except historians, standing in his shadow. The Franco-Russian alliance had been created by the vengeful enemy France to crack Germany like a hapless acorn in its stern pincers. France had been Germany's enemy for centuries. France had left Germany a smoldering ruin in the Thirty Years' War, much of its population butchered. France had invaded it, had conquered it, had subjected the German people to the brutal domination of its kings and even its emperor. Yet centuries of humiliation had been haughtily avenged in 1870 at Sedan, where as Bismarck had so cavalierly wired his wife, "Yesterday, the French lost 100,000 men and an emperor." Not only had the province of Alsace and part of Lorraine been torn from prostrate France, Bismarck had further ground into the dirt the face of the French nation by proclaiming the creation of the German Empire on French soil in the Hall of Mirrors in the Palace of Versailles. Finally the brutal Prussian boot had come down on helpless Paris with a triumphal march down the Champs Elysées, sealing forever a hatred and almost maniacal desire for revenge that would be the holy grail for every French government for the next half century. To defend their fatherland, the Germans of 1914 rallied enthusiastically to their erratic, unstable Emperor Wilhelm II, called "the Great" by no one, least of all historians.

The only reliable ally of the German nation was the polyglot Austro-Hungarian Empire, populated by a dozen or so nationalities, none of which felt any degree of unity for the national state except the Austrian minority, who regarded the other nationalities as conquered, inferior peoples on whom they must force superior Austrian culture. The emperor of this peculiar nation was the octogenarian Emperor Franz Joseph, whose Hapsburg ancestors had forged this empire at the expense of both its Christian and Muslim neighbors, claiming to be the defenders of the former and the implacable foes of the latter. In 1914 everyone realized that this state Benjamin Disraeli had so aptly called "the China of Europe" would hardly survive its emperor's death. He was genuinely loved and admired by most of the various peoples he ruled, and he would be the last emperor to whom the majority of the multi-national population would give its blind allegiance. He alone was the political glue that counteracted the centrifugal forces of nationalism tugging at the heart of Vienna. All knew that on his death his empire would shatter like a stem of Czech crystal into a myriad of pieces, and Wilhelm II knew best of all that the Slavic and Hungarian minorities would then never fight for the cause of the German Empire. Given the belief that war was inevitable sometime in the future, it would best occur while the various nationalities could still be induced to fight for the emperor they loved.

In both Great Britain and France, the war was greeted with the same eagerness seen elsewhere. In France it was the long-sought war of revenge that would right the injustice of 1871. Wild crowds thronged the squares in an almost festival air and shouted, "À Berlin." The tension of half a century had been released. The stain of its lost provinces had been steeped into every French schoolchild, and each knew the day of reckoning would finally come. That long-awaited moment had now arrived. To the British the motives were more complex and less emotional. It was the showdown that had been long coming with the increasingly aggressive Germans, who had insisted on embarking on a policy of colonial empire that necessitated large navies to defend it, and large foreign navies were ipso facto a challenge to the British island nation. Britain's major line of defense had always been that geographic curiosity that the British have had the impertinence to call "the English Channel." In conjunction with its fleet, the Channel had served the nation well, as no successful invasion of Britain had been made in over eight centuries. Yet the German desire in the 1890s to embark on her *Grossflotpolitik*, a plan to build a great navy, had driven Britain into the arms of France, since it is the cardinal tenet of international politics that the enemy of my enemy is my friend. The Entente Cordiale of 1904 was not a firm military alliance but only a diplomatic agreement to support one another's claims in Africa; yet as the years passed and other naval agreements were added, the "friendly under-standing" had virtually hardened into an alliance. Finally Germany's invasion of Belgium was the last straw, and England went to war, ostensibly, over the 1839 treaty of Belgian neutrality. Yet the "scrap of paper," to use German chancellor Theobald von Bethmann-Hollweg's metaphor, had not really catalyzed Britain's entrance into the conflict; rather it had been the equally false notion that England's security could be threatened easily from the Belgian coast. Napoleon had somehow fixed in British minds that Belgium was a pistol pointed at the heart of England, and whereas the French emperor had been unable to launch a successful invasion from even the much closer coast at Calais, the fear was real to the British mind in 1914. To the Englishman living in the twilight of the Edwardian era, the invasion of Belgium was merely the penultimate step to the invasion of his homeland. The British soldier went to war so eagerly that a draft system was not necessary for over a year and was not implemented until 1916.

What of the Russians? When the German Empire declared war on Russia at 7:10 P.M. on August 1, 1914, the Russian capital was in the grip of strikes and general labor unrest. Some have felt that these disturbances were the beginning of a revolution. Yet with the announcement of the German action, there swept spontaneously across Russia a genuine patri-otism and enthusiasm to meet the German threat. The barricades in the workers' sections of St. Petersburg came down. The next day the square before the Winter Palace, which had seen soldiers on Bloody Sunday in 1905 fire on unarmed workers and their families, was filled with loyal subjects. When the emperor appeared on the balcony, that vast heteroge-neous throng of bankers, metalworkers, cobblers, teachers, cab drivers, and even nobles fell spontaneously to their knees and sang "God Save the Tsar" with a volume that must have shaken the very foundation of Tsar Peter's great city. For the first and only time in his reign, Nicholas II was at one with his people, both spiritually and politically. As one puzzled journalist at the time wrote, "Russia is unrecognizable, or rather that haunting beauty of Russia which those of us who lived here . . . feel and love, has suddenly shown forth radiantly from out of the heavy clouds of failure and defeat that had hidden it for so many years."[5]

The alliance for which Russia fought so valiantly was created in the same manner of a dance partnership formed when, after all had chosen their partners, the two left on the sidelines went out on the floor together by default. Both had been left standing by 1890 as a result of a combination of Bismarck's departure and William II's bungling, and a marriage of convenience had been forged unenthusiastically. The two powers had come together solely because each feared isolation, the only interest whatsoever they had in common. Their governments could not have been more divergent politically, and nowhere in the world did they have common interests. Russian imperial activities lay in the Far East and in the Balkans, two parts of the world where the French either had little concern or hardly felt threatened. France was interested in an African empire, a part of the planet from which geography and climate had largely excluded the Russians. France was advanced, progressive, the birthmother of the Enlightenment; Russia still wallowed in a stygian ignorance and economic backwardness that had produced only 45,000 miles of railroad by 1914 for a nation covering one-sixth of the dry land on this globe. Even the younger and much smaller United States had 375,000 miles.

It is easier to see what the French found beneficial in the alliance. France was impressed with the size, and hence military capabilities, of the Russian colossus. In war the Russian hordes would sweep into Germany from the east, assuring French military victory in the West. "The Russian torrent," *Le Figaro* was to call it in the early days of the Great War,[6] and Marshal Ferdinand Foch would refer to Russia's "innumerable reserves" in 1916 after it should have been evident that they did not really exist.[7] France came to place too much confidence in Russian numbers, but as journalist Charles Rivet wrote of the time, "It was impossible to swim against the current, when French newspapers at every possible opportunity wrote fatuously that the 'innumerable *muzhik* [a Russian man],' 'the gigantic forest of Russian bayonets,' etc., constituted the 'greatest force in Europe.'" The French press's constant extolling of the power of Russian numbers came to embarrass even the Russian foreign minister Sergei Sazonov, who was said to have exclaimed, "They are advertising us in a way that would be indecent for a patent tooth powder."[8]

To be sure, the French held no affinity for the Russian giant beyond its ability to be exploited as an ally. "Russia for me is only a diplomatic and military entity," a prewar French ambassador noted, "and the fate of 180 million *muzhiks* does not interest me."[9] To the average Frenchman the absence of democracy, the prisons, the soldiers' whips, and the road to Siberian exile were all of no consequence. All that mattered were the hordes of mythical Cossacks who would sweep westward crushing the German armies, thus enabling France to pick the dual plums of Alsace and Lorraine, which it had lost in a war it did not deserve to win.

The myth of Russian invincibility was as curious as it was inaccurate. Russia alone had won no war against a major power in two centuries. Its one recent military victory, the Russo-Turkish War of 1877-78, had been against the Ottoman Empire, the so-called sick man of Europe, and the conflict had been described by a British journalist as a war between "the one-eyed and the blind." Yet the respect for Russian arms was universal among the British and the Germans as well. Even after the early years of the war showed that the giant had feet of clay, the cry "*Kossaken kommen!*" would send a ripple of fear through any German regiment. The basis of this reputation stemmed from the Seven Years' War in the eighteenth century, when simply due to their vast numbers, the Russians had overwhelmed the superb but smaller forces of Frederick the Great at the battles of Grossjägersdorf and Kunersdorf. They had even been able to take and burn Berlin. It had not mattered that the Russian army of that day was so poorly disciplined that some units had to be brought into battle in chains. The vast numbers and the leaders' insensitivity to their soldiers' slaughter had simply been too much for Frederick's smaller armies to withstand. One British observer of the time noted of the Russian soldiers, "They cannot be defeated. They must be killed."[10] In addition, the brutality of the depraved Russian soldiers on the conquered Prussian provinces of the Seven Years' War added to the fear. Russians wantonly burned villages, destroyed property, and raped the population of both sexes. Their numbers also made a great contribution to Napoleon's defeat a half century later. Thus was born the legend of the invincibility and terror of the Russian steamroller, despite much evidence to the contrary. The pitiful performance of the Russian military machine in the Crimean and the Russo-Turkish War of 1877-78 did nothing to tarnish the belief in the might of the Russian juggernaut. Add the damning evidence from the Russo-Japanese War of 1904-5, and one wonders why Frenchmen had any faith in the Russian alliance.

Also puzzling is why no one had taken into account the invention of high-explosive shells, rapid-fire artillery, machine guns, and an assortment of other instruments of destruction not available to Frederick the Great's generals. These new weapons of death could render impotent large numbers of men, especially those who did not themselves widely possess these weapons. The Russian general staff itself was taken with the myth of Russian numbers, and Vladimir Sukhomlinov, the Russian minister of war in 1914, had once sternly admonished professors at the Russian war college for teaching the superiority of firepower over the bayonet and the saber.[11] Soldiers themselves were taught that their chief weapon was "the breast of the living soldier," as one told the British Russian expert Sir Bernard Pares.[12] Yet the "breast of the living soldier" would prove defenseless against the machine gun. Furthermore, the Russian war machine so poorly armed was further weakened, as Charles Rivet put it, "by the incompetence of the governors and the growing discontent of the governed."[13] This crippled structure would be exposed shortly after the war began on the battlefields of East Prussia and Poland. Yet despite all the evidence, the French continued in the pre-war years to have supreme faith in the Russian army, just as they would view the Maginot Line as invincible two and a half decades later.

The famous *rouleau compresseur* in which the French placed so much confidence consisted of 114 infantry divisions, but that "great, gray slope of men," as Tennyson called it, was, with modern weaponry aside, a decidedly inferior institution due to generally poor leadership and a rank and file, over half of whom were illiterate. One authority on the Great War has noted that the Russian infantry could hardly execute the simplest maneuvers.[14] The infantryman was dressed in a calf-length gray-brown overcoat, a peasant shirt of the same color called a *rubashka*, belted at the waist with military pants tucked into knee-high boots. Greased linen or cotton footcloths took the place of socks. Each soldier was armed with a 7.62-mm. repeating rifle about six feet long and weighing nine and a half pounds. With the regulation amount of ammunition and other equipment, the Russian soldier went into battle weighted down with a burden of almost sixty pounds.[15]

The astute observer Leon Trotsky noted that an army is always a copy of the society it serves, with the difference that it gives social relations a concentrated character, carrying both their positive and negative features to an extreme. He then added, "It is no accident that the war did not create one single distinguished military name in Russia."[16] Although the war created no Russian Fochs or Joffres, it did reveal a number of competent, intelligent leaders, who under a different system and commanding troops that were well supplied with modern weapons might have become generals of Ferdinand Foch's caliber. Yet on the whole, the creator of the Red Army is correct in his characterization of the mediocrity of the Russian officer corps. The institution did not generally lend itself to the promotion of talent. One Russian general of the time rather accurately portrayed the Russian military leadership as being plagued with "much adventurism, much ignorance, much egotism, intrigue, careerism, greed, mediocrity and lack of foresight, and very little knowledge, talent or desire to risk life, or even comfort and health."[17] The buddy system prevailed, as it does in any society, yet with the general sycophancy and antidemocratic nature of the prewar Russian nation, the result was disastrous. An example can be made from a conversation between General Feodor F. Palitsyn, who later figures prominently in our story, and Grand Duke Andrei Vladimirovich in 1915, on the eve of the fall of Warsaw to the Germans. When the grand duke asked Palitsyn what the high command planned to do to save Warsaw, Palitsyn replied that he did not know. Pressed further, he told the grand duke that there were "some good, very excellent ideas," but when asked if they planned to attack, the most amazing conversation ensued:

"No, that's absolutely impossible."

"Then you mean to stand?" the grand duke continued.

"Good God, no! When we make a stand, they can hit us wherever they wish."

"Then you mean we must retreat?"

"God save us," Palitsyn replied. "How can we retreat? According to all theories, you lose more during a retreat than during an attack."

"So what are we going to do?" Andrei Vladimirovich asked in amazement.

"I don't know," was Palitsyn's reply, "but there are some very good, very excellent ideas."[18]

Even taking into consideration that Palitsyn might have merely been telling the grand duke to mind his own business, the anecdote has a true ring about it. Many similar examples of incompetence have been told too often for ineptitude not to have been a dominant element within the army of the tsar.

Moreover, there existed a veritable chasm between the officers and the men, as well as a rigid sense of hierarchy within the officer corps itself. The officers treated the common infantryman little better than a slave, and the soldiers' whole relationship with the officer in charge was one of humiliation and subservience far beyond the normal requirements of military discipline. When in time the soldiers' fear turned to hatred, this distance between officers and men made reconciliation, to say nothing of the reestablishment of control, impossible. Yet if the leadership was poor and the Russian military methods antiquated, the Russian soldier did in part compensate for these shortcomings. Of the physical qualities and sheer bravery that comprise a good soldier, the common Russian infantryman was unexcelled by any European counterparts.

Twentieth-century liberalism demands that we not speak of a peoples' national characteristics, fatuously reasoning that doing so results in the unavoidable corollary that suggesting differences among ethnic groups implies that one is somehow inferior to the other. No reasonable person should accept the latter part of the premise any more than he should ignore the first. Being reared with the confines of a culture cannot help but produce a general *Weltanschauung* in an individual. It has nothing to do with the blood in the individual's veins, intellect, or the color of eyes or skin. It is simply a collection of mental attitudes derived from exposure from childhood to certain values and ideas. For example, Russians are extraordinarily generous. They are warm and wonderful to the individual stranger but very suspicious of the collective, anonymous foreigner and his motives. Maurice Paléologue, an astute observer of the Russian scene, noted that gentleness is a major part of the Russian national temperament. He felt that the Russian had no bellicose instincts and possessed a "very warm heart." They never glorified war. They are charitable. For a *muzhik* to refuse alms to anyone asking him "in the name of Christ" means that he is absolutely penniless.[19] Sometimes cruelty will surface in a Russian but only under sudden stress when he is threatened. Then he will sometimes lash out with an animal-like fury, only to become gentle again when the threat has passed. Add to these traits an unfathomable religious faith flavored with almost pagan superstition, a fairy-tale concept of a tsar, and the absence of anything that could be described as formal education, one has the basic composition of the Russian foot soldier who marched off to war in 1914. This naive, trusting figure knew no fear, would hesitate at no battle challenge.

Almost everyone summoned to the banners of the tsar's army went gladly, and thousands not summoned sought to enlist. Millions died without hesitation in assaulting enemy trenches that they could not possibly have taken with the weapons they had, and hundreds of thousands died attacking positions of the enemy with no weapons at all. They advanced without questioning until their bodies lay in giant hecatombs of human flesh entangled in the barbed wire before the German machine guns. Had this marvelous raw material been properly trained, well armed with the most modern weapons, and led by officers they loved and respected, they would have reached Berlin long before the British and the French had ever reached the Rhine.

Such was not to be the case. The Russian leadership thought of its soldiers as natural warriors not in need of much formal training beyond some rifle instruction, basic drill, and the teaching of discipline. The latter was maintained with brutal, inhuman punishments worthy of an earlier time.[20] Yet this "training" produced some of the most obedient, unquestioning soldiers of the twentieth century. The only counterpart that might rival their devotion was the automatons of Nazi Germany, and it is highly doubtful that even the soldiers of the Third Reich would have submitted to the needless slaughter in the one-sided fight that the Great War Russians endured for as long as they did.

These traits and training produced a Russian soldier whom Colonel, later General, A. W. Knox, who spent the entire war with the Russian army and then wrote two volumes about it, described as being "very much like an Indian buffalo." He would go anywhere he was guided or pushed but would not wander into uncomfortable places on his own.[21] The London *Times* embroidered on this theme by writing that the Russian soldier was "about the simplest human animal that has survived the process of civilization," mainly because civilization had not been successful in spoiling him. The Russian *muzhik*, it said, with his blind obedience and unreasoning reverence for the tsar, is "finer material than more highly trained troops of other nations. He fights like a lion for the pay of a drudge," the article went on in praise, "and his pension, when he returns broken from the war, would be ludicrous if it were not . . . coupled with a license to beg . . . ." Noting that the Russian soldier was religious, the *Times* added that he was "intemperate if given the chance" but "fights quite valiantly without his vodka." His speech is "rarely obscene and never blasphemous," yet his talk is that of a little child." Although he thinks slowly, he is most curious and eager to learn. "He is stoic to pain." In concluding, the *Times* fingered a major component of the Russian soldier's loyalty: his blind devotion to the tsar for whom he would "fight against the evil one himself. The *muzhik* will always lay down his life for the tsar unquestioningly. He will not ask the reason why. Of such is the kingdom of Russia!"[22] The New York *Times* interviewed a German officer that same year on the various characteristics of the soldiers of the various enemy nationalities. Of the Russian, the officer said, "The Russian [soldier] is terrible . . . . They come in lines ten and twelve deep . . . so controlled by their own momentum that they cannot stop. They will go anywhere into anything again and again, as if they did not know how to be afraid." The only thing one can do, the German officer added, was "to slaughter them and pray you will have ammunition enough to keep it up . . . ."[23]

The Russian summer of 1914 was highly unusual. The heat was intense in a climate usually given to pleasant days and cool nights. Mysterious swarms of dragonflies filled the vast land for the first time and hung like storm clouds over the seemingly endless fields of wildflowers that grew in such great profusion that year. Wildfires ran out of control throughout the northern forests and in the peat bogs, creating a dense smoke that hung over both St. Petersburg and Moscow, casting a pall over Russia's capitals. In the villages peasants shook their heads and said, "This bodes no good."[24] When word reached the countryside in August that Russia and Germany had gone to war, rural folk noted that they had seen it coming.

The Great War of 1914 to 1918 is one of the more curious events in the history of mankind. Oceans of ink have been used to debate its causes, the validity of any of which can be diminished when it is realized that the war that occurred was not the war the soldiers and diplomats, emperors and kings, prime ministers and presidents thought they were starting. It was generally believed that the "next war" would be a short struggle of rapid mobility, for after all, had not all wars for a century been short? "Home before the leaves fall" the soldiers all shouted to their families in August 1914 as they marched toward an enemy who felt the same way. Both sides prayed to the same god for victory, with the equal assurance that that god was on their side. Like helpless actors in a play the script of which they seemed to have no role in writing, the leaders of the nations in 1914 helplessly played their parts as hourly Europe lurched toward war until all the major countries on the continent were sucked into a gigantic maelstrom that lasted for a horrendous 1,561 days, toppled four monarchies, destroyed a centuries-old social structure, decimated thousands of towns and villages, and left a number of dead that God alone could count. As for the misery the war caused, it cannot begin to be calculated. The dead can be buried and forgotten and the villages rebuilt, but for the survivors the mental scars could not be erased except by death.

Since all people recognized for half a century that this war "had" to be fought, each side had a scheme to fight it. The French plan was called, rather unoriginally, Plan 17, since it had been the seventeenth one concocted since 1871. It called for a dramatic lunge into the heart of Germany, relying heavily on French élan, which Colonel, later General, Louis de Grandmaison had taught the French general staff would somehow carry the day against German machine guns and the most deadly new inventions of the giant Krupp Works of Essen. Russia had two plans, A and G, for Austria and Germany respectively, identifying the nation to receive the brunt of the much vaunted "steamroller." Activation of each would depend on the early actions of their respective enemies. Germany's was by far the most daring. Named the Schlieffen Plan after its creator, General Alfred von Schlieffen, it called for avoiding an attack through the Alsace-Lorrainian frontier, which the French had heavily fortified. Instead, Schlieffen suggested a holding action there of two armies on the Franco-German border, while the major force of five armies, seven times as powerful as the static force, would push through unsuspecting Belgium, Luxembourg, and the panhandle of Holland, making a wide sweeping arc to the south and west of Paris, swinging through France like a scythe and outflanking the French armies, which would be expected to be concentrated in the direction of the German frontier. The unfortunate French would be then smashed between the flanking force and the static force in Alsace-Lorraine. Schlieffen had reckoned that to accomplish this dynamic manoeuver would take virtually all the forces that Germany could mobilize, and he allotted the drive in the West only six weeks to complete the defeat of France. Then Germany would turn these victorious forces eastward, where they would then defeat the slower-moving Russians, who would take, Schlieffen figured, at least six weeks to place an army into the field. The architect of this grand scheme died in 1913 and, supposedly, in his death delirium, had whispered in his last moments of life "to keep the right wing strong." The plan was changed, however, by his successor Helmut von Moltke "the Younger," the nephew of the great Helmut von Moltke of Franco-Prussian War fame. The elder Moltke was probably the only German military leader since Frederick the Great who could have made Schlieffen's plan work. The younger, on the other hand, was not the leader his uncle had been. He was somewhat less decisive and infinitely more sensitive, and the changes he made in the plan after the war began came to be its undoing. He reduced the superiority between the "hammer" and the "anvil" from seven to one, as Schlieffen had outlined, to three to one. While this alteration may have destroyed any chance for success, the unforeseen actions of France's ally Russia proved equally decisive.

When the war began, the French commander-in-chief, the phlegmatic General Joseph Joffre, had dutifully launched Plan 17 and had calmly watched the French armies unsuccessfully batter themselves bloody against the German defenses in Lorraine. He had early ignored the admonitions of General Charles Landrezac, commander of the Fifth Army at the Belgian frontier, that the major thrust of the German army was coming through Belgium. When the usually unflappable Joffre finally realized that Landrezac was right, it was almost too late, because all that stood between Paris and the major thrust of the German army was the already mauled Fifth Army, which had been double-teamed by the German Second and Third Armies at Charleroi on August 22-23.

Methodically and expertly Joffre finally shifted troops westward and France was saved.

At this point a second change was made in the Schlieffen plan, which ended any chance for victory. France's Russian ally had mobilized much more quickly than Schlieffen had thought possible, and by the third week in August two Russian armies were crossing the East Prussian frontier in a pincer movement designed to crush the German Eighth Army, which Schlieffen had placed in the East as the only insurance against any unexpected Russian offensive. Since either of the two Russian armies was larger than the one German force in the East, von Moltke panicked. It would make little difference for the Germans to take Paris if the Russians reached the banks of the Elbe. To guard against this possibility, von Moltke removed several corps eastward from the "hammer." When Joffre finally laid down his dinner fork and issued his ringing call to stand on the Marne, the Germans no longer held a large numerical superiority on the Western Front. After a week of battle, the German army began to retreat, "inflecting" its right wing "to the rear," as the official communiqué read,[25] and the so-called miracle of the Marne had occurred. Yet a large part for the price of the victory had been paid by the Russian ally whose early, hastily executed offensives in the East had so jolted von Moltke's nerve. The results were the disastrous Russian defeats of General Alexander Samsonov's army at Tannenberg and General Pavel Rennenkampf's army at the Masurian Lakes in August and September 1914. Bismarck's fear of a two-front war had proved valid, and even in death he was once again proved right. As for the French, all of the effort to create and maintain the Franco-Russian alliance, all the money loaned, all of the business ventures tried had been worth it. The Russian offensive in the East was undeniably a major factor in the French victory on the Marne.

The Russians had been pleased to play the sacrificial role they would be called on to play so often in the Great War. The Russian foreign minister Sazonov told Maurice Paléologue, "Samsonov's army has been destroyed [at Tannenberg] . . . . We owed this sacrifice to France as she had showed herself a perfect ally."[26] When Pierre Marquis de Laguiche, the French liaison officer with the Russian general staff, expressed sympathy for the Russian defeat at Tannenberg to the Grand Duke Nicholas Nicholaevich, the commander-in-chief of the Russian armed forces, the Russian leader merely replied, "We are happy to make such sacrifices for our allies."[27] In 1917 the foreign minister of the Russian Provisional government, Michael Tereshchenko, stressed this sacrifice when he told Sir George Buchanan, the British ambassador, that

"France, he was sure, would never forget that Russia had sacrificed 300,000 men to save Paris . . . ."[28]

When Russia formally left the war in 1918, however, France did forget, but its generals did not. Joffre wrote after the peace had been signed that when he learned on the evening of August 18 that the Warsaw and Wilno armies would go on the offensive the next day, he was delighted. "Russia was surpassing all our expectations . . . ," he wrote. "For this act of comradeship-in-arms . . . the tsar's army and the Grand Duke Nicholas had a right to France's undying gratitude."[29] General Foch, who would eventually receive the German surrender, was even more emphatic: ". . . we could not forget our allies on the Eastern Front, the Russian army, which by its energetic intervention, had drawn upon itself a large portion of the enemy's forces and had thus enabled us to achieve the victory on the Marne."[30] A Russian historian writing in Paris in the 1930s quotes Foch as saying "If France has not been wiped off the map of Europe, it is above all to Russia that we owe it."[31] General Maxime Weygand, who in World War II would have reason to appreciate an ally that would relieve pressure on a beleaguered France, asked rhetorically in his memoirs after the Second World War, "What could have been achieved on the Marne, or even at Verdun, without the counterweight and action of the Russian armies?"[32] Albert Thomas, the French minister of munitions in 1916-1917, also shared a favorable opinion of Russia's role at the Marne.[33]

The major component in the Russian sacrificial action had been Tsar Nicholas II's dedication to the Allied cause. Marshal Foch had spent a great deal of time with him in 1910, and he came away from the sojourn feeling that Nicholas was a sovereign of "unshakable integrity." Foch felt sure as to the use the tsar would make of the army at his disposal, but the French general left Russia with the feeling that it was prudent to base French dependency on its ally on things of which they could be certain and not on the intentions Nicholas expressed.[34] At Tannenberg that intention had proved to be worth much more than Foch could ever have imagined.

The war, however, had progressed only a few months before Russia developed a more alarming shortage that would make it even more dependent on its allies. Joffre had inquired about Russian preparedness as recently as September and had been informed that Russia had the resources for a long war.[35] On December 18, 1914, however, as the Russians were just yielding to the Germans the great textile city of Lodz in Poland, General Mikhail Beliaev, the chief of staff at the Russian war ministry, informed Paléologue and the British ambassador, Sir George

Buchanan, that although there were sufficient men to replace losses, due to a lack of rifles and munitions, France and Britain could not expect their ally to go on the offensive before the spring.[36] The French had assumed that by that time the Russians would have long been bivouacked in Berlin! Beliaev had said that the Russian armies needed 45,000 rounds of ammunition a day, while the maximum Russian output was 13,000. Furthermore, the Russians had 800,000 men in uniform with no rifles with which to train them. Beliaev noted that steps were being taken to increase national output and orders were being placed abroad, but for the next few months, the military situation would not only be difficult but dangerous.[37] The two diplomats were stunned by the news. An exasperated Paléologue wrote in his diary, "I learned yesterday that the Russian artillery is short of shells! This morning I learned that the infantry is short of rifles."[38]

Russia's unpreparedness for the Great War was not a malady of that country alone. None of the nations was ready in 1914 for the war they had so eagerly entered, for no one had any idea that it would last as long as it did nor consume the mountains of resources that it devoured. The major difference between the Russian problems and those of the other powers was that once it became obvious that Russia could not sustain a major effort at the current level of industrial productivity, it was unable to adapt to a war industry. French, British, and German industry moved quickly to shift factories from consumer to war productivity. Russian industry, in peacetime way behind Western counterparts in production and efficiency, fell further behind under the strain of war, and very early shortages reached alarming proportions. In the fall of 1914 Mikhail Rodzianko, the president of the Russian Duma, visited the front and learned firsthand from Grand Duke Nicholas just how bad the situation was: "I have no rifles, no shells, no boots . . . ," the grand duke told the Duma president. "Go back to Petrograd and get my army shod . . . . My troops cannot fight barefoot."[39] Russian factories produced only 165 machine guns a month in the fall of 1914; while the number grew to 1,200 per month by December 1916, the output remained woefully inadequate. Shells needed for the artillery, the part of the defense system not considered very important before the war, had been estimated then at what would seem to be the adequate number of 500,000 per month. After the battles of August 1914, the calculation was tripled and then doubled again at a time when the Russian shell production was hovering around only 35,000 per day, or slightly over a million a month.

The area of weaponry with the most serious early deficiencies was in rifles. By the first December of the war, soldiers were already ordered if wounded to give their rifles and cartridges to a noncommissioned officer or to any other soldier before going to the rear to be treated. Troops had few rifles with which to train, and many were sent to the front unarmed. When training rifles were available, they were often obsolete Berdan relics from the Russo-Turkish War of 1877, and even then there was only one rifle to every ten draftees.[40] Many had to fight unarmed until they could pick up the rifle of a fallen comrade. The overall problem was exacerbated by the soldiers' careless treatment of their weapons. In retreat they often threw them away, and when in camp rifles substituted for tent poles and as coverings over their trenches. In an effort to counter this waste, the military leadership offered bonuses of six rubles for each Russian and five roubles for each Austrian rifle retrieved. Yet the use of foreign weapons, both captured and imported, created a supply nightmare. A battalion might have sprinkled among its ranks ten different rifles, making ammunition supply virtually impossible. It was mid-1915 before Russian rifle factories were producing even as many as 40,000 standard weapons a month.[41] In the summer of 1915 Alexei Polivanov, the Russian minister of war, confided in his diary, "Rifles are now more precious than gold."[42]

At first, the Russians pretended to the French that they had plenty of arms, but then puzzled their ally by a request for rifles. In a cabinet meeting on February 2, 1915, Abel Ferry, a French undersecretary of state, reported that although Russia claimed to have 1,200,000 rifles in reserve, it was asking France for rifles to arm one and a half million men. An attaché present reported that France's inability to supply this number had caused an air of desperation among the Russian military. Ferry wrote in his journal, "A month ago it was announced from Russia that she had five million rifles. Between five million and 1,200,000—where is the truth?"[43] From this point until the Russian military collapse in 1917, Russia was largely dependent on its allies for war matériel, was chronically short of fighting equipment, and because of it suffered staggering losses unknown to the other belligerents. This dependency forced Russia to make military sacrifices to please its allies in order to keep the trickle of supplies coming. Russia became the horse of the alliance, with Britain and France the most demanding riders, spurring on their ally to attempt impossible feats, leaving the blood of a Russian generation on the battlefields of Poland and Galicia and laying the basis for the "jolt from the outside" that would bring the revolution.[44]

Early 1915 saw little improvement. By the summer of that year, the Russian artillery department had placed orders with Russian artillery firms for about 9,000 field guns but had received only 88. One recent researcher has noted that Russia could not produce an average of two artillery shells a day for each gun. Only a 1,000 rifles a day were made when the army need was three to six times that number.[45] Joffre claims in his memoirs that, in 1915, the French started sending the Russians 2,000 76-mm shells a day, reaching 100,000 for the month of May alone and 225,000 for June and the months following.[46] These figures seem a bit high if for no other reason than the difficulty, if not outright impossibility, of shipping this number monthly to Russia. Moreover, at the time of the great retreat on the Eastern Front in 1915, weapons factories could replace only one of every three lost rifles, and the Russian general staff estimated that it would need up to 2 million rifles to cover the losses and to arm new recruits that year. Privation had been so great that in a report in January 1916, General Mikhail Alexeev, the Russian chief of staff, felt it noteworthy to mention that the rifle situation had improved to the point that 70 percent of front-line troops now had rifles. Yet by the end of 1915 Russian munitions factories produced only half of the monthly need of 200 million cartridges. When the war began, Russian arsenals had only around 500 cartridges stored for each rifle. The reserve did not reach that level again until mid-1917,[47] when the army could no longer perform as an effective fighting force. After the 1915 retreat, the Russian army needed 3,000 new pieces of heavy artillery, yet between August and the end of October, Russia's factories delivered fewer than 800, and they produced less than half of the shells needed for these guns.[48] In desperation, the Russian government ordered all Russians in Petrograd in November 1915 to surrender to the police any rifles in their possession for use at the front.[49]

It is not surprising that in its critical condition Russia should have called on its allies, who must have appeared to have overabundant resources. As early as the spring of 1915 hard negotiations ensued between Lord Herbert Kitchener, the British secretary of war, and Grand Duke Sergei Romanov, the inspector general of the artillery.[50] In November Major James M. Blair, acting British military attaché in Russia, called for an immediate shipment of 150,000 rifles with 400 rounds of ammunition for each. He had spoken with General Polivanov and Alexander Guchkov, a Duma member involved in military affairs, and both were "very anxious that we should see our way to dispatching these rifles immediately."[51] In October the French and Russians signed a protocol stating that the French government would continue to make monthly advances to Russia for payments for munitions manufactured in France at the most favorable prices.[52] At an Allied conference in London in November, Thomas asserted that France had sent Russia almost 400,000 rifles in the last few weeks, and furthermore the French minister of munitions pledged one-third of all 4.2 Howitzer production for 1916 to the Russians.[53] A report in the French archives shows a breakdown of 39,000 1907-model rifles promised out of a reserve of 316,826 rifles in French arsenals, in addition to 80,000 Kropatchek repetition rifles already given and 300,000 of the 1874 nonconverted rifles. The English had supplied the Russians with 60,000 rifles and over 15 million cartridges.[54] To these were added 120,000 Winchesters from the United States, a number from Japan, and 300,000 Vetterlis from Italy.[55]

From this point onward, the archives are flooded with mind-numbing list of shells of various sizes, rifles, cartridges, revolvers, barrels of black powder and saltpeter, cannons, and all sorts of instruments of destruction designated by the French to be shipped to their ally. How much of the listed matériel ever arrived on the Eastern Front is impossible to say. It can be stated with certainty only that the British were able to help little, being barely able to meet the minimum needs of their own army,[56] and the French bore the brunt of supplying their Russian ally. The shipments did not, however, constitute gifts. The Russian allies bought each shipment that left Brest or Le Havre for Murmansk if by no other means but by French loans. Even the tsar spent his fortune deposited in British banks on armaments, leaving himself impoverished had he ever been successful in escaping to the West,[57] and rendering meaningless the tales of Romanov treasure in British banks.

Yet the problem was never completely solved, and the Russian paucity of weaponry was never completely corrected despite the gigantic quantities of war matériel finally produced by the Russian war effort or shipped by the Allies. Alexeev noted in mid-1916 that the shell output, especially for the larger guns, presented a "quite hopeless picture,"[58] and by the end of 1916, there were only two heavy guns for each half mile of front. In France, by contrast, there were twelve pieces of heavy artillery for the same length of trench. A Soviet scholar has determined that during the war, the Russian army fired four times fewer shells than the French forces and three and a half times fewer than the English.[59]

The demand on the Western Allies was, therefore, maintained, and between May and December 1916, the Russians placed orders in the West for almost 40 million shells. If French archival sources are to be believed, the Russians received an incredible 23 million of those, a highly unlikely figure.[60] Russian archives cite about 8 million three-inch shells having come from France by January 1917, with 740 guns of all calibers, plus a stunning 8.4 million hand grenades, 796 airplanes, and 1,884 vehicle engines.[61] At any rate, the Russian demand was apparently so great that in the summer of 1916 the French began to lie about their shell production in order to stop sending so many. Although the French government publication on the French army in the First World War reported 57,500 per day, the French claimed to their Russian ally that their daily output was only 10,000.[62]

While Russia had a shortage of weapons, its French allies quickly faced a deficit of their own for which no amount of increased industrial production could fulfill: an acute shortage of men. Since the French had last fought a major war, new and more deadly weapons of destruction had been devised. Moreover, to make matters worse, they had decided that the sluggish action of their armies had cost them defeat in 1870, and by the outbreak of the Great War the French planners had fallen under the spell of the aforementioned General Grandmaison, who had convinced the general staff that what the French called élan, the spirit of offensive attack à outrance, was the only certain recipe for victory in the next war. The spirit of attack, attack, attack would carry the day. The entire rationale of Plan 17 was based on it. All French soldiers were trained in it, taught to believe in it, and hundreds of thousands of them eventually died because of it. Grandmaison had somehow overlooked the introduction into warfare of the machine gun, and when French soldiers in their red and blue uniforms attacked shoulder to shoulder in the battles of the Frontiers (August 6-September 5, 1914), élan proved to be a poor weapon. The spirit of attack of 1914 would have served that nation very well in 1940, just as General Maurice Gamelin's policy of defensism in the Second World War would have stopped the German attack in the first with many Frenchmen's lives being spared in the fields of Lorraine and Champagne. Mankind always begins fighting the current war like he fought the last one, until events prove so brutal or disastrous as to convince him that he must change. Winston Churchill placed French casualties in the Battles of the Frontiers and the Marne, losses between August 6 and September 5, at a staggering 330,000 killed, wounded, and missing in action, with the so-called race to the sea, Artois, and Yser adding another 125,000. Stabilization of the front between December 1914 and January 1915, added another 74,000, for a total of 538,000 casualties in the first six months of the war.[63] A more recent study citing the figures of a special commission assigned to assess French casualties puts the number at 581,167 from the outbreak of the war to November 20, 1914.[64] By the time the butchery ended in 1918, France had sustained losses of almost 1,400,000 killed with wounded, captured, and missing bringing the total to almost 6 million casualties, or about 30 percent of the entire male population of all ages.

One horrifying account gives the story of a class of 100 boys who graduated from high school in May 1914. All but one of the class was drafted after the outbreak of the war, and by December, all ninety-nine had been killed. The one survivor had not been taken into the army because of an illness, but he joined later and eventually lost his life as well. In his memoirs German General Eric von Ludendorff, the warlord of Germany by 1918, commented that by 1916, France had already "given her children."[65] As a result of its stupendous casualty list, from very early in the war France had come to believe that more was needed from its ally Russia. As early as mid-September 1914, when Russia had just sustained the staggering defeats in East Prussia—saving France in the process— French president Raymond Poincaré wrote in his war diary that France would want "at least" to be relieved by Russia from the pressure that was on them, as though Russia was not doing its part.[66] This attitude continued to the end of the war and for some years after. To the French mind, Russia could never sacrifice enough, and France would always be willing to fight to the last drop of Russian blood. It was in this vein of thought that the idea of the Russian Expeditionary Force in France was born: The seemingly endless millions of *muzhiks* could be armed by the superior French armaments industry and sent to bolster the flagging French efforts somewhere on the French front from Flanders to Champagne.

The idea of some Russian troops in the West had already been suggested as early as October 1914, by a Major Campbell, a British representative to the Russian General Staff, to General Sukhomlinov. Campbell had felt that it would simply be good politics to station some Russian unit, especially a Cossack regiment, in England. Sukhomlinov liked the idea and authorized sending one Cossack company there,[67] but Lord Kitchener replied that, although he was very grateful for the Russian offer, he felt that cavalry would not function well on the Anglo-French theater and suggested instead the dispatch of infantry.[68] The image of Russian, French, and British soldiers fighting shoulder to shoulder would be an excellent impetus for Allied morale, and Campbell's suggestion may have come to him from someone in the British government, since the question had been bandied about there in August, possibly as a result of the story of Russians having already landed. The British government suggested three corps to be sent by way of the northern Russian port of Archangel on the White Sea in British bottoms, but the Russian government's response was negative because of the potential difficulties of climate, German submarines, and the slowness of transfer.[69] Another historian gives Sir George Buchanan the credit for recommending the plan in August 1915, although Buchanan makes no such claims in his memoirs nor is there any evidence in British archives.[70] In September 1915, when Bulgaria began making minatory noises for the invasion of

Serbia, the Serbian prime minister, Nicola Pasic, called on France to pressure Russia to send troops to Macedonia to impress Bulgaria and intimidate it into remaining neutral. Sazonov had told Paléologue that he knew nothing of any Russian plans to send troops to the Balkans, but Paléologue had thought the idea a good one and that Russia might also bolster naval activity off the Bulgarian coast.[71] David Lloyd George, soon to become British prime minister, also suggested a joint Allied force earlier in the year to Peter Bark, the Russian minister of finance, when the latter was visiting London. Bark had been impressed and had wired the Russian prime minister Ivan Goremykin that such an action would result in a declaration of war against the Central Powers by Greece, Romania, and Bulgaria. The Russian minister told Goremykin, "Such an army pushing against Austria . . . [would] ease our move into Silesia [and would] draw troops from the French front . . . ."[72]

If Russian ministers generally agreed to the merits of a joint Western venture, the Russian general staff did not. Questioning the competence of the politicians to judge such matters, General Nicholas Yanushkevich, the chief of staff of the commander-in-chief of the Russian army, sent a sharp note to Goremykin to that effect, adding "Please don't set this business in motion without consulting us. This is not the affair of Seignor [sic] Izvolsky."[73] Hostility from the general staff, coupled with Greek opposition, killed the matter for the time being, but the notion helped nurture the seeds for later.

Even as the discussions had gotten underway secretly in Petrograd, French publicist André Chéradame heard that Russians were to be brought as workers to France and wrote the minister of war to suggest instead that they be brought as soldiers. In a memoir entitled "How to Create a Reservoir of Russian Infantry in France," he referred to the Russians as "Human masses . . . vigorous and very desirous of doing battle against the *nemets* [German], the hated German," adding that their physical resistance was "enormous" and that their "adaptive ability" and "natural intelligence" were much greater "than is imagined in the West."[74]

Nothing was then decided, but throughout 1915 the British and the French continued to ponder the question of how to utilize to the maximum Russia's immense human resources. The problem of effectives on the French front had been disturbing, and Joffre noted that if a major German attack took place, France would be obliged to call the Class of 1916 (men turning eighteen in 1916) early. This problem, Joffre noted, was the origin of the "ingenious idea" of asking the Russians "whose lack of armaments prevented her from using a large part of her men" to send troops to the French front, where the French would arm and employ them.[75] A report in the papers of Paul Painlevé, the mathematician turned politician and the French minister of war in 1917, summed up the idea completely: "Unfortunately the effectives are in Russia, the matériel is in Western Europe."[76] Of the two, the shortage of arms was the more crucial. The Russians were in the more desperate situation, a fact that did not go unnoticed by the French. That position was underscored by the appearance in London and Paris of a group of Russian army and naval officers that became known as the Munitions Delegation. The group came accompanied by the ubiquitous Alfred Knox, arriving in London in early December after a journey of over five weeks. After meeting with and being greatly impressed by Lloyd George, at that time the British minister of munitions, they went to Paris, and from there to Chantilly to press their needs on Joffre and Foch, the latter of whom duly made notes of Russian shortages.[77] If the French had any doubts of Russia's desperate condition, the pleas of this group certainly removed them.

Shortly after the Russian delegation departed for the West, the new French prime minister, Aristide Briand, acted. Apparently having little difficulty in getting the cabinet to accept the infusion of Russian blood on the Western Front, Briand wired the French embassy in Petrograd on November 12, 1915, that he wished to send Senator Paul Doumer, a former prime minister and president of the Chamber of Deputies, to discuss the possibility of sending Russians to fight literally on the side of their French allies "to determine certain questions which deal with the closest collaboration of France and Russia in the present war." The senator would be accompanied, the French embassy was informed, by "a French general."[78] A man of Doumer's stature had been chosen because in the most recent rash of ministerial leapfrog that had plagued the Third Republic, Prime Minister René Viviani and Foreign Minister Théophile Delcassé had just been replaced by Briand, who held both portfolios, and the French government wanted to stress to the Russians that this shakeup would not result in any lessening of resolve. Doumer, who had also been governor general of Indochina, president of the Budget Commission, and chef du cabinet civil to General Joseph Gallièni of taxicab army fame, would become a powerful porte-parole lending to the cause all the moral authority necessary. Apparently to give additional punch to his mission, the Russians were not informed in advance of why Doumer was coming; the French feared that had they known the purpose of the visit, they might have stopped it.[79] On November 24, 1915, shortly before the Russian munitions delegation arrived, Doumer departed for Russia, arriving in Petrograd on December 4.

Yet before he had had a chance to importune the first official in Petrograd, Doumer had already made his first blunder. In passing through Stockholm, he had met with the Russian minister there and had taken the opportunity to blast General Joffre, whom he did not like and whom he wanted removed. In general Doumer had expressed extreme pessimism about the war effort, and the Russian minister had immediately wired Sazonov, who had told Paléologue, who had wasted no time in informing Paris. After asking if Doumer had instructions to discuss anything other than the exchange of military resources, Paléologue added, "It would be deplorable if the mission of M. Doumer would result in making the government and Russian opinion believe that France had no confidence in her generalissimo," who incidentally had just been made a marshal of France.[80] The next day Briand fired back a response to Paléologue telling him that Doumer must be convinced not to express these negative opinions to the Russian government because to do so might lead the Russians to reject the purpose of his mission, and the mutual exchange of their "military resources" was of utmost importance to France at this time.[81]

Paléologue, who seems not to have liked Doumer very much anyway, thoroughly chastised him on his arrival in the Russian capital for his Stockholm transgressions. Stressing Joffre's having been made a marshal showed the great confidence in which he was held by the French nation, Paléologue added that that should be enough for both Doumer and the Russians. Curiously, Doumer denied that he had said any of the things of which he had been accused, yet he still had to listen to a lecture, probably delivered in a somewhat condescending manner, by Paléologue on the finer points of keeping one's mouth shut on such delicate matters.[82]

Doumer soon met with the appropriate dignitaries: Goremykin, the prime minister; Polivanov, the minister of war; Admiral Ivan Grigorovich, the naval minister; Sazonov, and other figures. Presumably with each the French politician advanced his cause, pushing a "most focused cooperation" between Russia and France with their men and matériel and hoping to realize a possible accord on the point.[83]

On December 7, Doumer finally obtained an audience with Tsar Nicholas. Always gracious and charming, the tsar was generous with his banal remarks about Allied solidarity and intimate cooperation, casually dropping in the conversation that he immediately needed a half a million rifles. Doumer then raised the question of his proposal of men for arms, basing his position on the disproportionate French losses in comparison with its population. He also stressed French willingness to transport Russian troops and to guarantee their safety. The emperor, always eager to

appear sympathetic to an ally, agreed and expressed his immediate willing-
ness to work with the French in any way possible, adding that he and
General Mikhail Alexeev, his chief of staff, would give careful consideration
to the plan. As possibly an afterthought, the emperor suggested that
Doumer also speak to Alexeev himself. In conclusion, the tsar said, "The
thing can come off if we don't run up against insurmountable difficulties."[84]
With these words of encouragement, Doumer headed to Mogilev, the
Russian headquarters at the front, followed shortly by the tsar.

   If Nicholas was indeed genuinely in favor of sending troops to
France, those around him were not. Alexeev was openly hostile to the
concept in his meeting with Doumer. Besides the "insurmountable" transportation problems, he pointed out that the Russian armies did not have
enough trained reserves to enable large numbers of men to be dispatched
to the West. For that same reason he told Sazonov in November that
Russia could not send troops to Salonika.[85] The Russian front was a
principal one, and it could not be weakened. Alexeev, the son of a
commoner, had clawed his way over numerous aristocrats to the pinnacle
of Russian military power, an accomplishment of no mean proportions.
Trotsky's description of him as "a gray mediocrity, the oldest military clerk
in the army"[86] is unfair and untrue; Alexeev was one of the most highly
regarded generals in the Russian military. "My little cross-eyed friend,"
as the tsar called him, tended to be rigid, but he was by no means a
mediocrity, even if his vision might sometimes be clouded by his devotion
to country and crown.[87]

   In regard to Russian reserves, General Beliaev felt the same way.
In the talks with Doumer he had tried to assert the conviction that "our
effective contingent is not limitless, as they think in France."[88] Yanushkevich resented the notion that a great power like Russia was selling its
children to foreign countries like mercenaries, later writing that the
French had offered "one automobile tire [in exchange for] one battalion
of men."[89] Sazonov seems to have been generally insulted by the whole
idea, but apparently his major objections stemmed from his dislike of
Doumer, whom he dubbed "an enthusiast and an amateur" with "a want
of delicacy."[90] Curiously he never once mentioned the Russian force in
his memoirs.[91]

   At Mogilev long, animated discussions with Alexeev and Prince
Kudashev, director of the diplomatic chancellery at general headquarters,
ensued during which the Frenchman tried to allay Russian fears about
the weakening of their front, the difficulty of bringing troops by sea, and
the appearance of using Russian troops like mercenaries. Sometime later
the tsar arrived and another audience with him took place.[92]

After all the discussion, an agreement was reached, or at least Doumer thought it had been: In exchange for an unspecified amount of war matériel (one dispatch speaks about 150,000 additional rifles), the Russians were to send to the Western Front 40,000 men a month, weather permitting, until a contingent of 400,000 men could be assembled. The Russian soldiers were not to be dispersed among French troops but would have their own units and fight under the Russian flag, although there would be "*des officiers français*" with them. The French had been so eager for the additional effectives that a brigade of infantry was to be dispatched immediately. There was also included some vague understanding about troops being sent to the Salonikan front. Details of collaboration in France were to be finalized when the Russian troops arrived on locale, and the means for shipping them were to be decided between the respective ministers of war, with the French paying the bill for transportation and all upkeep.[93] Doumer again stressed the need to hurry, thereby under-scoring the air of desperation that had characterized the French negotia-tions from the beginning. At that point General Paul Pau was coming from France to serve as chief of the French mission at the Russian general headquarters, and Doumer even suggested that some Russian troops travel to France in the ship that was bringing Pau's entourage.[94]

Yet on the day Doumer left Petrograd, the Russians immediately began defaulting on their agreement. An admiral in the ministry of marine told Paléologue after Doumer's departure that Russia was experiencing the coldest winter in thirty years, resulting in even icebreakers' being frozen in the northern ports. Moreover, harbors were clogged with supplies, making egress even more difficult. Sending troops westward now would be impossible.[95] Doumer had known of this potential problem, but since the French boat *Champagne* plus three or four other boats had reached Archangel recently, he felt that shipping could still pass.[96] More-over, the admiral continued, there would be the added difficulty of keeping troops traveling in unheated supply ships warm. During a voyage at this time of year, temperatures could reach minus thirty to thirty-five degrees Celsius. Even if the ships bringing shells could be properly outfitted, there would still be the problem of getting Russian troops to Alexandrovsk, an icefree port, since Archangel was icebound. An addi-tional difficulty was the fact that mines must be swept.[97]

It is highly unlikely that these problems did not occur to the Russian command while the negotiations were being conducted with Doumer or even that they were discussed at the time. Yet by the time they were raised, Doumer had left and could not refute them. Apparently the Russians had begun to have second thoughts, or late in the business others began to add their objections. The Russian coolness to the entire project at the beginning had turned to outright hostility after the deal had been consummated. In early discussions with Paléologue in September, Sazonov had told the French ambassador that Russia simply did not have the resources to send troops. "Have you not considered the frightful losses that we have sustained in the past fifteen months?" he asked Paléologue. "I do not dare tell you what we have counted up in this retreat of three hundred miles," he continued. "There is certainly a limit to human forces! Our troops are stretched out, our effectives decimated. Do not ask any more of us."[98]

Moreover, the Russian foreign minister told the French ambassador that his "personal news" obligated him to doubt that the Russian High Command had engaged in principle to send ultimately 40,000 men a month to the French front. When Paléologue countered that his memory was quite clear on the matter, Sazonov replied that Paléologue had not been in on the discussions. Sazonov was so dogmatic that Paléologue felt that immediate clarification was necessary. He contacted General Pau and asked him to approach General Alexeev in the name of the French general headquarters to put the understanding into writing for the first time.[99] It is inconceivable that nothing of the agreement with the Russians was recorded, much less signed, and we have in the French archives only a memo of Doumer, composed on stationery of Petrograd's Hotel Astoria, that the 400,000 effective figure was the agreement. The Russians immediately, however, began denying that they had reached any such understanding, and it quickly became their word against Doumer's, who seems not to have had anyone with him from the French side to verify his story.

Several days before Doumer left Petrograd, General Alexeev had written to Beliaev, "Personally I see the fulfillment of the request of Doumer as completely undesirable." He felt that there was a moral question involved in making some sort of equation of men and arms, but he recognized Russian dependence on France and thought that something should be done, a token of some sort, from the "necessity and desire to preserve good relations."[100] To General Iakov Zhilinsky, the Russian military representative in Chantilly, Alexeev telegraphed, "Don't speak on this. Doumer has asked for 300,000 [sic] effectives, 30,000 [sic] every month. The request has been met with no sympathy." He did add, as he had to Beliaev, that perhaps a token force could be created, but he noted that he was against that as well.[101]

Apparently Paléologue's requested clarification from the Russian High Command never formally appeared, but, on December 23, Sazonov told him, "In that which concerns the desiderata expressed by M. Doumer, the military authority has unfortunately not been able to comply with the measure that they would have wanted." The figure of 40,000 a month was simply out of the question, the Russian minister said, adding that the tsar had never agreed, even in principle, to the figure. In fact, Sazonov added, "The figure of 40,000 has never been stated before him." His majesty had simply promised that he would present Doumer's request to the chief of general headquarters. The foreign minister did suggest, as had Alexeev, that perhaps a few troops in support of their allies, perhaps a brigade, could be sent to France if conditions out of Archangel permitted.[102]

A small, symbolic force was not what the French had wanted or thought that they had negotiated. Moreover, it would be of little value to them. Joffre later noted in his memoirs that the token force the Russians sent was terribly insufficient as a solution to the manpower crisis on the French front.[103] There is no way of absolutely knowing what had caused the misunderstanding, if indeed there had been an honest misunderstanding. Paléologue easily blamed Doumer, whom he criticized for not awaiting General Pau or a Captain Buchenschutz, a military figure in the French legation, to discuss the issue. Buchenschutz knew Russian perfectly and could have "control[led] and register[ed] the responses of General Alexeev."[104] Yet it is highly unlikely that the former French prime minister would have invented such a detailed story, and when told by Poincaré in January 1916 that Paléologue had gotten a different impression of what the Russians had agreed, he stated that he was ready to return to Russia to "assure the realization of the promises which had been made to him."[105] He was certain that the agreement had entailed an immediate sending of a small force, followed by 40,000 troops each month, until the Russians had an army of 400,000 men on the Western Front. Perhaps he took Nicholas's genuine willingness and sympathy as an acceptance of his proposal, thinking that only the tsar's word mattered. The last tsar often gave visitors the impression of his total agreement; only later did they learn that it was not so. It is also not far from the realm of possibility that some Russian official agreed to the 40,000 figure only to realize in the aftermath of *ésprit de l'escallier* that it could not be fulfilled. To deny having made it was better than to admit inability to deliver on the promise. At other times in history Russia's allies have thought that they had arrived at an understanding, whether it be numbers of men or democratic elections in Poland, only to discover later that the Russians had not seen it that way. In this case, the Russians probably agreed to Doumer's proposal while the French politician was in the capital and then thought better of it later.

Another problem catalyzed Russian hostility to the sending of troops. One official in the British embassy thought that the "ruling Russians" disliked the idea of their citizens becoming politically contaminated in

France and coming back home after the war as "free thinkers and social-ists."[106] Something similar had happened in 1825 after the Decembrists returned from France. The idea must certainly have been a factor.

The major reason for Russian resistance to sending an expeditionary force to France and Salonika, however, unquestionably lies in the fact that the Russians simply did not have the men to spare. It seems unbelievable that any nation could suffer the losses Russia had by the end of 1915 and still remain in the war. By July 1915, after the struggle was only eleven months old, Russian casualties numbered a million and a half.[107] The Russians were sustaining 150,000 casualties a month and were finding them difficult to replace. By the end of 1915, the total figure stood at a mind-numbing two and a half million.[108] Moreover, their 700-mile front running from Riga to Romania had to be manned; six and a half million men were required simply to hold it, exclusive of the needs for any offensives.[109] The 400,000-man contingent the French thought they had negotiated undoubtedly would have severely strained available Russian manpower. The picture of Russian losses worsened as the war progressed; one émigré source placed the killed, wounded, and missing in action at 6 million, a figure that does not include the millions captured in battle.[110] On the question of Russian casualties, General Paul von Hindenburg wrote, "In the Great War ledger, the page on which the Russian losses were written has been torn out. No one knows the figure. Five or eight million?" Noting that he also had no idea, he added, "All we know is that sometimes in our battles with the Russians we had to remove the mounds of enemy corpses from before our trenches in order to get a clear field of fire against fresh assaulting waves."[111]

While unable to fulfill their alleged agreement, the Russians did wish to show their loyalty by sending at least a token force. While Doumer was en route back to France and unaware that the Russians had reneged on the agreement he thought he had negotiated, the Russian government informed General Pau that a brigade of "elite troops" consisting of two regiments for an effective force of 7,700 men would be sent to France. The command would consist of one general, three colonels, six or seven *chefs de bataillon*, and an assortment of doctors, chaplains, and other service personnel with a total of seventy officers. The brigade would not have a company of machine gunners or musicians. One of the regiments was to be from Moscow, the other from Kazan or Omsk, and both were to leave Russia by the Far Eastern port of Dalny, if the Japanese would permit them to pass through Manchuria. Pau asked that three of his officers be allowed to accompany these troops to France, and the Russian govern-ment granted the request.[112] The government also allowed several higher-ranking officers to bring their wives, although apparently they followed at a later time. Embarkation for the troops from Dalny was to be set for February 28. The ever opinionated F. O. Lindly of the British embassy felt that even this scheme would not be realized.[113] For whatever reason, when the Russians finally did depart from Dalny, the British government was not even informed as to their actual destination.[114] Yet the Russians kept their word regarding this limited force. In the days of early January 1916, they began recruiting the first brigade of about 8,000 men, which the New York *Times* was to describe incorrectly as "picked men," most of whom, it added, had been awarded the Cross of St. George.[115]

The French were naturally disappointed in the small force that the Russians had sent them. Joffre noted that the number would hardly alleviate France's manpower problems, and moreover, their ally had gone back on a promise of a sizable contingent that might well have tipped the balance on the Western Front. Yet the French had at least in part achieved their goal: the exchange of arms, of which they had plenty, for men, which they did not. The French government also did not plan to allow the matter to rest. If they could not extract from the Russians 400,000 men, they might well obtain more than 8,000.

The whole affair had not been untypical of the nature of the Franco-Russian alliance. France's role had always been one of supplier of what was material, be it rifles or gold to build Russian railroads, while the Russians, in the French view at any rate, were expected to supply the humanity. The alliance had therefore functioned, once again, in the manner in which the French had hoped. Whatever disappointment the French might have felt about Russian unwillingness to deliver what the former perceived as the latter's greatest resource, at this time the French could hardly suspect that the day would come that they would thank *le bon Dieu* that the Russians had not kept their word.

TWO

A Debt Is Paid

Winter–Spring 1916

When the Russian troops entered Paris..., and our valiant soldiers marched through the streets and the Arc de Triomphe to the accompaniment of a thunder of frenzied hurrahs from the crowd, a woman shouted to them, "Now the debt is settled." My dear French sisters, such generosity and gratitude are very fine sentiments, but we do not sell our soldiers. They came to help you against the common enemy, to fight the common cause of all humanity, but with their blood and lives they have not settled the "debt." They brought their tribute of blood to the altar of fraternity, in the name of civilization.

—Princess Stephanie Dolgorouki[1]

Sold for Shells

—Title of the memoir of
A. Kozlov of the
Russian Expeditionary Force

And once again a new army is raised on the Neva.
Europe trembles at the fear of war;
The Bourse cries, "The Russians are coming, the Russians
  are here."

—from *Kladderadatsch*[2]

THE FIRST BRIGADE TO BE RAISED FOR FRANCE was composed of two regiments. To quote the cynical Leon Trotsky, its composition was largely "workers, clerks, and salesmen, elements that were of a proletarian or petty bourgeois background." The first regiment of the brigade, and the one to be the more historically important, was recruited largely in Moscow from the working-class regions of the city, where the citizens in their fledgling illegal unions had already been introduced to the ideas of Marxism and a sense of hatred for their capitalist masters.[3] Moreover, most members most certainly had had some childhood recollection and heard their parents' stories of the Bolshevik-led workers' uprising in Moscow in 1905. This background becomes extremely important as the story unfolds. The First brigade also contained elements from a regiment in Samara, the so-called City of Nobles, and was joined by a battalion and a depot battalion from Irkutsk.[4] Led by Colonel Mikhail Nechvolodov, this regiment was drawn from reserve units that had seen little fighting, much less been decorated, as the *Times* had told its readers. Attached to this unit was a drummer boy–mascot, whose name is alternately given by different sources as Ivan, Ignatiev, or Kostia, the only nonofficer member of the force given money for use in the canteen.[5]

The second regiment of the First Brigade was recruited from the lower Volga region around the city of Samara. Vladimir Rychlinsky was an aide-de-camp to thirty-eight-year-old Colonel Paul Diakonov, the officer commanding the regiment, and through a memoir he has given us a view of the selection process. He himself was chosen to join the unit because he spoke French, and in mid-January 1916 he went to Samara to begin organizing the group.

The regiment formed there was comprised of a number of ethnic groups from the Russian Empire, with native Russians composing only a small majority. The single criterion required of all chosen was that they be able to read and write Russian, and all day the soldiers passed before Rychlinsky having to pass only the one-question exam, "Do you know how to read?" The commandant of this regiment was Lieutenant Colonel Georgii Gotua, a major actor in the history of the Russian Expeditionary Force (REF).

One of the soldiers in the first regiment was A. Vavilov. He had come from a peasant family and at the age of nine was already behind the plow. At twelve his family had resettled in Siberia, and in 1912 he began working as a laborer on a canal project. He entered the Russian army in May 1915. Rumors came that these troops were going to be sent abroad, and one day in a review before a general, the first officer of that rank that Vavilov had ever seen, they were told that they were going to France, where they would be called on to sacrifice all for Mother Russia. As they left from Samara, where Vavilov had seen a street car for the first time in his life, they were serenaded by an ecclesiastical orchestra playing religious music. The townspeople, with tears in their eyes, watched their departure.[6] Vavilov's account is one of the very few personal inside views we have from within the First Brigade.

The supreme commander of all Russian forces in France was to be the aforementioned General Palitsyn, the Russian military attaché to the French capital. The second-in-command was General Alexander Zankevich, who would be the direct liaison with the force in the trenches, although he would be comfortably billeted in Paris. The overall field commandant of the First Brigade was Major General Nikolai Alexandrovich Lokhvitsky, chosen for his military record as a recipient of the Order of St. George of the Fourth Class. Except for what one letter written in the 1920s might reveal, little of a personal nature is known about the inner workings of this man, since nothing but professional and official correspondence has ever come to light. Pictures of him show a handsome, short, slender officer with a strict military demeanor who carries himself well and erect while others are slouching. His most salient physical feature was a pair of intelligent, haunting wolf eyes.[7] Although shortly after arriving in France, President Poincaré awarded him the *croix de guerre* and the cross of the *Légion d'Honneur*, he does not seem to have been an officer of any distinction, and a writer close to the time described him as a "timid man who feared responsibility."[8] He did, however, belong to a most cerebral family. His grandfather was a philosopher and man of letters who was a close associate with M. M. Speransky, the prominent Russian statesman, in the early nineteenth century. His father, A. V. Lokhvitsky, was a famous jurist who taught law at the University of Moscow according to some sources, at the University of St. Petersburg according to others. One of his sisters, Mirra, was a poet, and the other was the famous satirist Nadezhda Alexeevna Teffi, who wrote in the Russian émigré press in Paris after the war.[9] In October 1919 a report from the French security police stated that Lokhvitsky was the only general in the Russian army of Jewish origin,[10] but this statement is not correct.

Each regiment was composed of three battalions of four fighting companies. Attached to this Russian brigade were also three machine-gun companies with twelve guns in each, 180 staff officers, 8,762 soldiers, and eventually 185 French soldiers and 96 officers.[11] Along with the force was the usual contingent of secretaries, cooks, blacksmiths, engineers, photographers, service personnel, as well as automobiles, musical instruments, a portable disinfection car, a rolling field kitchen, and even some sewing machines.[12] The supplies included live cattle to be slaughtered along the way.[13] Very careful calculations as to space on the transport ships was made, granting a stiflingly close allocation of only two cubic meters for every ten men.[14]

Joseph Noulens, the French ambassador to Russia after July 1917, wrote in his memoirs that the troops sent to France were chosen from "all the regiments," and usually the colonels charged with selecting these men used this opportunity to rid themselves of their "hotheads."[15] Although there may well have been some cases when the officers used this method, we have no real evidence on the manner of selection anywhere. Whatever means of choosing the men may have been employed, it would hardly have been sufficient to have caused the problems that later destroyed the brigade as a fighting force.

On February 2, 1916, the second regiment began to leave in large railroad cars that could hold forty men and eight horses. The officers were housed in an old second-class Pullman. From extant pictures, it must have been a most unpleasant journey. The trip to Darien on the southern coast of Manchuria took slightly over three weeks, and the soldiers amused themselves by singing as they rode along. The weather was bitterly cold, and at a stop in one Siberian village Rychlinsky left the car and got frostbite almost immediately on his nose.[16]

The first regiment left Moscow on February 3, a day after the second, and General Pau reported to his government that these men would arrive in Dalny by the end of the month.[17] They more or less linked up at Orenburg with the regiment from Samara and became mixed together.

In this disjointed manner, the Russian troops traveled eastward across Siberia, but not as rapidly as they might have hoped. The program called for continuous nonstop movement, but, in the wartime conditions of Russia's railroads, that was impossible. Meanwhile Paléologue continued to orchestrate everything for the troops' departure by ship for France: schedules, ships, arrivals, supplies, and the negotiations with the Japanese. On January 18 the French navy requisitioned three boats at Saigon, the *Amiral Latouche-Tréville*, the *Himalaya*, both passenger liners, and the *Sontay*, apparently a troop transport of 12,000 tons designed for voyages in the tropics, and dispatched them to the Manchurian coast.

Soon the various chosen ships began arriving in Dalny. The first to reach the Manchurian port was the *Amiral Latouche-Tréville*, which was to serve as the flagship of the little armada. It was soon followed by the other two. The *Atlantic* and the *Amazon*, both French vessels stationed in Yokohama, were commandeered, but the *Atlantic* was in need of repairs, so its joining the fleet was delayed. Both finally arrived in Dalny, however, by mid-March. The Japanese slowness in responding to requests for passage through Manchuria and, then, their subsequent halting of individual units at the Manchurian border contributed to the fractured nature of the brigade, and when the infantry was allowed to cross into Manchuria, they had to transfer into unheated Japanese cars. The officers were assigned to an unheated American car. At night the men made charcoal fires, which intoxicated the soldiers in the closed compartments. The Japanese who greeted them gave the soldiers cold tea and rice wine, and the Russians were astonished by the toughness of the Japanese who stood in the open in the wind at minus 20 degrees Celsius.[18]

As the troops straggled into Dalny, the task of boarding the ships and allotting the men began. The date of February 29 had been set for the beginning of departure, and miraculously on that day General Lokhvitsky and the *Latouche-Tréville*, overloaded with 1,600 men, set sail for France. Because at this point the remainder of the brigade was still scattered across eastern Siberia, it continued to leave in dribbles. On March 2, *Himalaya* left with 2,500 soldiers, followed by the *Sontay* on March 12 with 2,400. Two Russian transports, the *Tambor* and the *Yaroslav*, with 1,550 men between them, preceded the late-arriving *Atlantic* and *Amazon* with 622 men. By March 18 the last of the transports had finally left for France.[19]

Pictures of the ships show them to be densely packed with men in what must have been incredibly uncomfortable and dangerously unsanitary conditions. As the ships moved into warmer waters, health problems did indeed arise. On March 10 the French ambassador in London asked permission of the British admiralty to land the force in Hong Kong and Singapore "as troops are crowded and the French admiral is considering transfer of some of these to another ship in one of these ports." Shortly afterward Lokhvitsky wired the admiralty asking to disembark 900 men from the *Himalaya* at Djibouti or Aden to prevent an epidemic from occurring on board.[20] The *Himalaya* stopped in Hong Kong, giving the men a much-needed break from the torrid conditions, and some of the other boats stopped in Singapore by March 16, after having landed in Saigon eight days before.[21] When they stopped in Singapore, the weather was so warm that the boots of the soldiers allowed shore-leave sank into the warm asphalt of the streets.[22] Pictures show the officers on shore in dress whites wearing pith helmets. Enlisted men's pictures show them in the traditional Russian soldier's dress designed for climates much colder than that of Southeast Asia. Meanwhile, General Lokhvitsky posed for the usual upbeat propaganda photos, including one in which he is cheerfully sampling the soldiers' food on the deck of his ship.[23]

Shortly after the first of April, the *Himalaya* and the *Latouche-Tréville* sailed through the Suez Canal and stopped at Port Said after a voyage that, surprisingly, had drawn little if any attention around the world. This secrecy was all the more amazing since the Russians had dropped numbers of troops in several places along the way and conscripted other boats to pick them up. The press in London had been formally notified a month before; demonstrating a unique professionalism, the journalists had kept silent for security reasons because they had been asked to do so.[24] Even the Russian minister in Port Said was kept in the dark as to the troops' destination and sought information from the British government.[25] There arrived at Port Said from a different direction a small sack of mail that had already reached France for the troops, and at Izvolsky's request to the British government, had been dispatched to Egypt for delivery.[26]

Whatever advance work was done in itself could not have generated the near-hysterical reception the Russians received on arriving in France. The heroic defense of Verdun was at its height, and the landing of Allied soldiers on French soil might certainly mean that indeed "They shall not pass!" Marseille had waited expectantly for several days and was decorated in a blizzard of bunting. The first two ships, the *Latouche-Tréville* and *Himalaya*, had been delayed for two days by having to "dodge torpedoes" (another account gives the more likely villain to be a storm), so that the exact time for their arrival was unknown. *Le Matin* reported to its readers that crowds thronged the quay staring expectantly at the horizon, and when at about 2:00 P.M. the *Latouche-Tréville* entered the harbor, the crowd erupted in an orgiastic cheer and was restrained by the police only with great difficulty. Bands played "God Save the Tsar" and were answered with the politically contradictory *La Marseillaise*. Shouts and cheers were answered with the same from the other side. A number of French military dignitaries from both the army and the navy, as well as M. Doumer, who could feel that he had been the father of it all, went on board the *Latouche-Tréville* to be received by Lokhvitsky. They were accompanied by Colonel I. I. Ignatiev, the military attaché of the Russian embassy in Paris, and by the Russian consul general in Marseille, a man with the very un-Russian name of Salviati. While this welcome was taking place, into the harbor sailed the *Himalaya*, whose appearance gave the reception an unneeded boost. The *Latouche-Tréville* moored to the strains of the Russian national anthem, played by a French naval band, and Lokhvitsky disembarked, ironically, near some astounded German prisoners of war working on the docks. He reviewed some French troops, and the Russian general was received with full military honors by General Alphonse Menassier, the military governor of Marseille, and General Pierre Guerin, General Joffre's representative.

Vollies of cheers followed on both sides, and French and Russian artillery roared in exchange of salutes. From the assembled civilians, who were so noticeably absent from the official greeters, there were constant cries of "*Vive la Russie!*"[27] The Russian officers were given automobiles for their use in Marseille and were treated to a luncheon by General Hyacinthe Coquet, commandant of the Fifteenth Military Region.

The event was replete with the usual toasts to patriotism, bravery, and unity. After dessert General Joffre's order of the day was read. It was a stirring encomium to Russian valor and the usual "devotion to the common cause." It praised the Russian soldier, "selected from the bravest of her armies and led by the best-known officers," and the order called on French officials to "welcome them as brothers." Joffre also ordered the French soldier to "show them how warm is the feeling you have for those who left their country to fight on our side." He concluded with the ringing words, "I bow before the Russian flags, upon which there soon will be inscribed the glorious names of our victories."[28] Lokhvitsky replied to Joffre's praise with a toast to the president of the French Republic, General Joffre, and the "glorious French army." "I drink to our future victories," he added, "which for us are certain."[29] A copy of more or less the same text praising the "indissolvable union which exists between the two armies" was sent to General Pau to be communicated to the tsar. Back down to earth, Joffre added the instruction to Pau in a later paragraph: "You would well like to profit from this occasion to bring up again the decisions taken on the subject of dispatching a second brigade . . . and notably on the conditions of transport and the approximate date of departure."[30]

For the 9,000 "hardened veterans," which one Western paper falsely described as "elite" troops "blazing with decorations won upon the field of battle," the journey could not have been pleasant. For them their mere arrival must have engendered more delight than the ringing phrases of welcome. Many were sick and some had died on the ships and had been buried at sea. The soldiers were, however, impressed by the welcome of the crowds, and it was a relief to see soldiers "on this summer [*sic*] day" in new clean uniforms instead of the dirty gray greatcoats they had worn since Dalny.[31]

Among the first to leave the boat was the mascot Ivan, who drew much attention in the Western press. As the soldiers left the boats, they were each given a Lebel rifle and a copy of the soldiers' newspaper *The Russian Soldiers' Friend*, which always showed on the front page a somewhat effeminate *poilu* (affectionate slang term for a World War I French soldier) touching fingertips over various military banners and flags with a Russian *muzhik*.

This particular issue informed the Russians of the fall of the Turkish city of Trebizond. For some time this house organ would be the only contact most of these Russian soldiers would have with the outside world.

Editorial reaction, not only in France but in Britain and the United States as well, gave the impression that with the arrival of these soldiers, the millennium had come. Since the number was not made public, and since rumors augmented their count until they had become a veritable human tsunami (several papers reported 250,000), it is not surprising that the French thought that their manpower problems were over. Moreover, newspapers and journals described in detail every conceivable point of curiosity about these soldiers: the buttons on their shirts, the creases in their trousers, and the precise position of their various insignia, and from the press reports it would be hard to imagine that even one of them was smaller than the giants in the biblical land of Canaan. *Echo de Paris* was almost sexual in its enthusiastic representation. Under the headlines "HERE ARE THE RUSSIANS!" the paper described them with the words "What beautiful men! What magnificent bearing! What young faces, their good pure eyes!"[32] *Le Bonnet Rouge* was a little more subdued, but not by much. In an article beginning with the words "Russians in France!" the writer spoke about rumors of "a new powerful force" for which everyone had heard and waited, and then forgotten. "Then suddenly when we no longer have these day-dreams, when the enemy blocks the Dardanelles, when our *[sic]* port of Archangel is blocked with ice at fifty-four degrees below zero," *Le Bonnet Rouge* prepared its readers, "the Russian soldiers arrive in France to fight in the trenches in the West on the side of their French . . . brothers-in-arms." The journal also noted the German prisoners of war on the docks and observed that in their ranks was a certain confusion. "*Russen! Russen!* [They said.] It is no longer *Deutschland über Alles!*" The convoy of prisoners of war passed these Russians with the air of being "beaten, discouraged, [and] destroyed." After a description of the disembarkation, the whited-out columns of the censor deprived the reader of any clue as to the destination or planned utilization of these "beautiful giants."[33]

The editorial cartoonists had a field day with the Russians as well. In the *Westminster Gazette* there appeared a cartoon showing a caricaturized Kaiser Wilhelm looking shocked at a Russian bear coming over the horizon. Captioned "What a Surprise!" the cartoon had the Kaiser saying "It can't be! Yes, it is a bear. How on the earth did it get here in the West?"[34] With a little more majesty, *Le Matin* produced a gallant-looking Russian soldier stepping out of an Easter egg engraved with the Romanov two-headed eagle, as if he were hatching out of it. Entitled "France's Easter Eggs," the cartoon was captioned "The Russians have disembarked at Marseille."[35] *Echo de Paris* was more subtle yet nevertheless powerful. A cartoon on the arrival of the Russians showed a *poilu* shaking hands in the trenches with a somewhat bewildered, newly arrived Russian soldier, who was dressed more in the fashion of how he would have been perceived to be dressed than how he actually was. (*i.e.,* he was wearing a Cossack hat). The French soldier is saying to the Russian "You don't speak French. I'm going to teach you. Say, *'On les aura!'* [We'll take them!]"[36]

   This enthusiasm infected the populace when a company of these Russian soldiers marched through the streets of Paris on the national holiday of July 14 to great acclaim. "Oh, they will surely save us" one Russian observer heard throughout the crowds.[37] Marshal Foch noted the landing with less enthusiasm. His notebooks make no mention of the Russians' arrival until the day after and then only state that the papers were full of the news of their landing. He did, however, effusively praise the Russian victory at Trebizond, noting that this victory gives "good hope for the Russian campaign of 1916."[38]

   The soldiers assembled on the dock and began a triumphal march through Marseille. The streets were jammed with cheering French citizens, and they threw presents of chocolate, fruit, and flowers to the soldiers, including oranges, the first that most of these men had ever seen. They were herded into the Place de la Préfecture, which Private Vavilov called an "orchard." Here a field kitchen had been built under a tent by an organization formed by Doumer called The Friend of the Russian Soldier. A simple lunch was served to the men, who were required to stay within the park. The reasons for detaining them were probably good ones, but the soldiers could not understand why they were held "like some kind of animal." Hundreds of French citizens had followed them from the docks and had surrounded the park in which the Russian soldiers ate, watching them with an understandable curiosity. Many had tears on their faces as well as smiles. Yet being observed in this manner did not sit well with the Russians, many of whom felt that they were objects under examination.[39] After lunch a company of colonial troops led them through the streets to the strains of "*Sambre et Meuse*," played by a navy band. Through a blizzard of flowers thrown from balconies, they marched to the bay of Estaque and Camp Mirabeau, where they were to be quartered for several days before being sent north to the front. In the tents erected for them, the soldiers found copies of a Russian newspaper, probably the one just mentioned, and postcards on which to write home. The French had erected an Orthodox church there, presumably rather quickly, for the Russian soldiers to have a place in which to worship. At Mirabeau each soldier also was assigned a *marraine de guerre*, a "godmother of war," that curious

French institution to emerge from the Great War. These women sent letters, knitted socks, and provided home cooking and sometimes other more personal favors when the soldiers were on leave.

After packing their effects that evening, some soldiers made music. One had a violin, another an accordion. Others went to the camp canteen to spend what money they had. As the soldiers went about the business of getting used to their new environment, Sergei Solomko, a war artist sent by the Russian government, made sketches of them.[40]

An American, Lee Meriwether, a special assistant to the American ambassador in France, was in the south shortly after the Russians landed. At one point the car in which he was riding had to pull aside to make way for a contingent of passing Russians. They had approached the car with a long sweeping stride, Meriwether later wrote, with the men singing as they marched "a weird somber Slavic song." To the American, every Russian was tall. "If they could only fight as well as they look," Meriwether mused, "what wonderful soldiers they would be! But they can't, which is why I hear many Frenchmen say they hope for the best but fear the worst, so far as Russia is concerned."[41]

After several days they boarded two trains, with over 800 Russians in each. Both departed in the early evening of April 24 with their destination being Camp Mailly near Troyes in the Champagne region, where they were to be given further training before going to the front. Instead of going to Champagne, a few Russians detoured by England to make a courtesy call, and they were reviewed by Lord Kitchener. Lokhvitsky meanwhile detoured by Paris to make the usual round of official visits and receptions.[42]

On April 25 the second group of boats of the little armada straggled into Marseille at 10:00 A.M. Word of their arrival "ran through the city like a trail of black powder," *Le Matin* reported,[43] and a crowd quickly assembled on the dock to greet this second wave with cries of "*Vive la Russie!*" General Menassier boarded the vessel and reviewed the men on them. More arrived on May 2, and within a week of the first arrival, all of the Russians of the First Brigade had landed in France.

Back home a Russian newspaper, *Vchernoe vremia*, correctly described the soldiers' reception as one of "heroes with a sentiment of sincere sympathy and admiration for their courage."[44] All along the route to Mailly from Marseille, crowds gathered to receive them. Up the Rhone valley, at Avignon, at Valence, at Lyon, throngs assembled at the stations to cheer them in the same hysterical fashion that had been exhibited in Marseille. At one station, the soldiers were allowed to disembark, and quickly a crowd of Frenchmen gathered. The Russians were asked to sing "God Save the Tsar," and the French then sang their national anthem.

Their destination, the camp of Mailly-le-Grand, had been built in 1903 about halfway between Troyes and Châlons near the railroad that joins those two cities. The post was about ten square miles and had been located there because the terrain was deemed ideal for special military instruction, which the Russians would undergo to condition them for the peculiarities and the different tactics of fighting on the Western Front, such as defense against gas attacks. Moreover, their method of assault was far less cautious than that of the French.[45] Also, the Russians had always been able to retreat large distances, due to the vast size of their country, a luxury the French could not afford in their smaller theater. They had to be taught that in the West each square foot of land was precious. Joining them would be a regiment of artillery (nine batteries of four French 75's), sapeurs, two ambulances, a hospital section, a sanitation group, an auto-mobile section, and an administrative convoy.[46] Attached to assist them were 190 French soldiers and officers, and 146 additional men, chosen because of their ability to speak Russian. Later the Russians would be transferred to Mourmelon-le-grand, a camp closer to the front.

The first Russians arrived at Mailly at 4:40 A.M. on April 23 and were greeted by a crowd of French soldiers, light cavalry, artillery men, and infantry. In charge of the event was a Colonel Speransky, who received the official greetings since Lokhvitsky was still in Paris. There was much playing of the respective national anthems, and tea was waiting to refresh the Russian soldiers. After they had drunk their tea, a moving Easter mass followed in which, *Le Matin* tells us, the Russian soldiers participated in one voice. Mail was distributed, and then the Russians performed traditional dances to the great amusement of the French soldiers.

Some Russians asked if Verdun had fallen, and, when they were told that it had not, they asked where it was. When showed the direction, their eyes stared at the horizon as if it were possible to see it, and then, *Matin* reported (most probably for German consumption), they said they had been told that they would be fighting beside the French troops there. At 10:30 a lunch was served of cakes, Easter eggs, and champagne. After-ward, arm in arm with the French soldiers, the Russians strolled through the streets of Mailly, where the local population greeted them well.[47]

As the French would have wished, the Russians' arrival did not go unnoticed by the German government. One Russian memoirist struck home by writing that the Germans would not be deceived, realizing that the appearance of these troops was merely a staged masquerade for psychological reasons.[48] The German press, however, came closer to the truth. The Berlin *Lokalanzeiger* called it a "transparent comedy, the wretchedness of which is too transparent for it to produce any sort of uneasiness. . . ." Further hitting the mark, the paper noted, "The fact that the French and their allies welcome this sham support with such enthusiasm only proves how bad the state of things must be in France."[49] The Frankfurter *Zeitung* added, "As nothing comes of the Russian attempt to relieve the French by an attack on Hindenburg's [the Eastern] front, the Russians send a deputation of heroes who have, no doubt, been embarked in two ships in order that their small number may not become known at once to everybody." Ignorant of the crowded conditions on the five Russian ships, the German paper continued, "We respect Latin feelings all the more because it can only be desirable for us if the Russians turn as many of their men as possible into Vikings who travel half round the world in search of a battlefield, which, in our opinion, they could just as well find at home."[50] A military critic of the *Berliner Tageblatt* likewise hit the mark. Referring to the Russians who had landed, he noted that the French, "who are easily impressed and deceived," were jubilant, but he realistically added that the German soldier had learned how to deal with these "bravest of the Russians" in Galicia and Poland.[51] In Washington, the German diplomats expressed no fear of the influx of Russians on the Western Front, correctly reading it as a sign of French weakness.[52] Generally the Germans had focused on the problem: the French shortage of effectives. By July 1916, the French had sustained over a million casualties (606,000 killed),[53] and it should have been clear to any objective observer that French ecstasy was a result of the belief that the infusion of Russian manpower would stem their own losses.

Certain Allied elements, however, were not so pleased that the Russians had arrived. When word reached the Russian Workers' Club in Paris, an organization of leftist expatriates at 12 bis Rue de la Reine-Blandu, "some lively recriminations" resulted. In their meeting on April 20, "about thirty members" commented very unfavorably on the news.[54] The venerable French diplomat Paul Cambon saw little point in bringing the Russians to the West, especially since it led them to make claims to which there was no truth. To a friend he wrote that there could be "nothing more ridiculous" than to import Russian soldiers to fight in France. He added, "We have on our front 8,000 Russians, that is to say, an insignificant force. Yet in Russia everyone says that it is thanks to the intervention of the Muscovites that we are able to stop the *Boches*," noting that as a result all over the world they think that French reserves are exhausted since France is obliged to turn to Russia. "It would be worth more," he noted, "to send this bunch to Salonika or, where it would be of better value, to Trebizond, where the Grand Duke Nicholas does not have enough forces."[55] In May he wrote that France had only "honeyed words" (*paroles de miel*) for the Russians "who rendered such imaginable services and we reserve our bitterness for the English without whose concourse we would not have been able to resist at Verdun. . . ."[56]

Surprisingly, one of the sharpest French critics of sending Russian troops into France was the French ambassador to Washington, Jean Jusserand. Before the Russians arrived he had wired his opposition to their coming, stating that instead of giving the manifestation of fraternity, it merely underscored the sad nature of French forces. If the Russians wanted to show their solidarity with the alliance, it could be done so more strikingly with an anti-German offensive on their own front. German propaganda, he warned, would have a field day showing quite correctly that France must be bleeding at every vein, adding that the Germans had already notified press agencies that they had captured French soldiers from the 1916 class, which had had to be called early. Moreover, the diplomat felt that the use of Russian troops would only underscore the Russian belief that they were doing everything in the war effort, noting that they already were claiming that they had saved Verdun and, strangely, even the Suez Canal. When the Russians did arrive, Jusserand was quick to report that the German agents and the Germanophile press in the United States saw Russian effectives in the West for what it was: proof of the exhaustion of the manpower of France and encouragement for the cause of the Central Powers.[57]

Moreover, French opposition was not confined to Jusserand. There was some hesitance in certain military circles as well. In a memo to the ministry of war, an unidentified French military attaché expressed serious, practical doubt about how well the Russian soldier would function in France. Noting that they were used to fighting in large expanses, the attaché observed that Russian soldiers did not see the necessity of solidly holding in "determined circumstances." Russian soldiers were not used to trench warfare like that in the West. "While not throwing off on their courage, which is not disputable," the attaché continued, "I doubt the solidarity of the [Russian] troops before a rather serious artillery bombardment." To counter this possible problem, the anonymous attaché suggested that small groups be taken to Verdun to see the action there and that small groups of Russians be dispersed among French soldiers.[58] Being used to giving way in such tense situations might make Russian soldiers in the West a liability, not an asset.

As the weeks passed and more and more reports came into Paris of Russian assertions that they were carrying the French war effort in the West, animosity began to grow against the small force. Report after report from French missions abroad complained vigorously of Russian diplomats and officers' bragging that their troops in France were single-handedly saving the French nation.[59] Colonel Jacques Langlois described this distortion as a "veritable explosion of chauvinism," and he reported to the French government that "the most inaccurate rumors circulated." For example, Russians in Russia spoke easily of the role of their troops at Verdun, of 300,000 having disembarked. One Russian officer with the Marseille landing was astonished to learn that his unit was the first to arrive, having been told that it was the fifth dispatched to France.[60]

The inaccuracies, or outright falsehoods, can probably be attributed largely to the Russian press. *Rech*, the generally reliable house organ of the liberal Constitutional Democratic Party, spoke of a clearly nonexistent "official communiqué" that told of great numbers of Russians fighting at Verdun, in Champagne, and on the Somme. "The Russian troops, it seems, are in the most important and the most dangerous sectors in France," it told its readers, adding that this "communiqué of our allies tells us that they [our troops] have participated in the heroic defense of Verdun . . . that they are also on the Somme"[61] *Novoe vremia*, a more conservative journal, spoke of the naval flag, the flag of St. Andrew, flying in the Mediterranean as if it were the standard of hundreds of ships instead of only the few that were there.

The inaccurate accounts of the role of the Russian armies in France were widely repeated and believed outside of journalistic circles. General Pau reported of hearing repeatedly that thousands of Russians were fighting at Verdun, which was infuriatingly compared to the Russians' rather inept defense of Warsaw the year before. The general military line had it that "the French are not able to do more, so we must aid them."[62] In one of the principal churches of Moscow a priest went so far as to inform the congregation that "if France is victorious, it will be thanks to the 300,000 soldiers that the Imperial Government had decided to send to her aid." The reporter of this statement was French consul general Gustave Engelhardt, who concluded his report with a request for instruction as to the attitude he must observe when in the midst of Russian society people who made these ridiculous statements.[63] Such stories could only engender hostility among the French, and these mendacious claims about the salvation of France made the problems that later came with the Russian baggage all the less palatable.

Not having forgotten the promise made to Doumer in December, the French decided to try again to induce the Russians to send more soldiers to France. A Senate report written on April 1, 1916, recognized that

Russia had contributed extensively to the war and that its sacrifices "as ours" had been considerable; yet the memorandum added, "One must hope that she is able to put soon . . . an important number of units in order to realize tactical results."[64]

In order to bring this flow about, René Viviani, a former French prime minister and perennial holder of cabinet positions, and munitions minister Thomas, a prominent socialist of some modest international renown, suggested in mid-April that they be sent on a mission to Petrograd with the goal of renewing the call for more Russian troops.[65] The French government liked the idea, and several days later President Poincaré wrote a letter to Nicholas II bemoaning that fact that there had been so little interallied visiting, noting that only the Russian minister of finance, Bark, had been in the West. The French president suggested that he send Viviani and Thomas to "examine with their Russian colleagues the problems for which it would be useful to search together for a solution."[66] Even the sometimes dense Russian tsar probably divined that some request was coming.

These two representatives were highly respected in France. At this point Viviani was the minister of justice and vice president of the Council of Ministers, as well as a member of the *Garde des Sceaux*, but he also had been the minister of foreign affairs and had accompanied Poincaré in his famous trip to St. Petersburg in the summer of 1914. A baker's son and a disciple of the socialist Jean Jaurès, Thomas was by far the more dynamic of the two. He was also very conceited and quite the opportunist. As Trotsky sarcastically put it, he was "a friend of everything victorious." Alexander Kerensky, the prime minister of Russia at one point after the revolution, described him as strikingly reminiscent of "a Russian intellectual who through his own effort had just escaped from a peasant background."[67] Given the Russian dependence on France for shells, choosing the minister of munitions to plead the case for the French might have been as metaphoric as it was practical. Thomas was known to be a rugged man with whom to deal, and his reputation for a sledge hammer approach to problems had preceded him. Some of the higher officials in Russia literally dreaded his coming. Knox tells us that General Beliaev "positively trembled" when he told the British colonel that he had been assigned the task of dealing exclusively with "the invader."[68]

Like many Frenchmen at the time, Thomas had no patience with the Russian steamroller's failure to reach Berlin. During his trip, the outspoken Thomas unloaded not only on Colonel Knox about what he called "Russian slackness," but to Mikhail Rodzianko, the President of the Russian Duma, as well. To the latter, Thomas sarcastically noted, "Russia must be rich and sure of her forces in order to permit the luxury of a government like yours, because your prime minister [the incompetent Boris Stürmer] — he is a disaster and your minister of war [General Dmitri Shuvaev] — a catastrophe."[69] A great champion of the proletariat at home, Thomas called for compulsion to make currently striking Russian coal miners return to the mines and bitterly condemned Russian labor for the habit of leaving their work for three or four days as if there was no war. "Everywhere I go I see numbers of men doing nothing," he once fumed on his trip, "and yet Russia complains of a shortage of labor."[70] The bombastic French socialist believed his main objective was to whip the Russians into shape and to get them to fulfill their role for the war effort. Part of that could easily be more men for the French trenches.

The two ministers left for the Russian capital in the end of April 1916, traveling under the telegraphic code name Uranus. Going through England, they crossed the North Sea to Bergen, Norway, then went by train to Stockholm, finally arriving in Petrograd just before midnight on May 5. The announcement of their arrival in the papers the previous day, especially the mention of Thomas, who was well known in working-class circles, had caused quite a stir among all political parties.

On arrival the men were taken immediately to the Evropeiskaia Hotel, where a late supper had been prepared. Paléologue joined them, and while eating, Thomas outlined to the ambassador the four main objectives of their mission, the accomplishment of any one of which would have been a major coup in itself. In addition to gaining from the Imperial Government major concessions in regard to Polish autonomy and a more accommodating stance in regard to Romania on the part of the general staff, Thomas and Viviani were going to "ascertain the military resources of Russia and try to develop them" and to "*insist*" on the dispatch of the 400,000 men to France that Doumer had thought he had negotiated in December.[71]

The French ambassador felt little optimism for the general success of the mission, but for the dispatch of the 400,000, he expressed no hope at all.[72] From the beginning, Alexeev had opposed the scheme anyway and had convinced the tsar that it was a mistake. Paléologue did feel, however, that with persistence, Thomas might be able to secure the dispatch of a few brigades.[73]

The next day, May 6, Viviani, Thomas, and Paléologue left after lunch for Tsarskoe Selo to meet the emperor. On the fifteen-mile trip to the tsar's palace, Viviani seemed anxious and apprehensive at how the tsar would receive his requests, but Thomas was in high spirits and quite taken with himself at the prospect of appearing before the Russian tsar. "Good old Thomas," he boasted at one point, "so at last you're going to stand face to face with His Majesty the Tsar Autocrat of All the Russias!" Yet on meeting the emperor, Thomas became quiet and remained in a somewhat embarrassed silence at first, especially after Nicholas II, in unexpected humbleness, pointed proudly to his *Croix de guerre*, noting that he was unworthy of it as it had also been given to the heroes of Verdun. After these and other pleasantries, the men got down to business, and Viviani began presenting his shopping list. He was most eloquent and charming. Paléologue wrote, "When he drew a picture of France bled white and suffering the irreparable loss of the flower of her race, he found tones which moved the emperor deeply." He discussed Verdun, during which the tsar interrupted him, saying "And to think before the war Germany used to say that the Frenchman is incapable of being a soldier!" Viviani replied, "The fact is, Sire, that the Frenchman is not a soldier. He is a *warrior* [italics in original]!" Thomas then finally entered into the conversation, underscoring all that Viviani had said. The emperor was most gracious and spoke positively. Apparently he had been impressed. He did say, however, that he would take the advice of his generals on the matter of additional troops for France when he returned to headquarters at Mogilev that day, adding that his military advisors were not inclined to be affirmative.[74]

Meetings in the capital on the following days with ministers of the Russian government did not, however, meet with equal sympathy. Despite the fact that General Shuvaev tried to kiss Thomas on the mouth *à la mode russe* at the end of their meeting, he showed no enthusiasm for the project, and Sazonov demonstrated his usual hostility. Stating "quite frankly" that Russia had no men to spare, he made the argument that given the length of the Russian front, the Russian Empire had fewer men per half mile of trench than the French republic had. Moreover, Russia's enormous losses and the great demands of Russian industry and agriculture added an additional burden. On a more arcane note, the Russian minister observed that the Russian peasant did not perform well away from his native soil. For him the matter was settled. On the day the French ministers departed for the front, Sazonov told the British ambassador that he doubted that they would be able to induce the Russian general staff to send more than an additional brigade to France.[75]

On the evening of May 9, the two French ministers left for Mogilev to lay their case before the Russian military high command. They arrived the next morning and immediately began their round of meetings. The tsar had preceded them, and on the day of their arrival wrote in one of his typically laconic and uninformative letters to his wife that Thomas and Viviani had had "prolonged conferences" with Alexeev, Beliaev, and "others," but then only added that he had sat between the two at dinner, thus avoiding the necessity of having to talk to each of them separately.[76]

Alexeev received them coldly. In addition to being hostile to their mission, the Russian general was a strict military man who felt that civilians, especially a foreigner who was both a socialist and an atheist, had no business interfering in Russian military matters. He also resented what he believed to be the French opinion that they alone were fighting the war. Viviani immediately handed Alexeev a letter from Joffre and asked him to read it at once, obviously expecting some discussion of the message and to return with a reply. The general, however, read it without comment. Viviani then mentioned what must have been the contents of the undiscussed letter that Joffre planned an offensive between July 1 and July 15 and would like the Russians to join in it with him. Alexeev curtly thanked Viviani and said that he would take the matter up with Joffre by means of regular military channels in Paris through General Zhilinsky.

There then followed a conference over which the emperor presided. Viviani made his appeal for the 400,000 troops in 40,000 monthly installments, the number Doumer claimed he had already negotiated. As the discussions ground on, General Alexeev and Grand Duke Sergei, the head of the Russian artillery service, became more compromising and the talks became less tense. Ultimately the tsar, by now won over by the two French ministers, asserted his will, and a decision was reached. In addition to the brigade already sent to France and the one due to leave for Salonika in June, five brigades, each 10,000 strong, were to be sent to France between August 14 and December 15. Paléologue congratulated Viviani on his success but wrote in his diary, "But we are still far from the 400,000 men which Doumer made us hope for."[77]

Yet the Russians did not give these new brigades simply for Allied solidarity. They held the French to their earlier suggestions of men for matériel. In exchange for the numbers mentioned, Russia asked for 100 French 75's, 150 of their 90-mm pieces, 60 of their 120-mm pieces, 400 pieces of 48 lignes (4-inch guns), 300 pieces of 42 lignes (3 1/2-inch guns), 80 to 100 pieces of 220-mm, and 36 11-inch guns. With these were to be literally thousands of shells representing unrealistic numbers to be produced daily by the French war industry.

Generally agreeable, the French nevertheless said that since Verdun was under heavy siege, they could not send any weapons of 75-mm, 48-ligne, or 220-mm caliber at this time, but they promised to furnish these later. Thomas also observed by way of reply that some of these requested weapons had been agreed upon already in an Allied conference on March 28. The 90-mm pieces were already in England en route to Russia, awaiting the arrival of a Russian officer to inspect them. In France an order was to be placed for 1,850,000 rifles, 50,000 of which were to be delivered in June, with the remainder coming in 300,000-monthly deliveries through December.[78] France also had to furnish a number of cars, draft horses, saddles, and a host of other useful equipment. The agreements included a most precise timetable for troop shipments that need not be recounted here, especially since the Russians never made much of an effort to follow it.[79]

The major business completed, the trip became a goodwill mission with great propagandistic opportunities. Back in Petrograd, the two ministers were feted by the president of the Duma at a banquet at which the great Russian singer Chaliapin sang *La Marseillaise*. They also lunched with Grand Duchess Maria Pavlovna, around whom had gathered the members of the imperial family hostile to the Empress Alexandra and her clique.[80] From the capital they went to Moscow and then Tula, visiting factories that made arms and other military hardware, including a former perfume factory that had been converted to manufacture poison gas.[81] On June 17, after a dinner for 350 guests, the two French ministers departed for Archangel by train to meet their boat *La Champagne*, an old English steamboat that had been *débaptisé* in order to be shown with a French flag. In one last demonstration of Allied solidarity, the two ministers stopped en route at Vologda, where Mrs. Viviani bought some Russian lace for publicity purposes from lacemakers specially convened at the station. They had to be led out of the White Sea by two icebreakers, which on the evening of the second day themselves became jammed in the ice. In the night, however, they managed to break free and made it into open water. They arrived in Brest after having spent ten days at sea. By that evening the delegation was back in Paris.[82]

When the two Frenchmen arrived home, they probably were a little disappointed at not receiving the 400,000 Russian effectives that Doumer had negotiated, but 50,000 men would be a help. Yet as Joffre pointed out, it would hardly solve their manpower problem. Moreover, the Russians had reneged on one deal. What would prevent them from defaulting on another? Paléologue was logically a bit skeptical. He wrote in his diary, "Thus the results of Viviani's mission may be reduced to the sending of 50,000 men to France or rather a promise to that effect."[83] As it turned out, the French were no better in fulfilling their part of the agreement than the Russians. In August the French had to notify Ignatiev that they were unable to fulfill the monthly production of 100,000 shells promised for several of the gun calibers.[84]

In the negotiations for troops for the French front, the Russians agreed to dispatch several brigades to Salonika in Greece as well. This port had become a repository for much of the detritus of the Gallipoli campaign of the year before in hopes of forming a force to attack the Central Powers in what Churchill would a generation later describe as "the soft underbelly" of Eastern Europe. The two allies decided that a second Russian brigade, destined for Salonika, and any subsequent men sent westward would leave from Archangel on the White Sea. The physical danger to any units was greatly increased, of course, since any troop transports would have to pass through the submarine-infested North Sea, but the shorter distance and the reduced cost would make the risk worthwhile.

By mid-April, however, the Russians had said little about sending the Salonikan brigade, or the additional promised troops, for that matter. Alarmed at the disturbing silence, Pau raised the question in a meeting with the tsar. Nicholas replied that the preparations were continuing but that he could not state a specific time for the brigade's departure. The tsar mused about the value such a brigade would have in the Greek panhandle, noting that he felt that its natural place would be at the side of the First, already in France. In hopes of accelerating the process, Paléologue asked his government if he could inform the Russian army that the transport of a second brigade could be accomplished by the French navy after the first of June, since the passage from Archangel should be possible by the latter part of May. Shortly afterward, Paléologue sent a second dispatch informing the French government that, already by May 8, a ship had passed through the straits of the White Sea, so it was now possible for the transport of the troops to begin.[85] These deliberations became moot, however, when at the same time as the dispatch of the second note, the Imperial Government informed Paléologue that the Second Brigade would not be ready to depart for Salonika before mid-July.[86] Since the French would arm them, rifles and artillery would accompany the transports so that during the voyage the Russians could familiarize themselves with the weapons they would be using.

By the first of June the brigade was ready. As the troops began assembling in Archangel, however, it became obvious that the French had not sent sufficient transports. The French foreign minister, Philippe Berthelot, instructed Paléologue to petition the Russian admiralty for the use of the liner *Tsar*, which was scheduled to leave next for the United States with several hundred immigrants. Instead the government offered the *Lechikachev* and the *Catherine II*, and with these two bottoms, the transport was adequate. The first boat with 73 officers and 892 men departed on July 4, arriving in Brest on July 18. Ultimately the number of all ranks that departed was 8,762. The officer in charge was General Mikhail Diterikhs, former quartermaster general of the armies of the

Southwest Front and later a prominent figure with the famous Czech Legion in the Russian Civil War.[87]

The troops were greeted with the same hysteria that the others had seen in Marseille. All through France, the Russian troop trains were greeted with the usual enthusiasm. Dietrichs wired back to St. Petersburg, "Within the borders of France from Brest to Marseille, along the railroad, the progress [of our troops] was a complete triumph . . . ."[88] The first train carrying about 1,200 Russians arrived on the Mediterranean coast on July 21. On July 24 the first of these men began embarkation for Salonika to perform on another stage of history.[89]

The schedule for embarkation called for the departure of the Third Brigade (the first negotiated by Thomas) from Archangel on August 14, the Fourth and Fifth on September 14, and the Sixth and Seventh on October 14. After October, due to weather conditions, passage through the White Sea would become difficult if not impossible, and transports would have to depart from the Kola peninsula. Paléologue reported that the Russian general staff had begun to express doubts about the dispatch of the Seventh since time was growing short. Six or seven days were necessary for travel from the place of concentration to Archangel, and troop movement was presenting a problem. In order not to impede the needed effectives, Paléologue telegraphed General Pierre Janin, commander of the French mission in Russia, to press Alexeev to try to minimize the delay.

The Third Brigade, the second one that would remain in France, was originally destined for Salonika. It was composed of bits and fragments from here and there and had been concentrated in Cheliabinsk and in Ekaterinburg, the city where the Communists would slaughter the imperial family two and a half years later.[90] All orders of the day originated from Ekaterinburg until the time of departure.[91] The Third Brigade was then placed under the command of Major General Vladimir Marushevsky with the two regiments under Colonel Vladimir Narbut in Cheliabinsk and Colonel Gregoryi Simenov in Ekaterinburg respectively. Each regiment had a three-battalion composition, and attached were six machine-gun companies and a reserve company. All components were taken by railroad to Archangel, and after some question about hygiene on some of the transports, all departed by the end of August.

Several soldiers of this brigade would later cross the stage of history. One such individual was a Captain Vadim Maslov, the last lover of the famous spy Mata Hari.[92] Risking capture and execution, she returned to France to rendezvous with this young officer, and it was in the hotel where they had had their trysts that she was arrested. A second figure was to play a major role in the history of his country: blond-haired, blue-eyed Private First Class (other accounts say "sergeant") Rodion Malinovsky, a machine gunner.[93] In the 1950s he became the defense minister of the Soviet Union under Nikita Khrushchev.

Marushevsky had been an old colleague of Colonel Ignatiev in the service academy and during the Russo-Japanese War. This tiny blond man had a wife, a brunette, who was two heads taller than he. Referred to behind her back as "the big umbrella," she had, according to Ignatiev, a superior air that gave her the right to dabble in her husband's military affairs, thus contributing to his ultimate downfall.[94]

Kozlov, a private in a machine-gun regiment that eventually became part of the Third Brigade, was stationed at Oranienbaum outside St. Petersburg on the Gulf of Finland. In his narrative, entitled appropriately *Sold for Shells,* he tells how his unit was first taken to Petrograd en route to departure. With a touch of melodrama that his memory must have added with time, he recalled that in Petrograd, a city in wartime overrun with soldiers, "People stared at us wondering 'What's their business.'" They went to Moscow by train in a journey that took two days. In the ancient capital of the Russian state they were housed in the Spassky barracks on Sukharov Square. A number of regiments were there from other places, but no one initially knew where they were being taken. To pass the time the officers led the men on pointless marches through the city singing and calling cadence while they marched. Yet soon they learned by mere chance that they were going to France. The officers of the assembled units lived in a nearby hotel and for music at one of their parties, they brought along several privates who could play *balalaikas.* At the party, the officers spoke to each other about their future life in France, and the musicians reported the information to their comrades on returning home.[95] Sometime later, at an assembly called at the barracks, an officer informed the men that they were going to fight in the west alongside their French allies.[96] After reading them a tribute from the emperor, the officer lectured them about how they were now entering "the Great Russian Army" and that to fight in the West was a great honor. In doing so they must not lose face by performing poorly. "Remember, gentlemen [he addressed the officers], remember, little brothers [he addressed the privates], that for these holy banners our children, our grandchildren, and our great grandchildren will read about and see all of our military service. Please try, gentlemen, please try, little brothers, to be worthy of the great kindness and trust held in us by the Emperor . . . so that our descendants will remember with pride our names and our service. . . ."[97] About two months later, Kozlov writes, the brigade departed for Archangel.

On the day of departure, the group was lectured by a Captain Ansiferov, who sternly told everyone that they were to "get with the program" and added that he did not want to hear a word about homesickness. Afterward, a priest put his blessing on the venture in a service that lasted about two hours, and the troops marched off to their trains. Several days later they arrived in Archangel. Due to a housing shortage in the city, the soldiers lived in wheat storage bins sleeping on piles of wheat that were also bound for the West. The soldiers joked about how they were "guests going with their own bread."[98]

One colorful addition to the Third Brigade was a young cub bear, who quickly came to be called Misha, as it seems are all Russian bears. He had been bought for eight rubles (one account states forty-five) by Captains Trachek and Cerniak of the 5th regiment (1st regiment of the Third Brigade) while in Ekaterinburg. Misha grew up playing with the soldiers in Russian khaki so the *horizon bleu* uniforms of the French soldiers' instilled in him a feeling of distrust, and he reacted hostilely to them.[99] This mascot went everywhere with the Third Brigade and became dearly beloved by them. He shared their food, their fun, and their privations on their foreign odyssey.

On August 7 the Russian government communicated to the French attaché that the Third Brigade was scheduled to depart for Brest on August 12. In an incredible breach of security, the French reported the fact to their government *en clair*. On August 6 a German submarine had been spotted northwest of Alexandrovsk near the mouth of the White Sea, and when on August 9 the Russian ship *Kovda* hit a German mine in the area, it was assumed that the German sub had laid it. English minesweepers in the White Sea rounded up others, but this incident delayed departure of the Third Brigade by one day. On August 13, however, the *Plata* left Archangel with almost 1,800 men.[100] By August 30 the last of the 10,000 or so men of the only other brigade that would serve in France had departed in the last of the seven-boat fleet that would carry them.[101] The ships were convoyed by torpedo boats into the Arctic Ocean and then left on their own. The journey was far from pleasant. Many men, on the sea for the first time, became seasick, which was aggravated by the food they were given, mainly lentil soup.

The voyage was marred further by an incident on the *Ekaterinoslav* that proved to be a harbinger of things to come. An administrator of transport, Colonel Edmund Krause, was much hated by the men for alleged German sympathies, most probably suspected more for his German name than any of his behavior. The captain had given him the job as signalman at a time when the ship was passing through what Kozlov tells us was "a most dangerous place." Krause, already unpopular, mounted a number of machine guns on deck "in broad daylight [?]" and was about to fire into the ocean, presumably for target practice. The captain stopped him, and when asked why he had planned to fire the machine gun, Krause allegedly gave the ludicrous reply, "It's necessary to frighten away the sharks following our ship." Everyone suspected that he really wanted to alert German submarines in the area of their location by the noise of firing. Later that night, an alarm sounded and all lights were extinguished after a German submarine had been sighted. All soldiers were ordered to put on life jackets. The boat changed course, turning northward at a right angle. A storm arose and they did evade the sub, but the turbulence worsened and the boat was tossed about on the sea. No one slept. The next morning the sea was calm, and the author could see icy mountains and vast empty expanses of water. The ship resumed its former course and the danger passed. At this point a group of soldiers turned on Krause and tried to kill him, somehow thinking that the machine-gun incident the day before had attracted the sub. They went after him to throw him overboard, but the colonel escaped, locking himself in his stateroom for the remainder of the voyage. This incident, however, did not end the Krause affair. In fact, the continuance of the Krause problem would alter the destiny of the Third Brigade.

The first ships carrying the Third Brigade landed in Brest to the same widely emotional reception as the others. On the quay stood a large crowd, among whom were some of the usual Russian expatriates. A priest prayed a prayer of thanks, but he hardly got out the words "Our Father" before he was drowned out by cheering and applause. That evening the Russian soldiers were showered with gifts of wine, flowers, cigarettes, and chocolate. Local newspapers extolled the virtues of Russian soldiers and wrote of how much they would add to the war effort. Soldiers responded to the tumultuous welcome and marched not to the hated "One, two, left, right, stronger foot" cadence of the drill field, but to "Eh, Dunya, Dunya-ya, Dunya, my berry."[102] From there the units boarded trains for Marseille from where they were to be transported to Greece.

Yet at a camp called Avgalades near Marseille, where the troops were billeted until they could depart for Salonika, an ugly incident occurred that was to alter the plan. The now-infamous Colonel Krause was haranguing his battalion about 11:00 P.M. on the night of August 28 when about a hundred of his men ran amok and brutally beat him to death, mutilating his body. They also attacked severely but not fatally another colonel who tried to come to his assistance. Due to the intervention of French troops, order was finally restored. A Soviet historian has tried to cite this incident as a sign of early revolutionary fever among the Russian troops, but it is much more likely that the attack was catalyzed by Krause's unpopularity.[103] Whatever its causes, the disturbance altered the destiny of the Third Brigade. Colonel Ignatiev in Paris first learned of the murder by a late night phone call from Colonel Valerian Balbashevsky, who himself had apparently received a call from someone in Marseille. Ignatiev had to get out of bed to answer it.

"Colonel, sir, there has been a major unpleasantness. Soldiers have killed the commander of the echelon of the Fourth [really the Third] Special Brigade. There was a disturbance in the camp. . . They have arrested with French help the 3rd machine gun company and taken it to the Fort. St. Nicholas." Balbashevsky noted that Ignatiev would find it difficult to come from Paris but asked if it would not somehow be possible since "the French are upset and the camp is surrounded with hussars." The next morning Ignatiev went to Chantilly to report the whole business to General Zhilinsky. Ignatiev arrived at midmorning to find Zhilinsky still asleep. Ignatiev then sought Joffre, who called the Russian uprising on French soil "unacceptable" and pointed out that such an incident was "food for the German propagandists: the French are shooting their own allies!" He ordered Ignatiev to go to Marseille to settle the matter. Thanking the French general for his confidence, Ignatiev decided that he should repair Joffre's breach of military protocol by at least informing Zhilinsky of what had transpired. Around noon he found the general now awake in a suite in the Rothschild's villa having his morning coffee and totally ignorant of the whole affair. In the latter's bedroom, Ignatiev reported the details of the incident to the general.

The Russian general acted as if it were hardly his problem. "They [he always referred to the French in this manner] wanted to get these troops badly enough," Zhilinsky said to the astounded colonel. "Let them administer these troops as they wish." In his memoirs Ignatiev wrote that he was furious at this attitude and what it meant to Russian honor and prestige, observing that "a fish begins to stink from the head."[104]

The French, however, quickly made it clear that although the incident had occurred on French soil, their government would not become involved, seeing it totally as a Russian matter. The Russians, therefore, would have to settle the problem, and Ignatiev was sent to Marseille with some officers from the First Brigade to learn what had happened and take appropriate measures. It took Ignatiev two days to travel from Chantilly to Paris, presumably due to the congestion of military traffic on the rail lines, and he left Paris for Marseille in the evening two days later. He was met at the station in Marseille by Balbashevsky and Colonel Krylov, the brigade's temporary administrator.

After making inquiries, Ignatiev pieced together what had happened. The soldiers, having received some sort of supplemental salary that day, had wanted to go into town to spend it, but they were refused permission to do so. A tense situation had developed and for some reason the unpopular Krause felt that he could defuse it. The colonel began to admonish the annoyed soldiers severely, and the dialogue turned ugly. A few from among the soldiers rushed him "like wild beasts," while others blocked his escape, and he was murdered. The brigade's officers, who apparently had been given permission to go to town, were routed out of their places of amusement by the French police but arrived after the incident was over and the men were back in their barracks.[105]

Ignatiev ordered Krylov to have the entire unit at attention at 6:00 A.M. the next morning, August 29. At exactly six the next day, Ignatiev and Balbachevsky entered through the gate of the camp and greeted the various battalions. According to Ignatiev, the soldiers gathered around him, and he spoke to them not from a prepared speech but "from the heart." He reminded them of the honor of the Russian soldier and their performance before foreigners. Then he asked them to hand over the murderers, giving them a rather lengthy six hours to think it over.[106] At this point, Ignatiev's memoirs, written after the war when he was serving the Soviet regime, turn vague. He records that he was never able to forget "the little bearded man" on the left flank of the line and then states that by 2:00 P.M. they had arrested four or five noncommissioned officers tied to Krause's murder. By 4:00 P.M. these men were already on board a train for Mailly to be returned to Russia for trial.[107] Four were executed in France.

Both Soviet and French archival sources tell a different story. A.L. Sidorov, one of the first fairly reputable Soviet historians of the Russian Revolutionary period, quotes a Soviet archival source indicating that Ignatiev threatened to shoot every tenth man in the battalion in order to get some cooperation. On the other hand, Paléologue states in his memoirs that every eleventh man was indeed shot, and a French archival source adds that Ignatiev wired his government, "[I] consider embarkation before the execution [of those] culpable and before having established general discipline, inadmissible." He suggested execution before the other troops.[108]

Ignatiev's faulty post-Revolutionary memory is not surprising for a number of reasons, yet the archival version, most certainly the truest account, explains both the "cooperation" that Ignatiev claims he received by talking to the troops and the strange vagueness in his memoirs. Not surprisingly, the soldiers' mood remained ugly after the event. The officers felt that embarkation at this point would not be desirable, and the Third Brigade was confined to quarters under the careful watch of its officers.

Meanwhile the Fourth Brigade concentrated in Moscow and Penza and departed for Archangel in September. These were, as events developed, to be the last of the promised troops ever to leave Russia. Yet even they did not reach their intended destination, for suddenly the Russian delays assumed a more permanent quality. The Fifth Brigade, also forming in Moscow and Penza, as well as the Sixth in Tula and the Seventh in Kazan, were ordered to halt, and the Russian government informed Joffre that it was rescinding its promise of sending any more effectives to the Western Front not only because the White Sea was freezing but also because German submarines in the area endangered the troops dispatched from these northern ports. Even the Fourth Brigade, which had by now arrived at Archangel and was embarking on four transports for the voyage to France, was ordered to disembark. Thus the Russian government informed Joffre that they were for the second time reneging on the promise for troops to the West.[109]

The French were dumbfounded. Why would the Russians once again break a promise that had been so solemnly given? As is often the case, one finds the reason by reading between the lines. The most important factor was most probably the staggering losses sustained by Russians in the Brusilov offensive of the summer of 1916. While a tactical success, the offensive had cost the Russians at least one million new casualties, and Alexeev was, by September 1, short about 200,000 soldiers. As early as June the tsar had written to his wife that "all available troops are being sent to Brusilov in order to give him as many reinforcements as possible."[110] This deficit was made worse in August by the entrance into the war and subsequent hasty collapse of Romania, quickly overrun by the Germans and Austrians, thus giving the Russians another two hundred miles of front to defend. These difficulties, added to the accumulated losses of over 5 million men and about 60,000 officers,[111] meant that the troops being dispatched to France were badly needed at home. There likewise must have been the Krause factor. This whiff of mutiny soon after arrival on French soil must have confirmed the fears of some Russian leaders of the infective nature of "republican France." Would not other troops sent there behave the same way? Given the fact that, as early as June, Brusilov desperately needed reinforcements, it might be wondered why the Russian government did not default on its promise sooner. Probably the answer lies again in Russian dependence on the flow of French artillery and shells. In the same letter just mentioned, Nicholas wrote his wife,

"This damnable question of ammunition for the heavy artillery is begin-ning to make itself felt again." To suspend promised troop shipments to France would most likely result in the cessation of the flow of shells just when the Russian army was advancing seriously against the enemy for the first time since 1914. Austria was reeling against the Russian onslaught, and the Russians were taking thousands of prisoners a week. To deprive Brusilov of whatever he needed, whether men or shells, was unthinkable at this time. To supply one might result in the loss of the other, and the quandary must have resulted in an enormous amount of soul-searching on the part of the Russian High Command in June 1916. Yet by the end of August, the losses incurred as the Germans buttressed their faltering ally made the decision increasingly less difficult to make, espe-cially as the September termination of the offensive ended the urgent need for shells but not for soldiers to fill the depleted ranks. For this reason probably more than any other, the flow of Russians westward ceased.

Having been successful once in changing the Russian mind on the troop question, the French tried again. Soon the French naval attaché met shortly with the Russian minister of war. Replying to the Russian con-cerns for safety, the French attaché made the not very valid point that Russian ships in the North Sea and the Arctic Ocean were no more endangered than those in the Mediterranean. Beliaev retreated into the fortress of tsarist prerogative, telling the French diplomatic officer that the tsar himself had given orders to disembark the troops already loaded to leave, so that ended the matter. Alexeev finally agreed, however, to allow the Third Brigade, currently being held in semidetention, to remain in France instead of going to Salonika as planned. The Krause incident probably had more to do with his change of mind than his desire to keep his promise. If the unit was inclined to some disciplinary instability, close confinement on a ship might make matters worse. The Third would be replaced in Salonika by the Fourth, which had not been contaminated, and Alexeev probably released it to that front when the French agreed to send the arms already reserved for the Russians for use on the Romanian front. The Fourth finally reembarked and left for its long voyage to the Aegean Sea. With its departure the erratic trickle of Russian troops westward ceased.[112] Based on his most recent understanding with Alex-eev, on September 17 Joffre issued the order for the Third Brigade to join the First at Mourmelon-le-Grand to form a division. Two trains carrying them left Marseille for the front in Champagne at 6:00 and 8:30 P.M. respectively on September 20, and these soldiers, who had thought that their destination would be the northern Aegean coast of Greece, soon found themselves in the trenches of northern France.[113]

Figures vary from source to source, but French government accounts place the total number of Russian troops sent from Archangel at 34,975 soldiers and 635 officers. If the 110 officers and 8,572 men sent from Dalny to Marseille is added, the total of over 43,000 soldiers and 745 officers left Russian soil to fight in the West.[114] About half of them, the First and the Third brigades, composed what came to be known as the Russian Expeditionary Force in France.

Although most of them eventually would return to Russia, many would never see their homeland again. A number would die and be buried in the soil of a land that came to hate them. Others would choose an unpleasant exile there after the war rather than return to their native land after the Revolution, which then was gripped in what one contemporary called "a nightmare in a lunatic asylum." They would marry foreign women and rear children who would speak a language their fathers could barely understand. Those who eventually did return home found a vastly altered Russia from the nation they had left. In their absence their country had shed its ancient political and social underpinnings and had taken a leap into a dark, unknown abyss. Some would return while their countrymen had turned on each other like jackals in a bitter civil war. Others came back after that war, when their country was prostrate and the land ravaged by famine. Their homeland had more than ever in its history become Nikolai Gogol's "flying troika" on a collision course with a brutal political destiny.

THREE

Postal Sector 189

July 1916–March 1917

Letters to Russia must have addresses in both Cyrillic and Latin alphabets. Packages must be accompanied by three customs declarations. They will be sent Brest-Archangel. All letters received in France must be addressed to Secteur Postal 189.

—Note de Service Postale[1]

When the Russian soldier is off his own soil, he is worthless; he goes to pieces at once.

—Sazonov[2]

Death to the two-headed eagle!
Sever its long-necked head with a single stroke!
So that it can never come to life again.
We have triumphed!
Glory to us all!
Glo-o-ory to us all!

—Mayakovsky[3]

ON ARRIVAL IN CHAMPAGNE, the transplanted Russians immediately began their transformation into Western front soldiers. Although the usual regimental strength in the Russian army was 1,000 men divided into four battalions of 250, each of the brigades in France was initially divided into two regiments of three battalions, like the French. Each battalion was divided into the usual component of four companies. An organization was created in Paris to assist the Russian soldiers with what at a later time came to be called "culture shock." To ease the transition, 1,000 copies of a standard French military vocabulary were sent to the two units by the French army. The reinstruction of the men at Mailly was under the general direction of the IV French Army's commander, the taciturn and morose General Henri Gouraud, a hero of the Gallipoli campaign, during which he had lost an arm and had had both of his legs broken. At the time the Russian force arrived, he was being considered as a replacement for General Maurice Sarrail, the commander of the Salonikan front.[4] Playing good politics, Gouraud visited the Russian church constructed near the front every time he visited the Russian units,[5] and he remained in continuous touch with the highest-ranking Russian military figure in France, General Zhilinsky.

Born in Riazan *Oblast* in 1853, Zhilinsky had followed the usual military career of the Russian gentry. He had good political ties, being a favorite of the Dowager Empress Maria Feodorovna and the minister of war Sukhomlinov, and he had used his connections to gain and hold a number of soft desk jobs while he rapidly ascended the chain of command. Apparently dull, he rarely took any initiative, usually relying on strict adherence to the regulations book to avoid complications with his superiors. Although calling him a "thorough gentleman," Sir Douglas Haig described him as a "very old man" and noted in his diary Zhilinsky's history of incompetence.[6] To General Edmund Ironside, later a figure in British intervention in the Russian Civil War, Zhilinsky was merely an "office soldier."[7] Joffre described him as being "neither very able nor frank."[8] After the East Prussian disaster, Zhilinsky had been named, again due to his court connections, as the head of the Russian military mission to the Allied Council in Chantilly. He served there with his usual sluggishness, generally displaying at meetings a stygian ignorance of Russia's military situation and avoiding decisions of any importance. He performed in this manner until he was recalled in November 1916.

Under Zhilinsky the direct command over all Russian troops in France was General Palitsyn. Palitsyn was a close friend and mentor of General Alexeev, who himself coming from nonaristocratic stock, had probably had his career helped by Palitsyn. Grand Duke Nicholas Nicholaevich had wanted to have Palitsyn as his own chief of staff in 1914, but the tsar had chosen the brutal anti-Semite General Nicholas Yanush-

kevich. A scientific soldier, before the war Palitsyn had begun a professional study of Russia's defense needs based on his careful study of
German defense installations and worked at it until he was stopped by
Sukhomlinov and his incompetent clique.

Palitsyn had been an advocate of retreat from the indefensible Polish
salient in 1915, which probably would have saved hundreds of thousands
of Russian lives had it been effected. When Grand Duke Nicholas was
removed from overall command and transferred to the Caucasian front in
1915, he took Palitsyn with him as his assistant to Armenia in 1916. It was
from the Turkish front that Palitsyn was transferred to France.[9] One day
not long after Palitsyn's arrival in the Caucasus, the grand duke summoned him to his office and told him that he had received a telegram from
His Imperial Highness stating that Palitsyn was to go to the Western
Front to oversee and lead the Russian Expeditionary Force. The grand
duke had already telegraphed that Palitsyn would go to Tiflis (modern
Tblisi) on October 17, 1916, and depart from there for France. On the
eve of his departure, he visited the minister of war, Shuvaev, who gave
him one directive in the meeting: "Do not interfere with orders [*ne
vmeshivat'sia v zakazu*]."[10]

Arriving in France, there followed the usual round of meetings with
major figures—Ambassador Alexander Izvolsky, Joffre, Briand, and
Poincaré. Then the Russian general was given a most spartan office at the
headquarters at Chantilly with only a few miscellaneous wall maps and
was cheerfully ignored. He participated in no meetings, saw no telegrams,
and was bypassed with news. This treatment continued until Alexeev
learned of it, and then matters proceeded normally.[11]

It is unclear even from Palitsyn's own account exactly when he made
his first visit to the troops he was commanding, but it apparently was not
until late January 1917, almost two months after he arrived. It would seem
logical to have gone there shortly after arriving at his station, yet he was
involved in the peripatetic scrambling to see various officials, and shortly
afterward, he departed for the Allied conference in Rome, which lasted into
January. Palitsyn tells us nothing about his visit to his troops in his memoir,
and he seems more interested in noting matters such as his encounter at
Châlons with the French General Henri Pétain, whom he especially liked.[12]

Directly under Palitsyn was commandant of the First Brigade
Nikolai Lokhvitsky, whose wife and two daughters appeared in France
with him, although there is no mention of their coming on the troop
transports. In the chain of command under him was the first regimental
commander, a Colonel Shchvolokov, the second regimental commander

Colonel Paul Diakonov, and the head of the *battalion de dépôt,* a Lieutenant Colonel Sevenard. Under them were 181 officers and 8,762 men of whom 84 officers and 8,577 soldiers were Russian. The remaining officers and men were French.[13] With the support elements of the brigade was, interestingly, a female physician, a Dr. Kroliunitskaia, whose husband was also a doctor with the same unit.[14]

By late April all parts of the First Brigade had arrived at Mailly for their special training, but the first week's work was interrupted constantly with troop reviews by dignitaries, both French and Russian. Yet those early days were used for the distribution of some weapons and ammunition as well as French steel helmets (with Russian emblems attached) and gas masks. The Western cuisine required some adjustment since the regular diet of the Russian soldier contained meat, potatoes, cabbage, and beets but usually did not include tomatoes, peppers, macaroni, or a large variety of fresh vegetables.[15] The quantities of rations were certainly adequate. The daily allotment of bread was 750 grams, about half a loaf, and the ration of beef was 400 grams, or about a pound. The diet also called for 800 grams daily of fresh vegetables, which were indeed abundant, yet these items might include lettuce and endive, something not known or appreciated by the Russian peasant's palate. There were also rations of tea and sugar, margarine, and buckwheat as well as the Russian nonalcoholic beer Kvas, which must have been difficult to obtain. For the infantryman there were 15 grams of tobacco per day, with 20 grams allocated for the officers.[16] In addition to the food and ammunition, the units were given quantities of horse fodder and even telephone equipment.[17] In the report outlining these early days, Palitsyn painted a very rosy picture. "Young regiments of both brigades are in excellent condition," he wrote to Petrograd, "abundantly supplied with all provisions. . . ."[18]

Soon after the arrival of the First Brigade, President Poincaré made the customary visit to review the Russian troops at Mailly. Along with Ambassador Izvolsky, General Zhilinsky, and General Pierre Roques, he left the Gare de l'Est at 7:30 in the morning of May 26 for the front. A fine rain was falling and the soil was soggy and muddy. Poincaré reviewed the troops of the First Brigade, which he described as *"très beaux hommes, manoeuvrant bien."* He passed the ranks crying out at each battalion three Russian words that he had learned to say in Petrograd and that mean "Good day, brave boys!" The Russians responded to the president's Russian with the appropriate reply. The president then gave the traditional decorations to the brigade general, the colonels, and the chief medical officer.[19]

The review completed, Poincaré visited the Russian chapel to see the icons. The priest made a short speech, which was translated by a

French officer and which affirmed that all Russian soldiers were Christians and thanked Poincaré for the chapel that had been built for them. The French president then visited the barracks, in which the men were singing Russian songs. In one barracks kitchen, Poincaré ate some soup, macaroni, and potatoes, which he found so pleasing that he described them in his memoirs as "very good." Finally, in a railroad car, a formal evening meal was served, which we can be certain consisted of more elaborate fare than macaroni and potatoes. The dinner entertainment consisted of groups playing alternately French and Russian music. Russian military units always seem to form choruses, and the REF was no different. Doubtless some of these groups performed for Poincaré. The Russian soldiers danced, and one of them demonstrated the astonishing talent of making the call of a nightingale.[20]

Palitsyn found the French supplemental training "with few exceptions" to be "excellent," producing a "warrior of good personal make-up," who performed his military duties "with valor."[21] This additional training for the First Brigade lasted between a month to seven weeks, a surprisingly long time, since the men were already basically trained in the use of military drill and less sophisticated weapons such as the bayonet. This training included a "Momento of Practical Advice" that was insultingly patronizing. In addition to telling the Russian soldier not to urinate in the communication trenches (presumably it was all right to do so in the parallel trenches), the pamphlet instructed the soldier not to expose himself to the enemy, always keep his weapon close at hand, and never fire his rifle unless there was something at which to shoot. No one was to fire at an airplane during the day unless ordered to do so by an officer, and at night it was forbidden to fire on a plane or dirigible, apparently whether instructed to do so or not. In a gas attack, Russians were told to don their masks, light some sort of brassier, close the dugouts, if there were any, and not to run or panic. In case of an air attack, designated by a whistle or a trumpet blast, the soldier was to hide under cover until the second signal was given.[22] To this basic tutelage was added additional rifle practice as well as machine-gun instruction with the Hotchkiss gun.

A major difference between the Eastern and Western fronts was the elaborate system of trenches in the West as opposed to the more casual defenses in the East, where the front had from the beginning of the war been more fluid. In some cases in the East, the respective lines were so far apart that no-man's land stretched for miles and frequently contained inhabited villages within it. After the series of flanking maneuvers in the West in 1914, called the Race to the Sea, the Western Front had settled down into static, close trench warfare that did not change appreciably until the last year of the war. Both sides built elaborate trench systems with bunkers, tunnels, connecting trenches, and communication trenches near one another, and a new type of warfare was introduced. The Russians had to be trained not only in the methods of fighting in and around trenches but in the art of building them as well. This schooling in trench warfare consisted of instruction in patrolling, observation, and occupation of enemy trenches, as well as defense against attack, the execution of mopping-up operations, trench raids (*coups de main*), and relieving a unit already holding a sector of trench.[23]

Despite the instruction, however, the Russian soldier never adapted well to the use of gas masks and the steel helmets, which they regarded as unnecessary encumbrances. French officers stationed with the Russian units had a great deal of difficulty making the Russians wear both, and members of the REF usually discarded them as soon as possible.[24] On the whole, however, the additional training turned the First Brigade into a first-rate fighting unit that performed well. When several companies of these troops marched in Paris on Bastille Day, the crowd was most impressed.[25]

The Third Brigade began arriving at Mailly on September 17, the first group of 1,050 men and 20 officers disembarking from the trains at 1:30 P.M. The remainder appeared over the next few days. The plan for their front reeducation was much the same as that of the First; the first week was devoted to vaccination and the distribution of equipment and the next five weeks designated for actual training. Weeks two through five were to be used for instruction of cadres while week six was for instruction together. This plan, however, was not even remotely followed. Colonel Marushevsky later bitterly complained that the Third Brigade spent only eight days in Mailly before it was sent to the front to relieve the First Brigade.[26] Verdun had taken a terrible toll on the French army, and the necessity of replacements truncated their training.

The First Brigade was ready to go to the front by the early summer 1916. General Gouraud had ordered that all officers were to have finished their training on June 16 or 17 and would be sent without their men for two days' duty in the trenches with the 21st Corps Armée of the IV Army to get a feel in advance for the kind of fighting they would be doing. They would then return to Mailly on the night of June 18 or 19 to rejoin their troops. All equipment would be readied to move on June 25. The men would be housed with a French unit, which was already located on the Suippes river, northeast of Reims.[27] The unit's artillery had as its area of surveillance the stretch of land between the Bois-en-couloir and the Suippes.

Private Vavilov asserted in his memoirs that the Russians had assumed they had gone to France not to fight in the trenches but to do garrison duty in the cities and function as guards, that is, to serve only as a link between the Russians and their allies. Yet at some point — exactly when is not clear — they were assembled, and a translator read them a letter, the authorship of which was unknown. It informed the recruits that they were to go to the front, and when the order to depart came, the first regiment was sent in troop trucks because some had to take position quickly at their jump-off camp at Mourmelon-le-grand, about four miles from their place in the front lines. The second regiment left Mailly for Mourmelon on foot in the direction of Soudon, then through the villages of Germinon and Villeseneux. That evening a heavy rain fell and progress was slow. The next day the regiment passed through Vraux and Jurvigny-sur-Marne, arriving at Mourmelon on June 27. After the men had been in the camp for a few days, they were taken to the front with the other regiment, which had arrived there several days before them. They entered the line on the Suippes river near Aubérive, where, according to the London *Times*, they occupied "an excellent labyrinth of trenches"[28] with the II Cavalry Corps under General Marie Antoine de Mitri. Two days later Vavilov participated in this first action and for the first time heard the hostile firing of cannon and machine guns and the explosion of shells.[29]

The sector, part of which they defended, stretched for eleven miles from Mourmelon-le-Grand-Aubérive on the east to the line Verzy-Prunay on the west. Lokhvitsky's command post was located on the highway from Mourmelon to Aubérive.[30] It would be impossible today to pinpoint exactly where the first Russians entered the French trenches. Most likely it was in the vicinity of Fort de la Pompelle, one of the emplacements defending Reims to the southeast near the village of Courcy.[31] In the tunnels and communication trenches there, the Russians memorialized their presence by writing their names on the wall in the Cyrillic alphabet.

The *Echo de Paris* reported the entrenchment of the Russians with the usual glowing propaganda. In an article entitled "The Russians in the Trenches," the French public was informed, "Here they are in the French trenches where they wanted to go. I have never seen soldiers so happy, so ardent to their task, so attached to their duty, so instilled with the noblesse and importance of their role!" Continuing in the same vein, the writer waxed as enthusiastic as the writers covering the first Russian arrivals. "Ah! These sympathetic and brave people . . . , so candid, so knowing, so valiant with their smiling and tranquil faces. How do you not attach yourself to them?"[32]

The anonymous writer of the article visited Lokhvitsky, who *Le Matin* stated was followed by his men as a veritable cult figure.[33] The journalist described Lokhvitsky as "young, vivacious, of lucid and calm authority." His French was spoken "with a finesse like his native tongue." As the writer arrived, the general was about to make what the author of the article thought was a stroll.

"Do you want to see my soldiers in the trenches?" Lokhvitsky asked the reporter. "I'm going this instant to make my usual visit. Go with me."

On entering the communication trench, Lokhvitsky and the writer encountered "happy" Russian soldiers making tea, which the Russians drank in great quantity. Having heard of the victories on the Russian front in the East (the Brusilov offensive in Galicia was moving forward very successfully at this point), they were eager to fight the Germans here and gain a victory too. On the return to Lokhvitsky's quarters, he told the reporter, "Now that our blood is spilled for the same cause and on the same field of battle, we regard the French as brothers and France as a second country."[34]

The Russians got into the fight soon enough. Their "military baptism" came on July 15, the day the reporter visited the trenches. Their initiation came not in the form of a full-scale offensive but as a *coup de main*, a probing action of limited objectives. The *Times* reported, giving no details, that on July 15 and 16 there was great activity on the part of both French and Russian patrols.[35] In raiding the German trenches, the Russians took a number of prisoners, who seemed dazed when they found themselves in the hands of the tsar's soldiers on French soil.[36]

For all the rosy pictures painted by French journalists of happy soldiers in idyllic surroundings, the Russian soldiers themselves did not find war in the trenches so appealing. Private Vavilov had thought that they would be able to sleep there like at home, but for three days after their arrival, they continuously received "small presents from Krupp," shells fired from the German lines. One fell on the observation point, blowing it to smithereens and scattering bits of human flesh all over their company.[37] Russian carelessness about wearing gas masks and helmets caused additional grief and rendered some of the ventures in which they were engaged more lethal. To make matters worse, within a few days shortages of fighting matériel had begun to be felt, and Lokhvitsky began complaining about the difficulty of getting weapons and shells to the general commandant of the Group West.[38] Generally, however, the Russians, like their French and English counterparts, adapted to the routine of trench life with the filth, the lice, the rats, and the constant fear of impending death. The first real taste of battle for the Russians came on

September 5, when they were attacked by the 212th German division in a murderous onslaught that lasted for twelve hours. Assisted by French artillery, which one author states fired 40,000 shells at the advancing Germans, the Russians repelled five attacks in the direction of Courcy and southeast of Reims toward Fort de la Pompelle.[39]

September 5 through 18 saw fairly intense fighting with the usual attacks and counterattacks. A *coup de main* into the German trenches on September 9 resulted in the capture of several prisoners, and a soldier and the group's officer, 2nd Lieutenant Tikhomirov, were recommended for decorations. In one incident, German fire fell on the 1st and 3rd battalion of the 2nd regiment just when it was due to be relieved. Lieutenant Colonel Gotua insisted that it continue in place, and losses were heavy.[40]

On October 5 (another account states October 16), 1916, the First Brigade was relieved at the front, and the men returned to Mailly for rest and more training after almost four months in the lines. During their sojourn they had sustained losses of between five and six hundred men. They stayed in Mailly for the month of November, where they again trained in new methods of fighting, and at the end of their stay, they joined in a grand war game with the French troops under real fire. Afterward they returned to the same sector at Fort de la Pompelle.[41]

Several miles northeast of the town of Mourmelon-le-Grand today is a Russian church adjacent to a cemetery for Russians who died in France. Near the cemetery is a large monument to the Russian dead. While most scars made by the trenches of the Great War have long since healed on the French countryside, on the other side of the Russian graveyard lies a copse of young hardwoods. Beyond lies an open field that stretches for miles to a distant wood. Among the trees are the rusty, decaying remains of a bunker that must have been part of a line of trench in 1916. We can only assume that it was near here that the Russian Expeditionary Force first saw action in France, and the first Russians must have died.[42]

In addition to the daily probings and clashes, the Russians had sharp exchanges with the enemy on July 16, July 27, and August 2. In the July 16 engagement, all of Nechvolodov's 1st regiment was in the line, with the second regiment in reserve, since one of its battalions was in Paris to participate in the traditional July 14 parade. At 7:00 P.M. on the sixteenth, the enemy began a strong bombardment of the Aubérive sector, which lasted for an hour and a half. At 8:30 the enemy emerged from their trenches and attacked the center of the 1st regiment, engaging the 1st battalion. They were met with artillery, machine gun, and rifle fire. In the initial attack, a Russian machine gun nest was destroyed with all of its gunners. At the signal of Lieutenant Bykovsky, machine gunners from the second line were moved forward, an action that mitigated the enemy attack. Then the repulsed Germans were counterattacked by the 2nd company of the first regiment, which advanced with the cry "It's us, the Russians!" By 9:00 P.M. all the fighting was over. Thirteen Russians had been killed, with thirty-six wounded, two of them officers.[43] General Dumas, a relative of the famous author, praised the Russian performance, especially the counterattack, and Bykovsky became the first Russian officer decorated by General Gouraud.[44]

A second daring encounter occurred on July 27 when, under cover of darkness, the first battalion of the 2nd regiment of Lieutenant Colonel Ivanov led by Ensign Guk attacked the German trenches without prior artillery preparation, using hand grenades to clear the way. They took some prisoners and returned to their own lines. Dumas wrote of their attack, "They proved their solid and serious valor and their ardent desire to perform."[45]

On the evening of August 2, a heavy rustle was heard before the position of Company 6, and the commander named seven soldiers to go out and investigate. In no-man's land they stumbled onto a German patrol. The oldest Russian among the seven, a Private Yushchenko, fell upon the enemy with his bayonet and almost single-handedly drove them away. A few Germans were killed, with some Russians receiving bayonet wounds. Similar encounters occurred during the nights of August 6 and 9. A reconnaissance mission into the German trenches was made on the night of August 17, where 2nd Lieutenant Blofeld was mortally wounded. Other short missions such as these were executed on August 24 and 25.[46]

Despite the success, there began to surface very early among the Russians a morale problem, which was not caused simply by homesickness. That would have arisen even on the Eastern Front, where the great distances and general transportation nightmares made home leave impossible for the common soldier. In France morale, however, was aggravated by the total isolation these two brigades experienced. On the Russian front at least a general flow of information from home came with the endless flood of recruits that were dispatched daily. After the arrival of the Third Brigade, most news and reliable ties to their homeland effectively ceased, leaving only the wildest rumors or leftist propaganda from the Russian émigrés in Paris as the source of their news.[47] Friction with the French likewise contributed to the problem, as the French seemed to use the Russians for especially nasty missions and behaved with a condescension often showered on their other allies as well. Moreover, release from the trenches was often not very therapeutic. Vavilov described the "rest" at the camp at Mailly as being worse than the "hottest fire of the trenches." "We lived in dampness," he recalled, and "the officers inflicted many brutalities." Often artillery fire could be heard from the front, a constant reminder of what they had left and to what they would return.[48] Add to this general annoyance the cultural and linguistic isolation, the different type of food, and the casual medical attention often given them by the French, one has an excellent recipe for a morale crisis, which with a few additional annoyances can develop into an irreparable collapse of the will to fight. These problems fertilized and supplemented the depression normal among soldiers and helped pave the way for the disaster that was to follow.

Except for an occasional and very restricted leave, the only source to alleviate the boredom and isolation was the aforementioned journal, *The Russian Soldier's Friend*, and a new sheet, *Military Newspaper for the Russian Force in France*, whose articles were as dull as its title. Like most such papers, the pieces were mostly propagandistic and of little value for informational purposes. The writing was, however, upbeat and optimistic, especially after the Russian Revolution, when the paper's name changed to *The Russian Soldier-Citizen in France*.[49] Then there appeared such articles as "The Soviet of Workers' and Soldiers' Deputies against a Separate Peace" and "President Wilson's Greetings to the Russian People" (issue no. 30,3/16 June 1917) The word "victory" and phrases like "collapse of the enemy front" were frequently used. One issue sported a picture of an English officer taking a turn at a Russian plow, and others showed French soldiers carrying French and German wounded. Each issue offered a French vocabulary lesson with the pronunciation of each word given as close as possible in Russian transliteration. The choice of words, while useful, was often somewhat lugubrious. For example, one May 1917 edition included the words "wind, rain, mud, dust, swamp," and phrases like "It's dark" and "It's cold." All issues contained many articles on the value of discipline.[50] This official journal was unofficially supplemented with papers printed by the radical Russian elements in Paris as well as an in-house rag published by the First Brigade in Mailly called *Otkliki voiny* (the Responses of War). The last was a rather coarsely done typed sheet depicting a sunrise over no-man's land with the saturnine addition of barbed wire on all four points of the front page.[51] This paper was much less patriotic and became vigorously antiwar.

On a higher level, some efforts were made to improve morale with the formation in June 1916, of a society of friendship called France-Russie, which sported as its president the perennial French politician Edouard Herriot with Russian ambassador Izvolsky as its honorary president. This organization met with some regularity for the exchange of ideas and general knowledge,[52] yet quite probably none of its work had much effect on the common soldier in the trenches, where most of the problems were festering.

These feeble efforts could hardly alleviate the Russians' perceived mistreatment by the French. From the time of their arrival in Marseille, the food given them was different from what they knew and often distasteful, although it probably was no worse than that given the French soldier. The bread they received on landing was spoiled and moldy, and except for the beer and wine furnished the officers, they were given nothing to drink.[53] In August 1916 an order was issued from General Maurice Pellé to the general commandant of the army of the sector in which the Russians were stationed forbidding the sale of wine to Russians even when on leave. "The Russian soldiers have never drunk wine in their country," the order read, "and some recent evidence has moreover shown the necessity to prevent in a total manner the sale of wine to Russian troops. I ask you," Pellé continued, "to give the necessary order so that the sale of this commodity be rigorously forbidden them."[54] The Russian writer Ilya Ehrenburg, at one point a journalist on the Western Front, wrote in amazement at the manner in which this rule was applied. He noted that when Russian troops arrived in a village to rest, the town crier announced to the accompaniment of drums that it was expressly forbidden to sell "grape wine" to the Russians. "In France," Ehrenburg wrote in amazement, "wine is given to children. The peasants were afraid to look out of their windows: the newcomers who could not be given wine must be savages, drunk before they had had a drink." Finally half a liter per day was indeed allotted each soldier, but often it did not reach him.[55]

Somehow the mistreatment seemed even worse near the front. When stationed in the village of Mailly, the Russians were forbidden to leave their prescribed boundaries, and when permitted to go into the village, every effort was made to keep them separated from the French soldiers by isolating them to certain canteens. Moreover, local merchants raised prices by as much as 20 percent just for the Russians. At one point the French military sold to the Russians at inflated prices straw that had already been used by Moroccan troops. A *Times* correspondent who visited the front was amazed that the Russians did not seem dressed for winter. Their uniforms consisted of regular khaki with French helmets. The correspondent felt that they gave the appearance of being colonial troops,[56] whom the French also treated shabbily. On a later occasion the Third Brigade did receive 1,350 tents but with no stakes or poles with which to erect them.

An additional factor in Franco-Russian friction was a major difference in cultural temperament and practice. The Russians, a somewhat
somber people, took seriously French good-natured jokes at their way of
life. The Russians ate then as now a buckwheat porridge (kasha), which
resembles coarsely broken, boiled oats. "You know, we feed cattle that
stuff," the French would say. The Russians learned to reply "What about
you? You eat snails and frogs. Our cattle at home would not look at
that."[57] Once a Russian detachment, having been relieved from the front,
arrived at a rest barracks behind the lines in which there were relatively
few latrines. The Russians complained to the French commandant who
sent two sergeants to examine the problem. After inspecting the facilities,
one of the French sergeants told the Russian in charge, "For two years
our *poilus* have slept here on these bunks and have never complained. And
you, having just arrived, you are griping. What pretentiousness! One
would think you were English."[58]

Of a more serious nature was the inaccurate reporting by some
Russian journalists that Russian soldiers had complained about corporal
punishment used on their regiments, saying that it had been authorized
by the French military. Since such treatment was regularly used in the
Russian army, it is highly unlikely that the Russian officers would have
asked French permission. Indeed, when one newspaper told of the flogging of Russian soldiers, the French government ordered the minister of
war to investigate. Yet what is believed to be the truth is always more
important than the truth itself, and the belief that this was occurring
helped crystallize both in Russia and in the trenches of northern France
a strong anti-French sentiment that would greatly influence the events
there in 1917.[59] Ehrenburg wrote that Lokhvitsky and his men were in
the habit of flogging any soldier who committed the slightest offense.
Colonel Gotua would make trench inspections by quietly sneaking into
lines in his soft Caucasian boots. If he encountered a sleeping soldier, he
would wake him by shouting. He would then inflict physical punishment
on the unfortunate infantryman.[60]

There was not, of course, any organized attempt to mistreat the
Russians, and indeed the French made an honest effort to stop price
gouging by posting in all stores and on main roads the lists of maximum
prices for which goods could be sold, and orders were given to the
gendarmerie to enforce the controls. To further improve the situation, a
commissary for Russians only opened with reasonably priced goods.[61]
Many of the alleged slights came as a result of the general dislocation
caused by war, and doubtless there were occasions when the French
soldiers also received stale bread and tents without stakes. The homesick

Russians thought otherwise, however, and for them that was all that was necessary. There were, however, individual acts of Allied camaraderie from time to time. When the military priest Sokolovsky had his arm torn off by a shell while on a reconnaissance mission to the German lines, his life was saved because a French medic gave him "generously" a blood transfusion, presumably of his own blood, since the medic was awarded the Cross of St. George for his act by the Russian government. There were other examples, such as French boy scouts' maintaining the graves of the Russian fallen. Yet the *fraternité de feu* of the trenches, when it occurred, was quickly forgotten in the rear and degenerated into the mutual ethnic pinpricks, which in time became outright hostility.

At a governmental level there occurred in the fall a major breakdown of communications that could only have further strained the relations between the two allies. On October 30, 1916, the French submitted a bill to the Russians for expenses incurred thus far by the REF. The sum demanded was 618,000 French francs, and with the request was a curt note stating that the French considered the account in arrears. It likewise suggested that the Russians begin paying weekly installments.

The Russians were stunned. The agreement that had brought the troops to France had included the proviso that the French would pay all expenses and support for the units. Oddly, months passed before the Russians responded by producing the agreement signed at Stavka by Thomas, Viviani, and Alexeev. The final months of tsarism were chaotic, and eventually it became the Provisional Government's job to obtain from the French official recognition that the Russians owed nothing.[62] Nevertheless, before the problem was resolved, the French sent a corrected bill for 802,634 francs, 382,320 of which were for blankets sent to the Russian army and 420,314 of which were for reimbursement for clothing, equipment and shoes. Other bills followed for feed bags, handkerchiefs, spurs, soap, leggings, and even grappling hooks, placing the total "debt" at around several million francs, apparently in addition to the 618,000 billed in October.[63] Meanwhile in March 1917 the French railroads called on the Russians to pay an additional 600,000 francs for the assorted internal transportation given the Russian troops after their arrival.

Ignatiev responded more quickly than his government, which on the eve of the Revolution had more pressing matters to attend. Reminding the French president about the original agreement, Ignatiev obtained the contents of the understanding of the initial contract, but Poincaré expressed the belief that there should now be certain charges for such things as heat and electricity.[64] French Minister of War Painlevé likewise suggested a number of items that should in the future fall as expenses to the Russian government, such as clothing and equipment. Finally in March a French colonel intervened to tell the French government that the Viviani agreement called for the French to pay everything.[65] In the fast-moving days of the young Provisional Government, someone found the time to search for the document signed by Alexeev and Viviani and present it to the French government.[66] At some point, some sort of revision of the agreement must have been accepted. There appears in the REF archive at Columbia University an undated document indicating that the Russian government was to pay salaries, for food, and for equipment and clothing, while the French were to fund expenses in the rather nebulous areas of "requisitions" and "damages."[67] The whole incident, however, had to have angered the Russians and further damaged Allied relations. Now that the troops were in France and could not be returned easily, the French seemed to think that they could change the rules since the Russians could hardly let their men go unclothed or hungry. Yet shortly, the collapse of order in Russia and the near collapse of discipline on the French front gave both the French and the Russian governments more important concerns.

In mid-October, the First Brigade was pulled from the line for a rest, having stayed there longer than French units usually did. Lokhvitsky's order no. 187, dated 2/15 (Julian then Gregorian calendar dates) October, 1916, expressed great praise and thanks for the men's service. "I deem it my duty to thank from the bottom of my heart all my comrades, and particularly those that I leave behind me, those who remain in this sector which is now for you a piece of native soil since the blood of Russia has reddened it." Lokhvitsky struck a chord on the impact that the joint service had had on the Franco-Russian Alliance, which he felt had been "sealed by a purple stamp of our blood shed together." France and Russia had now been joined in a still "deeper and more solid bond" like the one "which exists between blood brothers" and that "nothing would be able to break or destroy." He believed that the joint combat had created a "more intense sentiment" the radiance of which "will illuminate our way to victory, to glory."[68] When the First Brigade finally returned to the front late in November, it was placed under the V French Army in the sector of Ludes, somewhat northwest of Reims.

The Third Brigade had arrived at Mailly in September, after the decision to let it join the First. At 8:00 in the morning on October 16, 1916, it replaced the First at the front. The replacement unit was composed of the 2nd battalion of the 5th regiment under Colonel Ritov and two and a half battalions of the 6th regiment under Colonel Simonov, who was positioned on the left flank of the sector. The brigade's reserve under Lieutenant Colonel Anisimov was taken from the 5th battalion and one-half of the 6th. Marushevsky, of course, commanded the brigade. According to Ignatiev, he had adapted much more quickly than had Lokhvitsky to "the French order"[69] and worked better within the framework of the Western Front.

Outside of the basic humdrum of trench life, with the patrols, the probing, the counterprobing, little of a momentous nature seems to have occurred in the late fall and early winter. Most actions were minor, the most daring being a trench raid of 2nd Lieutenant Bogoslovsky. On December 15 the officer made a reconnaissance mission into the German trenches, quietly cutting the wire and slipping unobserved into their lines. He entered a bunker with two exits that could hold a hundred men and on a table discovered a stash of a hundred hand grenades, which he was able to take unobserved through the other exit back to the French lines.[70] Three days later the Russian units did attempt a *coup de main* in their sector. The morning attack was preceded by the firing of 58-mm cannons that made two breaches in the enemy barbed wire. At 7:42 A.M. two and a half companies from the 6th regiment went over the top. The right flank of the attack passed through the breach cleanly, but the left had to fight yard by yard with hand grenades. Both eventually got into the German first trenches, where there was hard fighting. The Germans counterattacked and sustained heavy losses. The Russians found and destroyed several bunkers before the German artillery opened fire on them, and they had to abandon their positions. Second Lieutenant Novikov and eight of his soldiers were killed, forty-two soldiers were wounded along with Lieutenant Kostin and the priest Sokolovsky. For their actions, General Dumas praised the "remarkable energy by the Russian infantry."[71] Probing of this type continued through the end of the year and into 1917.

On January 31, 1917, the Germans launched a gas attack that fell on three regions. The first, in the Aubérive sector, came on the 6th Russian regiment, the other two falling on French units. In Aubérive, the gas was discharged in three waves of thirty or forty minutes' duration with ten-minute intervals in between. The first fell at 4:00 A.M. The gas attacks were followed by a German infantry assault across no-man's land, but it was easily stopped by artillery fire. By 11:00 A.M. the front was quiet. There was no panic or disorder as the troops had heard noises and commotion in the German trenches for a week and expected that something was about to happen. In all, however, there were 1,980 Russian gas casualties, almost 20 percent of the entire unit. Two hundred fifty died and 277 were hospitalized. The attack had a more deadly effect than usual because it struck when the temperature was below freezing, and the gas was more lethal in cold weather.[72]

After a five-month stay, the Third Brigade ended its first duty at the front on March 12 and was replaced by the 185th Territorial Brigade. On March 18 the men were taken to rest on the banks of the Marne at Condé and Tours-sur-Marne and then to Mailly. When they returned to the front, they were transferred to the V Army to join the other brigade for the ill-fated Nivelle offensive.[73]

In May during the training of the First Brigade there occurred an event that might have helped Russian attitudes toward their allies: a visit of a Russian Parliamental Delegation to the West. The trip's objective was to buttress Allied unity and to demonstrate to the uneasy Western Allies that Russia was totally committed to the war. The delegation was composed of about twenty members from the State Council, the upper house of the tsarist legislature, and the Duma, the lower house. The Duma members contained a number of persons who were later to play a prominent role in Russian history: Pavel Miliukov, leader of the Cadet Party and later minister of foreign affairs of the revolutionary Provisional Government; Andrei I. Shingarev, a physician by training, a Cadet Party activist, and later the post-Revolutionary cabinet minister of agriculture and finance; Nikolai Markov, leader of the ultra-Rightists; Progressive party leader Ivan Efremov, who worked for the Soviet regime after the Revolution; and leader of the delegation, Ivan Protopopov, who later that year became minister of the interior.[74]

After visiting England, the members of the delegation crossed the Channel to France, where Izvolsky introduced them to Poincaré. At the meeting the French president made a short speech in which he referred to "battalions that [the Russians] have sent into France," and at a dinner the next day Protopopov told Poincaré that "the Russian people" wanted to send additional troops to France.[75] From Paris the delegates traveled to Champagne to review the two brigades, and their excursion included coming under fire from German mortars while with the Russian troops. A number of pictures appear in the photo album edited by Ernest Schultz of Duma members posing happily with Russian troops and their officers in the instruction camp, and they all have the air of being staged for propaganda purposes. What impression the visit made on the Russian soldiers is unknown, but due to delegation members' few references to it, clearly the visit was not an important part of their Western venture. Curiously, the visit with the REF has been recorded only in the above-mentioned pictures. Neither in his report to the Army-Navy Committees of the Duma nor in his memoirs does Miliukov mention it. In accounting to the Duma, Shingarev did note that the delegates had been very glad to visit "our own contingent in France at Mailly," where the men were training in order to take part "shoulder to shoulder with their French comrades in the general struggle." Adding that he hoped that their numbers in France would increase, he concluded with a statement of the fraternal feeling that "France and the French brothers" have for their Russian comrades-in-arms. He added that Russians were proud to see those "fine, alert, brave Russian troops" in a "country which is so dear to us." The statement was greeted by applause from the Left, Right, and Center of the Duma.[76]

The tactical victory of the Brusilov offensive in the summer of 1916 produced a short-lived euphoria among soldiers and civilians alike. Yet after the tsar called the offensive to a halt in September 1916, when the list of casualties numbered in the hundreds of thousands, a sense of defeat began to seep into the Russian psyche. Officers' reports indicate that discipline began to disintegrate as soldiers showed disrespect to command and mistreated horses, weapons, and other military property. Disorders began to occur in military trains. The number of desertions increased. It should have become obvious even to the most casual observer that the Russian army was beginning to disintegrate, yet sheltered by the officers under them, the leadership seems to have been oblivious to the problems. The one major factor that made the events of the 1905 Revolution so much more serious than those of 1917 was the loyalty of the Russian soldier to the tsar. There was widespread indiscipline in the armed forces in 1905, to be sure, the Potemkin mutiny being the most famous, but basically the army supported the emperor at that time. Yet the general paralysis late in 1916 of the Russian government, composed of incompetent ministers, made warnings go unheeded and daily led loyal men who might have been defenders of the regime either to desert to the opposition or to assume a position of neutrality. The helplessness worsened as the winter of 1916-17 came with its terrible food and fuel shortages in the cities. For the first time one heard the word "revolution" — not just among the intellectuals in their coffeehouses or among the revolutionaries in their underground hiding places but throughout the broad spectrum of Russian society. Revolution was discussed in the salons of both the middle classes and the aristocracy. Liberal politicians who dreamed of a democratic Russia and feared that a revolution would destroy their vision spoke of an upheaval in fear and horror. To those poor who stood freezing in lines all day for a loaf of bread, the possibility of revolution was just as real but it was discussed with favor. The regime augmented the wartime misery with its incompetence, while it allowed some to live as if there was no war. Inflation destroyed the purchasing power of the ruble, an economic problem affecting the poor most savagely. In 1914 one ruble had bought 14,000 food calories; by March 1917 it purchased only 168. In the words of Trotsky, "Everywhere it was going in the same direction—toward ruin."[77] On the eve of the catastrophe, the Revolution became real to both advocates and opponents. The only people oblivious to the impending doom were the highest government figures.

The crisis in the tsarist regime did not escape the Russians in France, although distance delayed their learning of the events in their native land. The collapse of the Russian army on the Eastern Front was due primarily to military conditions, which in the West were much better. At least there was ample ammunition, adequate artillery support, and a regular supply of food and some alcoholic courage. Yet one major element that destroyed the morale in France was at first missing in the pre-revolutionary East: defeatist propaganda from behind one's own lines, manufactured by the large number of Russian political émigrés who were not allowed to live in autocratic Russia but were permitted to reside in democratic France. Paris had for a century been the haven for dissidents who could not live in their own lands but found a home and hospitality in the radical communities of the French capital. When the Russian troops in France were given leave, something denied their colleagues on their front in Russia, they encountered in the cheap cafés and bars of the Latin Quarter of Paris hostile and bitter Russian expatriates. The tsarist regime had feared contamination of their troops in the West by contact with Western democracy. The virus that struck there, however, came from their own nationals.

The major hangout of these Russian malcontents was the Fourth Arrondissement, which had become sort of a ghetto of Russian émigrés. Some were probably in the employ of the Germans. Whatever their motives, they plied the Russian soldiers with drink and then planted the seeds of discontent against their sojourn in France and against their officers. They harped on the point that the soldiers' flesh had been traded for shells, and even aggravated their homesickness by reminding them of typical Russian food, which none had seen in a long time.[78] Their work proved a most powerful ingredient in the disintegration of the REF.

In the French police reports on the Russian radicals before the revolution, familiar names appear: Catherine Breshkovskaia, Victor Chernov, Boris Savinkov, A. V. Lunacharsky, Trotsky, and so forth. In one instance many of these dissidents gathered to celebrate the birthday of the famous nineteenth-century anarchist Michael Bakunin.[79] During the war, the newspapers and fliers that they scattered among the troops hammered away on pacifist and extreme political themes. The radicals, according to the French police, in effect commandeered a Russian library in Paris, La Bibliothèque Tourgenev, named for the great writer who at his death had left his books to the Russian community of Paris. The institution was a major gathering place for Russian soldiers.[80]

There had been some attempt during the war years to rid France of these "unpatriotic" Russians. Trotsky, for example, had been expelled in September 1916 by the Briand government.[81] When the Revolution occurred in Russia, many of the more important émigrés scurried homeward, assisted by the newly formed Committee of Immigration and by Georgii Chicherin, later to be the Foreign Commissar of the USSR, then living in London.[82] A number, however, stayed behind for what appears to be subversive reasons, and the French security police often were able to connect many to pacifist and German sympathies. These émigrés were the core of the group that spread propaganda among the Russian troops on leave. They gathered around the Paris Russian-language newspaper *Nashe slovo* (Our Word), until it was closed by the French ministry of the interior for its antiwar editorializing. It resurfaced late in 1916 with the ironic name of *Nachalo* (The Beginning). The individual credited by the French police for having founded the journal was one Vladimir Mecheriakov, alias Vladimirov, a native of the Russian city of Minsk and employed in Paris as an automobile chauffeur. He was a member of the *Société de Secours Réfugiés politiques de Russie*, believed by the police to be a front organization for leftist, subversive activities. In addition to sporting several addresses, he was, according to the police report, a member of the *Bureau russe de Travail* and the secretary and founder of the Russian section of *Chauffeurs d'auto*. The editor-in-chief of *Nachalo* was one Ovcée-Wendel-Sad *(sic)* Josephovich, alias Antonov, who lived at one of Mecheriakov's addresses. He belonged to and was the secretary of the *Bureau Russe de Travail,* as well as a member of other questionable organizations, and was a noted pacifist propagandist. Salomon Dridza, alias Dridzant and Lozowski, also living at one of Mecheriakov's addresses, was an advisor to and an important member of the organization *Le Comité pour la Réprise des Relations Internationals*, in which he seems to have been Trotsky's catspaw.[83] These men also formed the core of the group that gathered around what a police report called *La Bibliothèque russe* (Tourgenev?).[84]

Nachalo under its various appellations became a chief vehicle for the transmission of anti-Allied propaganda to the Russian troops, when it could reach them. The police confiscated the sheet whenever possible, and on December 24, 1917, they had even disrupted a planned fund-raiser given for it, to which "Geneva socialists"—presumably Vladimir Lenin and his crowd—had sent 200 francs. Yet even the expulsion from France of Mecheriakov in January 1918 does not seem to have slowed the activities of the journal.[85]

When a Russian soldier's letter critical of the war was intercepted by the military censors in March, the weekly *Nachalo*'s new editor, Drizda, made much of it and used it to influence the Russians on the French front, exciting them, the French security police thought, against the French Republic. In condescending fashion the police report voiced the opinion that such dangerous toys should be kept out to the hands of the "simple and naive spirits, like the majority of Russian soldiers."[86] This most recent activity led to the closing of the newspaper by the ministry of the interior on April 8, but a group under the undisguised name of "The Friends of *Nachalo*" opened it again under the appellation *Novyi epokh* (The New Epoch). The new paper was to appear daily, unlike *Nachalo,* which was published once a week. The fast-breaking events in Russia made news in a weekly stale by the time it appeared, and a new policy was needed. To supply financial aid for the Russian house organ, a group was formed called The Friends of *Novyi Epoch,* the membership list of which most assuredly must have been the same as the Friends of *Nachalo.*[87] Since the Revolution had created a government professing political freedom, all Paris émigrés could now return home, and the staff of the *Novyi epokh* used the paper to raise money to help many leave France. A major benefit was held in Paris in the Hall of Horticulture on April 16, 1917, and police informers estimated that around 500 people were in attendance. A concert opened at 2:30 P.M. with both French and Russian music, and after the performance about 200 participated in a luncheon. There were no speeches and no incidents. The police informer reported, however, that there were a number of Russian soldiers in the crowd.[88] They could only have been men from the REF.

In its short existence, for it closed on May 4 because so many of its staff had returned to Russia, *Novyi epokh* circulated widely and freely as a great pacifist propaganda sheet among the Russian soldiers, both at the front and among the wounded in the hospitals.[89] Unquestionably the activities of these Russian émigrés, whether their motives were driven by genuine pacifism or service to the Germans who paid some of them, had a detrimental effect on the Russian soldiers serving in Champagne. Alone the émigrés' activities probably would not have produced the problems that followed, but their propaganda, in conjunction with the other catalysts, made the events of May 1917 almost unavoidable.

The Russian Revolution is easily one of the two or three most salient events of the twentieth century, if not the most important one. In less than a year, it elevated a rather obscure economic doctrine, Marxian socialism, advocated only by a minuscule number of people in the Europe of its day, to a leading ideological force that would be a serious threat to the capitalist world that had gone unchallenged for centuries. The struggle that followed between the contrary philosophies went generally unabated until the advent of *Glasnost'* in the 1980s and led to a continuous confrontation, with varying degrees of intensity, between the world's two leading superpowers with the ever-present possibility of a nuclear holocaust. It is certainly arguable that had the Revolution not occurred and Russia been at the Peace of Paris in 1919, a collision between East and West still would have occurred as the former Allies divided Europe among themselves. Russia surely would have left Paris with something like the hegemony over Eastern Europe that it acquired twenty-five years later, incurring the enmity of former allies in the process. Only the ideological conflict would have been absent. Since it was not, a struggle for "world domination" followed on all continents over the past seven decades. Quite probably a capitalist Russia would have competed with the West for economic superiority around the world as well, but the struggle never would have assumed the intensity concomitant with an ideological confrontation, and the Communist domination of China would not have happened without the success of the revolution in Russia. Within the scope of Russian history itself, the impact is incalculable. Considering the horrors of the civil war, the slaughter in the collectivization, and the unknown hecatombs amassed in the Purges, none of which would have happened without the 1917 upheaval, the Revolution visited on Russia a nightmare unknown by many peoples in modern times.

The Great War, however, did not reveal the weakness of the system that was in transition; it revealed the inadequacies of the individual at the head, Nicholas himself, with his pathetically neurotic wife and her coterie of crackpots and faith healers. A stronger monarch would not have permitted the frightful paralysis that gripped the tsarist state by 1916, nor would he have tolerated the Stürmers or the Protopopovs, the incompetent ministers who were both the symptom as well as the cause. None of the previous four tsars, presented with the war from 1914 to 1918 and the same conditions, would have faced a revolution as did Nicholas II. Their respective political stances—and they range from moderately liberal to archconservative—have nothing to do with the failure of revolution to occur. Each was a strong-willed man who would have given Russia a firm direction in the war years. None of the previous four tsars would have tolerated a Rasputin and those bumbling elements that so discredited the regime and fueled the frustration that finally erupted in March 1917.

A people can endure much if they have strong leadership. The Russian people suffered much worse in the Second World War than they did in the First, yet there was no hint of rebellion. Granted the political machinery was different, but the man in the street always felt that the government was doing all that it could to lead the country in the difficult times, and right or wrong, there was always a direction. Yet in 1917, to the average Russian, the government was in a pathetic state of drift, making no effort to alleviate the misery generated by the war and even condoning "known" traitors in the government and around the imperial family. What is more, strong leadership would have alleviated some of the problems that caused the discontent. Instead rot from the top down poisoned every facet of the war, creating an anger and frustration that had no outlet except in the streets. The frustration with the regime, as in all successful revolutions, ran deep and cut across class lines. To greater or lesser degree, virtually every sector of society, either actively or passively, helped topple the tsarist government.

The danger of revolution is always that once begun, it cannot easily be controlled, and like a hurricane, it builds in intensity with the radical elements having at least a phase where they are in control. Moreover, revolutions in their inception are by nature often hysterical and usually unthinking. Their instigators can feel only their private frustrations, rarely giving careful thought to the consequences of their actions.

By early March 1917, however, the discontent in Russia was like the Volga, "broad and deep." Gaston Doumergue, a Rightist politician and president of France, and General Noel de Castelnau, who later plays a role in our story, had just returned to Paris from Petrograd early in March 1917, when they had dinner with Jules Cambon, the veteran French diplomat. Everything was in chaos, they reported, and there was the appearance of a complete absence of government. Prime Minister Nicholas Golitsyn, the last tsarist prime minister, was described by the two men as a *"fantoche d'opérette"* who "knows nothing, wants to know nothing, and asks everyone why they have put him there and whines constantly."[90]

Finally on Thursday, March 8, 1917, all the frustration, the anger, the suffering, and the desperation burst into one of the greatest and most sudden political earthquakes the world has ever seen. It was not planned, not rehearsed, nor was it led. In the words of the Duma president Rodzianko, "suddenly something seemed to snap, and the state machinery jumped off the rails."[91] The explosion, begun by a demonstration for women's rights, was intensified by the addition of 40,000 angry workers locked out by the management of the giant Putilov factory. Before the day had ended, bread shops and stores were looted and Petrograd was gripped by riots and demonstrations. The next day events intensified, encouraged by the casualness of the soldiers and cossacks to the disturbances. Yet by Saturday troops had fired on the crowds and the government seemed to be gaining the upper hand. There was sporadic disorder, and one unit had refused to fire on the mob and had to be disarmed, but all eyewitness accounts tell of calm streets on Sunday night. Yet late in the evening on Sunday, March 11, the Golitsyn ministry decided to prorogue the Duma until April, foolishly believing that the legislative body had somehow encouraged the parlous events. When the word hit the streets the next morning, the result was like pouring gasoline on a dying fire. The entire city exploded in open rebellion, and tsarism had crossed its Rubicon.

That afternoon a provisional government was formed of moderate, democratic, bourgeois elements, but at almost the same time was born the radical Petrograd Soviet of Soldiers' and Workers' Deputies composed of delegates chosen from factories and soldiers' units in the Russian capital. Since mobs in the streets during revolutions follow the most radical political elements, the crowds in Petrograd turned to the Soviet for leadership in the weeks and months to follow, and the Provisional Government's directives and orders were not obeyed by workers and soldiers until the Soviet told them to do so. Waiting for Marx's predicted second spontaneous revolution, the Soviet took no direct role in events. It did take a watchdog and hence obstructionist position, however, which crippled the leadership of the Russian government until a paralysis set in that was worse than the one before the February Revolution took hold.

Word of the events in Russia did not reach the Russian leadership on the French front until March 15, the day Nicholas II abdicated. On arriving at Beauvais from a trip, Palitsyn learned that "something serious" had happened back home in Russia, but he did not hear exactly what until the sixteenth. That day he was informed that Grand Duke Nicholas Nicholaevich, the former commander-in-chief until the tsar assumed command in 1915, had been reinstated and that the tsar had abdicated for himself and his son.[92] At first, Palitsyn tried to keep the word from the soldiers, but he wired the brigade leaders of events, telling them that it was necessary to fulfill the "will of Russia to carry out the struggle to the end." The telegram was marked "Secret."[93]

Of course it would be impossible to keep such earth-shattering news forever from the Russian soldiers in the French trenches. One soldier reported that they had heard of the revolution from a French newspaper, although they learned nothing at the time about the organization of the

"Soldiers' Committees," groups created by the Soviet to guarantee and protect soldiers' rights.[94] The Russian émigré and military newspapers probably quickly supplemented and even embellished the events. Adding word of mouth to other sources, news spread through the units very rapidly.

As the facts became known, there were joyous cheers among the Russian units in France and demonstrations garnished with red flags that seemed to appear from nowhere. Strains of the *Internationale* were soon heard. Somehow there quickly arrived the Soviet's infamous General Order No. 1, the Magna Carta of soldiers' rights that contributed greatly to the disintegration of discipline among Russian units everywhere. The order was a new set of regulations dealing with the relationship between the officers and their men, and there is nothing among the new guidelines save perhaps the creation of soldiers' committees that would seriously disturb an officer in any of the modern armies of the world. Corporal punishment was disallowed, and instead of the subservient *Vashe Vysoko-blagorodie* (Your Highmindedness), the soldier could address the officers with the simple "*gospodin kapitan*" or "*gospodin poruchik*" (something like Mr. Captain and Mr. Lieutenant). The officers remained in charge, but the disappearance of brute force made soldiers heady with their newly discovered liberties and translated into a lack of discipline not intended by the letter of the order. Officers were ignored and even rebuked by privates, and since there had been a decline in morale before the news of the Revolution, the order merely accelerated the disintegration.[95] Probably hoping for some sort of countercoup in the Russian capital, the officers in France dragged their feet on taking the loyalty oath to the Provisional Government. Not until March 29 did General Palitsyn as the commander of the Russian forces ask the French High Command for permission to swear allegiance to the Provisional Government.[96]

Palitsyn's order of the day on the eve of the oath-taking made a strong appeal to traditional Russian nationalism. After announcing the oath, Palitsyn reminded the soldiers that they were sent to France "to fight against the common enemy with the Allies' armies, to defend a common cause with them." As if looking over his shoulder, Palitsyn added, "The hour is approaching when, under the force of our combined efforts, the enemy will be broken. Remember that a good soldier is brave, obedient, and always faithful to his cause. Be strong in your oath and in your valor, in order that the land of Russia, which has sent you here, may be proud of you." He then added a word or two that implied that they might as well do their duty: "Russia has decided to prosecute this war to a victorious end, and we, her sons, must loyally execute her will. May Almighty God help us in our task."[97]

A report to the French government noted on April 13 that all had taken the oath, which had been accompanied by a statement, apparently the one just mentioned, from Palitsyn, and the ceremony had taken place in both brigades with the greatest calm. The soldiers had the choice of taking either a religious or civil oath, and, ominously, according to the report to the French government, every one of the soldiers elected to take the civil one.[98] Furthermore, any fears among the leadership regarding the soldiers' avoidance of the religious oath was augmented by the fact that half the soldiers refused to attend religious services on that year's Easter Sunday, the most important day in the Orthodox church calendar.[99] Whistling in the dark, the military newspaper *The Military Newspaper for the Russian Force in France,* the next day printed an order outlining the Provisional Government's policy of staying in the war. "Russia has decided to carry this war to victory," the editors told the soldiers, "and we, her sons, must willingly fulfill her will."[100]

Palitsyn later noted that it would indeed have been unusual to suppose that the events of such monumental importance "would not be able to bring a most strong impression for our force in France," but there was some delay in the resurgence of the open rebellion that so quickly afflicted the troops at home. Joseph Noulens, French ambassador to Russia after the Revolution was four months old, noted that, to Russian soldiers at home, after the Revolution all subservience seemed offensive. "They imagined that the revolutionary spirit instilled into them all knowledge by a miracle analogous to that of Pentecost." The regimental committees instituted endless discussions on all matters, no matter how far removed the soldiers were from a clear understanding of them. Noulens noted in describing a similar situation in the East that "some *muzhiks,* coming out of complete ignorance, having emerged from the depths of the Urals and the banks of the Volga, spoke endlessly, argued, deliberated, not only on the wishes of the officers . . . , but on the goals of the world war, . . . on the rights of France to Morocco and her colonies. Worse yet: certain soviets dared to deliberate on the surgical operations that were to be performed on soldiers."[101] As we shall see, the soldiers of the Russian Expeditionary Force in France were to come to this degree of "freedom," but somewhat later than the soldiers at home. French reports, however, while showing the Russian soldiers to be delighted with the alterations that the new regime had introduced to their lives, noted that general calm had been maintained. One general reported to Paris that no collective incidents of indiscipline or signs of disturbance had come to his attention nor to the attention of the French officers serving with the Russians.[102] Yet once these Russians in the

West grasped the significance of events at home, they would surpass in revolutionary ardor many of their brothers in Russia.

Prior to the report, however, several incidents occurred that were portents of the disaster to come. On March 19 a convocation of men from "the first regiment [of the First Brigade]"—the one that was recruited from the working-class neighborhoods of Moscow—met in the cellar of a glassworks factory near the front and arrogated itself the right to pass a resolution demanding to return to Russia; it designated a deputation to present its decision to Colonel Nechvolodov. When informed of the action, the colonel was so shocked that he fainted. The regiment representatives then became very upset and solicitously carried the stunned colonel inside his quarters. The soldiers then forgot why they had come there, and that ended, at least for the moment, their mission.[103] Whether this incident or the casual attitude that soldiers had acquired since the first of the year caused the change is unknown, but officers were ordered to mix more with their men to get to know them, something that the Russian high command had never considered necessary.

The junior officers had only a feeble response to this order. General Joseph Fournier, who reported all of these happenings to the French high command, expressed surprise. Since the tyrannical ties of the old army were no longer in place, the Russian officers, it would seem, would want to reestablish some other links with the soldiers to replace the old ones. Without a new relationship, dangerous developments could result since a hostile propaganda contrary to the discipline, and we have seen that it was brewing, might cause serious problems among the Russian soldiers whose "good, natural sentiments are unquestionable."[104] We shall see that none ever were.

After the March 19 gathering, Nechvolodov claimed in a memo to the company commanders under him that he permitted the meeting, as if he might have been able to stop it, because he had been assured that it was "loyal." "I have been deceived," he wrote later in a report. "The meeting had had a clear, revolutionary character." Nechvolodov forbade all such convocations and denied all men leave. Moreover, he ordered that soldiers attending such assemblies henceforth be arrested. Yet he showed his hesitancy by calling on the officers to reproach the soldiers who talked with the propagandists, adding that the officers were to treat them with an absolute firmness. He then revealed his real fears by asking the officers to report to him the next day on whether they felt that the units would hold together during the coming Nivelle offensive.[105]

What the officers reported is not known. It must have been in the affirmative since the Russians participated in the offensive, but events that occurred in the end of March and in April must have given strong cause for alarm. In a hospital at Montfleury near Cannes, where a number of wounded Russians had been taken, a nasty incident occurred involving a Russian lieutenant with the very un-Russian name of Zikaliotti. The officer had visited the hospital, apparently in order to pay the salaries of the soldiers there, but he took the visit as an opportunity to editorialize against the new regime in Petrograd. Telling the soldiers that the new government was "a bunch of Jews" and should not be trusted, Zikaliotti added that their salary would have been abolished by the new government but for the intervention of their general. He also spoke of maintaining loyalty to the emperor. A violent confrontation resulted and the officer was attacked and might have been seriously injured had it not been for the intervention of a Captain Caen, the French administrative officer, who spirited the lieutenant away to his office. Order was restored in the hospital ward, but not until several very angry Russians had made gestures of cutting off the officer's head. The French government report stated that Captain Lenail, commandant of the hospital, had learned that Zikaliotti had created similar unrest in other hospitals he had visited.[106] Eager to appear involved, the super-fluous tsarist ambassador Izvolsky summoned Ignatiev a month later and told him to investigate "*sans retard*" the Zikaliotti incident. Ignatiev informed Izvolsky formally that he already knew about the affair and that orders had been given for Zikaliotti's replacement and the return of the officer to his usual regiment.[107]

Although they were kept more effectively from the armies' zone, the radical émigrés in Paris found easier access to these hospitals, and police reports of early April tell of a "revolutionary library" that had been established at the Hospital Micheler, followed by the creation of a soviet on the model of those in units and factories in Petrograd. The émigré named Josephovich (apparently also known under the alias Antonov) was holding a veritable pacifist conference in Micheler when he was invited to leave by the officer in charge.[108]

Of a more serious nature was a plan among the men at the front to hold a demonstration in honor of those soldiers who had been tried, found guilty, and executed in September 1916 for the murder of Colonel Krause. The incident was closed when the call came to move to the front for the April offensive, yet since then someone had written on a Russian flag and on the cross that marked the graves of Krause's killers: "Honor and glory to those who have fallen victoriously in the struggle against the internal enemy—eight men of the 4th regiment." Another had written on their graves: "Here lie four victims." Moreover, on the day of the oath-taking to the Provisional Government, some soldiers had refused to march under the officers who had participated in the tribunal that had condemned the four men.[109] Unrest was definitely rearing its head.

In the early days after the men of the REF learned of the revolution, however, they remained basically loyal to the cause. The direct order to elect "soldiers' committees" had not yet arrived, and discipline remained intact. When the committees were finally elected after the Nivelle offensive, they quickly became schools to train troops in revolutionary tactics, and when they called for peace, social equality, and to be returned home, their demands fell on receptive ground.

FOUR

The REF and the Nivelle Offensive

April 1917

Yet at the same time he [Nivelle] was one of those luckless generals who from Mardonius and Varus to Benedek and Trochu, excite our pity, but can expect no mercy from the historian.

—Bernard von Bülow[1]

Among the Russian participants, the losses were great. . . . In far away France, where later they cursed and reviled the Russians, they left many abandoned eight-pointed [Orthodox] crosses. Now I often think: whether they were not all happier who died on the holy morning of Beautiful Easter, going out in a joyous blaze, never crossing the threshold of the fatal year [1917].

—Ilya Ehrenburg[2]

In war the victorious strategist only seeks battle after the victory has been won, whereas he who is declined to defeat first fights and afterward looks for victory.

—Sun Tzu[3]

Let your plans be dark and impenetrable as night, and when you move, fall like a thunderbolt.

—Sun Tzu[4]

GENERALS ARE FORGIVEN ANYTHING EXCEPT DEFEAT in the face of expected victory. General Joffre had commanded the French armies from the beginning of the war, yet despite the stupendous numbers of France's slaughtered youth piled before the German machine guns, by 1916 there had been no triumph. The hero of the Marne had become tarnished by the stalemate, and voices were crying out for new and decisive leadership. The bovine Joffre, whose calm reaction to the German invasion probably had prevented disaster in 1914, no longer projected the image of victory. Therefore, on December 12, 1916, the French high command removed "Papa Joffre," kicking him upstairs to the impotent position of chief military advisor to the government. The leadership replaced him with a politician's general, Robert Georges Nivelle, who had managed to convince the right people in the French government that he could by the same military means that had failed repeatedly under Joffre achieve a rupture of the German lines, carrying the war into Germany.

From the distant perspective of three-quarters of a century, it is impossible to comprehend how Nivelle persuaded anyone that his scheme would be successful when others conducted in the same manner had failed so badly. Not since 1914 had the insensitive hurling of men against a fortified enemy who had been warned by preattack shelling produced a major break in enemy lines from either side. Nivelle, however, hoped to concentrate large reserves to insure holding conquered ground, but any massing of troops could never go undetected by the enemy, thus further eliminating the element of surprise. If by some means men could be assembled secretly, the preliminary bombardment would telegraph the punch. Essentially the same tactic had been tried at the Somme the summer before, and the result had been 60,000 casualties on the first day, with only a few yards of blood-soaked mud changing hands.

Nivelle's plan, an attack on a twenty-five mile front after a nine-day preparatory bombardment, was sold to the French government only through the general's self-confidence and bouncy optimism, reinforced by the desperation of a people who were watching their country bleeding to death. Yet this offensive was the last step that broke the spirit of a great nation and paralyzed its foreign policy for the next two decades when the decisive action demonstrated during the First World War might have prevented the Second. The French leadership in 1917, however, was willing to try the same method once more in hopes that this time there would be a breakthrough to a decisive victory. Perhaps if the Germans had been at the breaking point themselves, it would have worked. They were not, and French history therefore took the sad road to Vichy. French optimism was indeed great that the Nivelle offensive would bring an end to the war. Charles Mangin, an illustrious French general who had been everywhere from Fashoda in 1898 to the Marne in 1918, spoke for France at the time when he said of the man and the plan, "We hold the method, and we have the leader. *C'est la certitude du succès.*"[5]

The plan of attack was presented to the French army in absolutely stupefying detail. Army maps covering the proposed field of attack present mindboggling minutiae, even to the point of detailing farm buildings, hedgerows, and drainage ditches. The written instructions virtually tell every French soldier where his foot was to be planted at precisely every hour of the attack. Units were ordered to place their right flank against a certain fence at a certain time and their left against a certain barn or wheat field. What is also amazing is the total lack of flexibility, which Palitsyn immediately noticed when Lokhvitsky presented it to him. The entire line would be affected by the failure of any one of the sectors to gain its objective at a given point. Moreover, success was dependent on the cooperation of the Germans to do their duty and fall back in great disarray, showing no heroics of their own.

For Nivelle, however, enthusiasm would be enough. After all, he had coined the slogan for Verdun, "*Ils ne passeront pas!*," and as one monument on the Verdun battlefield informs the present-day visitor, "*Ils n'ont pas passés!*" In his instructions to General Frédéric Micheler, coordinator of the Army Rupture Group, the collection of armies to be used in the offensive, Nivelle wrote, "I insist on the character of *violence,* of *brutality,* and of *rapidity* that must characterize your offensive and in particular its first act, the *rupture* seeing from the first blow the conquest of the position of the enemy . . . ." The instruction included the liberal use of words such as "*l'audace" and "ténacité"* (Nivelle's italics throughout).[6]

The offensive characterized by the now-bankrupt policy of élan, was to fall initially between the city of Reims and the canal of the Aisne and the Oise. The major assault would be led by the V, VI, and the X armies, the first of which contained the Russian brigades. With the VI Army, the V held the front from Reims to Soissons. These two armies had 5,500 pieces of artillery of various sizes and 200 tanks. To supply this enterprise, the French had constructed almost 70 miles of railroad.[7]

Yet the whole offensive had in effect failed before the first *poilu* went over the top because of a number of developments known but ignored by the leaders. The most important was the total absence of surprise. Yet it was not simply that the German intelligence could see a French buildup opposite their lines. On March 3 the Germans had made a raid on Maison de Champagne north of Reims and discovered on the body of a French captain a set of plans complete with scheduled goals. The same bad luck

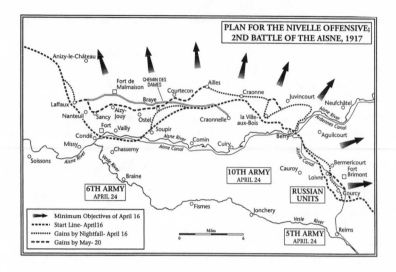

happened again on April 4, when a German storm trooper attack near Sapigneul resulted in the capture of a Zouave sergeant-major with another complete set. Yet if these happenstances were not bad enough, absolutely no attempt was made at keeping the offensive secret. It was widely discussed in the press, by schoolchildren, by war munitions workers, by idle men and women in the cafés, by everyone. We can only assume that Nivelle's general optimism had infected everybody, since no one seemed to think that secrecy was important. An additional factor that insured defeat, and the one that could not have been foreseen, was the weather in mid-April when the assault began. Cold rain and sleet had fallen all night before the day of the attack, turning the battlefield into a quagmire. Advancing against well-prepared German defenses under any conditions would have been difficult, but over a sea of mud, a successful attack became impossible.

The final element in the French failure was German preparedness. In the sectors on which the major thrust was to fall the Germans increased their troop strength from nine to forty divisions.[8] Early in February General Oliver Mazel, commandant of the V French Army, reported to Micheler that recent aerial photos showed *"grand préparatifs"* (italics in the original) in the Laon-Reims region in the German positions between the heights of Vieux-Laon and the region of Prouvais.[9] Since the Germans had made these preparations even before they had captured the plans, there intelligence must have been already aware of some sort of coming action. In April, after the Germans had obtained the plans, President Poincaré noted in his diary, "The enemy expects the attack because he had doubled [*sic*] the number of his divisions and batteries on the front of our Fifth Army (1st corps, 4th corps, 32 corps, 7th corps, [part of the 38th corps], and the Russian brigades). Nivelle and Mazel declare that this pleases them and affirms that we will be also able to take a greater number of prisoners." Then with more realism than had been shown by his generals, the president of the Third Republic added, "Their optimism scares me a little." Yet Nivelle's confidence allayed even the worst of Poincaré's fears for he concluded with "But confidence in success being, after all, the first condition of success, I do not let my apprehensions get to me."[10] France might have been better served if he had.

Meanwhile, the Germans continued to ready themselves for the attack. They destroyed the château of Evremond de Courcy, the gallant fourteenth-century French nobleman who died in a crusade against the Turks, because it might serve French troops as an observation post. The château had survived one attempt at demolition at the hands of Cardinal Mazarin in the seventeenth century and an avoided destruction by an earthquake a short time later. Philippe *"Egalité,"* the famous relative of King Louis XVI who had voted in the Convention to execute his own cousin, had once owned it, but when he himself fell victim to the guillotine during the Reign of Terror, the structure passed to the state. Crown Prince Rupprecht of Bavaria had tried to convince Ludendorff to spare it, arguing that to destroy it "would only mean a blow to our own prestige quite uselessly." His pleas went unheeded, and the historic structure was leveled with twenty-eight tons of explosives.[11] In the sector the Germans also increased their probing actions and *coups de main* after April 1. They launched a gas attack as late as April 14. Against the Russians in the sector, reports show that the German infantry was "calm," but there was a definite increase in enemy artillery activity.[12] The French V Army was given the objective of breaking the enemy front somewhere between Reims and Hurtebise, a sector of about twenty miles. It was stretched from La Pompelle to the east of Reims to three miles south of Craonne, a town at the eastern end of the *Chemin des Dames,* a road running east-west on which King Louis XV's daughters and other eighteenth century court ladies took rides. The order of its units from left to right was the 1st corps, the 5th corps, the 32nd corps, the 7th corps, and the first division of the 38th cavalry. On January 31, Micheler had written Nivelle some suggestions about the use of the V Army and the Russian brigades, asking for his concurrence. On February 4, however, both

Russian brigades were with the 38th corps, which was positioned in the vicinity of Reims from Fort de la Pompelle to Les Marquises. The First was in the midst of the corps, while the Third formed the corps' right flank. The orders for the corps cite a number of hills, towns, and villages to be taken, but the French command deemed this sector to be in "a region of less action" ("*une région de parcours facile*").[13]

After noting what hills would be taken and which villages should be attacked, Micheler concluded with "I add that General Mazel plans to reinforce the 7th corps with the [Third] Russian brigade, which operates around Courcy. . . . The Russian brigade would be relieved by the territorial troops." Mazel had felt, and Micheler had concurred, that this change would leave one Russian unit where it was and would employ them both on the village of Courcy with an appreciable saving of effectives. In February, therefore, the two Russian brigades were placed under the 7th corps under General Georges de Bazelaire, the First directly with the corps, the Third in reserve northwest of Reins. The 7th was assigned the storming of the *massif* of Brimont, on which there was a fort, overwhelming it from the north while simultaneously attacking it from the south and west. The specific duties of the First Russian brigade was to overrun the salient at a rise adjoining Courcy called the *Tête de cochon* and capture the railroad from Reims to Laon to the north of the village. Added to this assignment was an attack on Fort Brimont from the southeast and the taking of a glassworks at the edge of Courcy. In a report Lokhvitsky continued the instructions with six pages of incredible detail, and this directive was followed on April 6 with another memorandum of additional orders.[14]

Meanwhile, to reconnoiter the terrain, Lokhvitsky accelerated activity on his front. Late in March he executed a *coup de main* against the German lines and vigorously increased his surveillance patrols. Reports show much random firing of artillery at weak points of the enemy line with great care being taken to count the number of shells expended. In addition to daily sparring with the enemy, there was the usual repair of the trenches and other duties.

On March 24 a revised version of the plan placed the Third Brigade as a floating reserve northwest of Reims. On J plus 1 (one day after the beginning of the attack), it was to reinforce, depending on the circumstances, either the 7th or the 32nd corps. On the evening of April 13-14 it was to bivouac in the woods of the Château d'Hervelon, and on the day of attack, two hours after the assault had begun, the Third was to pass the St. Auboeuf farm in the woods to the west of the Tuileries of Couroy so that it could debouch rapidly either toward Cormicy to Berry-au-Bac, by

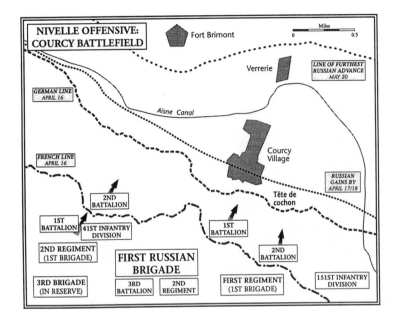

la Maison Blanche toward Godat, or by the Caron toward Loivre. Contact was to be established by telephone with both the 7th or the 32nd corps.[15] The Russians were to attack on the Comicy canal and the Brimont-Fresnes ridge, where the Reims-Laon railroad ran on a rise about six feet high. Meanwhile, the major French thrust was to fall on the north of Loivre.[16]

At noon on the sixteenth the 5th regiment of the Third Brigade under Colonel Vladimir Narbut and the 2nd battalion of the 6th regiment under Lieutenant Colonel Stravinsky were united there. The 3rd battalion of the 6th regiment was on April 16 to attack *Côte 108* with the 251st regiment of French infantry. At 4:00 P.M. the 5th regiment with its additional battalion was ordered to Couroy, a small village and wooded area directly west of Fort Brimont, almost four miles northwest of Courcy. The truncated 6th (the 1st and 2nd battalions) was ordered to Cormicy, a somewhat larger village on the line about twelve and a half miles northwest of Courcy. The 5th was placed under French General Noel Garnier-Duplessis and led to the front along the Neuville-Aguilcourt road. It departed about 10:00 P.M.

The night was especially dark and many of the companies became lost and marched all night before finding their positions. The 1st company was placed to the south of the Neuville-Aguilcourt road, the 3rd to the north of it, and the 2nd behind both in reserve status. By noon on April 17, all companies of thoroughly exhausted soldiers were in place in the line.

As for the 2nd battalion borrowed from the 6th regiment, on the night of April 16-17 it was placed to the left of the road with the 3rd Zouaves, with the idea of attacking on April 18. Yet this battalion apparently was delayed in taking position, because it was not there until 10:00 A.M. on April 19. On the night of the eighteenth, sometime between eight and nine o'clock, the 2nd battalion was attacked but repelled the enemy. About midnight Marushevsky took direct command of the scattered units in this sector, but he complained to the commandant of the 37th division on the "impossibility" of leading these scattered forces. He also reported that, having been active all day of April 16 and part of April 17, his men were "very tired."[17]

Lokhvitsky had complained somewhat about part of the scheme and demanded the addition of an artillery bombardment to continue for at least an hour during the first phase of the attack, to H 1hr.10.[18] Bazelaire agreed on April 11 to continue the barrage, and Lokhvitsky then requested more shells for his French 75's because the ones he had been given were expended in repelling a German attack on the night of April 8-9. Bazelaire immediately gave orders to fill the deficiencies, but he told Lokhvitsky that due to problems with transport, he could not guarantee their arrival before the beginning of the offensive.[19] The supply depot must have delivered some because the reports on April 12 and 13 show some artillery fire, although not too heavy, with sixty-two shells falling on the village of Courcy itself on April 12 alone.[20] On the 13th the Russians reported that the first and second German lines had been shelled, with modest damage to the barbed wire before the German lines.[21]

The mood of the Russian troops appears to have been very good at this point. Nothing in any of the reports indicates the unrest that was to come. Participation in the offensive had been passed in a vote by men of the First Brigade by a wide margin early in April,[22] and to most of the soldiers the revolution was still very far away. For now all seemed normal. The eve of the offensive was Easter in the Russian Orthodox Church. A most energetic priest, Andrei Bogoslovsky, went slowly along the trenches peacefully blessing his flock with a staff he had received as a present from the brigade in one hand and his personal Cross of St. George in the other, giving the soldiers a moving church. All night he repeated, "Christ is risen!" knowing that for many of the men, this service would be their last.

Many for the last time would answer *"Voistinu voskrese* [He is risen indeed!]." When the Russian troops entered German trenches the next day, Bogoslovsky was with them and remained there during the counterattack, cross in hand. He then helped carry two wounded to safety.[23] This remarkable clergyman enters our story again and again in the future.

At 6:00 A.M. on April 16, a French military force of fifty-four divisions, about 850,000 men, 2,300 heavy guns, 2,700 French 75's, several thousand machine guns, and 200 tanks was hurled against forty German divisions in what would be from that day to this the last great military offensive of the French nation. It was likewise to be the last great attempt at the use of élan, that belief of Colonel (by now General and *mort pour France*) Grandmaison that French courage was superior to German firepower.

The preparatory bombardment, which had lasted for almost ten days, Palitsyn wrote,[24] had done some damage to the German lines, but generally the enemy had pulled back from the falling shells. When the French advanced into the vacuum, they were met by 1,000 machine guns.[25] The rain and sleet that had fallen the night before broke for about two hours on the morning of April 16, and the sky even cleared, but it soon clouded over again. Although the rain held off, the low visibility made the work of the gunners and of aerial reconnaissance fliers difficult.[26]

The initial thrust of the attack was to be delivered by the V and VI armies. The V Army was to attack one of the strongest parts of the German defenses, an area that had not been altered during the Hindenburg withdrawal because the German high command deemed it to be sufficiently solid. The infantry attacked at the appointed time, and at first the fire the enemy returned was weak and irregular. The right wing advanced, gaining several objectives, but the left was stopped at the first enemy trenches by machine-gun fire from guns the bombardment had not eliminated. This problem was to be typical along much of the front.

Finally at 11:00 A.M. the tanks with the 32nd corps began moving for La Miette, a village to the southwest of Juvincourt. The others faced east toward the German positions, hoping to deter a flanking counterattack. The infantry did not follow because it was exhausted after five hours of fighting, and the tanks were supported only by cavalry. Little progress was made by nightfall, by which time most of the tanks, used for the first time by the French, were immobilized by either German shells or malfunctions. On the whole, the only successes were the breaking of several vigorous German counterattacks.

On the first day the 7th corps with the Russian First Brigade made, by World War I standards, substantial gains. Advancing between a mile and a half and two miles, the unit occupied part of the village of Courcy to the south of Fort Brimont. Bazelaire's 7th also took Loivre to the northwest and Berméricourt to the north.[27] Yet by 9:30 A.M. Bazelaire was already calling for reserves that Mazel did not have to give him.[28] As for the Russian First Brigade, it performed extremely well. Eager to show what Russians could achieve, it jumped the gun a few minutes before six on the morning of April 16 and began its attack on the heavily fortified town of Courcy, which by one account was buttressed by twenty-six rows of barbed wire. The first wave, covered by French artillery, pressed ahead so rapidly that the German artillery fire fell behind the advancing line.

Their immediate objective was the Aisne-Marne canal, which passed through the village and by Fort Brimont on to Neville and Berry-au-Bac. All battalions advanced without incident except the one on the left of the first regiment, which was struck with enemy fire. It had already sustained heavy losses, and the commandant of the battalion was *hors de combat*, so the command had been taken over by Captain Martin Ieske. The losses being considerable, he felt that the battalion could not continue to advance.

The battalion on the right of the 1st regiment advanced on the *tête de cochon* and encountered stiff resistance because the artillery preparation had not been completely successful. This battalion lost three-quarters of its effectives and was not able to engage for the remainder of the day, although it remained in the line. The center battalion enveloped Courcy from the south and southwest, the left battalion of which reached the canal on the edge of town and tried to make contact with the 2nd regiment. The left battalion of the first regiment took the 1st line but could not make liaison with the French 41st to its right until 3:00 P.M., when the canal was breached and liaison was made with the 41st.[29] The second wave was not so fortunate. It advanced just in time to receive the German bombardment and had to make its way through the falling shells. Despite heavy losses it reinforced the first, which was carrying the German first and second lines before Courcy.

From the safety of their bunkers, the Russian officers could see the vigorous attack on Courcy through their field glasses. All day the struggle continued up to and across the canal. By nightfall the town had been cleared of Germans, who responded with immediate counterattacks supported by artillery fire from Fort Brimont. The Russians held on, however, yielding no ground in the successive German assaults that night and on April 17 and 18. As a result of their valiant efforts, the Russians took 535 unwounded German prisoners, although Russian losses were heavy. Soviet sources report that 700 men were killed, 22 of whom were officers. The same source puts the wounded at a staggering 3,000.[30] If these statistics are correct, which they most probably are,[31] this action eliminated about half of the brigade, leaving some companies with only fifteen or twenty men.

At 3:55 P.M. the order came to clear the road between Courcy and 151 Infantry Division, stating that the entire brigade had to reach the canal. Yet by 9:00 P.M., only the *Tête de cochon* had fallen, and German artillery opened intense fire at 10:30 P.M.[32] Even with the halting of the advance, Lokhvitsky felt secure enough to move his headquarters up from a tower in the village of St. Thierry to the ruins of the château of Courcy.[33]

There are no clues today in the quiet, peaceful village of Courcy that such a fierce struggle ever took place. The canal, which was such a barrier to the attacking Russian forces, now seems small and insignificant. On a Saturday afternoon, the town is almost deserted save for several boys playing soccer on a dusty playground. The geological peculiarity on which Fort Brimont stood rises like a freak above the plains of Champagne. A paved road up the side of the small mountain to Brimont gives the traveler a panoramic view as far as the eye can see of fields and vineyards, kept in pristine neatness. Near the top of the mount near to what remains of the fort, the traveler who had been seduced by the tranquility of the country-side is brought sharply back to the reality of the history of the place. A wire gate bars the road, with a sign attached warning that it would be dangerous to proceed farther. Here in this halcyon, almost forgotten corner of France, many Russian soldiers fought, were maimed, and died. Moreover, it was in this quiet spot that their spirit, like that of their French comrades, finally broke, and it was here that the Russian Expeditionary Force fought with discipline for the last time.

It had been generally agreed among the leaders of the French military that if the heralded breakthrough did not occur quickly, then the offensive would be suspended so as not to become one of those typical meat-grinding attacks so characteristic of the war. Yet although it was clear to everyone at general headquarters by midafternoon of the first day that it was not achieving any of its objectives, the offensive was not suspended. The Second Battle of the Aisne, therefore, quickly became merely another human abattoir. On April 17, General Nivelle pressed on despite the failure to obtain objectives on all points.

Mazel's 1st corps before Craonne had begun to bend on the second day from vigorous German counterattacks, but the unit was saved by French artillery. The 9th infantry division to the right of this unit, however, made some advance toward La Ville-au-Bois, which was eventually taken. They had cleared the woods before them of Germans in an area called Californie with grenade attacks, but still the V Army was two to four miles away from the places that, according to the plan, were supposed to have been taken within three and a half hours of the beginning of the offensive the day before. About noon, Micheler informed Mazel that since the much-expected breach had not occurred, Nivelle was changing the orientation of the attack to the northeast, which would put the burden on the V Army.

Mazel was stunned. His men had already collided with a stone wall. The Germans had successfully survived the artillery bombardment and had crawled out of their bunkers to meet the French with murderous machine-gun fire. The troops were further demoralized by seeing their wounded of the previous day still lying unattended. At one place for 3,500 beds, there were only four thermometers, and for 4,000 wounded at one collection depot, there were only 900 drinking mugs.[34] The battering continued over the next few days at Caraonne, Mount Sapigneul, Mount Spin, and Chevreux Wood, and although they captured a large number of prisoners (Mazel reports 11,000), the French forces took little territory and occupied only a few insignificant villages as a reward for their efforts.[35]

On April 17 and 18, the Germans furiously shelled the newly taken positions, especially the line north of Courcy. The third battalion of the 6th regiment of the Third Brigade, the first of this unit to join battle, was sent to help defend *Côte 108*, a hill taken the day before. Meanwhile, the remainder of the 6th regiment was told to continue advancing on Courcy. When it did so, well-placed German machine guns at first halted this unit's progress, but the enemy guns were silenced by a *canon de 37* after the fourth try.[36]

Before Courcy, at 7:30 A.M. on April 17, after an artillery bombardment of the German lines, the 1st regiment of the First Brigade attacked in the direction of Courcy but was stopped by German machine-gun fire. There followed repeated attacks without much success. During the day Courcy was, however, rid of enemy effectives still on the west side of the canal, but all day the enemy fired on the captured Bastion de Courcy and the *Tête de cochon*. The account of the day's events reported that the troops "suffered very much from the bombardment."

A prisoner taken at 5:00 P.M. told the Russians that the Germans were massing north of the canal and planned to attack at 6:00 P.M. Enemy artillery had been feeble all day, but just before 5:30 P.M. a short intense artillery bombardment descended on the Russians, knocking out a number of the machine guns of the second Russian regiment, which had reached the canal the previous day. Infantry attacks fell on both regiments. The 1st regiment stopped the attack with machine-gun fire, but the Germans did succeed in temporarily penetrating the Russian positions before being forced back with a counterattack. At the end of the day, both sides diminished their efforts, with the Russians having sustained about 20 percent casualty rate in their units.[37] The *Times History of the Great War* described the Russians as having "rendered a good account of themselves."[38]

On April 18 in front of the canal and north of the Château de Courcy the Germans unleashed a heavy bombardment, but at 2:30 A.M. on April 19, the 3rd battalion of the 1st regiment pushed forward and captured twenty German soldiers and some military matériel. Liaison was also made with the French 151st on its right. At day's end, aerial photos showed the Germans reorganizing new lines and erecting new barbed-wire entanglements where they had stopped the Russian advance.[39] The First Brigade never advanced any farther from this point, yet by April 23, after the offensive had in effect been terminated, Mazel was still reporting that he felt that he could easily capture Fort Brimont.[40] Nivelle, refusing to admit that his offensive had failed, held a conference with Prime Minister Alexandre Ribot, Painlevé, and other military and cabinet figures and told them that his next operations would include an attack by the V Army on Brimont and on the crest that dominated the valley of the Ailette. Yet Mazel was now not so certain that Brimont could be taken, and Pétain had joined him in finding that such an attack would be "chancy, difficult, and bloody."[41] Doubts proved well founded, for by April 23 both Brimont and the glassworks at Courcy still remained in German hands, and the First Russian Brigade, having been badly mauled, had been removed from the fighting and was being held in reserve.

The full Third Brigade did not enter the battle until April 19. At 9:30 A.M. on April 16, the commandant of the 7th corps had asked Nivelle to allow him to use the entire Third Brigade as backup, but Nivelle refused because he had already decided to use it as support for the 32nd corps, which was scheduled to attack north of Cormicy at Sapigneul and Mount Spin, just south of Berry-au-Bac, at 11:00 A.M. that day.[42] One regiment (two battalions) was sent to the 32nd (the 40th division) south of the Aisne, but the remainder, the 5th regiment and one battalion of the 6th, Nivelle sent to reinforce the 37th infantry division in the 7th corps for the offensive on the eastern part of the Sapineul hill and the heights of Mount Spin.[43] Advances toward Mount Sapigneuil toward the northeast risked exposure of the flanks, so additional help was needed, which they apparently never received.[44] They took, however, the first three lines of German trenches and secured the heights of Sapineul and Mount Spin. In taking the latter they captured with hand grenades a German battery located on the forested slope of the mountain. Moreover, the Russians held, despite the German counterattacks, although they sustained an additional 200 casualties.[45]

At 3:00 on the afternoon of April 19, the attack against the Germans resumed, and the initial wave took the first German line. The second assault cleared this line and attacked the parallel trench, occupying it after a stiff fight. The Russians continued their advance to the third line, but there they were slowed by machine-gun fire from German guns that had survived the initial artillery bombardment. Only the 2nd company on the left was able to advance, the three others being held back on the right flank. The barbed wire before the 3rd battalion on the left was totally destroyed, and the unit easily took the first line and advanced directly to the parallel trench. The Russian troops took it with hand-to-hand fighting. The advance went well with liaison being maintained with the units on either side, and it reached the summit of Mount Spin, where it caught a murderous enemy fire. Meanwhile the 2nd battalion of the 6th regiment fought hard to take the first enemy trenches and then attacked the support trenches, but a German counterattack pushed it back to the first line.

The 3rd battalion of the 5th regiment and the 2nd of the 6th were merged later in the day due to the heavy losses. The 1st battalion was forced to retreat from the second enemy trench to the first, which had been partially occupied by the Germans, who had broken through and gotten behind the unit. To escape, they had to fight their way out with grenades. The 2nd battalion of the 6th regiment, having sustained heavy losses, retreated slowly under heavy German attacks.

Reporting the Third Brigade's retreat, the official account of the day's fighting becomes more and more vague. Other units also fell back, so that by 7:30 P.M. all Russian forces in this sector were at their original departure point and bracing for German counterattacks. Enemy losses were, however, heavy, Marushevsky wrote in his report, stating the unlikely consequence that all original enemy occupants of those trenches taken were either killed or captured. His report to the French government puts the best foot forward, but there was no covering the fact that at the end of the day, despite heavy casualties, the Russians were where they had begun in the morning. The battle continued in a desultory fashion until April 23, and in certain sectors sputtered on to April 25. It was finally suspended altogether amid loud claims of success that could hardly have fooled anyone.

Overall Allied losses had been large, but probably no greater than in similar offensives. Cyril Falls in his history of the Great War claims 187,000 French and 163,000 German casualties.[46] Both figures are probably somewhat high. A note on losses given to the French minister of war in May 1917 puts French casualties at 15,589 killed, with 60,036 wounded and 20,500 missing in action, for a total of 96,125 casualties of both officers and men. In parentheses after this statement are the words *"Russes et Sénégalais compris."*[47] Another note filed with the army in July by the Commission of Inquiry speaks of about 80,000 for four or five days, 30,000 of whom were killed.[48] Another document in the same collection puts the wounded in the V, X, and VI armies at 45,316, with an additional 5,274 sick, for a total of 50,590. Of these there was a surprisingly low figure of 7,278 casualties for the V Army by itself. Several pages later, the figure of 75,050 is given with the words *"1ère méthode de calcul"* under which someone has written two lines in a red pencil and the word *"fausse."*

As for Russian casualties, the figures also vary. How many Russians actually died will remain somewhat of a mystery since all sources, even various versions of the French reports that were classified at the time, do not agree. The figure most often quoted for the casualty list is 5,183, but other accounts giving different numbers for slightly different periods do not add to such a low figure.[49] In a report by Palitsyn, the count is placed at 4,472 men and 70 officers. French reports give the figure at around 5,000 killed, wounded, and missing. The May report just cited places the figure at 5,183.[50] General Marushevsky had asked for reinforcements even before the offensive, as had Lokhvitsky, and he reported a total casualty figure of 2,571 for the offensive alone. He included among these figures 880 wounded, 328 gas victims, and 1,355 sick from some illness. Of these, 1,505 were sent to the rear for treatment, and of these, 651 were returned to their units.[51] This exact number is given in a Russian source from the time, although it probably is based on figures given by the French. One definite number from one unit underscores the severity of the casualty rate. From the 5th regiment, 8 officers were killed and 7 were wounded. Two were missing. Among the effectives, 135 were killed, with 285 missing and 605 wounded. The casualties of the 6th regiment were not quite as heavy, with 4 officers and 91 soldiers killed and 13 officers and 570 soldiers wounded. The missing in action accounted for 122 more casualties for the one day's fighting.[52]

Both the French and Russian governments showered effusive praise on both brigades after the offensive, even to the point of mendacity. Delighted with the Russian performance, General Mazel noted that they had "brilliantly obtained all objectives of the attack," and he awarded both regiments the Military Cross with palms.[53] Of the Third, he observed that they had "gone brilliantly into the struggle . . . with great drive, despite the withering fire of the enemy." The Military Cross was likewise awarded to both regiments.[54] The order of the day for April 24 referred to the two units as "elite brigades" under the "energetic command of its leader General Lokhvitsky," who has "energetically achieved its objectives, has pursued its effort to its goal, in spite of high losses, *especially in officers* [my italics]" and "has succeeded in repelling all the efforts made by the enemy in order to drive him from the conquered terrain." The order of the day heaped fulsome praise on the Third, which it said was "superiorly led by their leader General Marushevsky and had the most brilliant attitude under fire," adding that it attacked "with the greatest bravery without letting itself be stopped by the most murderous enemy fire."[55] Two days before, General Nivelle wrote to General Alexeev that the REF "has especially distinguished itself," and added, "I would be happy if this would be reported to the leadership of the Russian army."[56] A week later Alexeev wired Palitsyn that the two brigades had performed "brilliantly" and that he was "happy to report to the Russian army about your dear brothers serving in regiments in far-away France, shoulder to shoulder with our glorious allies against a common enemy for right, freedom, and a brighter future of our people."[57] On April 25, Alexander Guchkov, then the minister of war in the Provisional Government, likewise sent a telegram of thanks to the men and officers of the two brigades "for glorious military deeds and outstanding valor."[58] Albert Thomas, now the French ambassador to Russia replacing the aristocrat Paléologue, told Russian journalists that the Russian force had "astonished France by its heroism."[59] All of this rhetoric masked the fact that by the time much of it was written, the Russian troops were in open revolt.

Whatever the losses inflicted by the offensive, they probably were not substantially worse than those sustained in many others, and as there was no element of surprise, it is nothing short of astounding that the slaughter was no worse than it was. If the total number of casualties was somewhere in the neighborhood of 90,000 to 100,000, the French army got off cheaply. Unquestionably the French had inflicted a staggering blow to the Germans, but the enormity of the list of casualties was not what so affected France. Rather it was the disappointment resulting from the military failure. In open discussion that preceded the offensive, a certainty was born that this effort would be the last demanded of the French nation and its army, that the long-awaited rupture of the front would occur that would recreate a war of motion that would carry the fight into the enemy's land. As the early optimistic reports of successes turned into the cold reality of failure, as the realization that the war was not to end in weeks but would continue to grind on endlessly as before, "a veritably tragic shudder," in the words of American Supreme Court

Justice Felix Frankfurter, passed through the French nation. Yet it was worse than simple despair—it was emotional surrender. Again to quote Frankfurter in a report to Secretary of State Robert Lansing, ". . . the whole nation came to believe . . . that 100,000 men were sacrificed through an offensive futile in result and generally as unwise in conception."[60] As the trainloads of mangled wounded came lurching into the Gare de l'Est, all of the frustration caused by the desperate, fruitless three-year struggle exploded in the government, in the press, in the streets, but most seriously at the front. In the armies there came one of the most widespread mutinies ever faced by a nation in which the mutinous army did not topple the government or give victory to the enemy. Units became drunk and disorderly and refused to obey their officers. Battalion after battalion informed its leaders that they would no longer go on the offensive. Replacement troops in the rear refused to board trains for the front. At their most passive, troops going into the lines would bleat like sheep being sent to the slaughter, and soldiers scrawled on trains carrying replacements to the front "*à la boucherie!*" and "*Vive la paix!*" At one point, one source states that there were only two reliable units in the French army between the front and Paris.[61]

From the end of the offensive until the French army stabilized, there were 119 cases of "collective indiscipline," to use the euphemism for mutiny. Between May 25 and June 9 alone, there were 80 such incidents, the worst occurring behind the lines, not in the trenches. Courts-martial brought in over 23,000 cases, but only 432 death sentences were pronounced with only 55 (some sources state 49) ever being carried out.[62] Yet these mutinies in the French ranks created the gravest crisis that the government of the Third Republic had faced since the Battle of the Marne. The most astounding aspect of the near disaster, however, was the fact that the Germans remained in total ignorance of it.

The blame for it fell, however, not on the real causes but on the innocent Russian brigades that had fought so well in Champagne. Governments of nations never want to admit that their armies violate their national allegiance. Disloyalty and treason are weaknesses of other nationalities, never one's own. It became convenient, therefore, to blame the Russians because shortly after the Nivelle offensive, they had a mutiny of their own. Writing in July, long after both mutinies were an accomplished fact, Mazel stated that he had misgivings from the beginning about the Russian Expeditionary Force because it "was sorely pressed (*travailée*) by the events in Russia." He added, "It was not necessary to risk it in complicated operations."[63] This statement was obviously employing hindsight to use the past to foretell the present, since these misgivings had not prevented the general from giving these units some of the most difficult and complicated tasks in the débâcle. Yet blame them the French did, despite the fact that the first French mutinies came several days *before* Russian discipline really cracked.

The major catalysts that provoked the mutiny of the Russian troops in France were much the same elements that destroyed the Russian armies on the Eastern Front, but with different twists. Geographic proximity gave the troops in the East a greater, more immediate knowledge of what was unfolding in Russia. Moreover, for them it was geographically possible to do what armies have always dreamed of doing: go home. As a result, throughout 1917 there was a steady stream of deserting soldiers passing from Petrograd's Warsaw Station, which serviced the front, to the city's Moscow Station, from which trains departed for the nation's interior.

The Russians in France, however, did not know what was really transpiring in the new Russia, and uncertainty was worse than reality. Memories of the wife left behind or the children last seen as infants placed a terrible burden on men trapped so far from their families. Moreover, it was impossible for them to "vote with their feet," as Lenin termed the mass desertions of the Russian armies. As for their role in the fighting, they felt that they had been given tougher sections of the front on which to fight while the French had it easy. They had no way of seeing the railroad cars full of untreated French wounded that were crawling to the rear to facilities hardly prepared to care for them. When Russians were placed into barns because there was no room in any other shelter, they assumed that the French soldiers were all sent to clean, sanitary hospitals. They had no way of knowing that thousands of French wounded lay unattended in the open air. They had no way of knowing that the *poilu* knew the same sense of frustration and bitterness that they felt: that they had been used, that they had been sacrificed, that they had been sent on another futile offensive in which there was no chance of victory. One newspaper reported perfectly the belief of the Russian soldier in France when it described the Russian units as having been "sacrificed without mercy by the high command."[64]

These sore points were hammered by the émigrés and German agents. The modus operandi of the pacifist agents was smooth. We have one account of how these provocateurs approached an officer, Yuri Lissovsky, when he was on leave in Paris. It was a bitter fall evening, and Lissovsky had on his overcoat, which hid his officer's insignia. He was walking down Boulevard St. Germain, and being relatively new in Paris, he stopped on a corner to get his bearings. Suddenly from behind he heard in perfect Russian the words "Confused, my friend? Where are you going and what are you looking for?" The voice was that of a tall, well-built male brunet, impeccably dressed, and about thirty years old. Lissovsky thanked him and told the name of the street. "Great!" the man said. "It is on this side of Montparnasse," and then the stranger began walking along with Lissovsky as if they both had the same destination. The man then began bitterly berating the French and said that if the Germans were bad, the French were worse. "Oh, I know them well, these masters. I've been in Paris for twenty years. For them you're only cannon fodder sold for a kopeck, for a centime. This is terrible. . . ."

At this point Lissovsky identified himself as an officer and stated that he knew where his duties lay. On learning what he was up against, the provocateur vanished into the night. Many Russian soldiers experienced these encounters, but the simple peasant soldier was most vulnerable to their arguments. Lissovsky states that by as early as January 1917, all the Russian soldiers understood that they had indeed been "sold for shells" to the French.[65]

French attitudes toward them and their treatment by average Frenchmen in the rear likewise did not help. After Nivelle, French soldiers and citizens met them with cries of *"Boches!" "Les russes avec boches!"* and *"Russes kaput!"*[66] Knowing how they had suffered, the Russian soldiers bitterly resented this behavior of their allies, and it merely fueled the explosion that was to come. Given the circumstances, it is amazing that the Russian mutiny in France was both as tame as it was and so long in coming.

After the offensive, when the two brigades had been relocated to the inactive I Army under General Noel de Castelnau, both Lokhvitsky and Marushevsky gave glowing reports of Russian morale. Perhaps they did not know any differently, but it is highly unlikely that they had not heard something of the revolt that had already begun to boil. On May 2, Lokhvitsky reported to the commandant of the I Army that "from all reports" the extensive combat of the recent offensive had shown that the soldiers of the First Brigade had "conserved all their combative valor." He reinforced what he was saying by adding that the men under him were "proud, proud to have fulfilled the mission which had been entrusted to them and having triumphed over the enemy." He went on to add that the losses they had sustained "had not affected them in any way" and that they "ask to participate in new offensives."[67] For his part, Marushevsky, in an account written when the Russians were resting in a quiet sector of Lorraine with the I Army, described the state of his troops as "excellent." Yet the commandant of the Third Brigade was a bit more realistic. He strongly urged that the troops be fully informed about the events in Russia "in order that no false ideas germinate in their minds." He gave to the French the first indication that there was trouble by adding that "it is necessary to educate *politically* [my italics] the troops, which are holding numerous meetings and conferences."[68] As both of these glowing reports were being written, the Russian Expeditionary Force was erupting into full mutiny.

Whatever the Russian losses in the April offensive, they were clearly awesome, and both brigades badly needed reinforcements. On May 1, a day that would become very important in the history of the Russian Expeditionary Force, General Marushevsky asked for an additional 2,800 men and 60 officers for the Third Brigade, and days later a formal request was made for reinforcements for both brigades, calling for an additional 50 officers and 3,000 men for the First in addition to Marushevsky's request. The report told the chief of the mission to "insist" on the dispatch of these replacements from Russia.[69] At midmonth the French also were asking for an additional Russian artillery division to be sent for which the French promised to supply the horses, technical officers, interpreters, veterinarians, blacksmiths, harnesses, and whatever other matériel would go with the unit.[70]

The Russian Provisional Government seems to have been more willing to oblige France than the tsar's government had been. On May 3, Stavka wired Palitsyn in Paris to dispatch immediately a plan for sending additional troops to France, adding that departure, however, would have to be delayed until the channel in the White Sea was open from Archangel, sometime after the beginning of June. The Russian command had already planned to send to France an artillery brigade originally destined for Salonika accompanied by assorted support personnel, but after its departure, the Russians would then send twenty-six companies of infantry to replace the losses in the REF.[71] This generous offer is probably indicative of the Provisional Government's desperate state of dependency on its allies; to continue to receive aid, it must demonstrate that Russia was committed to the Allied cause to the bitter end. Lenin put it more crudely: The Provisional Government, he wrote, were only the "simple stewards of the billionaire firms, England and France."[72]

Yet for all the noble Russian offers to share their human flesh with France, by the third week in May, the French were having second thoughts about accepting them. The French government asked at that time for a delay in sending replacements to the Russian units "because of the present happenings."[73] Within a few days, however, probably in part because of a fear that additional Russian soldiers would bring yet a fresh infusion of revolutionary virus to their own already-infected troops, the French ministry of war had decided that it did not want any additional Russian troops, delayed or otherwise. On May 27 the French wired the Russian war ministry that "in view of the agitation in the Russian force," France wished to refrain from further shipments of troops to the French front, yet added, "This order does not affect the force located in Macedonia for which divisions are able to be transported through France."[74] Amazingly, the French government did not inform Albert Thomas, then French ambassador to Russia, about the troubles among the troops in France

Regardless of the decisions of the French and Russian governments, however, the troops being sent might have had something to say about their dispatch. The Russian government had organized outside Petrograd at Novyi Peterhof a separate special artillery brigade under the command of a General Beliaev, brother of the General Mikhail Beliaev, who had been the Russian minister of war. A second unit was organizing at Luga. At the height of the preparations, however, the troops at Luga mutinied, arrested their officers, and announced that they would not allow themselves to be sent abroad. After this force revolted, the Provisional Government decided by necessity to reform the first "in sympathy with the revolutionary movement." The second was renamed the "first," and rotten elements were replaced with reliable soldiers of the other. Beliaev was placed in command of the new unit. He received orders to depart early in June, and a few echelons had already reached Archangel when he got a telegram from Petrograd ordering him "to stop loading, dispatched echelons to return."[75]

While still ignorant of the events in France, he wired his government on May 24 from Petrograd that the boats *Dvinsk* and *Tsar*, which were slated to take the first detachments of Beliaev's troops to France, had arrived in Archangel, and he wanted to learn on what date the boats carrying their provisions would arrive. Thomas also wanted to know if he was expected to buy provisions in Russia for these troops who were waiting to depart.[76]

The next day, however, Thomas sent a more urgent message to Paris asking for a different kind of information. Apparently certain Russian newspapers had published reports that indiscipline among the Russian troops in France had gained certain concessions for them, and Thomas had been besieged with questions. "Have denied the news," he wired the French foreign ministry, "but I want you to inform me on this subject and let me know as soon as possible if you see anything worrisome to continuing to hasten the dispatch of Russian troops into France."[77]

It is indeed peculiar that the French government had kept its own ambassador in Russia in the dark about the breakdown of order among the Russian brigades. Probably it had no special motive in doing so, unless perhaps it felt that if Thomas knew about difficulties, he might somehow leak the news to the wrong sources. He was, after all, on close terms with such figures as the Marxist leader George Plekhanov. At the same time Thomas also was not informed about the mutinies of French troops, and his lack of information might have been part of a larger secrecy program. Whatever the reason, given his personality he must have been more annoyed than he indicated in his dispatch at having to learn about the difficulties from Russian newspapers.

Two days later the French government wired Thomas that his information had been correct, indicating that "it is true that among the Russian troops in France some symptoms of indiscipline have been manifested." The dispatcher (the note implies that it was Jules Cambon) added with incredible understatement, "Their presence on our territory begins not to be without inconvenience." The note went on to state that given the conditions, the French government wanted to suspend all dispatches of Russian troops to the Western Front, but it added that this change did not apply to Russians destined to join the Army of the Orient in Salonika and to any that would not sojourn on French territory.[78]

Although among the troops in France the development of the mood of revolt lagged behind that of their comrades at home, it was nonetheless very similar. Like the disintegration in Russia, it was made worse by the Russian peasant's lack of sophistication. These simple soldiers had been told that they now had "freedom." To the common soldier, however, the word "freedom" encompassed an assortment of things that in reality it did not mean. To the *muzhiks* the idea meant that they no longer had to submit to the will of their officers. The tsar had sent them to war, and now the tsar was gone. For them the war was over. This belief led them to fraternize with the Germans.[79] When they were told that they could attend meetings, theaters, and concerts "equally with all citizens," they thought it meant that they could attend free of charge. This mentality produced chaos.[80]

Merely weeks before, they had feared their leaders. By May 1917 their leaders feared them. When they were removed from the line and joined to the I Army at Montmort and Bayé in a wooded terrain about twenty-five miles southwest of Épernay, they were already in a state approaching anarchy and could no longer be described as a fighting force. If their revolution meant that there was no tsar and they were now free, then what would be the use of freedom if they had to return to the trenches? As Trotsky pointed out, that was the genuine attitude of the Russian soldier everywhere after the revolution. It was not brought in from the outside, he felt. No provocateur could have thought of so simple and so convincing an argument.[81]

FIVE

Revolution Delayed:
The Russian Rebellion in France

April–June 1917

And because we concerned ourselves with nothing but finances in Russia, at the expense of the [Russian] nation, we saw that nation reveal itself in March, 1917, practically a stranger to us. . . . The fact is . . . the Franco-Russian Alliance . . . was a fraud, a painful political joke, for which the French middle classes put up all the money, and of which the Russian nation has suffered all the terrible consequences.

— Charles Rivet[1]

If there is disturbance in the camp, the general's authority is weak. If the banners and flags are shifted about, sedition is afoot.

— Sun Tzu[2]

Listen!
Each person
Even someone who is useless
Has the right to live.
You can't
You simply cannot
Bury him alive
In trenches and dugouts.
Murderers!

— Mayakovsky[3]

ON THE RUSSIAN FRONT, by the summer of 1917, the Russian army had simply ceased to exist as a fighting force. By the hundreds of thousands, they had deserted and left the trenches. The soldiers who stayed "loyal" remained sullenly passive. Had they been summoned out to stay the flood of deserters, they would have done little more than join them. Those who did remain in the front lines often had an unsigned truce with the Germans: They would stick their bayonets in the trench parapets in view of the Germans as if to say "We won't fight if you won't."[4]

There likewise existed in France by 1917 a genuine pacifist movement that was genuinely defeatist.[5] The drive was not in its own mind unpatriotic, just as the motivation for the antiwar movement in the United States during the Vietnam era was not per se unpatriotic. It was born of despair caused by the butchery on the Western Front and the painful privations at home. It was a cure-all mentality with little regard for what a negotiated peace would mean for France when signed while millions of German bayonets were firmly entrenched less than a hundred miles from Paris. The mentality was understandable nonetheless. The lack of a will to fight did not perish with Versailles in 1919 but remained to poison French politics in the 1930s and bring defeat in 1940. Of this malaise the Russians in France had their share.[6]

Because of the relative ease of their distribution, the émigré newspapers worked the major damage to official Russian authority. In the early years of the war, the most widely circulated was Trotsky's *Nashe slovo* (Our Word), which later seemed to be replaced in prominence by the aforementioned *Golos pravdy* (The Voice of Truth). It might well have been essentially the same paper; certainly it contained some of the same staff and had the same backing. Often seditious papers were suppressed by the French government to no avail. One Russian journal *Mysl'* (Thought) was closed by the police in July 1915, only to reappear as *Zhizn'* (Life). Even the great patriot Georges Clemenceau's journals were closed several times by the government only to reopen several days later under another name.

These subversive sheets hammered repeatedly on the theme of the injustice of Russians fighting in France. One such paper, *Social Demokrat,* published in Russia but which typified the work of those in France, attacked the very idea of any Russian soldiers in France. Categorizing the French as "valets of the former despot," the journal called on all Russian soldiers to remember their comrades on foreign soil and asked all to raise their voices to the defense of "our brothers sold to capitalists of an Allied country." Referring to the Provisional Government's members as "convicts," the paper went on to remind, by this time ad nauseam, that the tsar had sent them "as grain offered to capitalists of Allied countries." When they had asked to send delegates, the soldiers were reminded that they had "been sent to France [read: to the capitalists], and you will have no kind of rights." Then playing on white-black racism, the paper quoted the French as saying that if they insisted on sending delegates, "There is a division of niggers all ready to calm you down. . . . "[7]

For all of the efforts of the French government to stem anti-Allied propaganda and subversion, it made little effort to address the Russian brigades' genuine grievances. The few attempts at bettering the lot of the REF seem to have been largely freelance operations conducted by Russians, not the French. In mid-May a Russian journalist, a M. Brut, tried to counteract the antiwar indoctrination among the Russians by abandoning his role as a journalist and holding instead a conference among the assembled battalions. At this meeting he stressed the soldiers' duties. When he left the front, he seemed to think that the "illness" was not as critical as when he arrived. He was not received badly by the soldiers, and he apparently planned to create an organization of speakers to go among them frequently "to carry good speeches."[8] Since he appears no more in the police reports and since the climate turned precipitously nastier, we can assume that he never succeeded. In July, even after the situation had become hopeless, a Dr. Alexander Nikolaenkov, who had for some time been helping Russians passing through Marseille and who had been associated with certain anarchist groups and socialists opinions, organized a reunion of Russians in the area for the purpose of staying their disciplinary collapse. With the aid of the Russian vice consul in Marseille, he arranged an affair to which about fifty people appeared. When he spoke to the group, he largely addressed the soldiers, telling them to avoid political discussions and to remember that they were *Russian* soldiers and that they had come to France to do their duty. The police agent who reported the meeting opined that Nikolaenkov had given "some good advice to the Russian soldiers."[9] These feeble efforts, however, accomplished little to stop or even delay the revolutionary tide that had gripped the units. Given little support by the French government, whose early response to the Russian troubles was understandably a "hands-off" policy, any such efforts would have failed.

As for the French mutinies, they formally began on April 29 in Champagne in the X Army under the command of General Denis Duchêne, when a battalion of French troops resisted orders to attack. On May 3 a colonial division, which had suffered heavily in the assault on the *Chemin des Dames* during the Nivelle offensive, experienced incidents of insubordination because agitators had harangued the troops, telling them that munitions workers were earning 15 to 20 francs a day while they were risking their lives for a daily salary of only two francs. Between May 3 and May 20 there were many serious separate and independent outbursts, none of which were connected, but on the latter date, mutinies turned genuinely ugly. On that day there were major incidents of general insubordination in fifteen to twenty divisions. Soon 115 units, mostly infantry, were in varying degrees of rebellion, accompanied by drunkenness, vandalism, and general noisy disorder.[10]

Despite the fact that the French were incredibly successful in keeping the Germans from knowing about their mutinies, the enemy somehow received at least some hint of the problems with the Russian brigades. One newspaper in Germany (the report does not state which one) told its readers, "The Russian troops in France have become suspect. They have been carried from the front because their attitude has become bad." From this point the account became mendacious propaganda in telling its readers that Kerensky had ordered the shooting of mutineers and 150 had been executed. "The example had not settled matters: it is necessary to return the Russian troops to Russia from France."[11] It is amazing that the Germans could have learned about the Russian mutinies without learning about those of the French. The only probable explanation is that their agents had been actively working the Russians, with many visiting the Russians at the front, in the camps, and in the hospitals, and therefore they knew of the problem because they had helped create it.

The fact that French soldiers sang "The International" and shouted "Down with the War" made it all the easier to place the blame on the Russian soldiers, since soldiers on the Eastern Front were doing the same. The investigation held later by the French government "showed" that the Russian Revolution itself had been a major factor in the decline of French morale, not because of any revolutionary activity of the Russian brigades in France, but due to the realization that the revolution in Russia meant that there would no longer be any effective action on the Eastern Front, where hopeless offensives had saved France more than once.[12] The Russian brigades therefore were available to take the blame. In his memoirs, even Joseph Noulens, the French ambassador in Russia after Thomas had left, passed the onus for the problems almost casually onto the Russians. "Indiscipline is contagious," he rationalized. "The French army herself passed through a period of aberrations."[13]

Because the Germans did not capitalize on the French problems, the mutinies were not ultimately a factor in the outcome of the war. Marshal Henri Pétain, the general who had saved Verdun the year before by rotating troops for only a short duration through the murderous siege, was placed in command of the French armies after Nivelle was removed.

Pétain had a reputation among the common soldiers, from whose ranks he himself had risen, for not wasting lives in the hopeless offensives that had so characterized the war to this point. The average man in the trenches knew that with Pétain in charge, his life would not be thrown away. Moreover, Pétain himself visited the front lines, talked with the *poilus*, and sincerely listened to their complaints. He saw to it that they got better food and more rest far from the front lines where they would no longer hear the roar of the guns. Pétain also temporarily stopped all offensive military operations. For example, the V Army, where the Russians had served, was notified by General Marie-Emile Fayolle on May 27 that there would be "no important offensive action" in the near future. After that announcement, the French army began to stabilize,[14] and by the end of June a fragile discipline had been restored. By the end of the year, the French army was able to make limited offensives.

The collapse of Russian discipline had, as we have observed, different catalysts. The will of soldiers to keep fighting is maintained by a belief that they are fighting for honorable means, for God, country, freedom, democracy, or whatever had placed them on the battlefield in the first place. Yet by the third year of the war, for the simple Russian soldier, there was a plethora of so-called honorable means for *not* fighting after the February Revolution: The tsar who had sent them to war was gone; Russia had merely been used by its allies and would be used no more; the officers who had ordered them to attack the German machine guns had cared little for the loss of their lives and therefore deserved no respect from the men they led; and on and on.

Then came the ripple effect from Russia. The distance, to be sure, initially provided some insulation, but it arrived nonetheless in the form of changes, birthed by the revolution, in the relationship between soldier and officer. The first such reforms were the General Order No. 1 and the soldiers' committees that were formed to guarantee soldiers' protection from the capriciousness of their officers. To the unsophisticated peasant soldier these additions meant that suddenly officers did not have to be obeyed at all. With the arrival at the front of commissars (one veteran of the Eastern Front described them to this author as "Kerensky's damned students"), the disintegration began.

The situation was not helped by the fact that there coincidentally occurred at the time a turnover in leadership resulting in Palitsyn's recall. Apparently General Alexeev had decided early in April on the recall prior to the mutinies, and Palitsyn received word of his dismissal on April 19, in the midst of the Nivelle offensive.[15] His replacement was to be General Alexander Zankevich, but Palitsyn was to remain until Zankevich could assume control. Eleven days later Palitsyn received a curious wire from Minister of War Alexander Guchkov to the effect that the French did not have a preference between him and Zankevich, so he might remain in his position if he wished. Palitsyn, however, decided to return home.[16]

Alexander Zankevich had commanded the 146th regiment before he was named chief of headquarters of the 18th corps of the army and deputy chief clerk of the General Headquarters in Petrograd. He was only forty-two years old and had received three war wounds.[17] Like most officers in the Russian army, he was hostile to the soldiers' committees, and he favored Russian participation on the French front only with the "full abolition of the committees, [and] by the return to our former discipline."[18] Arriving in France on May 31, he must have quickly questioned the possibility of the unit as a fighting force because shortly after his appearance, he inquired whether willing REF soldiers could transfer over into French service,[19] indicating his belief that the force was indeed finished as an effective unit.

From the standpoint of the Russian officers and the French government, however, the most ominous innovation brought by the revolutionary changes was the soldiers' committees to guaranteeing soldiers' rights.[20] Under pressure from the Petrograd Soviet, Alexander Guchkov issued a notice stating "The new structure of the armed forces creates a system of chosen unit organization, which is to appraise each soldier of his civil and political rights. In such an organization is the company committee, regimental and army committees, and a disciplinary court. All of these are chosen by a general, direct, equal, and secret election. . . ."[21]

Committee powers consisted of the right to enter into relations with any political and social organizations outside the army, the right to intervene in the decisions in the differing relations between officers and soldiers, and the right of verification and control of the administration and dispatch of funds.[22] In short, the committees could in reality override the officers' authority. This change destroyed for all time the control Russian officers held over their men because it made officers' authority conditional.[23] No army can function democratically, and these committees quickly wreaked havoc on the discipline on the Eastern Front. They would shortly do their share of damage to the brigades in France, for whom the cry "To Russia" became the general slogan after the failed Nivelle offensive.

The formal order from Petrograd to elect soldiers' committees in France arrived on April 16, 1917, the day the Nivelle offensive began. Committees were not elected, however, until after the soldiers had been removed from the front. Two eyewitnesses who wrote were not precise about when the committees were first formed. Kozlov of the Third Brigade noted that it was when they were taken to "several villages in Champagne" (probably Mailly or Mourmelon) after the offensive had been terminated.[24] A participant in the First wrote how the soldiers first formed company committees, then battalion and regimental committees, with the regimental committees picking the brigade committee. He states that the brigade committee was located in one of the big villages near the front,[25] probably Mailly, which seems to have been a central meeting place of the committees.

French observers noted the hardly surprising fact that those elected to these brigade positions were always the most radical elements.[26] Watching in horror at the whole business, the French were most concerned about what the Russians might think that the committees meant in their relationship to their ally. Indeed, a French observer reported that one Russian soldier thought that the committees had legal force in Russian relations with the French army. The observer's report went on: "The danger is evident and must be exorcised as soon as possible; some energetic measures are urgently needed in order to prevent at any price the development of . . . disorder and preserve our troops. . . ."[27] By this time the French mutinies were already in full swing, and given the French high command's belief that the Russian brigades had caused their rebellion, the French ministry of war would only view these developments with the greatest concern.

Yet if the French government was alarmed with the potential danger from the soldiers' committees, the Russian officers were more so. The two internal eyewitness memoirs of the brigades mention Lokhvitsky's attempts to counter the committees' authority. Vavilov tells that to try to make them "dance to their tune," the officers ordered all brigades to assemble in the square for a meeting and review. Lokhvitsky made a long speech, which concluded with an order to retake a loyalty oath to the Provisional Government. Vavilov wrote that the soldiers' mood was against it, and very few took the second oath. Having failed in that manner, Lokhvitsky then took another tack. He announced to those assembled, "Those who wish to take the oath to the Provisional Government, stand where you are. Those who will not [take the oath], move away." Only the officers remained in their places, and Vavilov writes that "all" the soldiers pulled away. He notes that it was in part because most did not know for what the Provisional Government stood.[28] If indeed every single one of the soldiers refused to take the oath, it was due in part to peer pressure from what might well have been a majority. If a majority could intimidate a minority, no matter how large, to force unanimity on the simple taking of an oath, then it could force unanimity on a number of other issues, such as the refusal to fight. Whereas many soldiers probably did not grasp the significance of the matter, it could hardly have escaped notice of the officers.

Kozlov wrote that Lokhvitsky, appearing at one of the committee meetings apparently uninvited, confronted the authority question in the last week of April. The treatment of the wounded in the French hospitals was immediately put to the general, because many letters had been received from convalescent soldiers stating that they were being mistreated. Lokhvitsky became visibly indignant and responded with a denial. He acknowledged, however, that it was possible that "individual actions on the part of soldiers with their coarse tricks had led the French to excess."[29] Lokhvitsky apparently left without ever either convincing or being convinced.

Meetings of the soldiers' committees showed, however, that there was no unanimity on one relatively general matter, revealing differences that would play a major role in the future: What authority would the committees recognize? Kozlov noted that after the decision had been made to send a delegation to Russia, there had been an intense argument in his regiment's committee about to whom it should report in Russia—the Provisional Government or the Petrograd Soviet of Soldiers' and Workers' Deputies, the shadow socialist government in the Russian capital. Kozlov himself was for recognizing only the Soviet, and late in April, he was in a minority.[30] According to Kozlov, the soldiers' committee was dominated by "the Mensheviks," that is, the more conservative, orthodox Marxists, who were led by one Drobovich, the secretary of the committee and later editor of the newspaper *The Russian Soldier in France.* He was a supporter of the Provisional Government. From this point onward, there would always be a minority that would be contrary, thus reflecting a conservative-radical division in the force. Kozlov wrote his memoir some years after the events when he was living in a Russia ruled by those who had been victorious over the Mensheviks, so his account is most assuredly politically colored. At the time the "Menshevik-dominated" regimental committee would supposedly not report to the Petrograd Soviet, the Petrograd Soviet itself was controlled by the Mensheviks. Kozlov "remembered" that the committee's weak-willed nature was due to the influence of the shootings of the soldiers responsible for Krause's murder, yet this excuse was little more than a case of political editing after the fact.

A number of factors would indeed have made the regimental committees more conservative than the prevailing political mood in Russia, the most important among them being the simple distance from the Russian cyclone, the eye of which was Petrograd. The absence of boldness in those early days had more to do with the halting uncertainty of the situation and the newness of the path they were taking than with any ideological pattern that any of the leaders might have claimed to follow later. One strongly suspects that at the time, even Kozlov himself had no real clear understanding of Marxism and applied its principles to the events in France only after the fact and from the better-informed position of the political indoctrination that came after the Civil War. The temper of the committees ripened, however, in the next few months and indeed even overtook the pace of the revolution in Russia.

At the same meeting Lokhvitsky crashed, the committee decided to plan a major demonstration for May 1, the International Day for the Working Man created by the Second International. There was to be joint action with both brigades, and Kozlov was directed on April 29 to go the camp at Mailly to join what he calls the "weak-willed detachments and the center of the marching battalion of the 1st and 2nd brigades" for the preparations. He was given only a certificate of identification, a mandate from his regimental committee, and some sort of literature, which he does not specify. He must have had trouble establishing his credentials on arrival in Mailly ("without the proper documents, things were difficult," he tells us), quite possibly because he had to compete with someone else from his regiment who quite probably was duly authorized. Kozlov after all was from the more conservative unit. It would be a good reason for his muddying the details. He was, however, allowed to speak, and what he had to say was treated "with reservation," he tells us. The May Day demonstrations were discussed but nothing substantive was decided. Kozlov attributes this inaction to the fact that the committee's president was an "old corporal" named Bashilov, a clerk in civilian life, and he would not take any steps without the help of "the superiors." He also states the fact that the committee secretary, Drobovich, was "a Menshevik" also had something to do with the paralysis. Kozlov decided to go over the heads of the committee to the regiment itself and suggested a general meeting "for the guidance of the regiment." The committee agreed, and after he spoke to the full brigade (he switches from regiment to brigade in his narrative), his more aggressive plan was accepted and fulfilled.[31]

The committee decided on a central place to assemble for the demonstration. The larger crowd would clearly make a more definite impression.[32] When on the morning of May 1 the agitated soldiers gathered on a large field before the Châteaux of Montmort and Bayé, singing the French national anthem and carrying red and black flags, for revolution and

anarchy respectively, they triggered their mutiny. The historical significance of the music and the flags most certainly was lost on the majority of
the common soldiers, just as the privates in the Decembrist Revolt in 1825
who had shouted "Constantine and a Constitution" had believed that
"*konstitutsiia*" was Constantine's wife. To most of the soldiers of the REF,
the flags and the music simply stated that they wanted to go home. Whereas
few if any had a knowledge of Marxism, with their leaders it was a different
matter. Most were probably at least vague marxists, and like their comrades
at home, they won their following by playing on themes of discontent, not
preaching the finer points of Communist ideology.

Kozlov arrived after the demonstration had begun and learned that
the committee itself had come down on the side of "order," not for a more
forceful or riotous demonstration. A few officers participated (Koslov
does not identify them), but most did not. There were some patriotic
affirmations to the Provisional Government after which the mass of
soldiers separated into smaller groups.[33]

In the midst of this chaotic activity, General Palitsyn appeared,
ironically on a white horse. He had been watching the whole affair from
some distance and apparently decided that bold action was needed. Since
he had already been replaced by General Zankevich, technically he had
no official duties, but since Zankevich was not on the scene, Palitsyn felt
compelled to rush into the leadership void. French officers on hand made
themselves scarce so it would not look as if they had sent him. He arrived
at the crowd just as some radical orator was indulging in a tirade to the
soldiers, and he politely waited until the fellow had finished.

Palitsyn glosses over the whole incident in his unpublished memoirs
as if it had not happened, and given what followed, there is little wonder
that he omitted it. He rode among the soldiers, by one account, conversing
with them and ascertaining their needs,[34] but quickly trouble erupted.
Accused of trying to resurrect the old iron discipline, Palitsyn defended
his actions by laying the blame on regulations of the Provisional Government and on orders from the new minister of war. He was interrupted by
heckling from the soldiers surrounding him who shouted "Down with the
martinet!" and "Beat the old bureaucrat!" An orator took the floor and
harangued the crowd, which responded with great enthusiasm. Palitsyn
tried to respond but could not be heard over the roar.[35] Finally the hapless
general said pathetically, "Dear Friends, I am sixty years old and had
better leave." He fled in a barrage of insults,[36] leaving the rowdies in
control of the field.

Later in the day soldiers commandeered a staff car and after attach-
ing to it red and black pennants, rode wildly around the staff headquarters

of both General Lokhvitsky at Bayé and General Marushevsky at Montmort, yelling insults and obscenities with impunity. Then the other soldiers ran amok and even hurled abuse at some nearby French troops who had just returned from the front. Not understanding the language, however, the French soldiers thought it was a patriotic demonstration.[37] French peasants in the environs likewise marveled at the spectacle, and to Ehrenburg they expressed amazement at the curious Russian behavior. One peasant told the journalist, "I can understand their mutinizing. Everyone's sick of the war; our fellows are mutinizing, too. But why are there officers among them?" He also wanted to know why they were singing the French national anthem. "What a funny lot you are!" one peasant observed.[38]

After the May Day demonstration, there was no longer even any semblance of the old discipline in any of the Russian units. The collapse of authority was worsened by the fact that officers avoided their men as if they thought that if they ignored the disturbances, everything would calm itself. Kozlov tells of a meeting about which he had apparently just heard, since he could not have been present where a Colonel Zhdemov presided over a gripe session in which the officers reported how they had been insulted to their faces by their men and that they admitted that they now avoided the soldiers.[39] Disorder, of course, did not abate, and the officers were at a total loss. The most extreme case of this disrespect for leadership came, surprisingly, from the Third Brigade, where an ugly disturbance nearly resulted in General Marushevsky's murder. The unfortunate general escaped but did not stop running until he reached Paris, leaving his unit with no authority but the soldiers' committees. The French, on paper at any rate, solved the problem by uniting the two brigades into a division under Lokhvitsky's shaky command, not bothering to replace the now-absent Marushevsky.[40] The officers' ostrichlike stance certainly aggravated the situation. With no usual symbol of the old authority, the rebellion was not likely to burn itself out. Personal danger aside, these officers likewise confirmed to outside observers the low opinion generally held of the Russian officer. Henri Bordeaux of the French general headquarters opined when he saw the Russians leave the line what a fine body of men "these deep-voiced Russians" were. He felt that had they been well led, they would have made wonderful soldiers.[41]

By the time Zankevich assumed full command, the disorder in the units had become total chaos. The days consisted of endless meetings with much radical rhetoric calling for an end to the imperialist war and a return home. These sessions continued under the scrutiny of the French police, one of whose reports of a meeting on May 24 preserved for posterity the information that "Leninism," whatever the reporter thought that meant, had spread to the second regiment (the one recruited in Samara) of the First Brigade and the fifth regiment of the Third Brigade.[42]

On May 10, the radicals ordered new elections for a series of committees, one deputy for every fifty men and a separate Soviet of Officers' Deputies.[43] We do not know if these elections were ever held, yet the mere talk of them would hardly have tamed the disorder. Izvolsky blamed the French for the problem. On May 17 he wired Petrograd of further disturbances and reminded the government that he had strongly opposed the French request for troops. He had foreseen, he said, that the difference in the "manner, forms of discipline, etc., between the Russian and French forces would make problems," but he added that the composition, quality, and quantity of the officers had likewise contributed to it, as did the food and language problems. He strongly urged the government not to send any reinforcements to replace the losses, and he recommended stern measures to handle the problem.[44]

An observer visited the Russian camp and was "stupefied" that the new revolutionary methods adopted by the soldiers in Russia had been accepted so quickly in France. He was especially alarmed by the mushrooming of the soldiers' committees just as they had appeared in Russia. He was also upset over the pacifist and antimilitary propaganda that was freely distributed among the men. He especially noticed *Golos pravdy*, which he observed "seemed to be an organ in the mould of *Nashe slovo*," having no idea that it was the same newspaper under a different name. He said that at that time a majority of the soldiers had the paper in their possession, and he seemed to feel that they had acquired it on their furloughs in Paris.[45] In addition to having newspapers filter into the units, however, the Third Brigade itself in May acquired its own lithograph printing press[46] and was publishing a paper of its own.

In these early days of what seemed to be spontaneous disorder, leadership in the form of several men did emerge. The first was a Latvian soldier (by some accounts a Lithuanian) named Janis Baltais, who was chairman of the soldiers' committee of the First Brigade. Twenty-nine years old with the very unlikely civilian occupation of bookkeeper, he was a natural leader of men and held great influence over others. He had received the *croix de guerre*. As we shall see, later he was replaced by a twenty-five-year-old Latvian sergeant named Afanasii Globa of the 1st infantry regiment of the First Brigade, who in civilian life had been some sort of salesman and, if Trotsky is correct, was by religion a Baptist,[47] indeed both highly unlikely background traits for a revolutionary. Moreover, it is rather odd that the two men who emerged as the major leaders of the rebellion were not ethnic Russians but of Baltic extraction. A third major figure who was often near the center of power was a corporal of the first regiment of the First Brigade, Mikhail Volkov, age thirty-two, who before the war had operated a furniture store.[48]

Little is known of the mind or personalities of any of these three men as they left no known personal papers (this author only encountered two short items written by Globa, one published, showing a rather poor educational background, the other possibly written for him by someone else), and no detailed minutes survive of the meetings that they dominated. Beyond their considerable power to sway men, they will forever remain a mystery.

The first major manifestation of the Russian soldiers' new independence from their officers was the unauthorized sending of several delegations to Russia. A large committee meeting was soon held to pick five delegates to return to Petrograd to encourage the government, Vavilov writes, to bring the brigades home.[49] The first departed in April to the strains of bands playing music and in cars flying red flags, and by May 19, it was in Petrograd reporting to the Executive Committee of the Soviet. These deputies carried greetings and congratulations for the victory over the autocracy as well as accounts of the problems that the brigades were having in France. The first delegation told the Soviet that they were willing to carry on the struggle against the Germans but that the Russians in France wanted to do it on Russian soil.

A second deputation, probably sent to counter the expected damage of the first, left late in May with the instructions to report the events in France and to return to report on happenings at home. This group was composed of an officer and eight soldiers. Some of them were detained in Paris or London for some unknown reason, but the core eventually did find its way to the Russian capital.[50] It was supposedly a moderate group from what was the "loyalist" brigade, and these nine delegates had instructions to oppose categorically a separate peace. They favored pourparlers for a general peace, but they intended to remain "armed to the teeth."[51] After having arrived in Russia, however, both of these commissions spent much time lambasting France and calling for an end to the war.[52]

Ehrenburg states in his memoirs that at this point he himself received "delegates" in Paris from the Russian force. It is unclear whether these men were coming on their own authority to see him or if they were one of the groups of envoys that returned home. French police reports stated that his account of his visit to the front was published in *Birzhevaia vedomosti*, the newspaper of the stock exchange, which probably would not have published anything that was not positive even if Ehrenburg had reported it. Whether he sent an intentionally mendacious accoun⁺, or whether the editors at home changed what he had written, it is impossible to say. Yet an optimistic version of the Russians in the trenches in France is in direct variance with what he later wrote in his memoirs.[53] At any rate, the soldiers seemed to gravitate to him with their complaints, and they asked him to organize a commission of two soldiers, one officer, and a doctor, all presided over by a Colonel Bramov, to visit the hospitals, and for him personally to visit the Russian troops, as well as 400 escaped prisoners of war who were corralled in Brest.[54] Ehrenburg does not say whether he responded to this request, but he did wire Alexander Kerensky, now the minister of war, on their behalf on May 27, asking him to send a commissar to France with full military authority to inform the soldiers' committees of all government decisions originating in Russia about Russian forces.

It is impossible to know what effect, if any, these deputations or Ehrenburg's telegram had, but Kerensky did send what a Soviet historian called "a Menshevik lawyer," Evgenyi Rapp, with the title of Commissar of the Affairs of the Russian Forces in France, to handle the soldiers' complaints.[55] Kerensky instructed Rapp to inform the soldiers that he was working in their best interests and that land reform back in Russia would be decided by the Constituent Assembly, the legislature that was to be elected democratically later in the year to form a permanent government to replace the provisional one. Meanwhile, he expected all to adhere to "the fulfillment of their debt to their country and the defeat of German imperialism, which could be done only hand in hand with the Allies."[56]

Rapp possessed the radical credentials to win the confidence of the unruly troops. A lawyer from Kharkov, he had participated in the revolutionary events of 1905 in the radical Union of Peasants, and his efforts on its behalf required him to flee Russia. He and another Russian lawyer had established a legal practice in Paris on the Rue de Vanves. He had served, though somehow unofficially, as a soldier in the French army in the early months of the war as a member of a sanitation unit and later became attached to the Russian artillery commission of General Svidersky, where he found himself when the revolution erupted. Kerensky appointed him to this position several months later. He was probably a Social Revolutionary, a member of the party that claimed to speak for the Russian peasants. A French police report states that before the war he had been a member of the Cadet Party, a liberal democratic group founded in the events of 1905,[57] but this piece of intelligence is most certainly incorrect. His mission was to oversee the reorganization of the army on a "democratic basis"—the enforcement of General Order No. 1—and "to fight against any counterrevolutionary activity," meanwhile restoring the REF's "combative qualities."[58] According to Lissovsky, he quickly came to be regarded by the soldiers he came to help as a "bourgeois" and an "accomplice of the tsarist generals."[59]

The Russian Revolution accelerated the development of French and British animosity toward their Russian ally from whom they had so often demanded bloody sacrifices. French hostility toward Russia naturally fell hard on the units in France. A report on the situation in Mailly written in June bitterly reflected this attitude. The writer decried the "complete collapse of discipline ... where the Russians refused to submit to any rule." The account displays in horror the utter chaos, citing such conduct as soldiers' boarding trains at will, making nocturnal racket, refusing to salute, and fraternizing with German prisoners of war. What the author of the report found "most regretful" was the "absolute inertia of the Russian troops." This inactivity he blamed on the officers' lack of control over their men, who can ignore their leaders "without risk of refusal." The account continued to describe how even self-imposed authority was overturned. "The committees of soldiers themselves are overwhelmed and already disarmed by their electors who proclaim new elections." The French began to give some thought to transporting these men to some camp in the interior of the country "to isolate them from the extremists in Paris."[60]

French concerns about Russian behavior, however, went beyond their anxiety of just what the Russians might do: They feared contagion would spread to their already unstable army. Such dread was easy to understand when mutinous French and Russian soldiers were seen singing revolutionary songs together.[61] Foch had no difficulty blaming French discipline troubles on the Russian allies,[62] and whereas the general mutinies were kept a secret from both the French public and the Germans, at least one French newspaper blamed the Russians for trying "to undermine the morale of our brave colonial troops."[63] Yet one of Painlevé's reports honestly pointed out the reason for low French morale. In it he stresses general conditions such as war fatigue but makes no reference to any Russian influence.[64] French military leadership had been apprehensive for some time about the Russian question primarily because of the now-infamous soldiers' committees, which had blossomed after the Nivelle offensive. Both Foch and Pétain blamed them for the Russian problem, and late in May in an inquiry about the state of Russian morale, Foch especially requested information "on the organization of committees and on the influence they seem to want to exercise."[65] At the same time, Pétain raised the question with General Zankevich, saying that "due to the political nature of things, he was mistrustful of Russian troops with their soldiers' committees." Given the presence of this strange military institution, Pétain told the Russian general that he could not agree to retain the Russians on the French front. Zankevich wondered if there could be some pro forma use of the committees to give at least the appearance that they were functioning, and Pétain felt there was not, adding "As you know, the introduction of committees in your army has caused a number of cases of difficult breaches of discipline. . . ."[66] Zankevich responded that he would not deny this fact, and Pétain concluded by saying that he would agree to retain Russian troops on the front only if the committees were abolished, "that is, with the return of the former discipline." If this step were taken, the French general added, perhaps some of them could be used in the Foreign Legion.[67]

Some feeble steps, however, finally were taken to bring the Russians into line and at least to segregate them from the French. In the midst of this hopeless discord, the brigades' officers made a pathetic attempt in the May 27 order of the day to shame the units into some sort of stability. The document, probably written by Lokhvitsky, referred to the first communication of Guchkov, who had been driven from the cabinet in Petrograd, as "the first received by us here abroad from our country, our new, forever-free Russia." The order reminded them that they had not been forgotten: "They remember us, they think about us, and they sincerely call on us to do our duty here abroad, . . . helping them to carry on the war to victory. . . ." After a patronizing lecture on how there is no freedom without responsibility, the order ended with "Glory to the Great Russian Army, glory to the Great Free Russia."[68] Except for those suffering from stomach ailments, Russians were denied wine rations, and there were desperate pleas to soldiers to stop drinking voluntarily. Nowhere were they even permitted to buy alcohol. To prevent the men from fraternizing with the French, Russian soldiers were permitted to go on leave into Mailly only on Wednesdays and Fridays, the only days on which the French soldiers were not allowed leave there. They could go into town on Sunday but only until 1:00 P.M. When soldiers failed to obey this curfew, an almost pleading order was issued reminding them that "the violation of order in a foreign country resembles the violating the host's law" and such behavior "must not be typical for the soldiers of the Great and Free Russia."[69] A week later a sterner directive was issued informing the soldiers that forceful measures would be taken to curb any curfew violations. In order to depart from the compounds, any Russian soldier had to have a pass written in French. Any soldier found outside of the compounds without such a pass was to be subject to arrest.[70] Paris of course remained totally off limits.

The soldiers ignored all of these efforts and treated them with complete contempt, since they quickly realized that the officers who issued these commands could not begin to enforce them. A report on May 21 notes that soldiers without proper authorization were seen wandering in the neighboring villages, and there had been incidents where they had forced their way into houses and abused women.[71]

As if disturbances around the camps had not been enough for the French, problems in June intensified in the military hospitals about the country where some 6,000 wounded Russians soldiers were convalescing.[72] Unrest was usually a reaction to what the soldiers perceived as poor medical care. The only real account we have of how the Russians were treated in their convalescence comes from the Russians themselves, but even allowing for an embellishment of their mistreatment, it seems that the situation was not good. Given the French proclivity for condescension toward them, it is hardly likely that they handled the wounded Russians with more understanding. The food was not good, and their nursing care was bad or even nonexistent. Most of the Russian hospitals had no Russian-French interpreters, and only in a few of them did they have any Russian sisters of mercy. They were not able to converse with anyone about their complaints except each other, and the personnel were coarse and rough, to say nothing of being poorly trained. Operations, including amputations, often were performed without patient's permission, and in some hospitals the bed linen was never changed. Universally there seems to have been no Russian reading material,[73] thus making the radical newspapers even more welcome. Quite probably some of the supposed slights the Russian soldiers felt were merely problems that would plague any military hospital in wartime, and indeed the French wounded must have shared these problems. Lissovsky says as much.[74] Yet there is little question that the French were not giving Russian wounded the same care that they were giving the *poilus*. Early in May Marushevsky had complained about the frightful shortage of doctors,[75] and in many cases the "doctors" were only partially trained medical students rushed into service. Russian sources cite cases of beatings of wounded for complaining about the bad food and the filthy conditions of their rooms. One fault-finding soldier, a Private Bariatinsky, was thrown unconscious into a truck and hauled off to prison.[76]

Which complaints were truly valid is impossible to say, but real or imaginary, the mistreatment did exist in the minds of the wounded, and this fact, coupled with the relaxed authority away from the front, made the hospitals highly receptive to the radical agitators who quickly gravitated to such places. These radicals talked to the soldiers about the pointlessness of war, about the mistakes of the tsar and all the Romanovs, about the reactionary officers and the brutal system of the old army. They also criticized the French hospital administrators, nurses, and doctors. *Golos pravdy* and its successor, *Novaia epokha*, found their way to the hospital at Montpelier, then to Michelet in Paris. These papers' headlines often shouted such provocative messages as "Down with the War!" or "Long Live the Social Revolution!," and their articles reported such inflammatory, and generally incorrect, information as the fact that Russians held down an area at the front three times greater than comparable-size French units. Playing on racism, one journal reported that the same treatment was given to black units, implying to the Russian soldier that the French considered the Russians in the same light.[77]

As early as April 23 at the Michelet Hospital in Paris, the soldiers took matters into their own hands. They assembled and passed a resolution stating that the rules governing the Russian soldiers staying in French hospitals were to be based on the same as those of the Russian Revolution (whatever that meant), and Russian soldiers were always to have the privileges accorded soldiers in Russia. Since the military leaders had tried to curb the establishment of this reform, however, the soldiers themselves would work out a *vie interieur* in the hospital for themselves.[78] Their program established a system of governance under a committee that was to be elected and would deal with the French and hospital authorities in all matters relating to the soldiers. It even arrogated to itself the right to supervise medical treatment and the preparation of food. The resolution created soldiers' freedoms, such as the right each day to visit the local village and to receive freely visits at the hospital itself. The directive even ordered that uniforms given to the soldiers on departure must have been disinfected. Moreover, the soldiers would have the right to organize a canteen, a club, a library, and a lecture committee. Entertainments such as choirs, orchestras, chess games, and football would be allowed. Only the committee could inflict punishment or send soldiers back to the front.[79]

In short, the committee would, in effect, assume the entire direction of Russians in convalescence. How long or to what extent the French authorities followed this demand is unknown, but early in June French troops encircled Michelet, and despite the protest of the wounded, forced about 300 of them into tightly closed automobiles and scattered them in various hospitals throughout France. One of the wounded, protesting against the use of force on armless and legless cripples, was knocked down with a crutch onto the asphalt floor, which was soaked with the blood from the amputation of limbs.[80]

Word of the hospital disturbances was not long in reaching the Russian press at home, where, as we have seen, much was made of it, especially among the Leftist papers. Apparently it was taken seriously enough that Painlevé felt compelled to wire the attaché in Petrograd "categorically denying the cases of forced acts occurring in France in relation to the Russian brigades."[81]

The French government's reaction to these disturbances was surprisingly mild, especially given the potential threat to France itself. A memo stressed the necessity of explaining the problems that the Russians faced to the local French population. Since French citizens had seen the red flags, they had concluded that the Russian units had rebelled and made a separate peace, resulting in individual cases of bad treatment of Russian soldiers. "The solution," the report went on to say, in capital letters, "is to print in the popular journals some articles which make things clear to the population and to dispel this misunderstanding. We have already taken steps to this effect." Yet the report advised that propaganda needed to go beyond the local populace to the French soldiers as well, since the same misunderstanding existed in the French army. The Russians felt this same hostility from the French troops and received sympathy only from the black colonials with whom they always seem to have been placed to fight in the line. Furthermore, the memo suggested, again in capital letters, that the Russians should be placed more often with only the French units that had been reeducated. Likewise the French had to learn the new rules under General Order No. 1. Russian soldiers did not have to salute their officers when not on duty; therefore, in the same situation they did not salute French officers either. The memo advocated a quick restoration of morale and a speedy return to the front, since Russian absence from the front would give the Germans a valuable propaganda weapon.[82] These attempts to change French attitude, however, never succeeded. The Russian mutiny continued unabated and French hostility intensified. The French had nothing to do with the Russian soldiers except to scorn them, refusing them service in restaurants, stores, and shops.

In the midst of this friction, Russian and French officials tried to maintain the appearance that all was well. French Colonel Alphonse Lavergne in Petrograd issued a communiqué stating how proud the Russians were of their performance at Courcy, and a Lieutenant Pravosudovich of the 5th regiment of the Third Brigade wrote an upbeat report stating that the 5th, 6th, and 2nd regiments were "under control" and that only the 1st regiment of the First Brigade, and especially one battalion in that regiment, was rebellious, adding that even it was not in too bad a condition. This false account added that the officers hoped to determine who the ringleaders were, as if they did not already know.[83] Someone claiming to be "the Russian delegates" published a report in *Vecherniaia vremia* (Evening Times) denying any disintegration in good intercourse with the French, blaming the lie on those who wanted to discredit good Russo-French relations,[84] but the disavowal described much more fact than it exposed fiction.

During the spring of 1917, the French government made a number of changes in the officials who dealt with the Russians in hopes of improving relations. As has been noted, Paléologue, the French aristocrat who carried the name of Byzantine emperors, was replaced by Albert Thomas, whose socialist political persuasion made him popular among the Leftist elements of the Russian capital. No one was better suited, Ribot wrote, "than M. Thomas; he had already been to Russia with M. Viviani during M. Briand's ministry and had left behind him excellent relations everywhere."[85] He appeared in Petrograd bespectacled and with a reddish beard, which made him resemble very much the Russian intellectual returning from exile. On his arrival a crowd waiting at the station gave him an ovation, to which he smugly reacted as if it happened to him everywhere.[86] He carried Paléologue's dismissal with him. If he was well received by some, de Robien did not think that the cordial reception was universal. The journalist described him as looking like an "overfed bourgeois banker" who carried a "scented handkerchief."[87] He further annoyed the Russians when he spoke to the Executive Committee of the Soviet for two hours on what France expected from the "New Russia," which basically was "unreserved help."[88] Laguiche was likewise replaced by General Pierre Janin, someone who would also be more to the liking of the Soviet, and Captain Jacques Sadoul, a socialist lawyer, was sent on Thomas's advice to act as a go-between for the Petrograd Soviet and the French government. By 1918 Sadoul became so sympathetic to the Bolshevik cause that he joined their ranks.

After Thomas's brief stay, the short, balding Joseph Noulens, a socialist and former French minister of war from 1914 into 1915, was named ambassador. Despite his Leftist political leanings, he was very taken with the pomposity not uncommon in diplomatic circles and played his role to the hilt. Having seen him, Paul Cambon mused about the effect "this display of ambassadorial majesty will have upon the peasants' and the workers' committee."[89] In another letter he likened Noulens to a "Rajah," adding that he was astonished that "he does not want to make his entry into Petrograd on an elephant."[90] Notwithstanding Noulens's socialist background, Trotsky saw him in the same light as the aristocratic Cambon: "a bourbon who has learned nothing and forgotten nothing."[91]

General Foch, meanwhile, had already decided that the only chance of restoring order among the Russians lay in transferring them into the interior of France, and he ordered a study to be completed as soon as possible.[92] Major-General Marie Eugen Debeney had suggested Neufchateau, a rest camp in the Vosges. He proposed that no further troop reinforcements be sent except for officers, who should be dispatched as expeditiously as possible, and he recommended a new military house organ to counter the pacifist drivel coming from the various leaflets from Paris.[93] On May 25 the troops began leaving Montmort and Bayé to entrain for Neufchateau and General Castelnau's Eastern Army Group Command in the Voges, but the situation did not improve at Neufchateau. In fact, it probably worsened. Parisian agitators followed the troops there and convened meetings to excite the soldiers against their officers.

In order to restore discipline, the Russian war ministry sent to Neufchateau two agents with a rather vague portfolio. One of the men was one Morosov, about whom we know nothing except for his brief appearance at this camp. The other was Rapp, who had been named in March the Official Delegate of the Provisional Government concerning the Official Repatriation of Russian Political Émigrés but who by now was called the Military Commissar to the Russian Armies in France.[94] Palitsyn, who went to visit him, felt that Rapp was a decent and sympathetic man—after Rapp had assured the Russian general that he "warmly loved Russia" and that he realized that it was necessary to do everything possible to quiet the revolt among the troops. He then asked Palitsyn, "What do you think we should say to them?" Palitsyn, who himself had been singularly ineffective in dealing with the revolt, replied, "To the soldiers say that God is going to hold you accountable for your actions; to the officers, speak strongly like a boss."[95] The two men's instructions were to "explain the situation in Russia" and stress that Kerensky was "fighting for their interests." Knowing that all peasants wanted land, Kerensky instructed the two men to tell the soldiers once again that the land question would be settled by the Constituent Assembly to be elected later in the year. He stressed the need for the soldiers to fulfill their debt to the country and to the Allies.[96]

Reaching Neufchateau, Rapp immediately visited a soldiers' committee meeting at 1:00 P.M. with his assistant Morozov. He spoke of his mission and of how the Provisional Government wanted to learn their situation. He then introduced Morozov as "one of the military representatives of the revolutionary movement." At first the committee members were polite to Rapp and Morozov, and things went smoothly, but when the questions of their return to Russia produced vague answers, the meeting erupted into disorder. The soldiers' attitude was that they would not return to the front. They would fight no longer. Some chanted "To Russia, to Russia!" The meeting stormed on for two hours.[97]

Rapp courageously returned for a second meeting, which was open not only to the committee but to any interested soldiers as well. The mood was hostile and tempers ran high, so the leadership decided to finish the session in the open air. The "meeting," if it might be called that, was punctuated with shouts of "To Russia and nowhere else!" and "No more fighting!" The confusion was so great that Rapp could not speak. Kozlov, on whose account we rely for this meeting, felt the committee was really siding with Rapp and was no longer trusted by the soldiers, a highly editorialized view. Being swept with the tide, Rapp finally promised to ask the government for their return and left for Paris to do so.[98]

The French had other ideas. Wanting to rid France of this problem, they decided at the end of May to send the REF to join the Army of the Orient at Salonika, or at least use it as reinforcements for it. In any case, it would remove the Russian mutineers from France and away from French troops. A note written on May 30 warned, "The danger is evident and must be exorcised as soon as possible; some energetic measures are urgently needed in order to prevent at any price the development of these outbursts of disorder and preserve our troops while there is still time . . . [illegible] . . . all risk of contamination."[99]

The other option, of course, was to return them to Russia. This course was for some reason labeled "radical" by the note's author, but he stated that it would "end all controversy." Without doubt the majority of Russian troops in France would accept this option without hesitation and indeed "with a certain pleasure." Either choice, however, would present the French government with a major relations problem: If they stated the true reason for asking the Russians to take their own back, they would risk causing a tenseness with the Russian government. They would have to use other pretexts, such as the necessity of making room for the Americans, whose arrival made the Russians superfluous. Moreover, the Americans would need to be instructed near the front, so the Russians had to be moved to create space for them. The author added that they could mention the problems of supplying the troops and the difficulties that navigation in the North Sea would make bringing reinforcements. The latter was foolish, of course, because if it was arduous to take them one way, it would be tough to take them the other. Yet the note underscored the problem by stating the necessity to do something: "It is important nevertheless to remedy the present state of things and not let worse develop. . . . "[100] Of greatest importance, however, was the removal of the unruly troops from the front, after which these matters would be settled quickly, or so the French thought.

General Castelnau, who had himself lost three sons to the war, visited the Russian camp on June 4 and quickly recognized the unacceptable volatile condition of the Russian brigades. Although he was shown every respect and was received with full military honors without incident, he divined that the situation was probably beyond repair. In informing the ministry of war, Castelnau stressed that the Russian troops were no longer under their officers' control and were refusing to work. Acknowledging that they had not yet violently rebelled against authority, Castelnau wrote that they opposed their officers with simple inertia. He immediately concluded that the only solution was to return these troops to their own country; if that could not be done expeditiously, then they should be removed to an isolated camp in the interior from which they could not infect French troops.[101]

As we have seen, Foch had independently come to the same conclusion. On Friday June 1, even before Castelnau had written his recommendation, Foch stopped by the ministry of war on the Rue St. Dominique to urge Painlevé to act quickly. After considering Camp de Ruchard, which was currently housing Belgians, they decided to send the Russians to La Courtine, a training camp in a town of the same name in the 12th region about sixty miles southeast of Limoges, 2,000 feet up on the plateau Millevaches in south-central France.[102] General Louis Comby, military commandant of the French 12th region, received the instructions early in June to clear the area under his jurisdiction of all inhabitants in two weeks to make ready for the Russians. There were thousands of men there, including some German prisoners of war, but in ten days it was empty.

Placing rebellious Russians in this outpost far in the interior of the country, far from the war zone, would isolate the supposed contagion from French troops and also make it more difficult for the Paris radicals to find them. An untitled and undated memo in Painlevé's papers expresses concern that the decision to move the men would have unfortunate repercussions in Russia but asked: "How can they not be able to find some encouragement which will alleviate the rigor of this measure?" and "How can they criticize French prudence?" Perhaps Painlevé was thinking out loud.[103] Regardless of what the Russian government felt, the French could not leave these rebellious troops where they were.

Shortly after Castelnau's visit, an order circulated among the Russians that they were "to begin a new assignment." There was a nervous rumbling because of their ignorance of what the future held, and many feared that they would be returned to the front. If they were being moved simply to rest, then why could not they rest where they were? Why go to a new place? In a mass meeting the soldiers voted to refuse to move unless they knew exactly where they were being taken. Fearing that they would be separated and scattered in a number of camps, they also insisted on being kept together. In reply to their worries, they were told that they would move as a single unit to a new camp, one that was "comfortable [and] equipped for all situations." Therefore, in the first week of June 1917, the Russian Expeditionary Force began its journey to the camp at La Courtine.

The troops boarded trains to regimental music and were accompanied by seventeen wagons of materials and supplies. The men appeared orderly and well behaved under the command of a Russian second lieutenant. There seems to have been no officer of a higher rank present. Very quickly, however, the second lieutenant, rather worse for the experience, was hauled up to the French officer in charge by six soldiers. They, speaking for the group, were refusing to embark in the cattle cars sent to carry them, demanding passenger cars with no more than twenty soldiers to a car. The French officer responded that French law allowed thirty-six to forty French soldiers per car, even if wounded.

A Russian soldier replied, "Yes! The French treat us worse than pigs!"

Another added, "Still worse than Germans! Yes, the German prisoners also travel in France in passenger cars and in first class."

Another chimed in with "Yet the French military traveling in Russia are honored. . . . Nothing is too good for them! Not flowers! Not champagne! Not first-class wagons!"

The French officer agreed to talk to the station master, although when away from the Russians he instead called up the chain of command begging for a higher-ranking officer to take charge.

Meanwhile, French officers approached the surly Russians and said, "Don't forget that if French troops would do what you are saying, they would be punished to the full extent of the law. Now, since you are our allies, do not violate the laws of our country . . . , and don't show the sad spectacle of ill-discipline to the French . . . who shed their blood to save the freedoms that the Revolution has given us [sic]." At this argument, the Russians turned somewhat humble, but at this point a Lieutenant Malinovsky (not the future defense minister of the Soviet Union) appeared on a bicycle. He harangued the troops and was interrupted violently several times. Despite his efforts, the soldiers still refused to embark.

In the midst of the crisis, a group of Russians did investigate the wagons to see if they were as dirty as they had been told and returned saying that they were proper. A more moderate element called for an end to the talk, but Malinovsky resumed his diatribe and general chaos ensued. He finally convinced several soldiers who shouted, "What a shame! What an affront for us and Russia!" The whole question was put to a vote, and a majority decided to embark without conditions.

Yet when the officers tried to enter the one-first class car, they were stopped. One soldier told one of them, "Ah, you [he used the familiar pronoun] made the trip in first class under the old regime! You ride in cattle cars now." The trains finally departed to the strains of regimental band music.[104] As they left the station, both the Russians and the French sending them thought that they were beginning their journey home. Both were correct, but they had no idea how circuitous their odyssey to Russia would be.

SIX

A High Wall of Hatred:
The Encampment at La Courtine

June–August 1917

It [the Russian Expeditionary Force] did not want to fight either for Alsace or for Lorraine; it did not want to die for beautiful France. It wanted to try living in the New Russia.

—Leon Trotsky[1]

This war has brought much suffering and has caused the death of many young men, and why? For the bourgeoisie! . . . France is bourgeois also and would like to give us a bourgeois republic.

—Private Tikhomirov[2]

SITUATED ON THE PLATEAU OF MILLEVACHES in south-central France, La Courtine was in 1917 a sleepy little French village and agricultural center about ninety miles west of Clermont-Ferrand and about sixty miles southeast of Limoges in the department of La Creuse near the junction of the borders of the departments Haute-Vienne, La Corrèze, and Puy-de-Dôme. The French army had begun to use the vicinity thirty years before for training troops, and each summer the surrounding fields blossomed with white military tents lined in straight rows like the soldiers they housed.[3] La Courtine was a typical military town with its many restaurants, bars, and movie houses. For a short time after the war began, the post was used as a camp for foreign civilians and evacuees from Paris and the northeast, but in October 1914 it was returned to its original military use and became a training area for different kinds of military education, including noncommissioned officer training and machine-gun instruction. It also served as a detention camp for 2,000 German prisoners of war, but by June 1917, the core of the installation had been evacuated except for a company of the French 78th infantry regiment brought in from Guèret to guard the post itself.[4] Euphemistically called *troupes de protection*, the unit consisted of 142 men and 29 officers, and its commandant was a Lieutenant Colonel Farine. His chief function after the arrival of the Russians was to keep Comby up to date on the events in the camp, and his knowledge of the area's resources rendered him indispensable to the Russians.[5]

It is difficult to know exactly how many Russians ultimately went to La Courtine, since sources differ somewhat, yet most agree that the number of officers was 137 for the First Brigade and 113 for the Third, with 7,176 men in the First Brigade.[6] All agree that the Third consisted of 6,504 effectives. There were 2,507 men and 39 officers with the depot, giving a grand total of 289 officers and 16,187 soldiers, which were accompanied by 1,718 horses.[7] The camp was not large enough for all the soldiers to sleep in permanent housing, so the use of tents became necessary. The overflow was to be accommodated by crowding ten soldiers to a tent.[8]

The French authorities decided that the First Brigade and the depot would occupy the vacant barracks and that the Third Brigade would bivouac in the tents, which the quartermaster was to provide. The buildings housed an infirmary and a 700-bed hospital for both units, and the force's 1,300 tons of clothing with the depot were given over 4,000 cubic yards of space in the camp's magazines.[9] Zankevich recommended that a store for Russian effects be made available to his men, and General Jean Vidalon, commandant of the 5th region, approved its creation at Orléans.[10]

Zankevich was now in full command of the REF, the brigades of which had been combined into a division. Lokhvitsky as the division commander was over both Colonel Kotovich, commandant of the First Brigade, and Colonel Narbut, who assumed the duties of the now-vanished Marushevsky.[11] The individual with the highest authority, however, was General Comby. Born in Pompadour in La Corrèze into a distinguished family, he was the younger brother of Camille Comby, doyen of the lawyers of the Paris bar, and Dr. Jules Comby, a prominent physician also of Paris. He had entered St. Cyr in 1874 and the *École de l'état-major* in 1876. He became a career infantryman and was chosen as the commandant of the regiment at Limoges. In 1914 he headed the 37th division of the V Army under General Landrezac and participated in the well-organized retreat from Charleroi to Guise. His division fought on the Marne under the VI Army of General Michel Joseph Maunoury at Charlepont and Tracy-le-Mont. At the age of sixty-one, he was made commandant of the 12th region,[12] where it befell his lot to handle the Russian problem.

On June 15, three days before the first Russians began arriving, Lokhvitsky paid a visit to General Comby in Limoges while on his way to inspect the camp at La Courtine. After he had seen the proposed encampment, however, he returned to Limoges to report that he was quite pleased with the new quarters, telling Comby that they "exceeded all my estimates and make me hopeful of being successful in the enterprise of restoring in a good way my unfortunate division." Comby, impressed by the young Russian general, assured Lokhvitsky that he would help him in every way to attain his goal. Once the usual pleasantries were out of the way, however, Lokhvitsky leveled with the French general about his force. He described the First Brigade as "intoxicated." The Third was more disciplined, he reported, and he was depending on it to provide a stabilizing influence on the First. He added, however, that the decision of the French authorities to place the two brigades in the same camp was a mistake because of the different level of discipline between the two.[13]

Having met with Lokhvitsky, Comby then went to Paris to report to General Foch and Painlevé and to obtain instructions. Foch told Comby that he was to use caution and moderation — that is, to continue the policy used by the French so far — and that he was especially to avoid becoming involved in the Russians' affairs. Furthermore, Foch told Comby to keep him fully informed of Russians' activities. Years later Comby told an interviewer, "It was not difficult to see easily that not only the minister of war, but the entire government was concerned and preoccupied with this affair."[14] After the Russians did arrive, Comby followed his instructions to the proverbial letter. Although he was superior in rank, he acted only through the Russian officers, the contact with whom was made through General Michel Marie Lelong, the French *chef d'état-major* to General Lokhvitsky. He scrupulously eschewed any actions that the Russian's might interpret as evidence of impatience or mistrust. To avoid even the appearance of hostility he had ordered the security force at the camp to leave before the first Russian soldiers arrived, and he removed the barbed wire that surrounded the part of the camp that had held the German officers so that its mere presence would not upset the rowdies' sensibilities.[15] The French also did not attempt to disarm the Russians. Therefore, when they arrived at La Courtine, not only did they have their weapons, they had a full complement of light artillery. Given the fact that the officers had no material or moral authority over the men, their armed condition was a delicate one indeed.

Parts of the First Brigade began appearing at La Courtine on June 18,[16] with the last elements arriving a week later. Their appearance was somewhat disorderly, but they disembarked from the trains without incident. From their arrival, however, these Russian soldiers demonstrated a general disregard for order and refused to submit to rigid discipline. On June 28, when Lokhvitsky and Comby visited the camp, the men did pass in review and make the salute, and otherwise behaved satisfactorily, but in the next few days they became slothful and uncooperative. They lounged in the barracks, ate, and slept, but did little else. Any orders, if executed, were done unenthusiastically and indifferently. Work parties arrived late, if they appeared at all. Moreover, there were no military exercises to keep the men in a fighting mood. When Comby first asked Lokhvitsky why the First Brigade was not training, the Russian general gave the unsatisfactory excuse that he was waiting for the arrival of the Third Brigade in order to begin.[17] When finally ordered to resume training, the First Brigade flatly refused to participate in any duties or functions except the daily distribution of food. Early in July at one of its boisterous meetings it finally voted not to work or go on maneuvers, much less to go to the front. In a masterpiece of understatement, the French report of this insubordination ended with "The situation is strained."[18] Officers were completely ignored and the units even elected their own police force of two men from each company. Not surprisingly, there were soon reports of widespread heavy drinking and disorder among the soldiers.

This tense situation existed when the first fragments of the Third Brigade began arriving on July 5. A light rain was falling as the battalions disembarked and formed ranks, and the first soldiers passed along the avenues of the camp in good order, marching to regimental band music. The first men wore their packs on their shoulders in the correct position, with their assorted cooking utensils dangling from their bodies, and they marched evenly, shoulder to shoulder, singing as they went. Yet this was as far as the good impression went. After those orderly units, there followed a confused group of stragglers. Many were already drunk, and they left behind on the railroad platform much of their equipment in a tangled mass of samovars, mattresses, umbrellas, and the like.[19] Arriving in their bivouac camp, the soldiers of the Third Brigade pulled down the tents and repitched them in scattered locations more to their liking, often against walls, attached to trees, and beside each other, to the great despair of the camp adjutant. Settled in, the soldiers visited the many canteens in and around the post, and then ignoring the instructions not to go into the village of La Courtine before 5:00 P.M., they "stampeded" into the streets of the town, flooding the bazaars, movie houses, and cafés.[20] Observers noted, however, that their attitude was better than the first soldiers to arrive and that they seemed in better spirits.

André Obey, a French officer who became a well-known French literary figure after the war, was among the French guarding the Russians at La Courtine. He observed the Russians without the apprehension of the French military establishment. *"Bons Enfants"* the writer called them for the "exquisite" manner in which they pretended not to understand the discreet questions posed to them by the French authorities. He was fascinated with their "large naive eyes" through which it seems that one peers "to the very bottom, into their brains without deflection." Obey watched them gallop off to the village riding bareback on their small horses with their long swishing tails. He was pleased with their casual gestures and jokes, which he felt showed how at home they felt among the French.[21]

The sole source of recognized authority over the soldiers, if it might be called that, remained the soldiers' committee of the First Brigade, which had itself created militia to keep order. It called itself formally the Detachment Committee of the Russian Forces in France, despite the fact that in reality it represented only half of the soldiers. In the committee, authority was supposedly shared by a general, who apparently was never designated, two commandants, and two "deputies" from the ranks elected as delegates from the regiments. Comby felt that "this bizarre organization" only encouraged discipline problems,[22] and although the committee at this point was not really radicalized, it showed no signs of controlling the soldiers' behavior. At no point did it issue orders against the brigades' actions. French ministry of the interior reports about the committees describe endless meetings with loud, directionless, paralyzing debates. The Detachment Committee, moreover, daily bombarded soldiers with broadsides couched in the flamboyant rhetoric that always accompanies revolutions, with frequent use of such words and phrases as "brotherhood," "equality," "salvation of the Revolution," and the like.[23] In addition, there were large, very animated gatherings throughout the camp that were difficult to distinguish from meetings.[24]

Next came stories of disturbances outside the camp. Many incidents began to occur of arson, trespassing, and petty theft, such as stealing chickens and bicycles. In La Courtine a Russian soldier caused a disturbance by trying to enter the Hotel Modern because he had seen some Russian officers there; in order to calm him the hotel manager had to give him a bottle of beer. Frequently large numbers of Russian soldiers gathered in cafés, effectively taking over the establishments and refusing to leave when asked to do so.[25] One report lamented that the proprietor of a *maison de tolerance*, to use that marvelous French euphemism, was forced to close his establishment because the Russians seeking service there had "a coarseness and a revolting brutality," while intimidating everyone constantly "with revolvers and bombs."[26] A later account of what may have been the same incident records a further disturbance when forty Russian soldiers appeared at the same establishment demanding the ladies' services. In general, the accounts of Russian misbehavior are very brief, but the reporter of this event took great pains to give all the lurid details, waxing indignant at the potential mistreatment of these working girls.

Either suspecting that the soldiers had no money or that they might become too rowdy, the *patron*, a M. Courtine (perhaps a *nom de maison?*), denied them entrance. The soldiers then complained to their soldiers' committee, which immediately sent a detachment of men with fixed bayonets to force the opening of the establishment. The armed Russians quickly surrounded the house, posting guards at all exits, probably to prevent the hasty flight of any of the employees, and forced their way into the courtyard, kicking down doors and other barriers. They were resisted by several "*garçons*" employed by the place who seem to have been the only line of defense for the virtue of the ladies working in the house. One of these gallant lads received quite a beating at the hands of the impatient Russian customers, who were brought to order only when the *patron* took the dangerous action of firing a shot into the air. His energetic protestations, supported by the rallied "*garçons*," resulted in the Russians' retreat, but only to the outside. They blockaded the place until the next morning, permitting no one to enter or leave. After several touchy encounters with the French authorities the next day, a Captain Grinfeld from the soldiers' committee arrived and convinced the Russians to return to camp without attention of the establishment's employees. The historian of the affair added, "I will not say that they did it with good grace." The incident upset the community because it showed the flagrant abuse of power of which the Russians were capable. Despite it all, M. Courtine reopened his place of business the next evening, but it continued to discriminate against the Russian soldiers.[27]

As usual, Obey regarded the Russian behavior a little more sympathetically as well as dramatically. He noted that when darkness fell on the countryside, the Russians, who slept all day, mounted their horses and sauntered off into the countryside with "the hills, all black against the gloomy sky [reverberating] with echoes . . . from their galloping about. . . ."

"Who goes?" cries the French cavalry sentinel.

"Comrade Russkii."

A great joyous figure, clear in the twilight, appears above the head of a horse. The sentinel, not having any orders, replaces his bayonet and the Russian passes at a gallop in an odor of saddle and harness leather with the hooves of the horse clattering on the cobblestones of the village street.[28]

The locals, less inclined to melodrama, panicked at the sight of wandering Russians, so on July 2, Comby established a perimeter of confinement for them. Individual Russian soldiers could visit Limoges, Guéret, Tulle, Ussel, and Clermont-Ferrand only with special passes, and all roads in the 12th region were ordered blocked to Russians. Yet they still seem to have gotten through the encirclement.

When Russians were stopped and interrogated by the French, the exchange was often comical. The French soldier might ask the Russian, "What are you doing in your camp? Do you [familiar] understand? In your camp?" The Russian repeats laboriously,

"In . . . your . . . camp. . . ."

"Yes—ja—oui—si. In your camp at La Courtine. Understand?"

"Comarades—oui. . . . Russkii. *Voilà.*"[29]

By the second week in July, the prefect of La Creuse had had enough. In a letter to the minister of the interior he wrote, "The solution to the problem is evidently more complex but the retention of the status quo seems to me to have grave consequences. . . . The inhabitants are very alarmed, and if up until now they have shown patience, it is doubtful that they will continue to do so. . . ."[30] Goaded by Comby, Lokhvitsky finally issued the order to resume military instruction and drill in order to curb the soldiers' wandering around the countryside and general misbehavior. This move instigated the first incident of genuine rebellion. When ordered to appear for exercises, the First Brigade refused, responding through the soldiers' committee that they would not fight in France and therefore would not drill there. Lokhvitsky could do nothing.

Early in July the situation grew more complicated because of a totally unexpected development: a rift between the two brigades. The split was, in retrospect, something that might have been anticipated, given the difference in the social composition of the two units. It unexpectedly saved the situation. The First Brigade, especially its first regiment, containing its large element of left-leaning Muscovite workers, caused the first problem. In the early days of disorder near the front, the Third Brigade was merely sullen and uncooperative, while the First was openly hostile and rebellious. The behavior of the First was always marked by rampant drunkenness, idleness, the firing of rifles at random, and the terrorizing of local citizens. It was the First that eventually elected a soviet. These different moods led to friction between the two units.

Even near the front agitators from the First had visited the Third Brigade to encourage them to join their more active indiscipline. When the Third arrived at La Courtine, 5,000 to 6,000 men of the First marched, preceded by a band, around the Third's encampment, singing and shouting. Although discontented, the Third did not share the First's degree of rebellion, and its members eventually were harassed and insulted by the men of the First. Tension between the two units mounted. Within a day of the Third's arrival at La Courtine, only the slightest provocation could have triggered a rupture. That spark came in the form of the roughing-up of a captain of the Third Brigade by some soldiers from the First. The officer in question commanded a company of machine gunners, and on hearing that one of its officers had been taken prisoner, the unit decided to "liberate" him. A formal clash was averted by the captain himself who ordered his would-be rescuers to stay put, and he was released shortly as a result of the intervention of a committee of the regiments.[31] Lissovsky tells a somewhat more detailed account of the same incident, stating that the First Brigade had organized a protest demonstration with music and red flags, and when officers tried to prevent it, a fight started. It stopped only due to the interference of some Third Brigade machine gunners who threatened to fire on the crowd.[32] Differences between the stories aside, there are sufficient similarities to sketch an account that seems real enough. From this point onward the rift between the two brigades widened into open conflict, and the French police from this time forward referred to the two brigades as either *"vrai"* or *"faux"* Russians, that is, the Third and First respectively.[33]

The First Brigade memoirist Vavilov presented a pair of different and unlikely reasons for the discord. One was the question of the dispatch of Russian soldiers from France into Russia. The First Brigade was eager to return, but Vavilov felt that the Third favored remaining in the West and fighting. That statement was overly simplistic, although there clearly was a sizable element in the Third Brigade that would have followed orders to return to the French trenches. The other bone of contention as seen by Vavilov was the attitude toward weapons, a factor not mentioned by anyone else. The First Brigade was reluctant to surrender its rifles before returning to Russian territory, whereas the Third Brigade "did not agree." Vavilov did not explain this difference further, merely adding "The

Third Brigade believed their officers and were too trusting in them."
Vavilov noted that in each brigade there were those who did not belong
to the majority. In his unit he refers to the minority as "traitors," "collab-
orationists," "flunkies," and surprisingly "NCOs." He noted that there
were also several recipients of the Cross of St. George among the "traitors." He felt that they hoped that by being loyal they would return home
more quickly.[34]

Since one of the two brigades seemed more likely to take officers'
orders and submit to discipline, the thought soon surfaced in the official
leadership to separate the two units. It took no great perception to realize
that to divide the more loyal brigade from the more rebellious one would
likely restore control over one of them and reduce the hostility by half,
because as long as the more radical brigade was near to encourage dissent
in the more orderly one, there could only be trouble.

Within days of the Third's arrival, both were informed by the
officers that the force was to be divided. Zankevich merely stated that
part of the men would be under him and the remainder would be under
the Provisional Government, whatever that was supposed to mean. The
soldiers asked the officers for clarification and were informed that the
separation was only temporary to "find out the mood." They were assured
that later the two parts of the force would be reunited. Even soldiers in
the Third Brigade, however, questioned whether to obey orders to follow
this directive, and they asked the guidance of a Lieutenant Sagatovsky,
an officer whom they apparently trusted. Sagatovsky replied that he did
not know what to tell them and that this question would be put forward
at a gathering of the officers after which he would be better able to answer.
The lieutenant left, apparently for the meeting, and the men never saw
him again. The decision probably had already been made at this point.[35]

Kozlov writes that a "majority" of the Third Brigade refused to
leave, yet their independent actions belie this statement, for on July 8, at
8:00 A.M., to their band's playing *La Marseillaise*, the Third Brigade,
without orders from any officer, marched out of the camp of La Courtine
to the taunts of the First. Departing were about 6,000 men, accompanied
by 400 soldiers from the First. They moved northward to the small village
called Felletin, about seventeen miles to the north of La Courtine. There
had apparently been a vigorous debate during the night among the soldiers
of both units about what to do, and the agitation had become so great that
the military committees were summoned to referee the discussions. The
Third Brigade, tired of being intimidated by the First and told that they
were to be separated anyway, took Zankevich at his word and put a

considerable distance between themselves and their former comrades. From this point onward, Lissovsky wrote, there developed between the two different units a "high wall of hatred"[36] that sundered the rebellion and effectively made bringing it to an end possible.

Louis Poitevin, who wrote a history of the rebellion, noted that General Comby had authorized the departure only after Lokhvitsky had advised him of the desires of some men to abandon the camp and distance themselves from the First Brigade. Lissovsky, on the other hand, stated that "in order to prevent infecting the Second [meaning the Third] brigade," which he not totally correctly states "remained loyal to the Provisional Government" and "was still willing to fight wherever necessary," Zankevich separated the two brigades. Yet the Third Brigade was obviously detaching itself on its own and more than Zankevich had planned. The French archives contain a blizzard of telegrams to the Russian Third Brigade from Zankevich and Comby ordering them to stay put in La Courtine.[37] Both the Russian and French high commands could hardly have wanted a 6,500-man Russian force, even had it been disciplined and friendly, wandering around at will in the interior of France.

Comby himself rushed to Felletin from Limoges on the morning of July 11, arriving about 10:00 just as the wandering brigade was pitching camp. Lokhvitsky had taken to his bed, suddenly having developed heart problems. He did rise to receive the French general and apologized for not having executed the order to remain in the camp. "I realize that I disobeyed you," he told the French general, "but the excitement in the Third Brigade was such that I feared at any moment an armed conflict." Years later Comby remembered saying that he was only able to reiterate the order to return to La Courtine the next day,[38] an order that Lokhvitsky knew could never be executed.

Comby returned to Limoges and wired the ministry of war details of these fresh events, and the next day, at 10:00 P.M., Lelong phoned to say that the Third Brigade had not returned to La Courtine and that Lokhvitsky was ill, something that Comby already knew. An hour later Comby received another telegram, this time from Zankevich in Paris, stating that, after having seen Painlevé, it had been decided to "let" the Russian force at Felletin remain in place, as if they would have obeyed orders to return. The next day at 10:00 A.M., a formal, and pointless, command came from Zankevich to the Third Brigade telling it to remain at its bivouac until further instructions. Comby asked for a clarification of all these missives and was told to await General Vidalon, who would be arriving soon to appraise the situation.[39]

Vidalon, Zankevich, and Rapp arrived in the Millevaches plateau on July 14 and, after a hasty inspection of both La Courtine and Felletin, issued a broad order to all Russian brigades to submit to the authority of the Provisional Government and its agents. The command included orders to the officers who had fled the First Brigade to return and resume their duties. The La Courtine committee as it was constituted was then abolished and new elections were held in order to eject the old members. The newly constituted committee lost no time in rejecting the directive.[40]

At a loss for what to do, Vidalon left that evening for Paris, where he told the minister of war that urgent measures were needed. Painlevé had other problems, and he decided that for the time being he would maintain the status quo.[41] Since general slackness still existed among the Third Brigade at Felletin, Painlevé reasoned that its discipline was better than it would be if attempts were made to force it to return to La Courtine, where bitter and angry at being coerced, it would receive an additional infusion of rebellious sentiment from the First. Moreover, the reunion of the two units could have explosive results because of the animosity now existing between them. It was best to leave them where they were.

After the departure of the Third Brigade for Felletin, whatever might have passed for order and calm in the First disappeared completely. Typical was an occurrence in which a number of soldiers from the First attacked and looted a local inn when the innkeeper refused to remand to them several customers who had incurred their wrath. Protests that the hunted people were not there did not save the *patron* from a brutal stabbing that he miraculously survived.[42] Until this time there had been no life-threatening violence on the part of the Russian mutineers, and this and other such incidents were a clear indication of the change to an uglier mood. To further stress their independence and rebelliousness, the First passed a curious resolution stating that it would exclude the Third from repatriation when the time came to go home as punishment for their "criminal error" of disloyalty to the revolution.[43] Perhaps more important, Baltais, with help from Volkov and others, led the energized First Brigade at a division committee meeting on July 16 to elect a Soviet of Soldiers' Deputies of the Camp of La Courtine. The mass meeting was adorned with banners bearing the slogans "Down with the Provisional Government," "Down with the War," and "Long live the Soviet of Workers' and Peasants' [surprisingly no "soldiers'"] Deputies."[44] For want of any other recourse, Lokhvitsky himself followed Vidalon to Paris and returned with Zankevich and Rapp.

Rapp is a somewhat mysterious figure whose agenda remains obscure. He was a tall, thin man, with a brown beard and hair that was speckled with gray. One French government account states that he was a Russian who had descended from a French Alsatian immigrant to Russia during the period of the First Empire.[45] He lived in a luxury apartment at 14 Rue Stanislaus with his wife, Jéann, and their three small children. As for his character, there are reports that he mishandled some funds at one point in his career and provided legal counsel to some sleazy characters.[46] In several reports the French police state that he was a "bolshevik," but that charge probably is not true. The French security police carelessly placed that label on any individual who did not seem to them to be totally for the war or who had Leftist leanings, and since they had blamed Rapp for the troubles among the wounded in the hospital at Cannes, where he supposedly told the soldiers to obey the committees and not their officers,[47] he acquired that label. These commissars were instructed to oppose any counterrevolutionary activity in the army, and French security may have misconstrued some of Rapp's phrases as being "pro-Bolshevik." Zankevich explained the situation to Rapp and "Professor" S. V. Sviatikov, the High Commissioner of Russia Abroad.

Sviatikov had been sent to France in June 1917 by the Provisional Government in part to report on the business at La Courtine, but with the other dubious jobs, according to Matvei Sevastopoulo of the Russian embassy in Paris, of discussing the foreign policies of tsarism, watching over the embassies, and controlling the military attachés. He was a lawyer in the Court of Appeals in Petrograd and a member of the same bar organization as Kerensky, with whom he had cordial relations.[48] He was a large blond man who wore glasses and spoke French, according to Poincaré, "rather badly." When he met with the president in September 1917, he expressed the desire to see the creation in Russia of a military dictatorship to restore order,[49] so he could hardly have been sympathetic to the freedom of expression of the Russian brigades. He arrived in La Courtine on July 7, just as the two brigades had begun to separate from each other, and he presented himself to the Russian soldiers with all the pomp of a Roman emperor. Palitsyn remembered that he received big bouquets of flowers and strutted around like a "big bureaucrat," making a bad impression on the soldiers, who, Palitsyn, later wrote, "did not like to remember Sviatikov."[50]

Zankevich and Rapp visited Felletin and engaged in a gripe session with the soldiers of the less rebellious Third Brigade, and they were received with some hostility. Even the officers bombarded them with questions, especially wanting to know why a telegram sent to the Provisional Government requesting repatriation had gone unanswered. Zankevich told them that he personally had sent the wire (no such dispatch appears in the archives), and he offered to send another accompanied with all their questions.

The soldiers overall seemed to acquire some respect for Zankevich but maintained a strong resentment toward Rapp. Zankevich appeared to have won some to his side by his promise to send a telegram and to fulfill some unspecified personal agreements to better their living conditions. When he left again for Paris, however, the fourth machine-gun regiment of the First Brigade took a more bellicose stance and passed a three-part resolution stating that it would not just await a Provisional Government response but would harass Rapp until it got one, that they would categorically refuse to fight on the French front, although a small percentage apparently wanted to do so, and that they would no longer take military assignments, performing instead "cultural-educational duties [?]." In the other regiments, all orders were accepted at first; thus the action of the machine-gun regiment was the first official, unspontaneous act of rebellion.[51]

Zankevich's account, reported to Kerensky the same day, is somewhat different and a little more detailed. It also is either confused or mendacious. He informed the Russian minister of war that on July 21, he arrived at the camp and ordered all soldiers who were willing to obey the Provisional Government to come out of the camp at 10:00 A.M. Almost the entire Third Brigade (he refers to it as the Second) did so, but only 200 or 300 men of the First appeared, the rest remaining in their barracks. To all of them he presented three options: to stay in France, to fight on the Russian front, or to be forced in line with repressive measures. In the discussions that followed, he got the impression that the soldiers unconditionally wished to be returned home, where they would be willing to fight. The Provisional Government's representative correctly focused on the major element of unrest: the ever-troublesome first regiment of the First Brigade. Zankevich told Kerensky that the second regiment, the more conservative, was "merely a toy in the hands of the first."[52]

In the days that followed, a number of individuals with less authority tried to persuade the men of the First to shape up. One anonymous officer tried to convince Baltais and the other rebel leaders to encourage the soldiers to follow regular orders. He talked with them for three days, but they would not budge. At one point Baltais told him, "The unit does not want to fight on the French front and demands to be returned to Russia. Return us to our native land. There we are ready to fulfill our obligation." He added, parenthetically, that while in France, the unit would not do any daily drills "since we have nothing else to learn." Efforts were likewise made by a fifty-year-old émigré named Ivanov, whose revolutionary credentials consisted of having spent twenty years in the Schlüsselburg prison outside Petrograd. He too was unsuccessful. One soldier told him after his plea, "Well, we believe that you sat for twenty years under Nicholas [during the time of Tsar Nicholas II] in Schlüsselburg, but we are in the French trenches. . . ."[53]

Meanwhile, the Russians continued their extracamp excursions, referred to as "regrettable acts" by the police. One citizen, a M. Parvoteaux, had his donkey stolen (it was recovered unharmed), Russian soldiers stole fifteen francs' worth of firewood at one place, a bicycle was taken at another, and some onions disappeared from a garden. One Russian was about to relieve a French peasant of some rabbits when the owner was awakened by the furious barking of a watchdog. Confronted by the peasant who was armed with a revolver, the Russian fled down a nearby railroad track on which he stumbled and fell. After picking himself up, he vanished into the darkness.[54]

There was, however, another side to the stories of misconduct. Poitevin, who interviewed the inhabitants of the area several years after the affair at La Courtine, concluded that early police reports of Russian misbehavior were greatly overstated. Seeming to have gone almost door to door among the local population, Poitevin reported that the public response was always the same: The Russian *muzhiks* were most certainly "primitive and mystical," but all were very gentle. He received stories of how the Russian soldiers took quickly to the little French children and found the greatest joy in playing with them. The French remembered them as always being "honest" and "proper," much more so than the Americans who occupied the same camp in 1918. To those interviewed by Poitevin, the Russians, passing their time singing and playing their mandolins and balalaikas, seemed more like an encampment of bohemians than an army. They did get drunk sometimes, but when they did, they usually just lay in the road to sleep. Poitevin found no one who reported any acts of violence.[55] Even the police report of July 11 seemed to think that many of the stories of atrocities were rumors and embellished retellings of minor events.[56]

The truth about Russian misbehavior must lie somewhere in between. The Russians probably committed few if any outrageous acts, but the strange, almost childlike curiosity of the simple peasant soldier led him to investigate the local gardens and barnyards. Yet the uncontrolled wanderings of the Russian soldiers disturbed the French government sufficiently that the original zone in which certain Russians were allowed to go on leave was closed by mid-July, and from then on no one was able legally to leave the perimeter of the camp.[57]

Official efforts to pacify the men continued from all political quarters but were as futile as ever. Even the Soviet in Petrograd made an attempt with an order that arrived about the time of the decision to send the men to La Courtine. "Comrade Soldiers at the Front!" it began. "From the eye [*litso*] of revolutionary democratic Russia, we greet you warmly. You have settled accounts for the crimes of the tsar, who sent you to fight without weapons, without shells, without bread. . . . The War was not necessary for our laboring country. We did not begin it. The tsars and the capitalists of all countries began it." Yet after this antiwar diatribe, the order called for unity in the war effort and was signed by Kerensky and one Romanovsky.[58]

In July the Petrograd Soviet followed this directive by sending westward a delegation, which also visited the soldiers in France. Calling themselves the Argonauts of Peace, this group had really come to the West to rally support among the socialists for the Stockholm Conference of World Socialism to unite the international labor movement to end the war. It consisted of four Social Democrats, all of whom were Mensheviks, and one Social Revolutionary. This delegation of Russia's political Left preached the contradictory line of peace while calling for support of the war effort, and the group was sent to visit the Russian brigades with the idea that they might restore some discipline to their ranks. They seem to have been a bit better received than other elements that came to restore order, but they too were unsuccessful. They tried to encourage the Russians to continue fighting, but they generally got nowhere.[59]

In August even the Third Brigade joined the pacification efforts by sending an appeal to the First for order. It came in a blizzard of leaflets that were placed on walls and distributed among the soldiers. "Comrades! Come to your senses. What are you doing?" it began. Pointing out the obvious fact that they had disobeyed the instructions of the Provisional Government, the Third Brigade informed the rebels that the government was inflicting the death penalty "on all traitors" because those who went against the orders of the government "hinder the work of the organized masses, the masses of which you are presently one." With intense melodrama designed to play on guilt, a commodity that seems to have been in short supply, the leaflet informed the First Brigade that "the heart of Mother Russia bleeds when it learns that the loyal and courageous sons . . . have violated her wishes and her laws." It offered to forgive those who had been led "unconsciously but not those who went the criminal way. . . . " Trying to drive a wedge between the militants and those who were less radical, the author of the memo blasted the ringleaders, implying that their actions were selfish. "We invite all of you, those who recognize their errors, who have remorse, . . . to furnish

their names to the Committee [of the Third Brigade]." Informing the
mutineers that they had been weak and cowardly, the committee's flier
reminded them that they still had time to retract their errors and "show by
their remorse all their love for Russia." It ended with the words "Now or
Never" and was signed "The Committee."[60] The First remained unmoved.

With the instability continuing, Rapp met with Zankevich in Paris
in either late June or early July and briefed him on the entire situation.
Sviatikov was also present. Both Rapp and Sviatikov had been given
instructions by the Provisional Government's premier, Prince Georgii
L'vov, transmitted through Zankevich, to take whatever measures were
necessary to end the unfortunate affair, and they naively thought that
words would be sufficient. On July 17 the three men (some sources do
not include Zankevich) descended once again deus ex machina on both
Felletin and La Courtine with the firm certainty that they could bring the
matter well in hand.

First, Rapp and Sviatikov visited at Felletin the troops of the Third
Brigade, of which only about 200 men refused to pass in review. Sviatikov
spoke to the assembled unit afterward; he was eloquent, telling the troops
that they should not tarnish the honor of Russia and cautioning them not
to injure the interests of France. Playing politics, he praised their love of
liberty and called on them to continue the war to a victorious conclusion.
He seems to have been received well[61] and left feeling he had won them
all over. He then went to La Courtine to try his luck with the more radical
First, arriving there about 6:00 o'clock that same evening.

If Sviatikov had come to the conclusion that he held some special
talent for calming troops, he was rudely educated to the contrary at La
Courtine. Not one of the soldiers appeared when called out for review.
When Sviatikov tried to speak to the soviet that had been elected, he was
shouted down with taunts and the usual cries of "March! Forward! To
Russia!" His references to the necessity of loyalty to their ally France
provoked the most violent protests and accusations of bad treatment.[62]
Eventually a dialogue was established in a camp auditorium between the
government representatives (Poitevin states that Zankevich was there)
and a number of soldiers, yet it was hardly constructive. The discussions
consisted of protests, recriminations, and lamentations. The whole affair
must have been an excruciating experience. Sviatikov could have had no
doubt that all military discipline was irreparably lost from the First
Brigade and that the Russian officers could not possibly restore order with
the means at hand. Desperate measures were clearly needed.

Sviatikov returned to Paris and suggested that the authorities ask a
delegation of officers from each brigade and a couple of the committee

leaders of the most rebellious soldiers to go to Paris for a conference. Only the officers eventually went, and they assured the high commission of their personal loyalty to the Provisional Government. Some reared with monarchial sentiments saw the revolution as a great misfortune yet wanted to continue to serve the country in its disarray. They suggested to Sviatikov that military exercises be restored and that the rebels be separated from the "loyalists." Then an ultimatum to submit should be presented to the radicals, and if they refused, then they should be subdued by force. At some point the ringleaders should be arrested in order to leave the revolt leaderless.[63]

After seeing the officers, Sviatikov met with two of the principals, Baltais and Volkov, at that point still the ringleaders. The two rebel chieftains complained about the conservatism of their officers and were especially censorious of Palitsyn, whom they criticized for keeping from them the news of the events in Russia. They grumbled about conditions among the wounded in the hospitals, the necessity of tipping French hospital personnel to get service, the poor administration of the post, and the absence of letters from home.[64]

Sviatikov affirmed that the general's indecision when the regimental committees had been organized had indeed provoked distrust and the soldiers' protest, and he agreed to pass their grievances on to Zankevich. He even offered to wire their complaints to the Russian ministry of war in Petrograd as well. In reporting to both Zankevich and the Provisional Government, he stressed the necessity of "ridding the Allies of the nauseating spectacle of these troops in complete dissolution." He saw as the only answer the immediate repatriation of the most rebellious, but since returning only the mutinous elements would foment rebellion among the soldiers remaining behind, he strongly recommended that all troops be repatriated. He added the near-impossible condition that returning the troops to Russia should be done only "after discipline had been restored in all units." That state could be achieved only by the use of capital punishment, which was not then legal. As a final note he added that at all costs the French were to play no role in any disciplinary activities.[65]

As was his wont, Zankevich took no immediate action on any of Sviatikov's recommendations, probably because he realized that none of them was remotely feasible under the prevailing conditions. Hoping to gain time, he suggested an exchange of telegrams on the question with Petrograd.[66] Sviatikov, however, quickly became annoyed with the Russian general's inaction and obtained an audience with Poincaré in which he reported what was taking place. The French president seemed rather out of touch or otherwise uninterested in discussing the problem with the

Russian commissar. He assured him that Zankevich, "a sage and prudent man," would handle the entire situation and keep the French out of it, which was obviously his most pressing concern.[67]

While the Russian authorities were making their quixotic attempts to restore order, the French government was moving swiftly to prevent the dispatch of any additional troops, and hence additional problems, from Russia. Poised to leave Russia for France early in June was the artillery brigade at Novyi Peterhof led by General Beliaev. On June 12 Ribot wired the French ambassador in Petrograd to stop them, explaining to Thomas "Given the present state of morale of those which are already here, there would be grave problems to augment the number. Under these conditions, neither the brigade of artillery nor the 3,000 workers should leave . . . [Russia]."[68] Foch and the ministry of war were amenable, however, to allowing these troops to pass through France and to go to Salonika just so long as they understood thoroughly the guidelines of French discipline and that they would conform to the French authorities' rules. Passage through France would be executed very quickly, and any change of their destination would not be open to question.[69] As for the return of the troops in France to Russia, that was under consideration.

Thomas wired on June 18 that the troops had been halted, despite the fact that some had already boarded the ships, but the Russian war minister refused at first to allow those troops embarking to be reassigned to Salonika. For some reason, however, late in June the Russian ministry of war changed its mind and accepted the sending of the troops under the French conditions. At the very end of June this artillery brigade was ordered again to depart, as was another heavy force (*groupe lourde*) that was restationed in Vologda.[70]

It is curious that the French government, having witnessed first-hand the unreliability of Russian troops abroad, would have even suggested that additional Russian troops be sent to Salonika, where they themselves had soldiers participating in the diversionary action. This behavior is all the more peculiar since at this same time the French government began making serious noises about returning the REF troops in France to Russia.[71] An explanation for the confusion might come in Thomas's report to the French cabinet on the reaction in Russia to the news that the French had refused to allow more Russian troops in France. The French ambassador had noticed that the Russian press and the Russian public had been disturbed that the French had not seemed to want additional Russian soldiers on their soil. Concerned, he informed Paris that at a time when "we must obtain from the Russian army a renewal of goodwill, when we demand that Russia send us . . . some Serbian divisions and elements of Czechoslovakian troops, it would seem bad policy to show no interest in a corps already found, ready to leave, and in good state in all points of view." He also noted that to give the appearance of hesitating to use these troops would not be politically wise. Thomas had suggested that some excuse be advanced for not accepting them (lack of boots, or some such thing) to offset the bad feeling that it had engendered.[72] The need for effectives on a more urgent front — Salonika — would soothe the hurt feelings in military circles, and this reasoning probably explains the French willingness to send them abroad.

Meanwhile, at La Courtine the conditions worsened, the Russian soldiers continued to threaten the two nominal symbols of authority, the French attached to their brigade and their own officers, few of whom were still around. On July 7 some Russian soldiers made prisoners of several French officers in a canteen, claiming that now they would be the "masters."[73] Nothing ugly seems to have come of the incident, and perhaps it was more of a joke played on the outnumbered Frenchmen than any overt, hostile act, but it could hardly have added to the stability of the situation or soothed French concerns about the Russian question. As for the Russian officers, they continued to be shown no respect and often were abused both verbally and physically by their men. Typical was the incident on July 6 when Russian soldiers from the 1st regiment of the First Brigade struck a captain of the 1st company of the 6th regiment of the Third and ripped off his epaulets. Had not some of his own men come to his aid, he might have been seriously injured.[74] Yet the Russian officers' plight was not improved by their own behavior, which was hardly conducive to being granted respect. Lissovsky wrote that they were generally inactive and spent much time in Paris, where they prodigally spent their salaries.[75] French reports have those in La Courtine raking about the town's hotels and bars, spending no time with their men. Yet the author admitted that if the officers had tried to lead, it would have been unfortunate for them. Many literally barricaded themselves in the Hotel Terminus in La Courtine, closing the iron shutters to their rooms.[76]

As the Russian troops intensified their demands to go home, the French government was all the more determined to return them, and late in June or early in July (the exact time is unclear), it instructed its embassy personnel in Petrograd to open discussions with the Provisional Government on the possibility of returning to Russia the expeditionary force that it had received so joyously the year before. According to Lissovsky, Zankevich had decided as early as late June to ask the Provisional Government to return the brigades, since they appeared "desirous of fighting the Germans only in Russia."[77] He probably made his wishes known to the French. General Castelnau had already suggested repatriation, as we have seen, and throughout July there continued negotiations between Foch and various officials in both France and Russia. The decision to request formally their repatriation was made at meetings of government and military personnel on July 6 and 7. The committee had decided that "the maintenance of these troops in France presents some grave impropriety," and it determined that sending them home was the only answer. The repatriation was to include 16,500 soldiers, with an additional 320 officers and an assortment of 1,400 Russians of diverse categories who were at Brest, making a total of about 18,000 persons. A survey of transports revealed, however, that both units would not be able to return together. One could probably depart in August, while the other could not leave until October. In his directive Foch expressed a special interest in immediately packing off the First Brigade "in which had occurred all the acts of indiscipline."[78]

At the moment of the decision, there were three transports, *Tsar*, *Tsaritsa*, and *Dvinsk*, en route from Archangel to France, and Foch hoped to use these ships to carry the Russians home. On arrival, however, it was found that they were unavailable for the transport of troops, and several other ships, the *Kursk, Umona, Melbourne, Porto*, and *Orenoque*, were found as suitable backups. The *Kursk, Melbourne, Orenoque,* and *Porto* were being repaired but would be fit by the end of July. The *Umona* had just left the Orient on July 3 and was on its way to France. Foch felt certain these transports would be the means to return the rebellious brigades to their homeland.[79] As the summer passed, the French diplomatic correspondence regarding returning the Russian force developed an air of urgency, bordering sometimes on desperation. One note of Foch's dispatches marked *"très urgent"* stresses the point that the round trip to Archangel took a minimum of sixty days. The White Sea would freeze over in October, after which repatriation would be impossible until the following summer. The containment of mutinous Russian soldiers for yet another year would result at best in a nuisance that the French government definitely did not need.

The major obstacle to repatriation, however, did not come from the early Arctic winter or the paucity of transportation, but from the Russian Provisional Government itself. Foch had not suspected that there would not be any problem from the Russians about returning their troops, and on July 10, almost as an afterthought, he wrote to the prime minister, "I do not think that the idea of a departure for Russia . . . will raise, in Petrograd, any serious objections. The Russian government understands certainly that because of the growth of a number of English divisions and the arrival of the American contingents, we are presently in a position to return to Russia the units which she generously had sent. . . ." Foch then advised that the prime minister pose to the Russian representative the repatriation of the brigades so that "he will be able to give definite orders to the First Brigade to embark in the month of August."[80] Not only did Foch misjudge the mood in the government in Petrograd, he was totally oblivious to the Russian motives for stalling.

On July 13, Ribot instructed Ambassador Noulens in Petrograd to raise again the question of repatriation with the Russians, giving the rationalization that Foch had mentioned. He also suggested the months of August and October for the return of the First and Third brigades respectively. Yet added to these words for the ambassador were those not intended for the Russian government: "The attitude of the troops which refuse to obey their leaders renders urgent their departure. The minister of war eagerly insists that a solution be gotten [without? —word illegible] delay."[81]

Noulens must have received the telegram the same day it was sent and acted on it immediately, because his response to the Russian reply was also dated July 13. The return dispatch consisted of a cover letter to the formal Russian rejoinder, which for some reason is not in the archive. Exactly what it said cannot be determined, yet from the last paragraph of the ambassador's letter, it is clear that the Russian reply was not enthusiastic. "As you will see [from the enclosed communication]," Noulens wrote, "the Russian government does not share our manner of seeing this problem."[82]

On July 25, Noulens received another instruction from Paul Cambon's brother, Jules, the general secretary of the ministry of foreign affairs, stressing the urgency of returning the Russian troops. "It is *indispensable* [italics in original]," the French diplomat informed the ambassador to Russia, "that the first of the units be embarked at the beginning of the month of August in order to avoid loss of time and to utilize in the best conditions possible the [available] tonnage. . . ." Noting that contact with other Russians should be avoided, he added confidentially, "the attitude of Russian troops in France . . . is such that it is absolutely essential that their departure not be delayed."[83]

Meanwhile, on June 28 Zankevich received a telegram from Kerensky, at that point still the Russian minister of war, in reply to the troops' quest for repatriation, stating that the return of the REF to Russia was "categorically denied. In view of the unrest and breakdown of discipline in the First Russian Brigade in France," the self-important Russian minister continued, speaking of himself in the third person, "the military minister finds the necessity to restore order in the most decisive manner, not stopping with the use of armed force and leading to the introductory position of military-revolutionary court with a law restoring the death penalty."[84] Kerensky's orders, delivered with all of the pomposity of which he was so capable, would be laughable had they not been so pathetic. The impotent Russian minister's schoolmarmish directives are similar to those of Adolph Hitler during his last days in the bunker, when he persisted in sending nonexistent divisions to attack. By June 1917, Kerensky could not discipline the troops he had at home. The disastrous offensive on the Eastern Front was about to begin when Kerensky was writing his threatening orders to the command in France, and he later admitted that he held his breath when the order to advance in Galicia was given because he could not be certain that the troops on the Eastern Front would obey orders to attack. Yet he was demanding a crackdown on mutinous troops in France when he could not control the ones under his own direct command. Moreover, he ordered the use of capital punishment, which he denied to his generals on the Eastern Front. From his Olympian heights, Kerensky continued to bombard Zankevich all summer with demands that order be restored.

By the end of July what had been obvious to Zankevich since the first of June was finally becoming known to the French: The Russian general was powerless to impose order. As Russian impotence became more and more apparent, the French authorities came to realize that control over the units could not be established without their own involvement. Yet still they hesitated. In early August the French told Zankevich that they would intervene only after "the failure of Russian military attempts." To use French force against the small Russian units would give the Germans a deadly propaganda tool to employ against the Allies. The French, therefore, applied pressure in subtle ways, such as discontinuing the mutineers' salaries and intercepting alcoholic beverages destined for the camp. Ribot, however, questioned the potential for success of these modest steps, since the mutineers still had arms. "If their mutiny degenerates into open rebellion [?]," he wired Noulens on August 11, "we would be brought to the constraints of using force."[85] Yet first they would permit Zankevich to try to restore order.

Chaos continued to reign. On July 27 Mikhail Tereshchenko, now the foreign minister, speaking for Kerensky, wired Sevastopoulo to inform the Russian officers that discipline was to be restored "with the most decisive means," including the use of force and the implementation of the death penalty. On the question of repatriation, Tereshchenko noted that if order was restored and the undesirable elements expunged from among the troops, they might be sent to Salonika, where "the reinforcement of our troops is highly desired." Returning home was out of the question.[86]

These instructions materialized in La Courtine as Order No. 34. Whatever force was required to establish calm was to be supplied by the Third Brigade, and all who did not submit would be regarded as traitors to the country.[87] Kerensky had been erroneously informed that "under the influence of the Petrograd events and the application of more forceful means," improvement in the army had begun.[88] The information was probably in reference to the stabilizing of the Third Brigade at Felletin. While quiet, it could hardly be described as being disciplined. Petrograd continued to remain totally ignorant of the true situation in France, and the Russian government seemed oblivious of the fact that no authority outside of the French army could reinstate iron discipline to the Russians in France.

Zankevich was caught between two fires. His government refused to repatriate the troops he could not control, and he had to face the French authorities who demanded that he control his troops. In his reply to Kerensky on August 10, he agreed to pursue the possibility of sending them to the Salonikan front, knowing full well that this option would scarcely be acceptable to the soldiers, especially those of the First Brigade. He agreed to a short deadline for unconditional submission to his authority, one that he clearly knew could not be enforced, especially after the men received the announcement of the transfer to Salonika.[89]

On August 12 someone appeared at la Courtine with an order from the Russian Provisional Government, which was revealed the next day as Order No. 34.[90] It was Zankevich's most forceful ultimatum and the result of his having been goaded by Kerensky and Tereshchenko to bring matters to a satisfactory conclusion. Order No. 34 called for surrendering arms and submission to Provisional Government's authority.[91] Most rejected it. He wired later that his troops had refused to obey, stating that "of the 9,000 men [in the First Brigade], fewer than a thousand have laid down their arms." Then he added pathetically, "The remainder did not submit to my demands." He informed Kerensky, who now wore his third hat since the revolution, that of prime minister, that in order to restore discipline, it would be necessary to court-martial 100 leaders and about 1,500 men, "the most unruly and rebellious element." This action Zankevich was powerless to take. What was more, to accomplish this goal, he felt he would need French help and told Kerensky that on September 5 he would surround the camp "with French arms" and starve them into submission using force if necessary.[92]

On July 30 a French committee of the war ministry held a meeting devoted to the Russian question, and the assembled included Pétain,

Painlevé, and Foch. These three simply wanted to send the Russian troops home, but it was pointed out that orders had come from Petrograd to restore discipline first.[93] If the Russian government had to accept these troops, they wanted them under control when they arrived on Russian soil. The Provisional Government had enough rebellious troops under its direct command, and it certainly did not wish any additional contagion. Faced with this intransigence, the French changed policy. Whether the rebels were repatriated or not, the French wanted the mutiny in the First Brigade crushed, and they decided to take firm measures to do so.

The days of separation of the two brigades had had an increasingly quieting effect on the soldiers of the Third at Felletin. Elements of insubordination still remained, but defiance consisted of tame actions such as the soldiers' committee disallowing servants for officers under the rank of colonel. A French journalist, M. L. Malterre, observed these men, who he said had come to Felletin "almost as savages," become "sweet, gentle and sociable." As they settled into a quiet routine, the antipathy in the village subsided, and they even came to be liked by the local citizens, especially by the merchants, who felt that their presence was a windfall for business. Their visits into town, often accompanied by their bear mascot Mishka, were welcomed, and the denizens came to appreciate the gentle, melancholy nature of these Russian soldiers who patronized their stores and played games with their children. The evening air was often filled with the sound of their mandolins and balalaikas as they played their doleful Slavic folksongs. Years later Maurice Dayras, a lawyer from nearby Aubusson, remembered how they gave concerts in their camp and organized sporting events for the local population. On July 14, 1917, the Russian band gave a performance and hosted a festival in the hall of the local school to which the entire population was invited. Everything was free to the guests, including the refreshments.[94]

For the soldiers of the Third Brigade, a casual evening routine began to develop. Almost every day at five o'clock, some of the men would visit the neighboring town of Aubusson. Led by a man on horseback whom the soldiers jokingly called their "pope," the men laughingly skipped and danced into town. To the great amusement of the town's citizens, the horseman executed all sorts of gymnastics like a circus performer. To their amazement, the Russians would bypass the cafés and bars and enter the hairdressers' shops and the perfumeries, where they bought up all of the lotions and eau de cologne, which they gulped down with great relish, preferring it to wine. They also used it to wash down sandwiches made of bread on which they spread toothpaste they had bought. They would then assemble in the square and sing their native songs to the great delight of the French, who would gather around in a great circle and laugh at Mishka's dancing and other antics.[95] What was nothing short of a friendly relationship, therefore, developed between the Russian soldiers of Felletin and their French neighbors, and as the days passed and the rebellious nature of the Third Brigade further subsided, this warm association grew. Many years later locals had only fond recollections of the Russians who had been there.

The detachment's Soldiers' Committee met almost every day,[96] and the more conservative hue of the "*Felletinois*" was evident in the committee's calls for obedience. On July 13 the committee issued its first summons for order and explained to the soldiers the reason for the separation of the two brigades. With the eloquence of a Tolstoy, the author of the committee's July 13 statement began by saying "The Great Russian Revolution has swept Mighty Russia . . . from the front line trenches to the desolate and distant forests of Siberia," and then proceeded to speak of the "impending" elections of the Constituent Assembly, which would soon bring new life and order to the Russian state and end the dark autocratic past. Informing them, incorrectly as it turned out, that the elections to the assembly would take place in September, he added, "Here this historical process will also come to pass in the Russian detachments in France." The author then turned his attention to the "dark forces of our regiment," which he then strangely went on to say did not exist any longer. Yet the reference was clearly to the First Brigade, for he went on to note "We have found in ourselves a love for the RUSSIAN REVOLUTION *[sic]* and in the name of it on the 24 June [July 7 on the Gregorian calendar] we broke firmly from this dark force. . . [i.e., the First Brigade]." He then concluded with the stirring and often heard slogan, "Long Live the Russian Revolution!" and "Long Live the Constituent Assembly!"[97] Another appeal of the same flavor was issued on August 5. Reminding the soldiers how near to "our hearts is the deficient state . . . of our dear country . . . and our fathers and brothers struggling for freedom at the present minute under the influence of dark forces that seek to ruin . . . ," the author cried out, "Down with the instability *[shatanie]* everywhere!" and added, "We do not wish to be traitors to our country; move quickly for the front — we demand this!"[98]

The Third Brigade soldiers' silent acceptance of these calls to discipline and the resumption of fighting in France did not, however, mean complete submission. Yet at least they were not electing soviets and driving off their officers. Among them there was at least a nucleus of stable material with which the Russian officers and the French command could work. Isolated from the troublemakers of the First, the men of the Third could be perhaps re-created into an effective fighting force.

Meanwhile back in La Courtine, the chaos continued unabated, and anarchy reigned. There were all sorts of infractions of the camp boundaries as Russian soldiers continued to maraud about the surrounding countryside unchecked, and bursts of gunfire often broke the quiet of the night. Across the headquarters building stretched a banner that proclaimed, "Down with the War!" The camp was flooded with tracts condemning the "bourgeois war" and quoting Tolstoy's pacifist condemnations of war. Some observers believed that the soldiers were provoked by German agitators, but thoroughly infected with pacifist propaganda, they hardly needed German propagandists to agitate them. They were totally committed to returning home, and the socialist arguments against the war gave them an intellectual justification. Baltais seems to have been adept in keeping the tension stoked to the highest level, and the French unwillingness and the Russian officers' inability to intervene merely fueled the problem. The soldiers were hostile to any outsiders, save agitators. Former comrades who returned to retrieve their belongings risked injury.

In August the Provisional Government continued to little avail to send individuals, some even with "Leftist" credentials, to try to calm the rebels. A priest visited the brigade and was nearly shot. He had gone to give a sermon in which he enjoined the soldiers to do their military duty and was challenged for his efforts by some fanatics, who spit in his face. Regaining his composure, the ecclesiastic raised the cross above his head and in a loud voice hurled anathemas at them and pronounced an excommunication against them. A group of furious soldiers threw themselves at the priest and beat him until a group of believers placed him under their protection. His defenders took him through the woods to the Felletin road under the guise of getting him out of the camp, but once out of the reach of their comrades, they joined him in his flight to safety.[99]

Not surprisingly, the rebellious First Brigade tried to make contact with the Third after the latter reached Felletin, yet the accounts of such attempts are vague and in some cases inaccurate. Vavilov wrote that Baltais and his vice president, Volkov, went into the neighboring camp at Felletin on July 21 for conversations with their former comrades. Vavilov remembered that they were arrested and held temporarily until they agreed to return to the front.[100] Kozlov reports of another effort at contact when "some representatives . . . went on horseback" and met with some members of the Third Brigade. According to Kozlov, they were surrounded by officers and a few soldiers, who took their horses, called them "spies," and sent them packing back to La Courtine on foot.[101] One other account mentions an effort at communication, tells of marching out to music, and speaks of arrests, but there is no mention of Baltais.[102] Given the general chaos that reigned in the La Courtine enclosure, it is quite possible that several deputations went on their own or simply out of curiosity. None of these attempts appeared to have had an adverse effect on the Third Brigade, which seems to have remained immune to any contact with these missionaries of disorder.

One important development that did occur as a result of these attempts, however, was a change in the rebellion's leadership. It is odd that someone as astute as Baltais would have trusted the opposition, yet he apparently did. Lissovsky wrote that Baltais emerged with about eighty men in response to Kerensky's order to submit,[103] but it is highly unlikely that he would have done so considering that he was leader of the rebellion and that his hero status among the rebels continued unabated. If he emerged with eighty men, they were for his protection, for he certainly had no intention of submitting. We do not, however, know the objectives of this twenty-nine-year-old charismatic bookkeeper when he and Volkov went out on July 25 to talk with the representatives of the Third Brigade, but both were arrested when they left the protection of the La Courtine camp.[104] They were taken first to Courneau, a camp about 150 miles from La Courtine near Bordeaux, and finally to a prison on the Île d'Aix off the coast of France between Bordeaux and La Rochelle.

On Baltais's disappearance, the leadership of the First Brigade passed to another Lett (Trotsky calls him a Ukrainian),[105] Afanasii Globa. He appears to have been a natural leader.[106] Some who knew him said he was only of average intelligence, yet this large, striking, blue-eyed, blond man had the charisma that makes men follow. He possessed for the soldiers a revolutionary mystique, and with his oratorical abilities he dominated soldiers of all ages in the unit. He was driven by an implacable hatred for all officers, whom he considered to be incompetents.[107] The only known photograph of him taken after he had been incarcerated reveals a tall, handsome man with a slight smirk on his face and a contemptuous slouch. He obviously was being forced to have his picture taken. Apparently he spoke some French and came to be received in the homes of some of the citizens of La Courtine, where he was regarded as some sort of savant.[108] He also quickly acquired a French mistress, the wife of a local French soldier who was at the front. Vavilov described him as being "less stable" *(menee ustoichiv)* than Baltais,[109] which probably means more radical.

As the new leader, Globa established the iron discipline that had eluded the officers. He limited drinking and forced the soldiers to take good care of their weapons. In dealings with the former command he was firm. To one of Lokhvitsky's orders to surrender arms, he is supposed to have curtly replied, "We are not children."[110] As the French troops tightened their control around the camp early in August, his resistance hardened, and he remained to the end the implacable foe of all authority but his own. All else about him remains a mystery, yet to the end of the whole affair, the rebels never challenged the leadership of this enigmatical Lettish Baptist salesman.

Early in August the French and Russian authorities took an action that indicates that they knew their statements about the loyalty of the Third Brigade were not completely true. It was also the first move to create a force that would do their bidding. On August 10 the brigade was transferred in fifteen trains to the camp at Courneau, the one to which Baltais had been taken initially. Senegalese troops had to vacate the post to make it available to the Russians. There is little information about why the move was made, but the indication is that the "*vrai*" Russians were far less ready to go to the front than their leadership had indicated. The nearness of the First Brigade might have been a factor in the move, but the ease with which their deputies had been dispatched indicates that their proximity was not a major problem. A Soviet historian, giving no source, has written that the soldiers were transferred because they had become "more dangerous."[111] Yet as early as July 24 Foch had suggested moving the Third to Courneau (and the First to Archangel, where the Russians could handle the problem),[112] so there must have been trouble that was not apparent to the authors of the glowing reports of their great discipline and patriotism. Poitevin, who has been wrong on several points, states that the Third was moved because it had expressed the desire to return to military exercises,[113] which for some reason could not be held in Felletin. This explanation is doubtful. On August 4, Zankevich, leaving Lokhvitsky in total charge of the unstable situation, had returned to Paris, where he admitted to the French authorities that he was powerless to reestablish order in the First Brigade by using the Third Brigade in the shape it was in, and he asked that the Third be transferred elsewhere, where for some reason he seems to have felt that discipline could be enforced.[114]

The French government does not seem to have looked favorably on Zankevich as a leader. About his suggestions to move the men, Painlevé caustically pointed out to the prime minister that the feckless Russian officer had not even employed the "energetic measures recommended by his government," adding "It is not surprising that his action has produced no result."[115] Painlevé continued to stress the necessity of French noninvolvement beyond "indispensable aid." It must in all cases be General

Zankevich's actions that brought the crackdown, not any moves of the French.[116] For whatever the purposes, on August 10 the transfer to Camp Courneau took place, leaving only the soldiers' committee and a skeletal officer staff behind in Felletin. If there was any opposition within the unit to the move, it has not been recorded.

Courneau appears, from a picture in Ernest Schultz's pictorial history of the Russian Expeditionary Force, to have been rather primitive. The camp was composed largely of what seem from the picture to be tarpaper barracks with thatched roofs. On arrival there followed the usual tasks of organizing supply dispatches, latrines, and the general work involved with a move. Leave was granted to the towns of Arcachon, Cazaux, and La Teste; a grocery store in Arcachon was designated for the Russians to patronize. The camp then became a sifting station to winnow the remaining troublemakers. Troops who would fire on command were to be singled out.

There are no details about what was actually done there. The control over these men seems to have continued to improve but never became total. Some of the misbehavior seen in other camps occurred here, and at one point twenty-two of these Russians were sent to prison in Bordeaux for what must have been serious acts. Yet those who were deemed willing to return to the front, or fire on their colleagues in the First Brigade, returned to Felletin, now under the command of Lieutenant Colonel Valerian Balbachevsky. Poitevin states that the sifting operation did not go well in the beginning, for he reports that only fifty-one soldiers returned to the new camp after undergoing the cathartic effects of Courneau.[117] This number, in view of later events, is unlikely, or else the standards to measure renewed discipline were later relaxed. Yet reports show that things were improving. The colonel commandant of Courneau reported that the discipline of the troops "is *considerably* [his italics] better," adding that even the officer corps was showing some life, and the numbers of soldiers absent without leave had declined by the end of August.[118] Soldiers did scandalize local French tourists by swimming nude in Lake Cazeaux, generating many complaints,[119] but less and less serious trouble seems to have happened. Although all the malcontents were not totally expunged, by early September a new, basically reliable fighting force had been reborn.

SEVEN

The Battle of La Courtine

July–September 1917

France, Mother of Liberty, of Equality and of Fraternity, has sold herself. Do you comprehend, Mother of Liberty, all the cowardice of your command, you, who have been the guide of world civilization. . . . Your hand has stopped temporarily the march toward freedom and culture of an entire country. . . . It is because of your gold that the blood of the Russian people is still going to flow.

—Maxim Gorky[1]

If a general shows confidence in his men but always insists on his orders being obeyed, the gain will be mutual. . . . Vacillation and fuzziness are the surest means of sapping the confidence of an army.

—Sun Tzu[2]

—J'ai vu l'adjudant, dis donc. C'est contre les Russes qu'on marche. Paraît qu'y chambardent le camp de La Courtine.

—Ah bah! les Russes, —murmurai-je; mais j'avais trop sommeil.

—André Obey[3]

IN JULY 1917, Joseph Noulens became the Third Republic's third ambassador to the new Russian state in as many months. His immediate and only major task during his brief tenure in the last months of the Provisional Government was to convince the Russians that they should allow the two rebellious brigades to return. The French were thoroughly exhausted with the war effort and did not need the additional strain of mutinous soldiers on whom they could not use force. Kerensky, however, had enough unruly troops at home without adding two more brigades that, while stationed on foreign soil, had run amok and had gotten away with it. Moreover, Noulens arrived during the chaos of the July Uprising, a more or less spontaneous unsuccessful coup that the Bolsheviks had tried to lead. Sailors and soldiers were the major Bolshevik support in this failed attempt to seize power. Kerensky was not about to favor reinforcing the instability in his army with imported rebellion.

Yet the French government could no longer tolerate the presence of the armed, mutinous brigade on its soil, and the situation was rapidly becoming desperate. The First Brigade's officers would definitely never control them again, and if the French tried to starve them out of La Courtine, the armed Russian soldiers might take to plundering villages located near the camp. Noulens simply had to convince the Russians to repatriate their nationals, in Foch's words, *"le plus tôt possible."*[4]

On July 25, the day he offered his letter of appointment to the Russian government, Noulens raised with Tereshchenko for the first of many times the question of repatriation. As we have already seen, the Russian foreign minister was not sympathetic. The minister of foreign affairs was a young millionaire and an itinerant liberal belonging to no particular political party. He was a close associate of Kerensky and Pavel Miliukov, the leader of the Cadet Party, and he had entered the Provisional Government during the February Revolution as minister of transport. Besides Kerensky, he was the only individual to serve in all of the coalitions of that government. A virtual unknown, his name had brought laughter when it had been announced in March along with the members of the first Provisional coalition. When Miliukov, the original foreign minister, left office in May, Tereshchenko replaced him in the ministry of foreign affairs. Little is still known about him, although he lived into the 1950s. Except for one brief piece in a Russian émigré newspaper, he never wrote his memoirs.[5]

Noulens approached the question of repatriation with a great deal of tact, never mentioning the mutiny, about which Tereshchenko was of course well informed. Noulens used the official French line that due to the arrival of a large number of English divisions and the imminent arrival of the Americans, the Russians "so generously given" the year before were no longer needed by the French government. The French ambassador, as if ending the matter, extended a warm expression of thanks from the French government for "the service that the Russian troops have given the cause of the Allies," and added what he thought was the helpful bit of information that the First Brigade would be able to depart in the early days of August with transports that were now available. The exit of the other brigade "seems to be envisioned in the month of October."[6]

Tereshchenko responded vaguely with the promise to recall the brigades from France after "some semblance of order was restored," but neither Russian leader made any definite commitment.[7] This simple conditional statement, however, was enough to induce the French to act, and General Comby was immediately informed that "the decision having been made," he should prepare the troops for embarkation in August.[8]

Several days later, a visibly embarrassed Tereshchenko told Noulens that immediate repatriation was quite impossible because the ships going from France to Russia would be carrying much-needed *munitions and war matériel that was especially necessary to the Russian army at this moment* [italics in the original]."[9] Taken somewhat aback, Noulens pointed out that these ships were already designated to receive these troops, adding more realistically that a delay could lead to a "continuation of fresh incidents of which the REF are completely capable." Tereshchenko could only reply that Kerensky was committed to establishing a "rigorous discipline" among the Russian troops, and he said that the day before, the soldiers had been informed that the death penalty had been restored in the army.[10] Moreover, the Russian foreign minister added that General Brusilov believed that the contingents in France should be sent to reinforce the units in Salonika and become part of the Expeditionary Corps of the Orient. Brusilov's alleged objection was that the repatriated troops would compare the technical means (weapons, food, clothing, etc.) of the Russian army to those of the French and that would "sow discouragement in the units with which they came into contact."[11]

The idea of sending the troops as reinforcements to Salonika as a solution to the problem, already having dawned on the French, came to Russian awareness as well. Relocation would indeed be a solution: It would rid the French of their Russian headaches, and the Russians would care little if the troops were unruly in France or in the Vardar valley. At least they would be isolated and could no longer cause trouble between the Russians and their French allies. Exactly who made the decision is unclear, but by early August the Provisional Government was "persisting," to use Noulens's term, in asking that the Russian troops in France be sent on to Salonika on the Macedonian front.[12] At the same time the Russian government was inquiring about French willingness to supply matériel, horses, and transportation,[13] as if the decision had already been finalized. Foch and the French government came to an agreement, and the French general formed plans to send the units to the Macedonian theater by August 15. Foch, however, remained highly concerned about the state of discipline, and he wrote to the ministry of war a now-familiar refrain: "Discipline in these two brigades leaves much to be desired, and one is not able to dream of sending them to Salonika before the Russian authorities would have taken measures to reestablish order."[14] The troops never departed by August 15, but on August 25 the order was formally given, oddly enough from the desperate Tereshchenko to the hapless Zankevich, not from the Russian ministry of war.[15]

Just what exactly they planned to send is hard to tell — certainly not all of the First Brigade, unless discipline could somehow be established. Poitevin states that 2,000 men were brought to Courneau to join Beliaev's artillery units temporarily stationed there on their way to Salonika. In order to distinguish the two types of units, the artillery men wore yellow armbands on their left arms and the infantry wore blue.[16] Yet whatever troops were finally assembled to depart for Salonika, the soldiers would have none of it. Already in July, a Lieutenant Colonel Pantchulitsev reported that 200 Russians (it is unclear from what previously existing units these came) had refused to embark for Salonika "to fight for the French bourgeoisie,"[17] and a similar incident occurred even in the more conservative Third Brigade in August when it learned of its destination. In the words of Zankevich in a report sent to the French government, "A great agitation reigns among the [Third] brigade, unhappy about being sent to Salonika."[18] At the end of the month the Russian government finally retreated from its position and rescinded the order. The Russian government would not bring the troops home, it could not force them under military discipline, and it could not make them depart France for Salonika. The problem, therefore, remained a French one. It must have become increasingly apparent to the French government that if the brigades were to be controlled, it would be largely the French military that would do it, no matter how distasteful that would be. The ongoing crisis was a growing cancer, and with its own armies only recently having been in a state of mutiny, the French high command would hardly want as an example to their own troops a group of unruly Russians running amok. By August the French had realized that they needed to take a more active role in the affair.

Several weeks later the French government tried again, only this time directly with Kerensky, who had become premier in July. On August 13 Noulens sent a formal note to the new prime minister and did not mince words about the reason for repatriation. The missive stated that the Russian troops in France had refused to go to Salonika and that to get them to do so would require force. The note then revealed the major concern of the

French government: "I do not need to indicate the sentiment of horror that we have at the testing of the eventuality of a conflict at this present time between Russia and France. The employment of force is becoming inevitable. We dread the impression that it will produce in Russia and France [read: propaganda value it will give Germany]." Adding that Russian public opinion would not understand suppression of the brigades and underscoring the impact such action would have on the Franco-Russian alliance, the note concluded by virtually begging the Russian government to allow the troops to "embark as soon as possible for Russia."[19]

Kerensky's immediate response is not known, but the Russians continued over the next few days to stress in their orders to Zankevich to use whatever force necessary to quell the mutiny, including capital punishment, which Kerensky still had not allowed in Russia. Over and over in the instructions of the following days, the government in Petrograd used phrases such as "in the most energetic manner," "use of force," "the death penalty," "with the utmost severity," and so forth. The government also continued to suggest the now-dead notion of relocation to Salonika. Clearly it was interested in any option that did not include bringing them back to Russia. There was even talk of sending a "mission of more capable officers" to "speak with authority to the men," but Noulens dissuaded them from this course, stressing to the puzzled Russian leadership that this attempt would do no good. Although it is incredible, the Russian government seems still to have been unaware of the real depth of the rebellion, for it had even sent a number of regulations late in July for the punishment of various crimes such as brigandage, pillage, and pogroms as a means of intimidation for the unruly soldiers,[20] having no idea that the more serious offenses were going unpunished.

Fishing rather desperately for an answer short of repatriation, the Russian government decided to remove Zankevich, replacing him with "a person who would be able to speak to the troops in a more authoritative manner." As a further measure, the Russians proposed to expel from the army any mutineers who would not submit to discipline, depriving them of their pay and the right to vote in the elections for the Constituent Assembly. On hearing this proposed resolution of the problem, Noulens told the Russian minister that this measure would "bear fruit in a more or less far off future," but he added that it would make little difference in the present, where more direct action was needed. Noulens tried to explain to Tereshchenko, who was acting as if he were largely out of touch with the reality in France, that there was no authority save that of the French army to enforce the Russian government's orders, and he made it clear that the French were not going to intervene if at all possible.[21]

Quite likely the Russian government was indeed crying out for French help and did not wish to say so directly. When it made the stringent demands for order, Kerensky and Tereshchenko were certainly not oblivious to the fact that all discipline had collapsed among their troops in Russia itself. How could they think that by mere decree they could quell the mutiny? Their repeated recommendations of force in France, where they were totally impotent, probably was an indication to the French government that they would sanction, even welcome, French intervention. The fact that the French government had no desire to do so left Kerensky and Tereshchenko powerless to do more than bluster and fume at their officers, who had for the most part abrogated any responsibility and fled their duty. There is likewise the added ingredient that the Russians were fully aware of the situation in France and were merely using the pretext to prevent the return of these troops that they felt would merely be additional trouble. Clearly they did not want these armed men in their current state. What additional damage at home could troops in open rebellion cause? Kerensky and Tereshchenko did not want to learn firsthand.

With all the prodding, the Russian High Command, strangely through Tereshchenko, finally on August 28 issued a detailed directive on the problem. They once again ordered the leadership to take every opportunity to dispatch the brigades to Salonika. If this action proved impossible, both brigades were to be disbanded and placed under French discipline. The mutineers were to be judged by military justice, with the guilty to be dispatched to Russia. Those innocent, and it was presumed they would be docile, could then be sent to Salonika.[22] This move again proved unsatisfactory, and finally on September 9, the Provisional Government announced that it would repatriate the troops, disciplined or not, as soon as transports could be found. Zankevich received a telegram the next day ordering the troops home.[23] Whereas this action seemed to be a major Russian concession on the matter, it really meant little. No ships were available immediately, and, by October, Arctic temperatures would make the return of the troops impossible until the following summer. If it could stall another month, the Russian government would insure that the problem would remain a French one at least until the next year. By the time the Russians had issued the order, however, French patience had been exhausted and the situation had passed the critical point. When General Zankevich received his repatriation directive, the government of the Third Republic had already begun to place in motion other measures to rid itself of this utter nuisance.

Meanwhile, Zankevich continued going through the impotent motions of trying to establish order. Goaded by his own government and the obvious French annoyance with his performance, Zankevich finally, and with obvious reluctance, decided to have a showdown with the rebellious troops under his command. He had avoided an earlier confrontation because he knew that he could not force from them any obedience, but now he seems to have decided to act on one of those many orders to restore discipline. "Charged personally with the execution of the instructions of the Russian minister of war," on July 30 he promised his superiors to "apply the most energetic measures to reestablish order." If force became necessary, it would be supplied by the Third Brigade soldiers who were thought to be loyal. Expecting Zankevich finally to take some decisive action, Comby alerted his few troops to stand by in case of trouble.[24] Therefore, pressured from all sides, the beleaguered Russian general issued an ultimatum on August 1.

Exactly what occurred next is a bit obscure. A report dated August 16 chronicling the events concerning the first ultimatum from the French minister of war to the prime minister states that Zankevich and Rapp, having decided to appeal first to logic, went to the camp of the First Brigade on August 1 and ordered them to surrender their arms by 10:00 A.M. on August 3. The account states that about 1,000 soldiers from the First Brigade did so, joining the Third, but from the other thousands, there was no response. The report of the ultimatum to the French prime minister stated that on the next day (incorrectly reported as August 5), both brigades were told to stack their arms in a place indicated by the French guards by 4:00 P.M. The directive went on to state, "If they do not obey, they will be turned over to the *vindicte française*."[25]

Other accounts, mostly secondary, indicate that the demand to surrender arms was made only to the men of the First Brigade in La Courtine, not the Third.[26] The reference in the note to the prime minister to the Third Brigade was probably an error, since the Third was itself scattered at this time in a number of different camps, depending on each unit's degree of military reliability, and the major problem at that point was with the First, not the Third. The reference to the "thousand" from the First Brigade who had joined the Third seems realistic, since the reports to this point only tell of defections from the First to the Third. Vavilov's observation that the troops encircled in La Courtine consisted of the First Brigade and "a few thousand" men from the Third[27] would indicate that there were at least some members from the Third Brigade with the *"faux"* Russians, although "a few thousand" is highly unlikely.

It is difficult to believe that none of the Third Brigade would have sided with the First. Clearly a large part of the Third would not submit to discipline and had to be treated with sterner measures. Quite probably the author of the dispatch confused the First with the Third, because every indication is that the ultimatum was presented only to the First, not the Third Brigade.

The August 1 ultimatum began by informing the mutineers that Zankevich had received a telegram from the Russian minister of war which formally refused the return of the two brigades to Russia and stated the direction to Salonika. Furthermore, the order continued, in view of the absence of discipline, the ministry of war deemed it necessary to "reestablish order in these units." Since there was no other source of authority available, it would fall the mission of the Third Brigade to force the First Brigade to do its duty, "in order to avoid the use of French troops."[28] The command then called on the First Brigade to establish "its own iron discipline." Zankevich added that if it did not, the idea of freedom of assembly and soldiers' committees would be suppressed "by reason of their insubordination to the orders of the commandant." The "mutinous elements" would quickly be isolated and judged by a commission of inquiry, which Zankevich called a "tribunal of revolutionary form." The directive gave the soldiers at La Courtine forty-eight hours "in order to reflect and, in all conscience, to express their submission and their obedience to . . . the Provisional Government." As a sign of their submission, the First Brigade was to stack its arms, leave the camp, and reassemble at the Third Brigade's bivouac, near the village of Clairavaux. The deadline was 10:00 A.M. on Friday, August 3. Anyone remaining in the camp after this point "must be considered traitors to the country," and Zankevich warned that he would "take immediately on their regard the most rigorous measures." The order added that the terms of capitulation were in no way negotiable, and there would be accepted "no condition, no discussions, no requests." It was of course signed by General Zankevich.[29] Hardly unaware that the soldiers were unlikely to submit to the demands, a contingency plan consisted of refusing supplies to the camp and finally all-out assault by the Third. Apparently not trusting General Beliaev's unit, Zankevich asked Comby to furnish him with artillery and gunners.[30]

The response to Zankevich's demands was more indifference than outright refusal. Soldiers gathered in the square of the camp and the regimental band played *La Marseillaise*, although Poitevin states that 1,500 to 1,600 did repair to Clairavaux,[31] a figure that is probably high. Even if the number is accurate, that still left thousands in the camp who refused to submit. The problem had hardly vanished or even diminished substantially.

Zankevich did convene at Felletin the promised Commission of Inquiry—the only part of his threat that he made good—to ascertain exactly who the rebel chiefs were. The presiding officer was Colonel M. Isamov of the second regiment, assisted by a Colonel Savin, a Sergeant-Major Idoroveinin, and a soldier Shalkhanov. They drafted a list of leaders of the rebellion, which is somewhat different from the inventory that appears in the archive at Vincennes.[32] Surprisingly, the official French army list does not include Globa but does include a number of others not mentioned on Poitevin's list.

Aware that Zankevich could do little to enforce his order, the French began to prepare for a military struggle if one should start. Although they still hoped that the Russians could solve their own problems, the French high command had abandoned its hands-off policy. In his office in Limoges, Comby signed an order dispatching to La Courtine nine companies of infantry, four sections of machine guns, three sections of artillery, mainly French 75's, and three platoons of cavalry. These forces took their positions in the vicinity of La Courtine late in the night of August 3-4.[33] According to Sevastopoulo of the Russian embassy in Paris, the French had drawn from the front good military units in the form of one company, one cavalry unit, and one battery to supplement these troops sent earlier.[34]

At this crucial point Zankevich departed precipitously for Paris, from where he said he had to go to London for an inter-Allied conference, leaving General Lokhvitsky with the problem. He was merely passing downward the hopeless responsibility as Tereshchenko and Kerensky had passed their helplessness down to him. Zankevich's puffed-up attitude, however, had begun to take its toll on those officers under him, and the very day of his departure Lokhvitsky himself faced a minor mutiny from the loyal officers led by the 6th regiment Lieutenant Colonel Bromov, who planned to arrest Lokhvitsky and proclaim himself dictator of the disparate group at Felletin. To divert the revolt, Lokhvitsky convened all the officers in a meeting that very quickly turned ugly. There were insults hurled, reproaches given, and two colonels even came to fisticuffs. Bromov was finally relieved of his command but not arrested, which again demonstrated the pathetic paralysis of the Russian leadership.[35]

As a postscript to this first showdown with the rebels, there arrived within a couple of weeks an order from the new commander-in-chief of the Russian army, General Lavr Kornilov, making the usual demand for the restoration of discipline.[36] Two French officers were sent to the camp of La Courtine with the odious task of posting Kornilov's order there, it being too dangerous for any Russian officers to go. The French emissaries, however, were arrested immediately by the rebels on entering the camp but were released after several hours as a result of the intervention of the Abbé Laliron, the chaplain of La Courtine, whom French authorities charged to carry an energetic appeal for their release.[37]

The French government blamed Zankevich's departure for the most recent failures and formally complained to the Russians about his incompetence. Prime Minister Ribot instructed Noulens in mid-August to inform the Russian government of Zankevich's inability to restore order and the pathetic display of weakness exemplified by his leaving. "The French government is not able to assume the task [of leading the Russian Expeditionary Force] in the absence of any representative of the Provisional Government and Russian officers," the desperate prime minister wrote his ambassador. He went on to instruct Noulens to ask the Russian government to "repair the situation . . . and to assume the initiative and responsibility of all measures . . . [necessary]." The prime minister took an unusual step by urging his ambassador to tell the Russian government that if Zankevich were judged incapable to perform his mission, "it must be given to another representative of the Provisional Government." Zankevich's cowardly departure in the midst of such a tragic crisis had been irresponsible in the extreme, the prime minister felt, and according to Foch "proof of weakness, timidity and indecision." Ribot ended with a call for a new set of officers who would be capable of restoring order and ending this "veritable danger."[38]

Bypassing any proper protocol, Painlevé directly wrote Zankevich a stinging letter at the end of August outlining in unveiled contempt his numerous failures, adding in conclusion "The gravity of the acts will not escape you, and I ask you to inform me with urgency the measures that you envision to put an end to the situation which cannot be prolonged. . . ."[39] Even his country's own foreign minister was openly critical to the French ambassador, describing the mutiny and Zankevich's failure in terms showing that he was "profoundly indignant about it," noting that to end such a scandal one would need to "shoot about fifty mutineers."[40] Zankevich clearly had few friends and no real support. Had the situation been more stable, he would already have been removed.

In the general's defense, it might be noted that he took command after order had collapsed and after the corps of officers had lost all credibility with their men. Oddly, Zankevich was perhaps the only figure involved who did fully comprehend the situation. He knew better than Kornilov, Tereshchenko, Ribot, Foch, or Painlevé that no single officer

could resolve the crisis with mere words. Perhaps someone of the majesty
of an Alexander the Great or a Napoleon could have coerced them back
to order, but by the beginning of September, there existed no officer in
the entire Russian army who could have by his simple presence brought
order to these troops. Discipline could indeed have been restored if they
could have shot "about fifty of the mutineers," but there were no Russian
soldiers in France upon whom one could depend to staff such a firing
squad, and the French were wisely refusing to do so. Order had just been
restored in the French army after the dangerous collapse of its will to
fight in May by a judicious mixture of firmness and reform. Moreover,
France had a great officer in Henri Pétain, in whom the soldiers already
had supreme confidence. Yet even if an officer could have been found in
whom the Russian soldiers had such profound trust, he could never have
asserted control over them without force. Moreover, in the back of the
mind of every war-weary *poilu* was the understanding that if he broke,
the hated *boches* would rape his country once again. With that as a
stimulus, a popular general like Pétain could restore the fighting will of
the battered French soldier. Yet to the *muzhik*, thousands of miles from
his native soil, which he knew was torn asunder by a revolution, little
else mattered than the all-consuming desire to return home, to enter the
uncertainty and rescue loved ones. The Russians' natural anxiety was too
great for any Russian Pétain, could one have been found, to take them
in hand. They were simply homesick, and that desire took precedence
over anything else. This perception Zankevich was indeed capable of
understanding when no one else could. He had realized early that without
the use of force, the situation was totally and completely hopeless. Where
he is to be faulted as an officer is the pusillanimous way he fled from his
difficult situation, uncaring about the disgrace that he brought on himself
and his fellow officers.

On August 5 the leadership decided to name another deadline at
10:00 A.M. the next day, but by noon on the sixth, the situation remained
unchanged. Then Lokhvitsky made yet another of the now-tiresome
demands for the mutineers to come to heel. In Order No. 83 he announced
that his patience was exhausted, as if he had a million willing men to do
his bidding, and dramatically informed the rebels that the soldiers who
remained in La Courtine *"are no longer part of the force* [his italics]."[41] There
still was no response. Both Lokhvitsky and Rapp, moreover, had come to
the conclusion that the Third Brigade, or whatever "reliable elements"
they had in it, could not be absolutely depended on to fire on their
comrades if ordered to do so. They wanted to pass the need to enforce the
ultimatum to the French, yet Comby, adhering to his government's policy

of avoiding intervention, refused, although he instructed the French troops to redouble their vigilance.

The final acceptance by the French that they must play a more active role led them to form of a *cordon sanitaire* around the camp to prevent the spread of the Russian disease to the French population.[42] The encirclement was initially totally French, since large numbers of reliable Russian troops were not available. Yet Foch, fearing the potential contagion to the French troops, ordered that they be kept as far away as possible from the Russians "in order to avoid the danger of a bad example."[43] The French soldiers chosen for service were carefully selected from among units that had not been plagued by mutinies earlier that year and from among eighteen year-olds who had just completed their training. The morale of the group was high, and its ranks showed much general enthusiasm and good spirit. As for their task, it was at first simple. Painlevé telegraphed Comby that the French units around La Courtine were to, first, protect French territory outside the camp against all the mutinous enterprises and, second, to assist the Russian government in the repression of the mutiny without using force. Intervention was permissible only if the available Russian troops were completely unable to restore order and only if a representative of the Provisional Government requested their help in writing.[44] In short, they were primarily supposed to give the Russians some backbone.

Requests from the Russian leadership, however, were not lacking. In a meeting between Poincaré and a young Russian General Yankevich on September 1, a formal call for help was made to the French government. After thanking Poincaré for the *cravate de commandeur* of the Legion of Honor he had received, the elegant, perky Russian officer expressed embarrassment at the trouble caused by the Russian troops interned at La Courtine and asked Poincaré to use French troops to settle the matter. Poincaré refused. In his diary he noted that this intervention would give the Germans a good cause for a propaganda campaign against France.[45] Writing on this interview, the Soviet historian A. E. Ioffe interprets this refusal as showing "not only the underlying role of the French imperialists, covering their hands with blood of these soldiers, who had so recently fought for the interests of these very imperialists, but also the insincerity it demonstrated." Noting that ultimately French army, artillery, and soldiers were used to encircle the camp, Ioffe sarcastically writes that these actions somehow "do not count in his meaning of participation."[46]

Anticipating the future need, however, the French ministry of war informed Comby early in September to add to the 5,000 men already around the camp additional men from the Ninth, Thirteenth, and the

Eighteenth region.[47] Furthermore, on September 8 the ministry of war supplemented these units with the 19th regiment of infantry, the 21st regiment of Dragoons, and a battery of 75's. These three units would be gathered from the environs of Paris and sent to the area of La Courtine on September 9, when they would pass under the command of General Comby. The final complement of French troops was therefore a widely varying group divided among the sectors around La Courtine, with one unit in reserve.[48]

To force the rebels' final capitulation, Zankevich, who had finally returned from London, proposed a plan on September 7: If the last pourparlers did not result in a breakthrough by September 9, Russian artillery units would surround the camp. One more ultimatum would be sent to the rebels demanding the stacking of arms and full surrender by 10:00 A.M. on September 10. If this order failed to bring the desired results, then a blockade of the camp would be imposed and all provisioning of the camp would cease. Twenty-four hours later, the camp was to be stormed.[49] Any such plan would have to include the consent and active assistance of the French, since the reliable Russian elements were so few. Like Poincaré, Foch had expressed concern for the fodder for propaganda any French action would give the Germans and, in Russia, the extremist elements against the Provisional Government. With the collapse of General Kornilov's attempted coup in Russia at the end of August, there had been a Leftist, anti-Allied resurgence that would have likewise found French suppression of Russian soldiers on their soil useful in their political war against the Provisional Government. Therefore, Foch again stressed to the French ministry of war that any direct French involvement in the matter should come only after a written request from the Russian government.

The major force for the attack, however, was supposed to be a revitalized Russian unit, and, as we have seen, for weeks the Russian and French officers had been screening Russian soldiers primarily from the Third Brigade to serve for the attack. The unit that was finally created was given the formal title The Free Force, although sometimes it was called the Second Special Brigade, and it was nominally under the direct command of Colonel Gotua. It consisted of 2,500 to 3,000 men. Although most of these effectives were volunteers from the Third Brigade,[50] some were doubtless from the First, since we have seen that in August over 1,000 men from the First had deserted to the Third.[51] General Zankevich did not think much of these "deserters" and was justifiably suspicious of their motives, although very few of them, if any, were spies designed to be a fifth column. Probably most were men who saw the bleak future for the mutineers and wanted no part of being on the losing side. This attitude did not mean that they held any strong loyalty for the Provisional Government; they simply wanted to save their own skin. They had been able to leave the camp only in small groups because the La Courtine Soviet had expected some defections and had posted guards around the compound to keep them inside. They had had to use a ruse of some sort in order to escape, and most of them left without their arms.[52] Even without these men Zankevich was not pleased with the quality of this newly formed Second Special Brigade, which he felt had "a little shaky mood," and he feared its reliability in attack.

What probably gave the new brigade some emotional reinforcement was the addition of the Beliaev artillery brigade, which had finally arrived in France from Russia on its way to the Aegean. It had almost been sent elsewhere and had been constituted, reconstituted, embarked and disembarked, and then embarked again. It was only supposed to pass quickly through France on its way to join the Army of the Orient at Salonika. Zankevich's reports show that he planned to rely heavily on it. At the time they were needed in France, they were in Orange, and since they had not been long in France, and the French government had seen to their isolation while they had been within its borders, they were "loyalist" in nature. That is, they would still do as they were told.[53]

Who first thought about using these Salonikan-bound troops is not known. John Reed, the famous American who worked as a propagandist for the Bolsheviks and who was nowhere near the decision-making process, wrote that it was Zankevich.[54] At any rate, the formal request to the Russian government came from Zankevich through Noulens to Tereshchenko. The Russian foreign minister replied that he would pass the request on to the proper authorities—Kerensky—and by the time Noulens reached the French embassy from the foreign ministry, there was already on his desk a note of approval from the Russian government.[55]

On September 12, Zankevich gave Beliaev the formal order to join all Russian forces and French units under the command of General Comby "occupying the line satisfactorily for the lines filled by the units of the Russian brigade."[56] These men were armed with French 75's and sent to the perimeter. Yet even these units from Russia had a taint of revolutionary democracy because the artillery soldiers' committee had earlier passed a resolution "to talk it over" with the *Kurtintsy*, the Russian term for the rebels in La Courtine, to make certain that all possible avenues had been taken to end the affair peacefully. After sending several deputations in and out of the camp, the soldiers' committee came to the conclusion that suppression was the only answer and asked for French weapons.[57] According to Poincaré, in addition to the 75's, they were given rifles as well.

There was no other recourse but to attack. Zankevich and Beliaev devised a plan to take the 1,000 soldiers who had fled the camp and put them under Beliaev's command. He was also given four field searchlights, over six miles of barbed wire, and a hundred rounds of shells for the 75-mm artillery pieces given him by the French.[58] He also was to have under his command 721 infantryman and 26 officers who had come with him from Russia and been brought from Orange to Aubusson. There were two companies of machine gunners, a battery of artillery consisting of six pieces of 75-mm served by Russian artillery men directed by French battery personnel—all for a total of 150 men. They were put through a special training course lasting five or six days. Zankevich quite probably hoped that the time consumed by this special preparation would give the *Kurtintsy* a chance to surrender. They did not.

After September 12, Zankevich began building trenches around the camp, and with the excavated soil he constructed batteries on all the points where there might be some chance of escape. These earthworks were laced with barbed wire at strategic points, and a large guard was established near a church among some tall trees. Orders were given with passwords. Sentinels were placed along the roads and at various intersections. In La Courtine Russian headquarters was installed in the Hotel de Souty, which was cleared of its guests and owner, while a French headquarters was established in the Hotel Moderne. Both centers maintained a formal distance from each other and were cool in their relations. A special telegraphic line was established between the Hotel de Souty and the attacking Russian units.[59]

At 3:00 P.M. on September 14, Russian troops occupied the heights west of the railroad bordering the La Courtine station, and to the north of the camp at the intersection of the railroad and the road to the west of the village of Bombarterie. These troops were led by Colonel Stravinsky and consisted of six companies and eight machine guns. This command was part of Sector West under Colonel Masse. On the Sector North under Colonel Fischer the effectives were six companies of Russian infantry and twelve machine guns. Sector East, occupied only by Russians, began with Sector North at Mont-Pinesu, Puy-de-Chambon to the crossing of La Courtine–St. Oradour with the ridge to the north of the village of La Courtine. There they stationed five companies and twelve machine guns. Artillery was to be four pieces on *Côte 795* to the west of the La Courtine-St. Rémy road, two pieces in the village of Le Coudert, near the route La Courtine-Sornac, for a total of six pieces. Special orders were given to defend La Courtine should the rebels attack. The leadership stressed to the men that discipline would be maintained at all times, and the machine guns should be ready to fire day and night until told otherwise. The Russian command post was south of La Courtine on *Hauteur 822,* and a Russian observation point was placed on *Hauteur 832* to the west of the village of St. Denis.[60]

The French troops were stationed in a rough concentric circle around these Russian troops. The reserve, the 19th regiment of infantry, the 21st dragoons, and the battery of the 246th artillery, was transferred from St. Armand into the sector including Poussanges, Croze, and Felletin. Colonel Barnard, commandant of the 21st dragoons, refined the details of the bivouac. These positions were ordered to be taken up by 4:00 P.M. September 14. The password to enter the sector was "Petrograd."[61]

The Russians were therefore strongly reinforced by the French. Should the attack falter or should the rebels try to attack from the camp, the French could give sufficient support to the Russians at any point on the line. The impression remains, however, that the French encirclement was designed as much to keep the "loyalists" in line as to give them added strength. The possibility of the attackers' cracking had certainly occurred to the French high command, and the French force was prepared to stop it if necessary.

Within the circle was the rebellious First Brigade, or rather what was left of it. Poitevin gives the number at 8,000, which with the reported defection of about 1,000 from the group would be essentially correct. Globa had made preparations himself by digging trenches and making redoubts to prepare for coming attack. His activities had the effect of creating a false rumor among the attackers that the First Brigade was digging a tunnel under them and planned to escape through it behind their lines.[62]

Yet both the attackers and defenders maintained toward each other a casual air of polite relations. The rebels readily sent their sick and later their wounded through the lines to the French dressing stations, and when they attended brigade meetings, they left their arms depot unguarded. The attackers noticed this oversight, and Colonel Farine suggested that some troops make a surgical strike to capture the depot, but the potential hazards of such a venture were noted and ultimately nothing was done about this opportunity.[63] In the midst of all these preparations, a "loyalist" officer with an automobile drove right into the rebel camp to get the large officers' tents in a warehouse there. He told the guard on duty that he wanted them but was formally refused and drove casually off.[64] Even a number of the rebels' horses, denied fodder, wandered out of their stables and around the countryside, passing through both lines in their attempt to find something to eat.[65]

Despite the casualness, however, both the loyal Russian and French leadership knew that this unenthusiastic standoff could not continue and decided that it was time for the final ultimatum. Comby dispatched secret orders to his troops stating that after the order to surrender or even after any fighting began, troops that submitted were authorized to leave the camp in all directions except toward the village of La Courtine, entrance into which was strictly forbidden. Close contact with the Russians was to be maintained. The prefect had earlier demanded the evacuation of the civilian population of La Courtine and several of the surrounding villages. They were encouraged to take their livestock and given careful directions on which roads they were to be sent. Half of the population of La Courtine was directed toward St. Rémy, the other half toward Felletin. They were told that their absence would be of a brief duration, and they would therefore need to carry only a little hand luggage. Train departures for inhabitants would be published the next day, and each family was instructed to prepare for the police a list of the number of persons leaving each house and the direction that they had chosen to depart. The authorities were instructed to stop by each house and collect this information. Those wanting to depart by other means could do so within a given twenty-four-hour period. A civilian guard made of La Courtinians was formed, and all who wanted to join were to present themselves at city hall. About fifty did so.[66]

The order to evacuate caused, according to Gabriel Cluzeland, an eyewitness, "riots in the streets." The citizens were afraid of what would happen to their houses and personal property if matters were serious enough to require their evacuation, and women and young girls cried as they departed. A long line of cars, carts, and streams of pedestrians left to seek hospitality in the villages of St. Rémy, Sornac, St. Setiers, and Felletin. At 3:00 P.M. on the day the last ultimatum was sent, all routes out of the camp were barricaded. From this point onward, the rebellion was completely isolated. The code word to be admitted out of the circle was to be Riga.[67]

The night of September 13-14, the night before Zankevich delivered the final proposition to the mutineers of La Courtine, was a rather raucous one in the encircled camp. The soldiers probably did not know that the last demand that they surrender would come on the morrow, but they knew that they had been completely isolated and they could not have helped but notice that the civilians in the surrounding community had been evacuated. Something obviously was about to happen. The camp soviet held a meeting, but if any minutes were taken, an unlikely event in any case, they have never come to light, so we cannot know exactly what transpired. We can be certain, however, that the debate centered on the new and very well disciplined ring around them. Excited voices shouted at other excited voices. Large numbers of soldiers watched this circus with neither approval nor disapproval, one observer reported. What is amazing is that with an attack clearly imminent, the camp was bathed in the bright light of its own searchlights, which were directed on the large crowds of rebels. A decision was finally reached to send a delegation to negotiate with the leaders of the forces facing them at their headquarters at the Hotel de Sauty. Then, utterly amazingly, several concerts were organized and the soldiers rather cavalierly sang well into the night, as is the custom of Russian soldiers, some haunting lullabies. Other soldiers recited their evening prayers according to the old order of the Imperial Army.[68]

The next day, Zankevich made his last appeal and delivered his final ultimatum. It was sent in person by Colonel Balbashevsky, who walked unescorted into the camp at about 3:30 P.M.[69] and handed it to Globa. Balbashevsky seems to have been an excellent officer. General Comby thought very highly of him and opined to someone that had he been in charge of the Russian force, the mutiny would never have happened, an extended overstatement at best. As he handed the paper to Globa, he supposedly said, "Well, Globa, I have told you that this would come to an end. It's coming to an end now."[70]

The ultimatum itself was addressed not to Globa but to the "Russian Troops in France." It began: "According to the specifications of the Provisional Government in the person of its president and of the minister of war, I have received the order to restore the obedience of the rebellious soldiers of the camp of La Courtine. I order the soldiers of the camp . . . to submit and execute entirely my orders. . . ." Then strangely Zankevich shifted to the third person. "They must deposit their arms at the interior of the camp on the lawn opposite the officers' mess. These arms will be received by the French authorities after the evacuation of the camp" went another peculiar twist. After depositing arms, the soldiers were to leave the camp in all directions except through La Courtine itself. Four assembly points were indicated, and all soldiers were to go to one of them: the village of St. Denis, a point on the road to Felletin, about a mile from the camp, to the north on the route of Beissat to the village of Daigne, and to the east on the road north of the pond of Grattadour, which leads to St. Oradour. Encampment and food was assured at all of these points. Anyone leaving the camp armed was warned that he would be greeted with fire. Any soldiers, whether armed or not, were to be shot if they tried to enter La Courtine. The directive went on to say that in order to give time to disassemble the camp, a deadline of 10:00 A.M. on September 16 was designated. Provisions were to be completely suspended on September 15, and after the September 16 deadline, the artillery would open fire. The decree continued with the admonition that anyone not surrendering by the deadline would lose the right to participate in the elections for the Constituent Assembly, that the allocations to their family would be stopped, and that all of them would be deprived of the advantages that would be accorded under the new democratic regime in Russia. Moreover, those who did not surrender would be court-martialed. The stern document was signed by Zankevich, Rapp, and the captain of the Russian Headquarters, Lieutenant Colonel Galichkin.[71]

The rebel response was not long in coming. After a mass meeting during which Globa harangued the troops, telling them that the French cannons were dummies and that the troops would never attack in earnest, the rebel leader sent a reply, not to Zankevich and those who signed the ultimatum but to the opposing Russian soldiers themselves. Globa had known that he could treat the first ultimatum with contempt, for it was little more than a warning. The second ultimatum, however, was enforceable because the rebels were surrounded by 5,000 well-armed troops with heavy artillery and French support. Whereas with the first ultimatum Globa could contemptuously ask the messenger, "Do you think we are children?" he knew that he had to take this order more seriously. There exist two accounts of the response. Both are lengthy, very similar, and highly melodramatic, and both were addressed to the soldiers of the Third Brigade, to whose nationalism they appealed. Exactly who authored the real response is impossible to say, but probably Globa did not write it completely.

One version began with a statement to the effect that now was not the time to talk about "our interests as the bloodthirsty German presses our Mother Russia from all sides." It asked instead rhetorically what their fellow Russian soldiers were doing at this time "raising their bayonets against their brothers," who were waiting with open arms with the intention "of joining with you and soaring together in the quickest way to the aid of our much-beloved country . . . [which] awaits our prompt return in order to defend against an adversary and dress our deep wounds." There followed appeals for brotherhood and a cry that bygones would be bygones. The reply played on their former comrades' emotions, stating that it would be a shame to raise their hands against their brothers and in the process become traitors to their country. They were reminded of the numerous calls to defend the Russian nation and were then asked, "Who is the traitor, those who advise the disposing of arms so that the ferocious enemy can then oppress our dear country? Do you want that from us?" After more patriotic rhetoric, the rebels called on their besiegers to come to the rebel camp under the leadership of "your officers," under whom they would go together to fight against the enemy and "succor our dear country." There were many professions of love and open-armed friendship, along with reproaches for turning against brothers. Calling for an end to their conflict, the author added the ludicrous notion that their fight was already the "cause of laughter of our ally France." After an appeal to the officers to join them without their stacking their arms, the reply concluded, "Come honestly and we promise to receive you with . . . *musique-en-tête.*"[72]

The other version, the one formally reported to the Russian government, had much the same flavor but with a somewhat different slant. Often outlining how they had shed "not a little blood in the fields of Champagne," the mutineers opined that they did not know who they are: prisoners or free men? They complained about being surrounded by French forces and about not being given bread or other supplies, with the result that they were hungry. "We have in Russia as is known over three million POWs, . . . and they are all fed there, but we citizens of a free Russia . . . go hungry." Stressing that they have done nothing wrong, the response concluded, "If we are culprits to our native land, then we will submit to the judgment of all Russia. Let our brothers judge us there, if we are guilty." It was signed by the brigade committee.[73] Both versions of the response are most cleverly worded and might well have had some effect on the soldiers, especially on the newly arrived Beliaev unit, but it is highly unlikely that any of them were ever allowed to see it. Father Laliron, the French Catholic priest who held the confidence of the mutineers, brought it to the besiegers. He arrived with the response at about 3:00 P.M. on September 15, "with a radiant air," in Comby's words. He seemed to think, or so Comby thought, that he was giving the French general the notice of the mutineers' surrender. Comby told him to return in one hour for the reply to the mutineers.

When the *curé* reappeared for the response, Comby told him, to his stupefaction, that he would not have an answer. The rebels had been given an order and they were only to accept it. There would be no negotiations. Laliron indicated that he must return to the mutineers with this non-response, and General Vidalon and Comby tried to convince the abbé to remain with them because he feared that the rebels might take them hostage. Laliron stated that he had promised to return with some sort of answer and that he therefore would do so. If they took him hostage, then so be it. In typical fatalistic and priestly fashion, he added that his life was worth little and that if the loyalists had to fire on a camp with him in it, then it had to be. "Fire when ready as though I did not exist," he told the two generals. According to Laliron, who later wrote Cluzeland, General Comby responded, "You are the representative of God and the minister of peace — I let you go free."[74]

If that was indeed Comby's response, it has a phony ring. Comby's personal account to Poitevin, given on the same page, simply states that the priest left agitated and returned to the besieged camp. Comby then sent the letter from Globa to Zankevich to keep him up-to-date on the whole affair.[75]

Laliron himself has left a confusing and rather unlikely account of his return to the revolutionary soviet of the First Brigade. He states that he reported the negative answer and tried to convince the rebels that they were not helping France (*sic*) by continuing the struggle. The Russians, most probably through Globa, replied that they would not remain under French officers, and Laliron supposedly replied, "Discipline commands you to submit at first to your [own] officers and then finally you will be able to ask to pass under orders of French officers." This admonition was not received well, and the soldiers shouted, "Freedom! Freedom!" The priest then told them that they were not yet ready for freedom and called on them to reflect on the gravity of their decision. "You will be the cause of a massacre among yourselves," he added, and he guaranteed that no submitting officer (*sic*) would be hurt. The reply was to the effect that they were all unified, and the abbé claimed he said, "So much the worse for you. Tomorrow there will be victims, and you will carry before God and the men the responsibility. That will be my last speech."[76] Globa was unmoved, and as the sun set, the priest began by foot his journey back to town after having received a military salute from the rebels.

Laliron's version seems too detailed. Moreover, it is self-serving and probably not completely accurate. Whatever he did do and say, however, he made the last peaceful contact between the rebels and the loyalists and definitely gave his all for a peaceful solution. The next day he celebrated mass at 9:00 in the morning for both Russian and French officers. One hour later the deadline of the ultimatum expired. This little clergyman never received any medal or recognition for his attempts at a peaceful solution. He died on December 30, 1930, and was buried in a small cemetery in his native village of Millevache.

The encircled *Kurtintsy* made an additional eleventh-hour effort at a peaceful solution by once again going over the heads of the Russian officers and appealing to the men themselves. The day before the final deadline expired, the rebels sent an open letter to their "comrades and brothers of the Third Brigade." Noting that the "longed-for day has come for the bourgeois and bloodsucking officers" who "wish to drink the blood of the glorious defenders of the country and freedom," the *Kurtintsy* reminded their comrades in the Third how many of them had died together at Courcy in Champagne and then observed how now brother was fighting brother, to the delight of the bourgeois officers who want the return of the old dynasty. Calling on them to join the First Brigade, they told their former comrades that they would receive them with "brotherly love." Labeling all officers "liars," the rebels appealed to their comrades not to obey their orders. Condemning those who were complying, they told them, "Leave us; you are not sons to us" but "murderers of our fathers, brothers and mothers."[77]

Again there is little likelihood that this appeal reached the ears of the soldiers surrounding them. Since the men had been carefully chosen for their job, it probably would have had little effect, but the officers who did see the missive could hardly have taken that chance. The pleas of the First Brigade were not, however, limited only to the forces surrounding them. Even after they were encircled, they wrote letters to various places, and, amazingly, some arrived at their destination. One letter written in August was published in Russia in *Izvestiia*,[78] containing a pathetic plea for help in a dramatic and partially untrue description of the situation. Calling for aid and stating that they were "oppressed by the bourgeoisie and our officers," the letter noted that the rebels were being starved and "were going barefooted and naked, surrounded by French forces like the German enemies," adding "They want to shoot us because we want to go home." They included with this note Kerensky's instruction of July 30 restoring the death penalty and calling for the brutal restoration of iron discipline on the French front. They sent a similar letter to an unidentified French newspaper which referred to the whole affair as a "shame for the country [France]," then asked rhetorically, "Is it possible your government thinks that all this will remain secret?"[79]

No help came, of course, and on September 15, Comby ordered half rations be given the encircled soldiers at noon and every day thereafter. The mutineers refused even the half rations, but Comby returned them, feeling that for propaganda reasons it would be better to have provided something.[80] For the rest of the day, things were quiet and, curiously, no order of the day appeared.[81] The besiegers must have been quite tense, but as Obey has told us, they were ready to do their duty. As for the besieged, they were probably calmer, primarily because they actually thought that their opponents would never fire on them. The loyalists for the most part hoped that force would not be necessary. Both sides came to be greatly disappointed.

Surprisingly, no in-depth official French government version of the final days of the La Courtine affair seems to exist. The notes of the ministry of foreign affairs, rather detailed before and very detailed afterward, are nonexistent for the three days of the battle. None of the rebels has left any dependable blow-by-blow account of events either, and we must depend mostly on Poitevin's work, which leans very heavily on Gabriel Cluzeland's notes, which are nowhere to be found, Colonel Gotua's account, and Zankevich's report to Petrograd. To make matters worse, Cluzeland left La Courtine for Limoges on Sunday morning, September 17 before the battle was over. The events must, therefore, be pieced together largely from bits and crumbs of information gleaned here and there.

The whole confrontation ending in the battle is interesting in that it was basically a dress rehearsal for the Russian Civil War to come, and the French role would be essentially the same: Loyalists of varying sorts backed by French artillery and bayonets opposed Leftist insurgents. In his history of the Russian Revolution, using perhaps a little literary license, Trotsky described the French role in a similar fashion: "Later on the French ruling classes organized a civil war on the territory of Russia herself, surrounding it with the barbed ring of the blockade."[82] Yet the significance of the incident passed unnoticed at the time, if for no other reason that it largely remained a secret. Only later, under a Bolshevik government, would the events of La Courtine be reported to the Russian public, and then not as news but as propaganda.

The morning of September 16 was clear with the sun flooding the countryside. The light made the long row of white barracks in the camp glisten and stand apart. For the most part the rebel soldiers stayed in their rooms and the camp appeared deserted. Occasionally several soldiers crossed the courtyards between the various buildings carrying out orders of some sort, but there was little other activity. Through binoculars a small group was seen milling around the latrine tempting the artillery that Globa had told them was fake. Cluzeland pondered the painful aspect of this task before the French soldiers who already had the difficult duty of defending the country in danger. "Why is it necessary in our country in the solitude of our *Massif Central*, which is like the calm heart of France, [to have] an unfortunate task to impose on our friends already additional suffering from the spilling of blood?"[83] he asked himself.

Shortly before the expiration of the 10:00 A.M. deadline that morning, Generals Comby, Vidalon, and Louis Brezet left their camps and went up onto the Rue de l'Eglise located on the right of a small road that passed by the parsonage and climbed the bank from which the panorama of the camp was arrayed before them. From there they had a clear view of both the *"vrais"* and the *"faux"* Russians, and from this vantage point they could direct the conflict between the two Russian forces. Among them were a few civilians, mostly local politicians such as Connevot, a deputy in the National Assembly, Rischmann, the prefect of La Creuse, Le Bihan, the vice prefect of Aubusson, and the Abbé Laliron. Around them a slight breeze blew over the unfolding battle that pitted Russian against Russian.[84]

By 10:00 A.M. there had been no response from the rebels. This time, unlike in the past, the order went out for the artillery to fire, and shortly afterward with the thunder of the guns, the Battle of La Courtine began. Pavel Karev, a rebel in the camp, and therefore not someone who really could have known, claims that the French artillerists were ordered to fire first and that they refused, stating that they had fought the Germans on the same side as these Russians and that they therefore could not attack them. Zankevich, according to Karev, who most assuredly never talked with the general, turned the artillery over to the Russian officers, who together with the French officers opened fire.[85]

Not only is the story unlikely, we know that the French were not ordered to fire first. Furthermore, we have seen to what great lengths the government in Paris had gone to avoid any involvement by the French military. It was also unlikely that after the days of preparations, the French artillerists would have been surprised when ordered to fire. Throughout, Karev's recollections have the flavor of having been the subject of much postrevolutionary political correctness.

The first shots fired, however, were four blanks from the French 75's in apparent hopes that the mere sound of artillery would induce the desired surrender. The next three shells fired were dud exercise projectiles fired off target and for range practice. They all struck a hill near the barracks. These first phony and trial salvos, however, merely confirmed the belief in the camp that the besiegers would not really attack and that the French cannons were "quaker guns." A few shots were fired closer to the barracks. The *Kurtintsy*, however, now feeling that they had nothing to fear from the attackers, poured armed into the streets of the camp with an almost festive air and cheered as other shells landed in the camp. Vavilov wrote that one shell fell into the crowd, resulting in three rebels' being wounded and nine killed,[86] a false statement, unless all mutineers who died in the entire three-day battle did so as a result of this one volley. The *Kurtintsy* did not return the fire, in part because they had no artillery, but instead responded with the camp orchestra's playing Chopin's

"Funeral March" and the French national anthem. These first few shots ended the morning round of the battle, and both sides took a four-hour lunch break.

In the afternoon the firing began again, but this time it was less of a farce. Obey wrote, "We are petrified. [When a shell is fired] we listen stupidly to the crickets chirping and count the seconds. Then . . . the shock of the explosion reaches us."[87] From this point to the end of the battle, Obey claims, probably somewhat exaggeratedly, that a shell was fired on the camp every thirty seconds in what he metaphorically calls "the Dance of the Cannons." The artillery attendants worked silently. The *chef de pièce* would raise his hand with an air of boredom, the cannon would quickly recoil, followed by the clicking of the ejection of the smoking casing, "all without speech."[88]

With the early-afternoon attack, the *Kurtintsy* began to realize that the fighting was real and the singing ceased. The resumption of the bombardment cut short a band's rendition of a Russian folksong with the ironic title "It is in vain that you are making this trip, my boy." There was a wild rush for cover into the more substantial buildings made of stone and brick, and for the first time it must have dawned on many of the defenders that they must either surrender or risk dying. Later in the day there was another lull in the firing to give any who wanted to surrender a chance to do so. By the time the attack stopped for the day at about 8:00 P.M., 160 men had given up.[89] Others had tried but had been shot by their own sentinels, one dying in the dirt of the road between the opposing forces. By morning the additional number that surrendered in the night was a disappointingly-small 200, probably because of a fear of being shot by their own comrades if they tried. In a chivalry rarely seen in war, however, all wounded rebels both inside and outside the camp were evacuated in French ambulances to a hospital in Ussel.[90]

General Brezet and General Beliaev, however, waited for the mutineers to strike their colors, but they waited in vain. The rebels remained defiant. All day there had been the exchange of fire from trench to trench, accompanied by the crackling noise of the machine guns. Even though the action had taken a serious turn, it remained somewhat desultory and halfhearted, with neither trying to make too great an effort to hurt the other. That night after the firing stopped, Globa had the bright camp lights lit, clearly revealing the defenses to the attackers. For the most part these places remained untouched by shell fire, indicating that the attackers were not seriously trying to destroy the camp and were still hoping for a peaceful surrender. Zankevich reported that only eighteen shells had been fired, with only one death and eleven wounded.[91] Although the rebels complained of no food, Zankevich seemed to think that they had ample supplies from the camp stores and kitchen gardens.[92] In his report to his government, Zankevich cited the 160 prisoners, noting that the small number was due to the mutineers' closing of all exits from the camp.[93]

On the morning of the second day of the siege, however, General Brezet intensified the attack. At 10:00 A.M. forty shells (Zankevich reported thirty) very quickly burst on the enclosure. Expecting an infantry assault, the defenders braced for an attack that did not come, and the besieging artillery only returned to their methodical lobbing of shells into nonstrategic places in the camp. The defenders' return fire consisted only of the usual music they had played for days. At noon the attackers stopped firing and continued only after a leisurely luncheon of three hours. Despite the casual nature of the fighting, however, inside the resistance was crumbling, and clearly resolve had seriously weakened during the night. Food was running out and by the second day of the battle, all that was left to eat was the hardtack and preserves in the regimental storehouse. According to Vavilov, the horses, which also had had nothing to eat, were restless, and on that day the *Kurtintsy* began to consume the meat of those horses that he states had died of starvation,[94] hardly the case after only two or three days without food.

By late morning (Comby remembered early afternoon) small white flags began to appear, and groups began to desert the camp, carrying with them personal belongings but leaving their rifles behind. By early afternoon, despite Globa's urging, the rebels began to surrender in greater numbers. Both as individuals and in small groups, the mutineers started to leave the camp waving their white flags. The number had become too large for those remaining to stop the desertions, and the fact that they did not shoot these men indicates that the hardcore elements must have realized that they were vastly outnumbered. A few of those leaving were drunk, but many seemed simply downcast. They formed, apparently without being told to do so, columns of four and marched off passively into captivity. In what could only have been a desperation move, the rebel leadership released that same day all their remaining horses, some 800 in all, and these streamed out of their pens and into the surrounding countryside. Most were rounded up and taken to a large nearby pasture, where there was water and grass on which to graze.

Comby later described those men who called it quits "sullen and resigned," except for a few who were drunk. One inebriated Russian approached a general to surrender and, when raising his hand to salute, he staggered and passed out at the general's feet.[95] No resistance came from one group of several hundred rebels who were left guarded by only a couple of soldiers and a corporal. Comby called the 19th battalion, a squadron of reserves at la Courtine, and another battalion at Malleret to guard the increasing number of prisoners. Around 7,500 to 8,000 men (Gotua reported only 3,500) surrendered that day, and they were herded to the north and south of the route to Eygurande.

Yet there remained 500 or so fanatical mutineers who refused to surrender and who barricaded themselves in the camp hospital and the officers' mess, from which they continued to resist as darkness fell, opening up with machine-gun and rifle fire.[96] Rain had begun to fall that day, and throughout the cold wet night of September 17-18 the 75's fired on the camp. The encircling Russians drove in the few mutineers still remaining in the trenches, most of whom left probably because of the cold rain rather than artillery fire. Zankevich reported that day that three had died and thirty-six had been wounded.[97]

During the course of the day some written communication had occurred between Globa on the one hand and Zankevich, Lokhvitsky, Beliaev, and Rapp on the other. When this curious statement was sent is unknown. Zankevich reported to his government that it had originated with Globa, written in a clumsy, uneducated Russian: "Your [*sic*] sacrifices are already too great," it began. "Wounds flow with blood. There is no help. They are dying from lack of medical care." He pleaded with them to stop the shooting and then invited them to "come and stack the rifles or tell us where to put them."[98] In view of Globa's repeated refusal to surrender, this note is strange indeed, yet it is unlikely that Zankevich would have fabricated it, since to do so would have had no point. It shall ever remain one of the mysteries surrounding this most unusual affair.

On the third day of the battle, September 18, another attack began about noon. According to Vavilov, the defenders were not able to clear away "our dead," and there was no place to put the wounded because the brigade police station was full.[99] Gradually the loyalists under General Beliaev advanced into the camp, taking building after building. As they surrendered more and more of the enclosure, rebels slipped out of the barracks and into the woods to the north. Barracks Grattadour and Laval fell to the invaders, as did the officers' mess. The fighting must have been much like the artillery fire as there were few casualties, although one loyalist did die by a rebel's revolver fire. By the end of the day the camp was taken but a few mutineers still held out in the Le Breuil barracks and the woods to the north. There the artillery rained shells somewhat indiscriminately.[100]

An unfortunate episode occurred on the last full day of the battle involving an army postmaster and his assistant, who must have been oblivious to the events of the previous days. As if nothing were happening, they approached as they had done every day the Le Breuil barracks with letters of the battalion from La Croix d'Echaron postal station. Amazingly neither French nor Russian sentries on either side stopped the two men before they arrived at the barracks. The Russian rebels opened fire on these unfortunate men, mortally wounding in the abdomen Sergeant Pierre-Marie Lemeur, a thirty-six-year-old father of six children, and shooting Sergeant Yves Féger in the thigh. Féger managed to turn the car around and head back under continuing rain of bullets, but Lemeur could only cry out *"Mes petits! Mes pauvres petites!"* Lemeur died in a hospital in Felletin and Féger spent five months recovering, only returning to the army in 1918. The vehicle on which the rebels had fired was an ambulance that bore the red cross.[101]

By dawn on September 19 only the woods to the north of the camp was in rebel hands, and by 10:00 A.M. a white flag went up and the last hundred or so *Kurtintsy* surrendered. The total number of captives was so great that not all could be searched until the following day. Orders were given to feed them since many had not eaten for several days. Poitevin states that there was an American general present at the surrender who congratulated Comby by saying "I did not believe, general, that you would get rid of this bunch of lice so elegantly."[102] The fact that the last of the rebels had taken refuge in the woods north of the town, however, led to a false legend that continued for years in La Corrèz that "savage Russian soldiers" still lived in dens and lairs not wanting to come out.[103]

The overall casualties were much lighter than Vavilov states, indicating the gentle nature of the suppression. Zankevich reported that by the end of September 18 the mutineers had lost only ten dead and forty-four wounded. He felt, however, the losses were worse because on the second day, those trying to escape were fired on by some of their own machine guns. Where he obtained his numbers, he does not say, and why those shot by their own men are not counted he also neglects to explain. As for the attackers, they lost one killed and three wounded.[104] Whether this number includes the unfortunate postmaster or not, Zankevich does not tell us.

The last 500 holdouts were formed into ranks after capture under French guard, and they received a stern tongue-lashing from Rapp. Of this number, 81 of the worst were isolated and sent to the Russian authorities at Bordeaux. The others were taken various places. John Reed claimed in his famous book *Ten Days that Shook the World* that the Provisional Government's "official report" was not true and that documents discovered in the ministry of foreign affairs proved its mendacity. Reed concludes, without saying were he obtained his information, that over 200 of the mutineers were shot in cold blood.[105] There is no evidence whatsoever to substantiate this tale, and the fact that we know that the most dangerous of the group were not executed indicates that Reed was merely doing his job as chief propagandist for the Bolshevik cause.

As for Globa, he had not waited in the forest to be captured but had tried to escape with his French mistress. A patrol of three loyalist Russian lancers caught them while they were fleeing down the road to St. Sentiers. When approached, he did not resist, and he and his lady friend were taken under guard to La Courtine. The woman had apparently joined him in the camp at some point before the battle had begun and had been living with him ever since. When the lancers returned with the two to La Courtine, she was released and allowed to go home to await the wrath of her husband when on his next leave. As for Globa, he strutted around until he was taken to French headquarters. When a general addressed him, Globa arrogantly replied that he was not taking any orders from officers. He joined the group sent to Bordeaux. Although the French government had captured Globa, it had not heard the last of this salesman turned revolutionary.

Despite the cautious suppression, the lightness of the casualties is rather surprising. As we have noted, officially ten Russians were killed and forty-four wounded. Lissovsky gives the same number killed but states that only five were wounded.[106] Foch wired the cabinet that nine had been killed and forty-six wounded, with the majority of those casualties having been caused by the fire of the rebels themselves who turned their machine guns on comrades who tried to escape the camp. Foch advised the government to inform the French ambassador in Petrograd so that he might correct any inexact versions of the casualty numbers made there by the enemies of France.[107]

Apparently only one Frenchman, the unfortunate Lemeur, was killed. Both he and Féger were awarded the Cross of St. George. None of the reports speaks of any dead loyalists, but *Rabochii put'* (The Workers' Way), a Leftist paper in Petrograd, reported that one of the attackers was killed and five wounded.[108] We do have an account of one loyalist having died, so the one reported in the Leftist Russian press was probably he. A service for the dead loyalist was held at 9:00 A.M. on September 19, and according to the Russian custom, the coffin was carried by officers.[109] On October 30, a week before the Provisional Government would become just so much history, it released a brief, factual statement that raised more questions than it answered and only gave the Left more anti-Allied propaganda.[110]

As the captives were led away, they must have wondered about their fate. In the old Russian army, most would have been executed, and they must have feared that this end awaited them. Vavilov thought about trying to escape but decided not to attempt it. "We just walked and walked, and walked," he wrote as he recorded his recollections years later. As he marched, he pondered life and death.[111] As for the French government, it must have breathed a collective sigh of relief that the Russian force was disarmed and under control. Most probably it thought that the problem was now finished. Few of the French ministers or generals involved in the affair of La Courtine could have guessed that their troubles with the Russian soldiers whom they had so eagerly "bought with shells" over two years before were really just beginning.

1. Russian Troops in Paris on the Champs Elysée, 1916 (Danilov, *Russkie Otriady*).

2. Section of Russian trenches on the Western Front (Danilov, *Russkie Otriady*).

3. General Lokhvitsky (Bibliotheque Nationale, Paris).

4. General Palitsyn reviewing Russian troops (Bibliotheque Nationale, Paris).

5. (Next page) Russian flag guard at a July 14 celebration, 1916 (Bibliotheque Nationale, Paris).

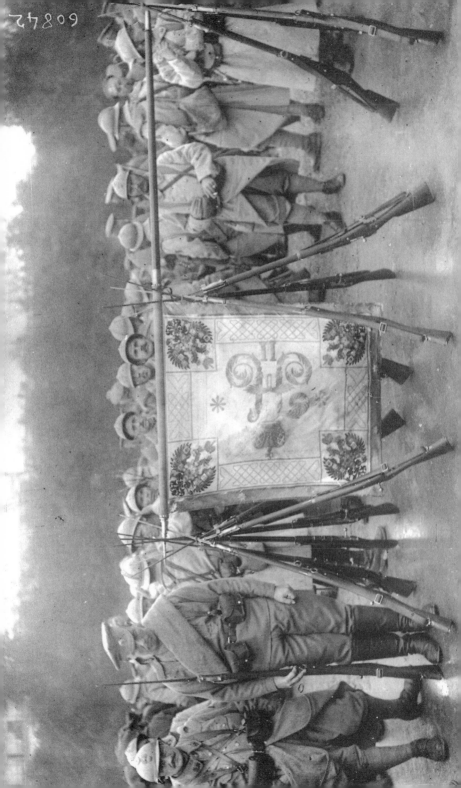

6. Russian wounded strolling in Paris, 1917 (Bibliotheque Nationale, Paris).

7. Globa, rebellion leader, in captivity (Poitevin, *Une Bataille*).

8. The Russian Military Cemetery and church at Mourmelon-le-Grand. (Courtesy of the Association du Souvenir du Corps Expéditionnaire Russe en France.)

9. The monument to the Russian dead at Mourmelon-le-Grand, courtesy of the Association du Souvenir du Corps Expéditionnaire Russe en France.

10. "France's Easter Eggs: The Russians have disembarked at Marseille."
Le Matin, 24 April 1916.

11. "Russian Brothers." The caption reads: "You don't speak French; I'm
going to teach you. Say: 'We'll take them!'" (Tu ne parle pas francais; je vais
de l'apprendre. Dis: On les aura.) *Echo de Paris,* 22 April 1916.

EIGHT

White Slaves of Capitalism

September 1917–January 1918

The majority of the soldiers want to return to Russia simply because they believe that since the Revolution their country has become the happiest on earth and the life there is comparable to that of a terrestrial paradise. The civil war, the famine, the horrors of the German occupation are for them only things invented by the Allies....

—General Jean Brulard[1]

We, Russian men, soldiers of the Revolutionary Army and citizens of a Free Russia, consider it insulting ... to pave streets, dig trenches, [and] cut wood, at a time when the national sentiment of the Russian citizen calls every one to rise for the defense of individual liberty of the whole world.

—Resolution of the General Assembly
of the Soldiers of the 2nd Russian Regiment[2]

They want us to work, but we will not go.

—Private Egorov[3]

"Tell me frankly, [Lokhvitsky said,] what reason you have for asking to return to Russia?"

"Above all, Your Excellency, [Rychlinsky replied,] the desire to see the blue eyes of my Natasha."

—Vladimir Rychlinski[4]

AFTER THE COMPLETE DEFEAT OF THE REBELLION, the "victors" quickly departed. On September 19 the 750 to 800 soldiers of the Russian artillery unit took their guns to Aubusson and then moved to Orange, and the battalions of "loyalists" returned to their camp on September 21 and 22. The French troops who refereed the battle were sent to the zone of the armies on September 23 and 24. Their departure left only a skeleton crew to guard the now somewhat docile *Kurtintsy*. The rebel brigade's troops, according to one Russian eyewitness, were robbed of their belongings and stripped of their shirts and boots,[5] a statement that is most assuredly false, since it will be shown that they were not terribly well disarmed. Yet legends were spawned. Years later locals made the preposterous claim to Poitevin that they had seen "convoys of wagons carrying dead bodies to fill up the trenches,"[6] and seven years after the mutiny, *Pravda* quoted a rebel soldier T. Dmitriev, remembering that over two hundred had been killed and in order to hide this "murder," the French reorganized the units of troops.[7]

There had already been, and would continue to be, a great deal of reshuffling of the Russian troops in France, but not for the purpose of hiding any French misbehavior. Given the potential seriousness of the situation and the general nuisance of the Russian mutiny to the French republic, the French army and government showed remarkable restraint in suppressing the affair. The natural inclination would have been to smash the Russian revolt quickly, but the French carefully and adroitly avoided such action because of the potential propaganda harm that could be done to them by Germany and in Russia. They took a great risk in doing so.

By September 19 the problem seemed over. Indeed the worst of the crisis was, but the French still had within their borders, two brigades of more than 15,000 unstable Russian troops, not counting several thousand housed in hospitals about France, that did not want to be there and whose government did not want them returned. By October the two original brigades were barely distinguishable. By mid-October there were 6,970 men at Courneau, most of whom were probably from the Third Brigade, 7,500 at La Courtine, probably all of whom were from the First Brigade, 300 at the prison at Camp Bourg-Lastic, and 249 in the prison at Île d'Aix. In Bordeaux there were 103 being held awaiting trial.[8] As they continued to churn these men around, the numbers in various places of detention changed almost daily. Moreover, these men had to be fed, clothed, and sheltered whether they were of any military or work value or not. There also remained varying degrees of order among them, from those who were completely patriotic and would have been willing, indeed eager, to return to the French front to fight, to those who were conscious agents of the German cause or of Bolshevism, the specter of which was beginning to haunt Petrograd in September 1917. Even if they had been sent home quickly, they would have to be segregated according to the degree of discipline of each soldier, with the most incorrigible isolated from the others to prevent any worsening of morale and behavior. After La Courtine, many headaches lay ahead for the French government.

The defeated rebels passed in review before the French and Russian headquarters in the camp that they had so recently defended. Standing silently in the square, the men were lectured like truant schoolboys by Commissioner Rapp, who, calling their behavior "unspeakable," told them that it pained him as an old revolutionary to have to help "suppress such an outrage to the Revolution."[9] Throughout Rapp's lecture, Lokhvitsky stood silently and said nothing. After Rapp finished, the unfortunate general slipped quietly past the others into the company barracks.[10] Poitevin noted that he was fighting back the tears.

There followed an interrogation of the soldiers that revealed little information of worth. Obey re-creates a conversation between a Russian soldier and his interrogator, who always spoke to the Russians in pigeon French (*petit-nègre*): "Cannons? Hou . . . Hou. . . . Bad, cannons. We not afraid, massié [monsieur]; we soldiers. Understand? We much hungry. Yes. Here is why. Understand?" They pull open their shirts and show their scars. "A shell explosion. . . . Machine gun ball . . . Courcy, yes. . . . Champagne."

The inquest did reveal an interesting set of perceptions from the mutineers. One peasant soldier from Perm *guberniia* blamed the revolt on the abdication of the tsar, an explanation likewise given by more sophisticated minds on the Eastern Front. Their oath had been to the tsar, he noted, and now that the tsar was gone, they owed no one any allegiance. "When we heard that the tsar had abdicated . . . and thought about it, [we thought] that for them [*sic*] the war had ended." He continued, "Indeed the tsar had sent us to war . . . , yet I still rotted in the trenches. . . . For three years I rotted. . . . But Kerensky again said about the war that it was necessary to fight again." Then he added, "Here it seemed to us that something was not right. . . . We are the dark people [*temnyi narod*]."[11]

The perceptions of the rebel leadership were somewhat more sophisticated, articulate, and of course more theoretical, although little detail of what they told investigators or wrote to friends seems to have survived. Baltais, who had been captured before the attack, seems to have gotten a little help from the Bolsheviks. He was interrogated by 2nd Lieutenant Janvich [Iulii?] Julievich Kolkovsky, the Commandant of the

Place Russe de la Courtine after the suppression. This lieutenant myste-riously used his position twice to suspend Baltais's inquest, on action that aroused police suspicion. Examining Kolkovsky's background, they learned that he lavishly spent great sums of money, although he had no income beyond his modest salary. The French police were able to deter-mine that he received his surplus funds from some mysterious woman, but they could neither identify her nor trace her whereabouts.[12] When Globa was asked to explain his actions, he replied that he had led the revolt in order to "save the revolution." He added, "We saved freedom. We were not able to do otherwise."[13]

The French and the Russian officers divided the mutineers into three categories based largely on each soldier's political reliability. The first group, Category A, were those who would not join a fighting unit but were otherwise not thought dangerous. About 7,500 of the First Brigade fell into this category. They were all placed under a company commander and were installed at Grattadour near La Courtine, where Colonel Farine remained at his post as camp commandant.[14] All of these were under the careful supervision of the French troops, although Vidalon advised that a special effort to see that black troops should not be used to guard the Russians. When these African troops had been used to control the muti-neers immediately after the siege, the radical Left in Russia had made much of the fact.[15]

Category B was comprised of the most culpable, the "incorrigibles," who refused either to fight or to work for the French. The French subsorted Category B, which numbered 549 men a day or two after the siege, into groups based on their degree of hostility, and 300 of them were sent under escort to Camp Bourg-Lastic in the 13th region (Clermont-Ferrand) on September 20, and 249 to Île d'Aix on September 21. In a directive, Foch described this category as "dangerous elements for public order," and ultimately most were sent to North Africa to isolate them completely from more stable Russian elements and the French troops. The first 81 of these, including Globa, were dispatched under heavy escort to Bordeaux to be placed under Russian military authorities, at least nomi-nally. Vavilov has left us a sensational account of the special treatment of the Category B "incorrigibles." The day of the final surrender on Septem-ber 19, the prisoners were led around until about 2:00 A.M., when they were taken into a little hamlet where the captors' headquarters was located. They were herded into a room in which they had to sleep on a cold asphalt floor. In the morning they were taken to a breakfast consisting of only a cup of water, although later they were given more substantial rations. At some point after breakfast they were returned to La Courtine,

which was well guarded by "the enemy" with "machine guns everywhere."
There they were left in an open square. September 21 was cold and rainy,
and the mutineers remained under the open sky. Some were given overcoats, some were not. Vavilov states that a group of 200 men huddled
together to keep warm. That next day they were taken to the station and
loaded into railroad prison wagons without being told where they were
going. Through the slats they could see only passing train platforms.
Standing on one of them was an old woman, Vavilov tells us, who at first
stood silently looking at the passing train, and then in what must have
most certainly been some postrevolutionary editing, cried out, "Bolshevik! Lenin! *les boches!* I spit in your face!" On September 22 they arrived
at a prison at Bordeaux. At 8:00 the next morning, they were given a third
of a pound of bread for breakfast, and that was to be the daily ration from
then on. Coffee was also served. For lunch they got beans, and for supper
only bitter coffee with no sugar.[16]

The captives in these two categories continued the previous lack of
discipline. For example, on September 24 two companies refused to
assemble for morning muster and finally did so only under the threat of
French intervention.[17] There are many reports of thefts and beatings
among the ranks of the mutineers, with the guilty men usually being
turned over to the Russian officers, who continued to do little to the
culprits. French reports are replete with incidents of officers avoiding
their duty, and their performance did not improve with the suppression
of the mutiny. This lack of control resulted in the natural disintegration
of cleanliness and hygiene in the camps, a problem that was less immediate
but potentially dangerous. Early in November Comby visited La Courtine
and reported that things were "less and less good." Noting that the camp
was not in proper order, he added that the "filth was piling up."[18] General
John Pershing, who also visited La Courtine, was disgusted with the
conditions and sloth there among the men, whom he described as a "heavy,
stupid-looking lot." He observed that they did not care how bad things
were so long as the French continued to feed and clothe them.[19] Moreover, if the men did not clean their own surroundings, it is not surprising
that they would not care for their horses. Major General James Harbord
of the American Expeditionary Force visited the stables at La Courtine
and was surprised to see 900 horses "poor and uncared for, standing in
mud to their fetlocks." He concluded with the observation that he had
never seen "a dirtier place than their [the Russian] camp."[20] Not surprisingly, the poor sanitation led to the outbreak of disease. Typhoid fever
appeared in both La Courtine and Courneau in October, and a French
health inspector was sent to Courneau to determine the cause. After an

investigation, he reported that it was the "lamentable filth" in the camp.[21] Added to typhoid fever were the additional headaches of venereal disease and chronic drunkenness. Both states of ill health indicate that guards did not strictly enforce the camp boundaries, although many cases of venereal diseases might have been contracted before the mutiny had been suppressed. A report to the French government late in November saw a "social peril" in the making.[22]

With the suppression of the mutiny there came from Petrograd a fresh echo of the demand from the impotent Provisional Government for the Russian officers in France to restore the old iron will. On September 27 Tereshchenko, who would not have to enforce his own directives, told Noulens that "a certain number of examples must be made among the mutineers who are arrested." The Russian foreign minister did not fear the adverse reaction to a firing squad, because he told Noulens that "events which are going to take place in Petrograd" will either permit the restoration of discipline in the army or give victory to "the elements of trouble." In short, the Russian foreign minister expected that there should be a showdown, a military-political armageddon with the Bolshevik-controlled soviet, and any repressive measures taken in France would not change the face of things in Russia itself.[23] Yet the French knew that its military would have to take any firm action that would be taken, and the repercussions would not be pleasant for either France or its allies. Something more in line with the gentle approach applied thus far was the only answer until the situation could be dumped into the lap of the Provisional Government with the repatriation of the troublesome soldiers.

The French military held a meeting in General Vidalon's office in the afternoon of October 20 to discuss a plan of action to be taken to contain the problem until the Russian soldiers could be shipped home. Lokhvitsky was present as a representative for Zankevich, who for some reason could not be there. There were also some individuals from the French army headquarters. It was at this convocation that Lokhvitsky planted the seed for the third grouping, Category C. He had already discussed the possibility with Zankevich, who had wired the Provisional Government about the mood of the men and suggested that a fighting unit be formed. Not waiting for a reply from Petrograd, Lokhvitsky informed the Third Brigade's committee that the response from the capital would be favorable and that they should be prepared at the first opportunity to take a sector of the front.[24] Whether Vidalon knew in advance of Lokhvitsky's suggestion or not, at the meeting the French general explained the need to him and asked if loyalist volunteers from the various groups could be sent to the lines and also if workers from both camps for various jobs could be recruited. He suggested that the remainder of the Russians be kept in Courneau.

Showing less enthusiasm for the project to the French than he had to the Brigade committee, Lokhvitsky replied that at present it was not possible to form battalions of volunteers because such orders had not come from the Provisional Government. On the other hand, he agreed that work units could be created and that 4,000 to 5,000 of the 7,800 *(sic)* effectives could be utilized.[25] The French officers accepted what Lokhvitsky had to say apparently without discussion or queries, or if they did have questions—and they should have—they do not appear in the report. After saying his piece, Lokhvitsky left and the French officers then began to decide what to do without any Russian input, any of which would have been rather useless anyway. Despite Lokhvitsky's fears, they decided to proceed basically with the plan to disperse the Russians in the manner in which they had outlined earlier. La Courtine had to be cleared because it was needed for Americans, who would be arriving soon. They also decided to accelerate the formation of workers' battalions and put those who refused to work in barracks guarded presumably by the French.[26]

Yet the situation at Courneau, while not as bad as that at La Courtine, was much less than desirable. The soldiers who inhabited the camp were basically those from the Third Brigade, who had been taken there for triage and had not been considered reliable. Soldiers came and went from the camp at will, causing trouble in the community. These supposedly loyal troops held continuous wild meetings, where all sorts of resolutions were voted, including one to arrest Zankevich, Ignatiev, and unit officers. One statement passed does support Lokhvitsky's contention of Allied loyalty: The soldiers would march to the front, but only under an officer that they had elected.[27] Not surprisingly, this camp likewise had become quite filthy. General Pershing inspected it, staying for about an hour and a half, and was as appalled at the terrible state, as he had been at La Courtine. For the conditions he raked over two Russian officers. In his diary he described the compound as "the most unsanitary place I have ever seen" and added later, "the [sanitary] conditions there may better be imagined than described."[28]

Lokhvitsky visited both Courneau and Île d'Aix with an idea of making recommendations for improving morale. He suggested the building of new barracks and supplying cutlery and plates. He found the food "a little feeble" and asked that it be increased. The soldiers themselves asked particularly for more potatoes. They also wished to receive a Russian-language journal of some sort.[29] Whether these recommendations were followed is not known, but if they were implemented, they did not accomplish their goal of improving morale.

Moreover, the problems of indiscipline and the unrest that the soldiers caused in the environs were exacerbated by the fact that the Russians had never been completely disarmed. Elements among these troops were not so reliable, probably because they had been infected by the lax attitude of both camps, and being armed made them especially dangerous. What was developing in Courneau was an irritation that was turning into a cancer not unlike that at La Courtine. The soldiers would not work, and since they were armed, it would have been difficult to force them to do so. In addition, the French were still paying them their army salary,[30] and this money gave them a greater inducement to venture into the community. There were the usual incidents involving Russian troops roaming the countryside around Courneau, and there was even a reported rape by soldiers Kiselev and Loshikarev in the town of Romoratin, where the local police arrested them. Surprisingly, the gendarmes merely handed them over to the Russian authorities, who sent them to Rochefort-sur-Mer.[31]

The unrest and the rebellious mood was reflected, as usual, in the correspondence, which the French assiduously read but allowed to pass both to Russia and to other groups within the Russian force itself. The political tone was always "patriotic," in the same sense that Lenin and the Bolsheviks were "patriotic," and always antibourgeois, which usually was synonymous with "anti-French." One Private Lashkin sent a note to his father in Russia that somehow arrived and was published in *Sotsial-Demokrat*. "Here in France our life is hard and nasty," Lashkin told his father and by extension his newly acquired extended readership. "We are all the time fighting with the French bourgeoisie and cannot get anything: they trick us all the time and worry us. Besides that," he continued, "our own bourgeoisie help the French. . . . If Russia leaves us here, then we will perish like worms. I would write you more, but you surely will not receive this letter."[32]

The fact that his father did receive the missive should have been some proof that much of what he said about French severity was not true. Even if mailed from a civilian post office, the censors would have noticed any address in Russia and could have intercepted it if they had wanted to. The free flow of mail merely reflects the gentle approach to the Russian problem that the French had used from the beginning. Russian charges that they were brutally mistreated are simply unfounded. As further evidence of French liberality, General Henri Alby of the prime minister's staff complained to Zankevich about the comings and goings of soldiers from Courneau to La Courtine and vice versa in order to obtain their effects or just to visit. The French certainly could have stopped this roving but did not. Instead of intervening in the cross-visiting themselves, they asked the Russians to prevent it with the probable knowledge that the Russian officers would make no attempt to do so.

Of more potential trouble to the French was the election at Courneau of the Congress of Representatives of Russian Troops in France. Exactly when and what gave birth to this curious organization is not clear. Its election appears to have occurred at Courneau just as the "loyalists" from there were finishing the suppression of their comrades at the camp of La Courtine, although something of the sort had already appeared in July. The "second congress" met from October 2 to 6 and was composed of sixty delegates representing four regiments, two *bataillons de dépôt*, and even the southern base at Hyères. Both Rapp and Lokhvitsky were present, certainly as observers. By a vote of twenty-five to five, with two abstentions, the "congress" had decided not to include any representatives from La Courtine because, in the opinion of a delegate Kolchugin, to include the *Kurtintsy* would bring "massacres" into the assembly. The president of the congress, Ensign Dzhornia, had likewise spoken against giving the *Kurtintsy* the right to be included because they had revolted, yet Adjutant Bachikov argued that a majority of the rebels had acted in ignorance and their civil rights should be preserved. A debate followed during which Kerensky was quoted and an analogy was made comparing the *Kurtintsy* to Germans. Exactly why is unclear, but the group did vote to give three places to military units in Paris and five to organizations in the south, presumably the hospitals. Whether the congress was to be a deliberative or consultative body was hotly discussed in unruly sessions, with the latter alternative being finally adopted.

Rapp delivered next a note of welcome praising the democratic organization of the army, which he asserted to be "an institution of the future" despite several inevitable false starts. Much of the following give-and-take seemed to apologize for the collapse of discipline, yet the congress did not seem remotely interested in calling for the restoration of the old authority of the officers. Discussion and debate tried to blame the problems on the absence of military work and training for the past six months, and in general the minutes seem to imply guilt for the military inadequacy.

Dzhornia then gave a report on the conditions of the REF and its hopes for the future. He retraced all of the military activities at the front and then rehashed the causes of the rebellion. He was surprisingly critical of certain measures taken to suppress it. His report was followed by one from Lieutenant Beliaev, a naval officer who seems to have somehow wandered onto the scene, on the possibility of repatriation into Russia in the near future. Essentially his position was that, given the large practical difficulties, it would be at least six months before there would be any chance of returning home. Finally Lokhvitsky and Rapp joined in the discussions.

Lokhvitsky reported that the news from Russia was bad. The Germans had taken control of most of the Baltic coast, and Finland had virtually declared itself independent. Returning home would be difficult. Then he made one of the typically patronizing speeches about soldiers' duties and how these soldiers were "representatives of Russia." He added, "Liberty is not liberty to do everything" and stressed that they must obey the Provisional Government, "not the Right or the Left." He noted that indeed the order was to return home—a doubtful interpretation of what was coming from Petrograd—but he again reiterated a caveat that they must remain calm and disciplined if repatriation was not possible. Delegate Ivanov (probably Ivan) Polosin, a doctor, proposed to accept Lokhvitsky's suggestion, and it was seconded by Delegate Vedensky, also a doctor. Lokhvitsky's motion, although he did not realize that he was introducing one, passed with twenty-two votes.

Lokhvitsky then raised the question of volunteers for the front. There was universal doubt about whether discipline would be maintained in such a force, and Dzhornia added that order had collapsed because "we are not accomplishing our duties as soldiers—all the rest is only a search for excuses." Then he added, "The union of officers and soldiers is possible only under falling shrapnel, and it is only under fire that we will restore it."

The delegates at the meeting also took shots at Rapp and the absent Zankevich. In adding that there had been the lack of a central democratic authority, Rapp was blamed for "not serving at his post," and the debaters accused him of ignoring the life and the needs of the force. General Zankevich was similarly criticized, and the belief was expressed that he must share the blame. The debate also criticized the officers who mostly held themselves aloof from the troops; finally they passed judgment on the soldiers who while not revolutionaries were too quick to forget the welfare of the whole for their own personal gain. It was clear that the general solution was the enactment of the order to send the troops home, a move that the French would have been only too happy to fulfill. A consensus seemed to be that they should elect a deputation of soldiers to the Petrograd Soviet, although no extant minutes signal who if anyone was finally chosen. The meeting then turned to criticism of officers and discussion of health problems, mainly venereal disease, which must have indeed been rampant given the amount of time spent discussing it.[33]

The new presidium of the group, also headed by Dzhornia, remained active after the congress. In the most florid prose, it sent greetings on November 8 to the now-deposed Kerensky, "the great leader of Democracy," and pledged "all our strength, blood and life to the end for you and our free country." It is unclear from their missive whether they knew that Kerensky had been overthrown the day before, yet the congress poured encomiums on the hapless leader as if he were some Russian messiah. Calling him "the one hope for salvation" to defeat the "Bolsheviks and the dark forces of counterrevolution, which have delivered a blow in the back of bloodied Russia," they implored him "to be firm and merciless with the enemies of Russia," pledging support to him "to [their] last breath."[34] It is a pity that Kerensky never received such a ringing affirmation of trust and support. Doubtless it would have cheered him, since he was not receiving such praise from any other part of the Russian political spectrum.

Like almost everyone else, the presidium ignored the Bolshevik coup and proceeded with preparations for the elections of the Constituent Assembly, which were already scheduled to take place in Russia between November 25 and 28. On October 26 a committee of nine men to direct the elections in France was created with some additional members elected in December. The new committee planned to hold meetings, lectures, readings, and distribute flyers to educate the soldier-voters in the functioning of elections.[35] A major problem was whether they should allow the former mutineers to vote. In what must have been a lively meeting on December 23, the election commission decided to delay any decision until it could get some advice or interpretation of a directive on the matter that had been sent in May by the now-defunct Provisional Government.[36] Meanwhile the soldiers' committees remained active, electing leaders, issuing proclamations, and handling such mundane business as book collections from the library, care of the horses, and even the procurement of warm underwear.[37]

This new "democratic" organization, the mere existence of which must have sent shudders through the French authorities, was basically patriotic, but hardly subservient or reactionary. Moreover, the congress had put its finger on some of the most pressing problems facing the Russian troops in France. Although it saw repatriation as a clear answer to the whole affair, discipline had to be reestablished first, not by force, but by remedying the irritants that had caused the difficulties in the first place. To the French military, the mere existence of the congress indicated a potential for future unrest, and there continued to be French suggestions for firm repression, which in reality could be the only successful means of restoring iron discipline at this point. The Russian troops in France had been out of control too long to submit by reason to discipline. At the end of November, Zankevich himself expressed the belief that discussion and logical argument with the Russian troops would not work, and he warned Foch that forcing Russians under French discipline would not restore the Russian will to fight. "The number of soldiers who will agree to act under your conditions will be `minimal,' he wrote the French general with more prescience than he usually demonstrated, "and the remainder will consider themselves wronged and will refuse to be employed as workers." This condition, Zankevich felt, would make necessary armed force "of which I am not disposed."[38]

Meanwhile, the sorting and relocation of the defeated rebels of La Courtine had moved at a casual pace. Two months after the battle, only 1,600 had departed on work details, the creation of which will be discussed later, so there was a scramble to find other places to send the balance of about 5,000 unruly men. With little supervision, these potentially dangerous soldiers later wandered freely about the villages and countryside and caused trouble, again showing that the French had placed no real restrictions even on the detainees after the revolt was suppressed. Moreover, these men lived in the slovenly manner demonstrated before when under no discipline. On December 9, Zankevich tried to crack down. After a necessary call for unity where "each strong arm must be strictly utilized for the goal of our success," he demanded that the soldiers of the camp of La Courtine join detachments to perform war work outside the zone of the armies under officers and under military laws "presently on the books. . . ."[39] With this order, the sorting process did accelerate, but even by the time in December when most of the men had agreed to be dispatched somewhere, 350 men still had managed to resist leaving La Courtine. On December 8 a regiment of cavalry (it is unclear whether they were French or Russian) was sent there to dislodge them, and General Comby ordered Zankevich to issue an ultimatum that either these men join a French work unit or be deported to camps in Algeria. The next day Comby used French soldiers to stop their wanderings, and he gave a final order either to join work details or be deported. The remaining rebels finally were dislodged on December 19, except for a group of 28, who at the last minute had agreed to work and had remained in the camp to be assigned to work details. There were also still at Laval 24 officers and 164 men willing to fight the Germans that had been established. In addition, two soldiers imprisoned at La Courtine would be dispatched to Île d'Aix.[40]

At the time of the Comby-Zankevich decree of December 9, about 5,000 men were still left in La Courtine. Of those, 3,300 were termed "incorrigibles" and eventually were sent to Algeria, with 1,785 volunteering for work details in various regions of France. With the expulsion of the last recalcitrant 350, the infamous camp of La Courtine was finally empty.[41] The barbed wire came down, and all arms were stacked. The weapons that had been confiscated were shipped off in eight wagons to the artillery depot in Angoulême. A report to the French government told its readers, "This affair can be considered terminated."[42] On December 20 the first Americans soldiers, 1,000 men from the corps of engineers, *musique-en-tête*, the French report states,[43] arrived at the camp.

Thousands of rather uncooperative Russians, however, were still on French soil. At the time of the Comby-Zankevich December ultimatum, in addition to the 5,000 at La Courtine, the French had in hospitals 1,867 sick and wounded, 518 who had been discharged, 1,194 convalescing, 106 invalids, 299 escaped Russian prisoners of war, 2,685 in work brigades, and at Courneau 139 officers and over 6,800 men. Thus over 18,000 Russian troops were still in France, even the most disciplined of whom were driven by the one overriding desire to go home. The rebellious forces of La Courtine might be subdued and scattered, but for the French government, the affair was in no way "terminated."

After the defeat of the mutineers in mid-September, a paramount problem faced the French government: what exactly to do in the long term with the thousands of Russians "*vrais*" and "*faux*" on their hands. The simplest solution, of course, was to send them home to whatever Russian government was in power. Yet the difficulty of finding a sufficient number of bottoms to transport them alone made this solution impossible, to say nothing of Russian unwillingness to accept them. Long after the end of the war the simple return of the Russian troops was the French government's first, most desired, and most elusive answer to the Russian question.

The inability to repatriate them immediately made another temporary solution desirable. The hard-core incorrigibles could be sent to Africa, but the simple soldier, whom the French government recognized had merely been led by the radicals, did not deserve or need this type of detention. Moreover, these men might yet be useful to the war effort. France was desperately short of manpower to perform physical labor in the forests, on the farms, in the factories and mines. As early as June 1917 the French minister of agriculture had requested to use some Russian soldiers as farm laborers since they were no longer at the front. The French government initially had rejected the idea because it feared adverse political propaganda, but by October it was giving it a second thought as some men were needed in the sugar works.[44] Even the Americans asked to use some Russian manpower. Pershing discussed the question with Foch and then formally requested some later in a letter. Noting the "urgent need of labor" for construction and terminal work, Pershing added that "negroes" had been sent from the United States for this sort of thing, but "this course is open to objections" since they would take space that could be used to bring American troops. "If the French government has no objection," Pershing wrote, "we would like to obtain a certain number of these Russians for use as laborers. . . ." The American commander-in-chief added that they would be paid $33 per month and would receive the same rations as American troops, thus absolving the French of having to care for them. The number Pershing suggested was 2,000.[45] Petitions soon began flowing in from all over France for some Russian workers — calls for fifty here or a hundred there. From this need a use for Category A came into being.

On October 16 Ribot made a formal request to Zankevich about the possibility of converting these soldiers into workers. Noting that the English would not return them and that they would not fight in France, these men might be used for work, since it is "indispensable and urgent" not to leave them inactive. The French prime minister suggested that Zankevich request his government's permission to form a division of workers from the able-bodied Russians who would not fight.[46] Already in the first week of October the French had designated a naval commander with the very un-French name of O'Neill to organize Russian soldiers for labor because he had been attached for a time to a Russian brigade and knew well the personnel in each unit. This Frenchman, who most certainly had descended from an Irish religious refugee, had been working with the French undersecretary of state for inventions, and the government asked that he be released for this job even before it approached the Russian government and military about the matter. A formal reply in the affirmative came on October 12 from both the vice minister and O'Neill himself, and within a day or two Zankevich received the formal request.[47]

The working conditions and terms, it was finally decided, were to be the same as those of French workers. The Russians were to be kept away from any contact with the Annamites, Indochinese who had been brought into France to do the same type of tasks as the Russians would be conscripted to do, and they were at no time to be exposed to enemy fire.[48] The salary of each laborer was to be three francs for an eight-hour day, paid weekly, with overtime pay for any work more than the required time. The Russian soldier-workers were to be provided food and comfortable lodging, with one day off a week. They were to receive one and a half times the daily rations of a soldier at the front, which was 350 grams of meat, 700 grams of bread, 5 grams of tea, 60 grams of sugar, 30 grams of salad, one soldier's ration of oil, 70 grams of wheaten rice, and a soldier's tobacco allowance. French labor rules would apply concerning accidents occurring on the job.[49] Major General Debeney, commander-in-chief of the armies of the North and North-East, probably spoke for all French commanders in the zone of the armies when, on learning that Russian workers might be sent into the area of his command, gratuitously suggested conditions under which they would serve. Debeney insisted that these Russians be under the authority of French officers who would have the same control over them that they would have over French soldiers.[50]

On October 20, Zankevich supplied from the internees in La Courtine a list of the special manual talents and work experience that could be found there. From over 6,000 men, not surprisingly a large majority, slightly over 4,000 had backgrounds in agricultural work. The second largest group were factory workers, only 350, a surprisingly small number, given the Bolshevik influence that supposedly had come in through proletarian elements. There were 304 carpenters and woodworkers, a curiously high 128 locksmiths, 94 iron and armament workers, 42 painters, a surprisingly high 50 brick masons, 11 plumbers, and 7 mechanics. There were 200 who were specialists in different odd trades that Zankevich decided not to list.[51] All in all, there existed an unusually talented and well-trained element. Getting them to perform, however, might be another matter.

The utilization of Russians for manual work for France was first formally announced at La Courtine on October 23. After the suppression, a "secret committee" apparently had been chosen among the soldiers to replace the official one now detained at Aix, and it replied to the work order with a resounding "*nyet.*" That same day the committee posted a notice in the camp calling on all the soldiers to refuse to work for the French government. "Comrades!" the broadside cried out "Many among us have shown a weakness by beginning to submit to the bourgeoisie. . . . Comrades, it is not necessary to agree to execute this particular work. Those who have signed are doing so at their detriment, as well as that of their comrades who suffer without reason. . . . Refuse [to sign up]!" A second broadside soon appeared that was even stronger: "Refuse categorically all special work and equally so any order to the front. They are deceiving us in telling that there are no boats. These are lies. They do not want to return us to Russia, to help our fathers and our brothers." Once again taking a swipe at the French bourgeoisie, the authors of the flyers informed their skeptical readers that the hour of their return to Russia was near and ended with a resounding "Hurrah!" for all that was going on in Russia and a general condemnation of tyrants, wherever they might be.

A third broadside was somewhat more ideological, scholarly, and dramatic. Announcing that they had not forgotten, nor would they be able to forget, the beating taken at La Courtine, it told its readers that there was only one thought: "To Russia! To Russia! Send us all to Russia as soon as possible." It accused the French of not feeding them, a false accusation, and of sending their "innocent" comrades into unknown places. Denouncing the colleagues who had begun to accept submission, the broadside asked rhetorically, "Is it possible that we would be so brow-beaten, so docile to the point of going to work for a salary?" and then reminded "Your liberty is more dear than all their copper coins." It cautioned that if they returned to Russia having done voluntary work, their brothers would look them in the eye and ask, "What have you done? You have worked for the French and accepted their salary and taken the last kopeck from your family." It ended with a final plea to refuse to sign and with the traditional chant, "To Russia! To Russia!"[52] The guilt laid on any soldier who might agree to join the work brigades was skillfully placed indeed. The documents show a clever talent for playing on the fears of the men and were hardly written by semi-illiterate soldiers. Many did not join, and they provided a large source for Category B.

Somewhat surprisingly, the first work order was no better received among the "*vrai*" troops at Courneau. On October 24 Lokhvitsky, in a generally depressed mood and considering resignation to seek service somewhere else, appeared there to issue the order to join labor units. He met with the regimental division committees to tell them about the plans for them to begin work, but the assembled majority decided to decline to do so, using the phony logic that it would be a shame for the young, healthy Russians to labor in the rear when Frenchmen over forty were in the trenches.[53] The Courneau camp commandant, Colonel Fonssagrives, having received word to the contrary, knew this reply to be merely a face-saving way of saying no, and he informed the commandant of the 18th region that "their beautiful sentiments, which leave me a little skeptical, are contradicted in a letter which had been brought to me by the censors." He enclosed an intercepted letter to the division committee in which a dozen Courneau soldiers declared their wish to join work details of which they had heard in order to help their country. Moreover, the letter stated that they did not wish to remain idle.[54] Fonssagrives was reading too much into the request to work, just as the committee was guilty of ignoring it. Surprisingly, some of the strongest opposition to the labor scheme came not from the lower ranks but from the officers. In December French Captain Duboin, commandant of the headquarters of the 1st Russian division, reported to General Vidalon that the element most opposed to nonmilitary work was the corps of officers who were always looking after their own interests. He noted that if the soldiers went to work, the moral position of the officers would be diminished.[55]

In short, from all ranks and for many reasons, there was opposition to contributing much to the French war effort. There were probably a number of motives other than political ones for this attitude, most notably the desire to return home as soon as possible. Joining French work units seemed permanent; at least it would probably mean remaining in France until the close of what appeared to be an endless war. Moreover, the revolution held out a vague promise of a new and better life; the change implied a brighter future. Yet, stranded in this little corner of southern France, the *muzhik* could not digest these finer points. He only understood that, to restate Trotsky's phrase, "He did not want to die for France; he wanted a chance to live in the new Russia," and no amount of verbal logic would have brought the soldiers into line at this point. As General Harbord said, only "lining them up and shooting every 100th man could probably bring the remanded to their senses."[56] Yet eventually many did volunteer. An updated list from Zankevich's earlier rendering showed the largest group to do so were those who chose to work in agriculture, a total of 440, no surprise since peasant farmers comprised the largest single segment among the Russians in France. By early November, however, 200 factory workers, 80 finish carpenters, 77 iron workers, 50 "chemists," and all but 8 of the 128 locksmiths — for a total of 680 workers — had come forward. Public works and manual laborers drew 575. From among the armament and factory workers, 200 volunteered, as did a number of automobilists, pit sawyers, cobblers, leather workers, tailors, lithographers, and miners. These groups came to a total of 2,355 out of 8,000 or so.[57]

Their departure was orchestrated by Lieutenant Colonel Cros, who was sent to La Courtine expressly for that purpose. They left in dribbles, beginning on November 5, for l'Eure, l'Eure et Loire, the Gironde, Provence, and Normandy, going wherever there was a demand for certain skills and work. They went to the farms, the mines, the factories, and the timber yards. Some days the exodus stalled because the men hesitated in the train yards, battling with their wills and consciences. Many left only because some form of work was preferable to prison or North Africa, their spirit of defiance not having lessened at all. By December 10 there were still around 3,000 left, but the exodus continued two days later in four trains that left at various times during the day.[58] With the departure of these workers, the diaspora of the Russian Expeditionary Force sent to France began, and as they traveled, many became lost to history. A number of them came to marry French women and never left the country that had been the object of their hate and mistrust.

Exactly what constituted the composition of a work brigade is difficult to determine because two different descriptions exist in the French archives. One memo states that the work units were to be constituted of 250 men led by noncommissioned officers divided into four units each under two Russian-speaking French officers, assisted by two interpreters.[59] Another recital the same month notes that the work detachment was to consist of about 500 men commanded by a Russian captain under whom was to be four Russian officers, either captains, lieutenants, or noncommissioned officers. If a number of companies were grouped in the same region, they were to be under the authority of a lieutenant colonel. Each company was to have a Russian-speaking French officer or a noncom and a secretary. All medical attention would be administered by French physicians.[60] Each worker was issued a set of standard equipment for his daily living consisting of a straw mattress, one pillow, two blankets, a water bottle, a satchel, a mess tin, and a knife and fork.

The initial behavior of those leaving to work was reportedly good. A dossier of correspondence dated in December 1917 indicates that there had been no trouble with the workers. Captain Duboin wrote on December 14, "The spirit of the Russian troops is improving daily. Despite the officers pulling on one side and the soldiers on the other, the great majority of the soldiers have decided to accept work [and] to obey the French government orders." Duboin, however, resumed with what proved to be an inaccurate description of the Russian soldiers' attitude toward France: "The soldiers are convinced that the French government will always have for them the greatest understanding in view of their former conduct. There is certainly with the majority of soldiers some excellent sentiments which will be able to be exploited. . . . "[61]

It was not long, however, before this optimistic and inaccurate perception began to collapse, and before the end of December 1917 there were the usual reports of drunkenness on payday and a "defeatist attitude" among those choosing to work. The minister of the interior asked all prefects to report any news of Russian workers' misbehavior, and in December most of the replies report trouble. Since most of the soldiers spoke only Russian, there was little interaction with the French population, yet supposedly those at a factory in Puy-de-Dôme were reported to have indicated "pacifist" ideas and in Lyon at Fort de Montluc in the Rhone valley, workers demonstrated "pro-Lenin opinions." One Russian subject, Lasota, called by the report a "revolutionary," sold radical postcards in Lyon and tried to make contact with French workers in the region, but the police were aware of his activities.[62] Often the men who had enlisted to avoid worse conditions became a great source of trouble in the fields and factories. As time passed, the problems with these workers increased and their value to France must have been negligible.

More interesting was the treatment and actions of Category B. Their number at first ran somewhere between 600 and 700. This group, however, could be subdivided into two groups itself: those whom the French generally labeled "irreconcilables" and the smaller, hard-core leadership that had led the revolt in the first place. The latter, we have seen, ended in the grim prison on Île d'Aix off the southern coast of France. It was originally decided to incarcerate the former in the citadel of Montlouis, but later the authorities decided to send them to North Africa.[63] In the meantime some were sent to various prisons, such as Labottière, Bourg-Lastic, or to the barracks Xaintrailles, which had been converted into a prison. For the hardcore, the prison at Île d'Aix seems to have become a sorting place, and from time to time large numbers were sent there. In October, Colonel Kotovich authorized the removal of 320, sending them nonstop by train at night. Colonel Lebedev asked that 74 soldiers still at La Courtine early in December be sent to join them.[64] By January 1918, there were 260 (one report states 258) men imprisoned there.[65] From this point to the end of the whole affair, the prison at Île d'Aix appears often in documents and reports, and numbers of both soldiers and officers seem to have passed in and out of its grim dungeons.

General Alby described conditions in the prisons of Xaintrailles and Labottière to Zankevich in a letter for the prime minister; if true, they must have been a shopping list advocated by the most vigorous devotees of prison reform of the day. Prisoners could obtain books and papers through the garrison's major and were allowed three free hours a day in the courtyard. They could buy items at the canteen if they had any money and were permitted showers once a week. Those at Labottière could shower only once or twice a month because the prison had only cold water, and the prisoners had to be transported some distance for showers to the depot of the 3rd Aviation Group. Their rations were the same food received by the French military but for some reason "in a more abundant quantity." They could buy tobacco and were given ample time to use it.[66]

The situation at Île d'Aix was definitely less comfortable. Soldiers there were given only a quarter of a pound of bread a day and only two ounces of meat with an ounce of dry vegetables (beans, rice, etc.). Potatoes and cabbage were also part of a daily diet.[67] As in the other prisons, soldiers were given the option to work or be sent to Africa with a salary of twenty-five centimes per day.

Those sent to Africa were dispatched to Marseille nonstop, and the government specified that they be guarded en route by white troops to avoid racial trouble. Those guilty of "crimes or offenses" were put in neither category but were retained indefinitely at Île d'Aix.[68] By the first of January, 258 had been screened there and 192 had finally volunteered for work. Fifty-four were banished to Africa and twelve were being held for misdemeanors of common law.[69] Yet for the ordinary soldier who had originally refused work, it seems that the French government allowed a prisoner's transfer rather easily. As early as November, a hundred who had been taken to Île d'Aix were allowed to leave and return to La Courtine, over Comby's objections, because they were recognized as having "good conduct."[70] Those who suddenly decided that they would work were released, and those who had been on good behavior for a least three months in the prison were recommended for workers' companies.[71] Sudden volunteers for work do not seem to have been examined too skeptically, and their abrupt conversion to discipline was accepted at face value.

Our best source for the trip to Île d'Aix is Kozlov's memoir. As a radical member of the Third Brigade, he had been an early participant in the mutiny in his unit. When he was sent to prison, he and the others who went with him were herded into two wagons between two passenger cars of a train and sent westward. At the various stops people looked at them like they were wild beasts. When they realized that the prisoners were Russians, the crowds were generally hostile. Kozlov asked the guard why they were so unfriendly and was told that the French government had been "spreading" false rumors that they were taking German money to cause trouble.

Arriving in Bordeaux at 2:00 A.M., the mutineers were put into specially prepared trams with their windows covered and closed. After riding through deserted streets for half an hour, the conductor blurted out in Russian, "What did you stir up in Courtine?" All were taken aback on hearing Russian spoken because until now, no one had addressed them in their native language. As soon as they tried to reply, they arrived at their destination. They were marched through narrow streets between rows of dark houses. Kozlov was placed into a bare-walled cell thirty paces by ten with forty-four other men. On the floor were straw mats for sleeping. Their overcoats had to serve for covering.

At 7:00 A.M. the next day, a sergeant ordered them out into the yard, and they were not allowed to return until five o'clock that afternoon. They were given no food that day but were fed the next. Breakfast was bread only, with soup for lunch and again for dinner. Meat was allowed them twice a week, but in such a small quantity that it was used only as an ingredient in the soup. They were not given hot water, soap, clean underwear, or tobacco. Kozlov wrote that dinner was at 4:00 P.M., and they had to go nineteen hours until the next meal, a lunch, which was served at 11:00 A.M. (Somehow Kozlov seems to have forgotten about the bread breakfast). He got so hungry that his "belly played a march." As for outside contact, they were allowed to write letters, but they never received any replies,[72] most probably due to the chaos in Russia, not a French failure to transmit their correspondence.

In the winter things worsened because of the bitter cold. Simply sitting in the cell was impossible because to keep warm, one had to walk since the stoves in the cells did not work. Periodically the internees were taken to interrogation to determine if they would work, and some weakened, Kozlov wrote, due to boredom and did volunteer. The radical elements would ask whether the work was for the war effort or not. Their interrogators would not answer but only ask in reply, "Yes or no?"[73]

After about a week, they were told that they would have a "visitor," and then Rapp appeared with Colonel Lissovsky. Rapp told them that he was there to learn what they needed, while Lissovsky was there only to "help" them with legal questions. The two interrogated the soldiers and seemed interested in their origins in Russia. They seemed especially concerned with those who were from Moscow or Petrograd because they were searching among the internees for the leaders, and they felt that someone from one of the two capitals would be the most likely to be a radical.[74]

The prisoners complained to Rapp about the lack of reading material and about the absence of mail. Rapp replied that he had written "everyone" about the matter of correspondence and had done all that he could do. Not many ships could leave Russia with mail due to the weather, but even if any could, the chaos that had overtaken the country by the fall of 1917 probably would have made delivery of the soldiers' letters impossible, to say nothing of the return of the replies. The internees never ceased to believe, however, that their letters were being intentionally withheld.

They also held political conversations with Rapp at one point. Rapp wanted to know, according to Kozlov, why they had fired from the camp, adding that it was necessary to expose those who were guilty. Then Kozlov asked him:

"If they fired from La Courtine, would they be judged?"

"Of course," Rapp replied.

"But who will judge those who fired on the camp and destroyed it? Aren't they a particular type of guilty?"

At this question Rapp visibly wilted. Then Kozlov continued, "It is hard for me to believe that you are a socialist."

Rapp responded that if people were against freedom and did not fulfill their orders, he felt that their freedom should be taken away, that they supported counterrevolution. Someone who had heard this statement cried out:

"What?! You're calling us counterrevolutionaries. You'd better look around you!"

Rapp and Lissovsky were never able in their investigation to get anyone to tell on someone else. The crowd, according to Kozlov, remained unified. Someone told Rapp, "Don't look here [for the guilty]; you should look in a mirror."

The two men finally concluded their investigation and returned to Paris to prepare the report for the indictments. On leaving they did promise to locate reading material for the internees and to try to obtain their correspondence. Kozlov, whose work, while valuable, is to some degree early Soviet, anti-Western propaganda, claimed that Rapp's promises were never fulfilled "unless one considers that the replacement of rice soup with that made from wormy green beans [fulfilling his promise]." He later admits that books and reading materials did arrive by early November, but they were not numerous because of the paucity of Russian-language reading material in France. Mostly what they were able to find were the lives of the saints and tales about medieval bogatirs, princes, and boyars. To Kozlov, the papers and pamphlets were worse than the books. They were given such propagandistic tracts as *Russia and the Defense of the Native Land*, *Organ of the Committee of the Struggle against Defeatism*, and *The Russian Soldier-Citizen in France*. Kozlov also writes about the brutality of the guards. He tells one story of a guard's taking a ruble from a soldier named Sinenka, who had somehow received it through the mail. When the soldier protested, the sergeant put him in confinement, and Kozlov never saw him again.[75]

The Russian consul general at Bordeaux made several visits, and on his second appearance he brought with him a General Branovsky, who spoke for the Russian military representative in Bordeaux. The two informed them that seventeen troublemakers were to be removed in seven days. That night almost none among them slept, and in the morning the guards gave them bread and jam for two days and divided them into four groups. They were taken from the prison under the guard of artillery soldiers and herded into trams. They boarded a third-class railroad wagon where they were put six to a coupé, each monitored by two guards. They were not told of their destination, but they knew that their stay near Bordeaux had ended.[76]

The prisoners traveled almost without stopping. At eight in the evening they came to Rochefort, where they marched to an empty artillery barracks. The sentries were forbidden to speak to the prisoners so they were completely ignorant about their fate. They were mustered out in the morning, given bitter coffee, and again marched off. In thirty minutes they found themselves down on the docks, where they saw a boat in which they sailed to a small island two hours out to sea. They were let ashore and marched for about a mile and a half, after which they came to a very simple two-story stone house, which they discovered had been a temporary prison for Emperor Napoleon I on his way to St. Helena. Here they learned that they were in Category B and that they were in the prison on the Île d'Aix, built about the turn of the seventeenth century. At Île d'Aix they encountered many of their former colleagues who helped them move into their sea-level rooms, which were dark and damp with one window and one door. A cold wind continuously blew in from the sea.[77]

The head prison supervisor was a Russian, Lieutenant Pavlov, who really was a figurehead. There was also an interpreter. The real commandant was a Frenchman who was a tyrant and full master of the island. Kozlov's colleagues who had been there awhile told him, "What he wanted to do, he did." Kozlov was most annoyed at the conditions and immediately began hounding the sentry to obtain for him an appointment with the camp commandant. Eventually he got one and the meeting was held in the presence of an interpreter and, for some reason, a French doctor.

Kozlov bitterly complained about the food and the absence of any eating utensils. In repeating what he said, the translator softened his language. The reply given Kozlov was that these things would be provided, so Kozlov also pressed for underwear, clothes, soap, and tobacco. The interpreter answered himself that there had been tobacco, but that it had been taken away because of the bad conduct, especially the soldiers' refusal to work. On hearing the word "tobacco" (*tabak* in both French and Russian), the commandant said, "Yes, tobacco indeed is not much, but for such there must be better behavior." Finally they were given a ration of it.[78]

Kozlov stayed at Île d'Aix only a few weeks before he was returned to Rochefort. It has been noted how easy it was to obtain release from the prison: One simply had to agree to work. Kozlov, who has been so damning of those who had agreed to labor for the French "bourgeoisie," apparently decided to do so himself, although he does not mention it in his memoirs. On landing in Rochefort, he encountered some American soldiers, who were surprised that the Russians were marching under guard. Somehow through the language barrier these soldiers managed to convey to the Russians the idea that the war would end soon.

Kozlov finally found himself at the shelter of St. Marie near the Swiss border, where he performed road work under the watchful eye of

French guards, whose Russian vocabulary consisted only of the word *"Rabotai!* [Work!]." They were seldom allowed breaks, and they were sometimes given moldy bread. Medical help was needed but was often unavailable, and their clothes deteriorated into unrecognizable rags.[79]

Yet there were those who did not "sell out" to the French and who stayed in Aix. In the French archives there exists lists of those still there by the summer and fall of 1918. The June 1918 list contains forty-five names. The number is less than half that by September. These hard-core elements became heroes to those of their comrades who had agreed to work rather than languish in prison. The list of the forty-five gives a great deal of information about those who were there. There seems to be no order to the roll except that of a degree of rebelliousness. Yet even with that as a criterion, Globa is only number twelve on the list.

About Baltais the marginal comment showed that he had behaved well since his arrival, but the note states that he continued to exercise a great influence over the other interned Russians. We are also informed that he is *"Très intelligent, mais bolshévik."* There included the recommendation that he should be separated from the regular group. As for Volkov, who had been arrested with Baltais, the comment tells us that he had also maintained good conduct since arriving at the prison but suggested that he be separated from Baltais "to whom he is very devoted." Globa was also observed as having a great influence over his comrades, and the report noted that he had behaved perfectly since arriving at the prison. Added in what looks like another handwriting at the end were the words "has reservations."[80] These few men were kept isolated until it was decided that they would no longer infect other units, and then they suddenly appeared in Africa.

Those who refused to work but who had not been singled out as having a leadership role in the whole affair were rather swiftly dispatched to the French penal colonies in Algeria. Zankevich had opposed the exile of these incorrigibles to the deserts because it "would have nasty consequences." It would be interpreted in Russia as an act of violence, the equivalent of sending prisoners to Siberia. Expressing this opinion to Foch in a letter at the end of November, he agreed with the obligation of Russian volunteers for work at the front, but he again advised against sending them to Africa.[81] If Foch replied to Zankevich's plea, the reply has not survived. The Russian general hardly provided a solution or a viable alternative to sending incorrigibles to North Africa, and by now Foch had no patience left for these Russians whom they were feeding and who would neither fight nor work.

The French government estimated that after all who had agreed to work or fight were assembled, the remaining group of about 5,000 would be sent to the North African contingent. There they could be held in concentration camps more easily isolated in the deserts than they could be detained in French cantonments. Moreover, in France they might escape into the forests or be subjected to any Bolshevist elements that might still be lurking. A letter to General Nivelle, now the commander-in-chief of French North Africa, alerted him on December 1 that the first of the contingent of 5,000 Russians would be directed nonstop to his care in Algeria, where they were to be lodged in Laghouat, Boghar, Médéa, and Aumale. They would bring with them their tents, cooking utensils, and the like.[82]

The planned date of departure was to be December 11. A unit of 150 French soldiers was to escort each block of Russians to the point of embarkation; there the French would be relieved by African units. The first trains were to arrive at La Courtine on day J and would transport the men in groups of 1,500 (1,280 Russians and 220 French escorts) to Toulon on J plus 2.[83] With delays, however, it was not until December 17 before the first Russians left Toulon on the ship *Canada*. On board were 1,561 Russians with 7 interpreters and a French escort of 4 officers and 245 men.[84] The next departure came on December 20, when 1,950 Russians boarded the *General Gallièni*, with another detachment arriving in two segments at Toulon the same day. The note informing the authorities of this schedule called for order and the total secrecy of embarkation. It also made the curious suggestion that a soldier's ration of hot tea be provided before departure.[85] Eventually these men were scattered over Algeria, mostly in agricultural jobs. It is odd that somehow they were induced to work there when they could not be forced to do so in France. This change in attitude suggests that they were treated more harshly in the isolation of the deserts, far away from reporters and their own government agents, than they had been in France.

Kreider, one of the camps in Algeria, at one time housed 2,500 Russians in tents. It was on the edge of a desert and surrounded with barbed wire. Winds blew constantly and the soldiers' food and clothes were full of sand. They suffered terribly from the heat, and the ubiquitous grit caused eye problems. They worked twelve hours a day, from 6:00 A.M. to 6:00 P.M., Sundays and holidays included. They were fed only twice a day an insufficient diet consisting of a bowl of soup with a little dumpling and several morsels of an unrecognizable meat. They were allotted a half pound of bread a day. There was no medical service for them, and these men were plagued with dysentery and malaria. Surveillance was maintained by black troops who beat them with the flats of their swords and with heavy riding crops, which reminded soldiers of the heavy Cossack *nagaiki* (whips).[86]

Even here the Russians must not have been watched too carefully since there are accounts of drunk Russian soldiers causing "scandal and disorder." In December at Boufarik, a rape incident led the police to make patrols and establish order. At Pont de l'Eau the same type crime occurred on December 23. After these incidents, liquor was forbidden the Russians in an effort to contain such misbehavior, but despite all the supervision, Bolshevik propaganda—genuine pacifist literature or perhaps materials spread among the Russians by German agents—managed to reach the Russians here as well. All this disorder eventually led local entrepreneurs, for whom the Russians mostly worked, to refuse their labor, especially since Russian workers sometimes sabotaged their work projects.[87] In July 1919, in Bone, a number of Russian workers went on a twenty-four-hour strike to protest the fact that they had not been repatriated, and on July 24 they issued a stirring appeal to the French people over the heads of their local oppressors. How wide a circulation it received is unknown, but it carried all the flavor of those declarations we have read before. Indeed, it probably had the same author.

"It has already been three years and eight months since the first echelon of Russian troops designated for France left Russia . . . ," the protest reminded its French audience. "All have fought on the front in France . . . [and] many have died, others have been crippled." After recounting the sad history of the La Courtine affair, the declaration continued: "When the camp was reduced, the survivors of repression were subjected to sad treatment, the anguish of hunger, and incessant interrogations. Many ended in prison. The majority forced to work in Algeria . . . [where] they fed us badly. . . . Several have died. . . . German prisoners return home, but we continue to suffer without the end to the situation in sight." Then in ringing martial tones, the appeal cried out, "Citizens of France! We are not murderers; we are men suffering in heart and spirit. For several years we have had no news of our country. . . . We are in a sense the white slaves of capitalism. . . . For us demobilization does not exist and among us are men forty-three and forty-four years old who have seven and eight children." Then the protest gave an ultimatum of its own. "If the French government does not give us a favorable response . . . , we would be obliged to refuse all work. . . . We are prepared to die of starvation in African prisons rather than continue to lead this same existence."[88] Nothing seems to have come of this appeal, but then it is unlikely that it received a wide readership.

In time the numbers of African internees grew and grew. By the end of the war French figures indicate that 8,775 men and 47 officers were incarcerated there. There they languished for some time after the war but not because the French did not wish to be rid of them.

There occurred in the midst of all this moving of all the Russian troops in the fall of 1917 an event that drastically changed world history. In the early-morning hours of November 7, the Bolshevik Red Guard seized important points in the city of Petrograd, including the telephone and telegraph exchanges, major bridges, and all railroad stations. It likewise surrounded the Winter Palace, the seat of the Provisional Government. Learning of the first moves of the Bolsheviks in the night, Prime Minister Kerensky drove out of the city in a Pierce Arrow (not in an American Ford commandeered from the American embassy, as legend has it)[89] to try to collect loyal troops to thwart the coup. The Winter Palace was defended by a contingent of cadets from a military high school and a battalion of female soldiers, armed not only with rifles but with arsenic tablets in case their virtue found itself under imminent assault. The Bolsheviks did not storm the building, a myth perpetrated by the melo-dramatic Eisenshtein movie *Ten Days That Shook the World,* but instead sent in their own soldiers one or two at the time until they outnumbered the unenthusiastic defenders, who casually surrendered. Knowing that the building was in Bolshevik hands, the leaderless Provisional Government awaited the inevitable in Tsar Nicholas II's private dining room. To appear busy, the impotent ministers spread maps on the table and were pointing to meaningless geographic locations when the Bolshevik soldiers entered the room to arrest them. The next day Vladimir Lenin, the brilliant, obsessed, neurotic leader of the Bolshevik Social Democrats, began to, in his words, "build the socialist order." One of his first acts was to begin the process that would take the exhausted Russian nation out of what was at that time the most devastating war in history.

The reverberations of this revolution influenced many develop-ments of the past, great and small. One of its lesser effects was the impact it had on the REF in France. When Poincaré heard of the overthrow of the Provisional Government, his only diary entry on the subject was simply "Bad news from Russia. The Maximalists [Bolsheviks] tri-umph."[90] It probably never occurred to him what impact the Communist seizure of power might mean to the Russian Expeditionary Force, since neither he nor anyone else felt that the Bolsheviks would last. As this presumption was the norm, the Russian embassy in Paris became the foreign ministry-in-exile for all the Russian embassies in Europe and the Provisional Government's ambassador to Paris, the famous trial lawyer Vasilii Maklakov, the foreign minister of some sort of phantom "Free Russia." He remained so until the French government finally extended formal recognition to the Soviet government in 1924.[91] This "foreign ministry" without a country found itself in the midst of the maelstrom caused by the Russian forces now stranded in the West.

Initially efforts were made to keep the news from the Russian troops abroad, but that proved impossible. Some who knew French had access to French newspapers, and once a few of them learned of it, the word spread quickly that the Bolsheviks were in power. At the prison in which he was incarcerated in Bordeaux, Vavilov learned of the October Revolution by an announcement, which produced a chorus of "Hurrah!" among the men. Panicked at the prospect of more trouble, the prison supervisor dispatched all the guards, but within several days the prison officials allowed the soldiers access to the kitchen to cook their own meals, and there was a general relaxation of the regimen imposed on them. Moreover, rations of bread, meat, and sugar were increased.[92]

Zankevich tried to minimize the effect the new revolution would have on the dispersed men still nominally under his command. In the order of the day of November 26, he told the soldiers not to obey the revolutionary government and to refuse to recognize "the group of persons who have seized from the governmental institution in Petrograd the authority of State Power. . . ." Continuing in the same vein, he added, "We do follow only the orders of the Provisional Government, which had named us and that represents us. The powers of the government . . . remains unchanged." Then he added the brief statement that Russian loyalty was tied "as in the past entirely to the Allies." The order was signed by Zankevich under the title of Representative of the Provisional Government to the French armies.[93] His order, of course, had no more effect than earlier ones. The problems in Petrograd could only energize those troops who refused to accept his authority, and it most certainly weakened the resolve of those who were neutral.

The mere existence of the force in France, with a number being held prisoner, gave the Bolsheviks a great domestic propaganda weapon. Even before the Bolshevik Revolution, Noulens had reported that "the papers malintentioned toward the Allies" had used the suppression of the Russian troops at La Courtine in an anti-French campaign "which twists the facts to our detriment."[94] In December he wired the ministry of foreign affairs that the troops were giving "the people of Smolny [the Bolsheviks]" a pretext for agitation against France.[95]

Yet the October Revolution presented the French with a new and different type of problem regarding the Russian force: one of legality. If the new government of Russia was not in favor of the war, were the troops who refused to fight still to be considered traitors? If not, could they justifiably be detained any longer? There was no way, however, that the French could allow thousands of uncontrollable men to roam freely about the countryside. Moreover, if the Bolsheviks took Russia out of the war, as they were trying to do, what then would be the legal status of these troops, which the French would have eagerly sent home but physically could not? The unrestricted submarine warfare since February 1, 1917, had taken a dreadful toll on Allied shipping, and whereas the convoy system had diminished that considerably, by year's end all of the sunken tonnage could not be replaced rapidly. Thus even with a radical change of government in Petrograd, the problem of what to do with the REF remained a French one. Furthermore, the geographic problems of repatriation ultimately made the matter worse for the French than the mere controlling of several thousand unruly soldiers.

In addition, the Bolshevik Revolution presented for the French yet another headache, or at least an old one of renewed intensity: increased leftist agitation. Some of it remained German-instigated, to be sure, but the French security police regarded it all as "Bolshevik." Regardless of the origin, the effect would be the same. With the October Revolution agitation increased in intensity toward the Russian troops in France, in camps, prisons, or work details. By one means or another these political incendiaries reached the soldiers no matter where they were.[96]

By the fall of 1917, Spain seems to have served as a conduit into France for new provocateurs and all sorts of subversives. It was, for example, through Spain that Mata Hari came and went into France. Because of Spain's strange role as a go-between for Germany and the peculiar activities of the Spanish ambassador to Russia, Count Villasinda, it is clear that the Spanish did some subversive work for the Germans. In October a woman, obviously of Russian origin and living in France, wrote in bad French to the minister of the interior to complain of deserters, "the most part Israelites," who spoke Russian badly. "These dirty fellows (*cette sales graines*) arrive here from Spain, and I cannot understand, M. Le Ministre, why they are allowed to flow through the border. . . ."[97] Other reports also speak of a Spanish connection. One known Bolshevik agent, Nicholas Lagoff, was traced to Madrid by the French police.[98] The ministry of foreign affairs informed the French minister of the interior late in September that another known Bolshevik representative had landed in Spain and had made immediate contact with the German espionage service there. The minister of the interior then asked the border guards at the Spanish and Andorean frontiers to inform him which if any Russian citizens had crossed the French-Spanish border on that day and to send him a list of their names and addresses.[99]

The reply stated that no Russians had crossed the border on that specific day, but the French minister continued to ask the question daily between October 7 and October 19, indicating that there must have been additional word of a major attempt to send Russian/German agents through Spain. Other police reports indicate that by October 1918 Barcelona had become a "Bolshevik stronghold."[100] The final French response to this threat was the closing of the Spanish border at one minute after midnight on October 30, 1917, to produce a *cordon sanitaire* against future "Bolshevik" incursions.

Regardless of whatever might enter from Spain, the French government had enough subversives with which to contend within France itself. Police reports indicate that these Russian subversion tended to make as their pied-à-terre the tea shop on the Rue de la Sorbonne, the Café de la Rotonde at the corner of the Boulevards Raspail and Montparnasse, and at Madame Demko's house at 4 Rue d'Ulon. A number of them held a meeting on December 11 at 6 Rue de Tournefort with the idea of organizing more effective propaganda among the Russian troops.[101] *Soldat-Citoyen* seems to have resurfaced by November and was publishing its usual inflammatory anti-Allied, anti-French propaganda for any Russian readers; it was suppressed by the French authorities on November 27. Moreover, police reports show list after list of "known activist Bolsheviks" still living in the Russian colony of Paris. Most of the names are unfamiliar unless they have appeared on other contemporary lists.[102] The paper *Otklitki zhizni* (Comments of Life) seems to have been the most active element of Russian Bolshevism in late 1917. It was a similar newspaper to the now-closed *Nachalo*, which the French linked to the mutinies of the Russian troops in May.[103] According to the French police report, "At nightfall one sees enter [the paper's office] the same individuals completely of the type of former Russian nihilists," whatever that meant. The report continues to state that "the direct surveillance of the press produced some results. . ." without stating what the results were.[104] The subversives made an effort to spread thousands of these sheets, which had a "prudently veiled" pro-Bolshevik editorial position. The paper was on shaky financial ground, however, and the French police had discovered that the editors had to extort contributions from their supporters.

The propagandists performed their destructive work well. Further disturbances in the fall of 1917 resulted in near-total anarchy. In Hyères there were 825 men and 765 in a hospital in Cannes, most of whom were from the Army of the Orient. Reports of hospitals in Hyères and Cannes show the usual accounts of indiscipline, with one report describing the situation as "urgent."[105] The report tells of the sick and wounded paying no attention to orders, climbing over the walls, going into town in groups, and staying away overnight. As always, some obtained revolvers, and, as usual, the officers had no control over them.[106] Black troops armed with machine guns were brought in to crush the disturbance in Hyères, where the hospitalized soldiers had elected a soviet, which stayed in touch with other units in France.[107] Yet it is unlikely that all this trouble was caused by Bolshevik agents-provocateurs. When authority collapses among unhappy soldiers, little is required to sustain the disorder. These soldiers simply wanted to return home, and likely much the same disintegration of authority would have occurred with or without Bolshevik agitation.

It is not surprising that the new Bolshevik regime would quickly use the mere existence of Russian troops in France, especially given why they had been sent there, as a propaganda tool. Noulens reported that the new Russian government demanded repatriation as soon as it had seized power; although Kerensky had systematically delayed it.[108] The suppression in which the French had played a large, albeit passive, role could only have antagonized the situation and given the Bolshevik government new fuel for their propaganda machine. Zankevich early expressed concern that the Bolsheviks would present the Russian troops as victims like Siberian exiles and take their anger out on the French in Russia,[109] which, as we shall see, is exactly what they did. Early in December Noulens reported to his government that the situation of the Russian troops in France had become for the new Bolshevik government "a pretext for agitation against France." The Bolsheviks had, as it turned out, reported to the Russian people the truth—the suppression, the imprisonment, the work details, and so forth— but they had not noted that the French had acted in a very gentle fashion as any other nation would have done under the circumstances. Yet accounts of imprisonment and other actions taken, presented in a one-sided fashion with unfair embellishments, could be a most valuable tool to mobilize the anti-French sentiment. Noulens discovered that "a doctor" had recently returned from France to direct the campaign against that country using the brigades as a propaganda source.[110]

The subject of alleged French abuse of the Russian soldiers was employed well and to quote the words of the French General Albert Niessel, it helped "turn the internal mood very ugly."[111] The Bolshevik papers loudly denounced the alleged mistreatment, and orchestrated demonstrations in Russia resulted in support of the soldiers in France. Even before the

Bolshevik coup, *Soldatskaia pravda* reported a general meeting of workers of the First Russian Fellowship of Aeronautics and Joiners during which it was decided to launch a protest against the soldiers' retention in France and "to obtain by all means the return of all forces into Russia where they will serve out general revolutionary business."[112] Early in December Trotsky, now Russian commissar of foreign affairs, published a letter from Zankevich, which must have been in the foreign ministry archive, complaining about the treatment of the Russian soldiers.[113]

On December 15 the French government sent a note to Noulens and Niessel in response to the former's inquiry of December 7 regarding the situation of the Russian troops in France. Exactly what reached the two men cannot be ascertained because on certain touchy subjects the French archival copies have been erased. In one document, for example, there are references to the soldiers who became *cultivateurs* and *entrepreneurs du bois*, but a part of a paragraph telling of the shipment of troops to Africa has been marked for deletion — and someone neglected to do it. The note does inform Noulens and Niessel that the steps were taken with the complete agreement of the Russian governmental representatives, and it ended with the words "Neither pressure nor violence had been exerted against the Russian troops, who receive a French salary and food superior to that of the French troops. Refute all news not confirming to the indications given above."[114]

There was one point of agreement, however, between the French and the new Soviet government: Both wanted the Russian Expeditionary Force to come home. The Provisional Government had delayed and stalled their return because of very real fears of how the troops might behave after their arrival in Russia. The Bolsheviks had no such fears. There was a genuine, more immediate problem: the shortage of transports to send them. Had ships been found before the October coup, the Provisional Government's opposition would have been a most serious concern. With the overthrow of that government in November 1917, that obstacle had been removed, leaving only the question of transportation, to which the French applied their energies with great seriousness.

The French approached their British allies for help. Even as early as late September 1917, one month before the October Revolution, the French had raised the question with the British of transporting the Russians from Scotland, and early in October Ribot nudged the French embassy in London to hasten the discussion because the White Sea would soon freeze and then the French would have the problem of the troops for yet another winter.[115] The British Committee of War discussed the issue of moving the Russians through England for embarkation in Scotland but did not act immediately, which resulted in another jog from the French government on October 3. Unbeknownst to the French, however, someone in the British government had decided the day before that they would not be able to help their ally in this matter, and the secretary of state for war was authorized to refuse the French government's request. The refusal, however, did not come until October 7.

The British reasons for refusal went beyond the shortage of tonnage, which indeed was real, to the realization that other problems would be involved, such as feeding and housing the troops once they arrived in northern Russia. A railroad had been completed in 1916 between Petrograd and Murmansk, Russia's one ice-free port, thanks to the Gulf Stream and the Norwegian Current, but the British gave the spurious excuse that sending thousands of men this way would seriously disrupt the shipment of war matériel already taxing the route to its fullest.[116] Jules Cambon, the French ambassador to London, reported to Paris on the day the secretary of state for war's letter was written but probably before he had received it that he did not think that the British would be able to find the necessary tonnage. From somewhere he had obtained the information that of five possible ships waiting in Scotland, one was docked for repairs, and two or perhaps three would be used for repatriating Russians living in Great Britain who had asked to do their service in Russia, leaving only one or two ships available. Moreover, no Russian naval authorities would allow any ships to depart for Russia that could not arrive that month; if they left later, the ships and crew would have to spend the winter there. The last transports of merchandise to Russia were to leave that week.[117]

The French continued such frantic efforts in London throughout October, their air of desperation increasing with each diplomatic note. Finally later in October the British government formally notified the French that they absolutely could not help. In a conversation between Cambon and Arthur Balfour, the British secretary made the most of the point that so many troops would congest their railroads, thus preventing the delivery of needed supplies to British troops.[118]

With this avenue of repatriation closed, the French then turned to the Americans with a proposal for a fantastic scheme. American boats were debarking troops in France and returning to the United States empty. Russians could be dispatched in these empty transports to America, thus freeing camps in France for Americans; once they reached America, these men could "be forwarded [!] on to Vladivostok." The minister of war requested the ministry of foreign affairs to present this request to the American government and to General Pershing as well.[119]

The American reply was not slow in coming. On December 6, Jusserand, who had opposed the use of Russians in France in the first place, wired his government that the American administration "expressed great embarrassment [?]" but refused to return the troops via America. The transfer of 16,000 *(sic)* ill-disciplined men across a continent would be very difficult and dangerous, the American government had felt, and one does easily envision unruly mobs of Russian soldiers terrorizing small towns from New York to California. Furthermore, a detour through Panama would immobilize for a long time urgently needed tonnage. The American government did, however, pass this request to Tokyo, to ask if the Japanese would be able to effect this transport, perhaps through Panama.[120] In March 1918 the French government was still pleading with the Japanese for help,[121] but once again it had come to a dead end.

Faced with having to contend with the Russian problem for yet another winter, the French finally exhausted the last of their patience. Through Zankevich on December 12 the French presented their own ultimatum to all the idle soldiers left in France, who were those mainly in Courneau. They had four options: They could perform work of some kind, they could join the forces in Salonika, they could fight in France, or they could be transported to North Africa. Their response had to be immediate. Zankevich went to Courneau and on December 24, he laid down the law.[122] Those troops who would fight would be used as cadres in French units employing some Russian officers. Rigid authority would be maintained. There would be a Russian base for administration, and on such matters as salary, the Russians would be treated the same as French soldiers. The troops were told that no soldiers' committees would be tolerated and that from then on they would be subject to French discipline. Those who would not fight would have to become military workers, either in the army zone or in the interior; in neither zone would they be exposed to enemy fire. Those who refused to make either choice would be summarily sent to Africa to labor like the ones who had gone before them.[123]

Many of these regulations had been stated policy before but had been enforced very lackadaisically, if at all. Now the French government meant business. Probably a major difference now was the fact that the intractable Georges Clemenceau had become prime minister. The seventy-seven-year old journalist turned physician turned politician never had much patience with nonsense, especially if that nonsense hindered his all-consuming goal of expelling the Germans from France. Clemenceau even cracked down on the Russian wounded in the hospitals, ordering that they too would work. According to the anonymous eyewitness writing in *The Russian Force in France,* those who would not work were forced into some sort of isolation in damp barracks under strict regimen. In January 1918, in a hospital at St. Malo, Soldier Bariatinsky was arrested merely for asking for a light in his room.

One immediate result of the French December crackdown was the final and complete disarmament of the Russian units. Either a very casual effort had been made to remove all weapons from the men after the siege, or the soldiers somehow managed to obtain others later, for by mid-December 1917 over 1,000 shells, almost a quarter of a million rifle cartridges, about half a million machine-gun cartridges, and over 4,000 revolvers, some of them Spanish, were taken from the Russian troops.[124]

By midmonth the new French authority also moved to segregate the malcontents at Courneau; the remainder they had planned to send to Salonika.[125] The "loyal" troops at Courneau, especially the 5th and 6th regiments, however, passed a resolution unanimously rejecting military service on *any* front. Lokhvitsky sent their refusal to General Louis Hallouin, commandant of the 18th region, who dispatched it on to the government in Paris. The text, although refusing to go to the front to fight, was rather moderate and legalistic in tone. "Given that the armistice has been concluded in Russia," it began, "the soldiers of the 5th and 6th Russian regiments in France do not consider themselves as having the right to participate in work at the front; feeling on the other hand that a person in France today does not have the right to do nothing at all, that each has the duty to get his own bread for his work, the soldiers of the 5th and 6th Russian regiments have decided unanimously to work in the interior of the country without any restrictions on individual liberty and *while preserving existing elected organizations* [italics mine]."[126] Since the French were not tolerating any "elected organizations," there was a major obstacle to getting these people into the labor force.

On the day after Christmas, Lokhvitsky tried to convince Hallouin that he should meet with the delegates of what the latter called "the soviet." The French general flatly refused. Since there is no record of a soviet's being elected from the soldiers of the Third Brigade, we can assume that he was referring to the soldiers' committee. He informed Paris that while he would not meet with soldiers' delegates of the soviet to discuss their proclamation, he did have to give the order either to work or to go to Africa to these very delegates, since their officers had no influence over the men. He suggested presenting them a choice: either work in France "without soviets" or be shipped to Africa.[127] Permission to make the offer must have come quickly, if indeed he bothered to wait for it, because he wired back on December 27 that he had already returned to the

Courneauois with the work-in-France-or-be-deported ultimatum. Giving little time for reply, Hallouin indicated to them that the first contingents would begin leaving the next day, making it plain that he was not waiting for any response from the "soviet" at Courneau. He added in his report to Clemenceau that he did not know how many would be "volunteer workers" and how many would be "recalcitrant."[128]

For whatever reason, it was not the next day but two days later before the first troops began leaving Courneau "without incident" and "in good order." Lieutenant Colonel Cros asked whether some Senegalese units could escort the troops to Africa, if such an escort was necessary, since the 18th region was short of other contingents.[129] Hallouin, who had been so firm with the Russians to this point, was obviously relieved that they had not resisted and even praised them, referring in a report to the "valiant Russian division in France" and adding, not entirely correctly, that the Third Brigade had "preserved its discipline and its military spirit." Apparently the first to depart were the most reliable, for he added in his order of the day that he hoped that those leaving "that day [December 29] and the next" would demonstrate the same example to the French and American troops witnessing their departure.[130] The police also noted that these troops had left "without incident."[131] Despite the efforts by General Hallouin and Commissar Mikhailov, who were sent by the Provisional Government to "assist" in restoring order, the number of "Irreductables" was a rather high 1,330, to which 54 still on Île d'Aix might be added. Of the remainder, 5,083 left to work in France, 300 remained in hospitals, and 277 volunteered for combat.[132] The camp, however, after a thorough cleaning, was finally ready for the arriving Americans.

It would be naive to assume that all of the 5,000 who had agreed to work for France had done so out of some sense of devotion to duty. A large number, we cannot ascertain how large, did so only to avoid the rigors of the African deserts, and they were still prepared to cause trouble wherever they went and would do so. Yet a quixotic sense of duty exists in some men, and there had always been an element among the REF, however small, that was prepared to go on fighting. Out of the 7,000 in the camp at Courneau somewhere between 250 and 300 asked to return to the front and continue the war. These men became the core of Lokhvitsky's third category.[133] It was a small percentage of the total number, but it was an interesting group. What induced these men to take this position probably differed within each man's soul, but a large factor must have been shame, however legitimate, at their comrades' recent behavior. Within the hearts of every one of these men must have been a desire to erase the blot on Russian honor, for not having remained in the war and for having abandoned Russia's ally. There was the added shame of their comrades' rebellion. These few would show that Russians had honor and national pride and would remain true to the Russian commitment. From this sense of duty and the shame of the Russian mutiny, the Russian Legion was born. Before the end of the spring of 1918, Russian blood would again flow into the already saturated soil of *La Belle France.*

NINE

This Little Piece of Russia

Winter 1917–Spring 1918

*I did not know Russia had been in the war. I guess you Russians
didn't do very much, did you?*

— A wealthy American woman[1]

*I would never have believed that we would have to drink from such
a cup [un tel calice à vider]. We will long remember those 'valiant
allies' as we called them on our arrival in France.*

— Private Mazharov[2]

*When I, a former prosecutor, see that many persons who made
propaganda in the Russian regiments in playing the game for the
Germans remaining free here, it revolts me. Everything must be
done to get the attention of the French and to open their eyes on that
which is happening because these gentlemen are serving defeatism,
not only among the Russians but also among the French soldiers.*

— Colonel Vladimir Lissovsky[3]

THE NEW YEAR BROUGHT an intensification of defeatist propaganda
that was now assuredly mostly German in origin, although it continued
to be labeled "Bolshevik" by the French security police. It speaks highly
of French devotion to civil rights that these individuals, so closely
watched and who had induced suspicions of being subversive, were not
summarily arrested, especially since many were obviously, if unprov-
ably, German agents. A focal point for these provocateurs was, of

course, the Russians now scattered all over France. A memorandum of April 1918 reported to the government that information had been gathered in Bern that a number of Germans were incorporated into the Russian troops then in France. One Russian deserter found in Switzerland claimed to be a German citizen and was sent into France to spread defeatist propaganda.[4] It is amazing that the French internal security forces ignored the evidence of German backing for these moves and persisted in blaming Bolshevism simply because the perpetrators were Russians. Many were by now Russian Leftists of some sort who were prostituting themselves for German gold, as Lenin did, and held little if any real allegiance to specific Bolshevik ideology. Whatever the motives, the net result was, of course, the same.

In March 1918 a "defensist," pro-Allied Russian paper *Russkii* (The Russian) had to cease publishing because of a lack of funds, giving the antiwar agitators a clear run of the field. To make matters worse, the disappearance of the pro-war journal came at a time when the Bolshevik-German-pacifist propaganda was intensifying and increasing more than ever among the Russian troops, who were receiving tracts hostile to France in ever growing numbers. One such flyer in March advanced the typical, logical, and oft-repeated argument that since Russia was now at peace with Germany, it would be a shame for Russian soldiers to continue to fight and die for France; such reasoning had gone over well with the beleaguered Russians on all fronts.[5]

This type of subversion was found everywhere in France where there were Russian soldiers. At Poitiers in the 9th region around Tours, two men and a woman, "all speaking many Slavic languages," were sowing discord among the Russian workers in the region.[6] Reports arrived that "revolutionary and antipatriotic propaganda" was discovered among the Russian soldier-workers in the department of La Vienne, and at the military Hospital Michelet in Paris, the Abbé Werterle discovered antiwar pamphlets among the wounded. Postal control then seized some letters and brochures in Russian with socialist leanings sent to the soldiers there by a defeatist organization located in Paris masking under the marvelous name the League of Revolutionary Defense.[7]

Even the Russian Red Cross came under suspicion, probably with good reason, since the Soviet government from the beginning was not averse to using reputable organizations for subversive work. The Russian Red Cross in Switzerland had used its position to propagandize elements in Zurich, and the Swiss government finally had to expel the institution from the country. The French government was advised that allowing the Russian Red Cross to enter France for any purposes would "not be without inconvenience" and that "it would be desirable to be able to avoid it,"[8] and in November Clemenceau made it plain that he did not want any agents of the Russian Red Cross functioning on French soil,[9] a position he would have to reverse in time.

Many escapees became for the Germans the source of *agents provocateurs* who circulated in France either to spy or cause trouble. The French in October 1918 learned that a group had sent thousands of francs to a colony of about eighty Russian deserters interned near Martigny,[10] and they would not have sent them money for altruistic reasons. Another source of help was what the French security police called the Swiss Bolsheviks, probably Swiss socialists or maybe even communists, who used various means to spread the word that the French had been mistreating the Russians in France, thus causing the desertions.[11] So many Russians went into Switzerland that, as early as March, the director of Swiss General Security contacted the French minister of the interior in hopes of getting it stopped. The French cabinet official replied that the flow of Russian deserters into Switzerland had not escaped his attention, and measures would be taken to try to stop this violation of the border.[12] Presumably they were.

As 1918 wore on and it became evident that the Allies eventually would win the war, Bolshevik propaganda began to shift from the antiwar theme and the treatment of Russians in France to opposition to the Allied intervention in Russia that was beginning to develop. Initially Allied involvement in the Russian internecine struggle had as its goal the opening of a second front in the East and the prevention of supplies earlier sent to Russia from falling into the hands of the Germans. Western leaders feared that the Germans might have demanded delivery in some secret clause of the Brest-Litovsk treaty that Russia had signed with the Germans in March 1918 when they left the war. As the Allies became more and more hostile to the Bolshevik regime, their motives for intervention, however, became more personal: the toppling of the Bolshevik regime and its replacement with a government that would honor the Russian war bonds sold in such profusion on the French money markets. Bolshevik propaganda naturally changed to reflect it.

Yet one major legacy of the hostile propaganda was the transformation of the anti-French attitude among the Russians that had always been there to strong dislike, and even hatred, of France. Aide-Major Lapidus in the Russian embassy noted in his report to Ambassador Maklakov that in his visit with a medical commissioner to the wounded some months before, he was struck by the "muted but evident hostility" to France of the Russian soldiers who had left the front. This attitude was also very much in evidence among those few who had been able to leave the country.[13] This antipathy was very broadly manifested among the radical Russian troops exiled in Africa but, amazingly, also among those who expressed a willingness to fight in France. One French report noted this animosity and even added that it was not "unjustified" because many of the vexatious problems, such as the concentration camp atmosphere around those performing labor, had never been rectified. The author of the memo expressed the fear that it would be "extremely regrettable" if these soldiers returned to Russia "propagating Francophobic ideas" and suggested that something be done so that the men would instead return as "friends of France."[14]

This enmity never lessened, however, and reports indicate that even the trickle of Russian soldiers who did return home were hardly off the boat before they began attacking France in the most hostile terms. The French *chef de mission* in Murmansk wrote Paris late in April to inform the government of the "extremely violent anti-French propaganda" made by the Russian soldiers arriving on the most recent ship.

From the Russians' arrival in France, however, there had likewise been among the French an anti-Russian bias. With the revolution and the collapse of the Russian armed forces, that antipathy turned to hatred. At first the French had, as did most Allies, seen the February Revolution as a positive ridding of the Russian government of corrupt, pro-German elements, but with the rapid disintegration of the Russian army and the concomitant danger to France, the attitude changed to one of hostility. After the rout of the second Brusilov offensive in July 1917, the French military used words such as "cowardice" and "spinelessness" to describe the Russian army, mocking the "steamroller that could not crack a nut." One letter read by the censor called the Russians "riffraff, from the tsar down to the lowest *muzhik*," curiously blaming the Russians for "landing them in this mess." Attendance at Russian classes in secondary schools diminished, and Russian officers were verbally attacked so viciously on the street that they were asked not to wear their uniforms in public.[15] Those Russians in hospitals and prisons were neglected and not given newspapers, journals, books, or movies. There were no official visits to keep them busy.[16]

Prince A. Lobanov-Rostovsky wrote that while taking additional training in the Vendée in late summer of 1918, he was stunned by the locals' frigid, unfriendly attitude. He suffered more than the others because he spoke French well and often understood the slurs and the insults. Once while in a restaurant, Lobanov-Rostovsky had "some French bourgeois" stop by the table and just stare at him and his Russian companions as if they were animals in a zoo. They stood and saluted, but the Frenchmen only turned their backs and walked away.[17]

It is strange that the French should have been so contemptuous of Russian failure, since the French themselves had butchered a generation of their own countrymen against the Teutonic war machine. The French never came to appreciate the degree to which the Russians had sacrificed for the common cause and the extent of their suffering in that war, just as the West never fully comprehended the Russian contribution in the struggle against Hitler a generation later. In neither world war could the West have endured the punishment meted out to the Russians, yet in both cases the West tended to minimize the Russian role, never comprehending the hardships Russia's troops and their citizens had faced.

To counter the hostile forces, Zankevich asked permission in the late winter of 1918 for the resumption of publication of *Le Soldat-Citoyen*, this time privately funded. Clemenceau had suspended it as an economy measure but had no objection to its being produced with private funds, although he warned Zankevich that it would have to submit to French censorship just like all other newspapers published in France. One objection raised by General Alby was the publication of the journal under the auspices of the Committee of the Detachment of Russian Troops in France. These committees were supposed to have been abolished by order on December 24, 1917, and the paper therefore could not be under any such committee.[18] Mikhailov obtained for the journal's resurrection a subvention from an unlikely source, the Young Men's Christian Association. The renowned organization agreed only after every assurance had been given that the publication would be "clearly ententophile" and that it would have the purpose of buttressing the morale of the Russian troops under French military authority.[19] Offices were organized at 46 Boulevard Saint Jacques in Paris. At times, however, *Soldat-Citoyen* strayed from the prescribed agenda, although not due to any Bolshevik influence. In May some article appeared (the report does not state its nature) that displeased the French authorities, leading them to take "necessary measures to see that no other similar article would appear again."[20] In November after the war had ended, however, a piece went so far as to criticize the French lodging and treatment of Russian wounded.

During the winter of 1917-1918, the French government completed its basic sorting of Russians into their respective categories. Archives of the various ministries involved with the different groups are replete with memos, lists of instructions, and directives for groups of soldiers combined together for whatever reasons. Meticulous care always was taken to document the comings and going of each group. The designation on which there is probably the most material is the labor contingents. In February the workers were all formed into companies and regiments as the basis for overall organization, and the French kept incredibly detailed records on both their work and their behavior.[21] Memos often were report cards with grades given for "*morale*," "*Situation matérielle*," "*Situation sanitaire*," "*Distribution de tabac*," and so forth, with marks awarded such as "*satisfaisante*" and "*bonne*."

Functioning only as workers safe from the line of fire, the Russians' grumbling, however, did not diminish. There were the usual complaints about the insufficient bread ration (two-thirds of a pound per day), absence of news from home, not enough tobacco, unkept French promises, and the desire to return home. In March some workers at St. Malo wanted to celebrate the anniversary of the revolution and obtained authorization for a meeting, but it quickly became political and revolutionary in nature and was stopped by the French. In retaliation, soldiers paraded the next day in groups sporting the *cocard à boutonnière*, a symbol of the French Revolution. The authorities took measures to restore order and ultimately no incident took place, but the occurrence is good evidence of the unsettled mood of those Russians that had chosen to work.

All reports of work battalions are sprinkled with accounts of desertions, indiscipline, and disorderly conduct, often resulting in transfers to Île d'Aix or North Africa of those who had first agreed to work but later caused trouble. Russian laborers, however, seem always to have been given freedom to roam about during their free time, and sometimes clashes with locals were serious. For example, sixty-five Russians armed with clubs caused a disturbance in a cinema at Fay-aux-Loges. At the forest at La Nièvre, workers revolted and refused to work, using the now-familiar argument that Russia's having left the war gave them no obligation to perform war labor. Formal strikes erupted in May among Russian cement workers in Vermenton and foresters in Mailly-le-Château.[22]

Such incidents were constant throughout the year in large cities as well as in many small towns and villages. Yet from the beginning the French sternly suppressed any disorder, and those refusing to work were immediately denied their salary. For continued reluctance to work, there was quick imprisonment or deportation to Africa. In the 1920s a Private Semenov told a *Pravda* reporter that in his unit, refusal to work resulted in execution. When his group refused to do what was demanded of them, the French officer in the field told them they would be shot. Some of the group, obviously not taking the threat seriously, replied, "Go ahead and shoot! We don't care. We will not work." Before the soldiers' very eyes, the French shot their leader, a soldier named Poliakov.[23]

Although the story has a true ring to it, the account is highly unlikely, for all unbiased accounts demonstrate that the French continued to treat the Russians with surprising circumspection. When they became ill, they were hospitalized under basically the same conditions as the French. In October 1918 there were among the Russians only eighteen mortal cases of Spanish flu, which would indicate that their medical care must have been exceedingly good. Moreover, to the very end of the year, reports continued to indicate these Russian workers were given a surprising amount of freedom, as accounts of incidents in towns and villages caused by conflict with natives appeared. In the end of December, General Alby complained about Russians coming by train from the armies' zone to Paris, where they caused trouble, clearly showing how little restraint was placed on them. Despite the extent of trouble, it was not until June 11, 1918, that all Russians, even those then fighting for France, were denied leave in Paris. Surprisingly, the Russian prisoners in Category B were allowed free access to the French mail system, and they seem to have corresponded freely with one another, written home, and petitioned Lokhvitsky and Zankevich for help. When it was not forthcoming, they sought assistance through the French mail service from a M. Tschopak, 46 Boulevard St. Jacques in Paris,[24] the address of the *Soldat-Citoyen* and one that appears frequently in police archives. Had the French been as ruthless as Russians later claimed, this freedom would never have been permitted. It is impossible to conceive inmates in Stalin's *gulags* being given the same privilege.

To the other Russian soldiers throughout France, the prisoners of Aix were heroes, who received, especially Baltais, Volkov, and Globa, from their former comrades-in-arms a flood of letters written with the greatest respect. They addressed their former leaders as "Most Honored Comrade," and they gave them the news of what was happening and even complained about their living conditions as if these generals of the rebellion could do something about it. The soldiers on the outside also sent them money. Colonel Barjonet noted in a memo in June that a soldier Ezhepatkin in a work detachment in Valençay had recorded in a letter read by a censor that sums of 122, 60, and 122 francs had been sent to Baltais. Barjonet was writing to inquire just how these sums could arrive.[25] Quite possibly some of these funds never reached the intended recipients, but another report states that soldiers had recently sent Baltais 70, Volkov 30, Globa 115, and one Faliavka 57 francs. A request from Baltais to a comrade at St. Pierre-des-Corps resulted in a return of 65 francs, 10 of which Baltais kept, dividing the remainder with his colleagues.[26] Usually, however, the "heroes" did not bother responding to the correspondence because, according to French speculations, they wished to foster the belief that they were not allowed to do so.

Baltais continued to have other friends in high places, the most conspicuous being General Nikolaev, the military representative of the Provisional Government to the French Army and the director of the Military Justice Service. For whatever reason, early in February, Nikolaev asked for the release of Baltais and his colleague Volkov as well as sixteen other unnamed Russian soldiers awaiting trial before a war council, to a work detail in the Bordeaux area. The specific request for the Bordeaux area sounds a bit suspicious, and the commandant of the 18th region was most hesitant to have these leaders in contact with other workers in the area because they could cause trouble. He asked that he be informed as to their destination if they were released.[27]

It is not surprising that there would be some escapees with so many Russians detained. Most of them were, of course, from among the workers in France who could not be guarded very closely and who were given leave to go into the villages and towns. General Maurice Baumgarten, commandant of the 16th region on the Spanish border, was fearful as early as November 1917 that idle workers would try to cross the Spanish frontier, and he suggested that they be given work as soon as possible.[28] Most of those who did succeed in fleeing, however, did so through neutral Switzerland, where the Bolshevik agents were very active from the beginning and most probably a support network already was in place. Contact could be made with Swiss sympathizers, and some landlords would rent to them. French reports state that the "deserters," when successful in crossing the border into Switzerland, went immediately to the German consulates, where they received help. They also obtained assistance from the Russian (now Bolshevik) legation in Bern.[29]

The winter of 1917-1918 saw the initiation of French diplomatic relations, albeit unwillingly and unofficially, with the new Soviet state. The French did not recognize the Bolshevik government, but in January 1918, however, there were 2,000 French nationals in Russia and about 20,000 Russian nationals in France. Some sort of contact would have to be established to deal with the problem of respective repatriation, if nothing else. Moreover, immediately upon seizing the reins of government, the Bolsheviks had started peace negotiations with the Germans. When, in January, the Bolsheviks received German demands calling for the surrender of much of their European territory and natural resources, a rupture of negotiations occurred. Russia might be induced to remain in the war. Given this turn of events, even the militantly anti-Communist

Foch favored limited cooperation with the Soviets, and for about two months, while it appeared that Russia might stay in the struggle, the French even agreed to help the Communist regime. Yet the thought of strengthening an army that might one day be used against French interests did not sit well with the military authorities, and even though later in March French officers in Russia were ready to go "on line" as advisors to Soviet Russia, Clemenceau stifled any such action. When General Foch became Allied commander-in-chief, the idea was dropped completely.[30]

Toward the end of April, Chicherin, now foreign commissar, terminated the brief honeymoon when he sent a note to Noulens at Vologda, where the Allied embassies had fled, stating that he had learned that members of the Russian Expeditionary Force in France had been sent to Africa, where they had been subjected to disciplinary punishment "in conditions of such rigor that it has already made object of debate in the Chamber [of Deputies] and in the press." The Council of Peoples' Commissars asked the consul general of France to present their protest to the French government and express the hopes that the government would transport the soldiers back from Africa and in the "immediate future" organize their return to Russia.[31] To avoid possible embarrassment, the French government advised Noulens not to respond, since to do so would give the debate that the Russians so wanted, but very shortly discussions with the Soviets would be impossible to evade.

In May the Soviets complained again about the treatment of the Russian soldiers, claiming that some had been sent to Hyères in December in unheated cattle cars, given boxes marked "medicine and bandages" that were empty, and in general received abusive handling by the accompanying French authorities.[32] To keep their countrymen abreast of these matters and no doubt to fan Francophobia, the Soviet government printed a long article in *Pravda* recounting the general mistreatment, telling the journal's readers accounts of alleged French cruelty, from the beatings of amputees to the serving of "repugnant soup."[33]

Chicherin, who must have been enjoying this game of unilateral debate, sent President Poincaré a letter via the representative of the French government in Moscow, once again denouncing the treatment of Russian soldiers in France in contrast to the treatment of Russians in so many other countries.[34] No reply came from the French government, so to keep the pot stirred for the benefit of Soviet Russia's relations with both Germany and France, the Soviet foreign commissar sent a public letter to the Russian soldiers in France informing them that the new Russian government had protested against any enlistment of Russian soldiers in the French armed forces. Chicherin called on all Russians in France to oppose "by all means possible" the incorporation of Russians into the French army and branded all Russians who would dare to submit to French authority "enemies of the [Soviet] Republic."[35]

As the civil struggle intensified in the new Russian state in the early fall of 1918, the Soviets sent another letter to Poincaré through Switzerland, one of the few nations that had recognized the new Russian regime, stating that its government was examining the prospect of repatriation through Switzerland and spoke of Red Cross help to facilitate the matter. The Swiss appended an addendum to the note stating that they had agreed to permit the passage of the Russians through Switzerland.[36] By this time the French were committed to the overthrow of the Bolshevik regime and did not reply to this overture.

In mid-October, angered by the lack of response and by growing hostility within France to their very existence, the Bolshevik government issued a veiled threat to the French government against those French citizens, especially embassy personnel, then living in Russia. If the French continued to oppose the return of the Russian troops, something that they were of course not doing, the Bolsheviks threatened retaliation against the French in Russia. At this point, all consular personnel were still at liberty to depart, except for Pierre Darcy, the commercial attaché, M. Mazon of the Political Information Service, and the commandant, M. Ducastel, who were being detained as insurance. While this game was being played, Maxim Litvinov, the deputy Soviet foreign commissar, was in Great Britain with a deputation, and the Soviet government informed France that these three Frenchmen, not any English personnel, were to be held as hostages for his safe return from Great Britain, as if the French government had any control over British policy.[37]

A month later the *Huntsend*, a British vessel that seems to have been regularly shuttling between France and Murmansk, was in northern Russia, and the British captain offered the French ambassador passage out of the country. In fact, he pleaded with him to board either his boat or the *Stephen*, which was also there. If he did not, there would be no occasion to leave for some time, and he might be detained by the Bolsheviks.[38] For whatever reason, neither Noulens nor his staff departed, and shortly afterward, the unofficial Franco-Soviet nonrelationship took a cruel turn for the worse, giving the new Soviet government an important trump card to play against the hated French.

The new year, 1918, saw an ever-increasing intensity in the paradox created by the Russian force and the French desire to send them home. While the Soviet government was making propagandistic hay from

France's having Russian soldiers on its soil, French memos dealing with their attempts to rid themselves of the Russians became more and more frantic. The new year did indeed see the beginning of repatriation from Western Europe, but only in trickles that did not begin to solve the problem for the French. At the end of January, about 250 discharged soldiers asked to be returned to Russia through Sweden at their own expense, and the French prime minister asked the foreign minister if he objected to repatriation of these men.[39] Most of these soldiers were officers from the First Brigade who, not wanting to fight for France, had nothing to do. A few Russian officers had found jobs in the armament or aeronautic ministries and some found places on the staff of Generals Zankevich and Ignatiev, the remainder, the 250, had no employment. If this small number would return and at the same time cost the French government nothing, it might be a beginning. On February 6 the minister of foreign affairs reported to the prime minister that he felt that it was acceptable to allow these men to be repatriated, if they paid the costs themselves.[40]

Early in February, Mikhailov wrote a memo to Clemenceau suggesting general repatriation through Vladivostok, beginning with the sick and wounded first, followed by the more suitable groups. Making an important point, he added, "It is necessary to decide the repatriation in principle and without delay to carry this decision to the knowledge of the troops," a point well made. Given the French desire to return the men, it is peculiar that they did not shout their intention from the rooftops. About a week later Clemenceau responded through Foch, who had contacted the ministry of the navy to ask for an examination of possible routes for moving the troops eastward to Vladivostok, to consult the Americans and Japanese about the possibility of letting them go westward and be carried in ships of those nations.[41]

In two direct discussions, Clemenceau accepted Mikhailov's suggestion to ship the men in small groups. They also agreed that the men should be subjected to amiable pro-ententist propaganda so that they would leave France with a good impression of their sojourn in the West. Both Niessel and Noulens suggested that in the process of repatriation, a deal be struck with the Soviets to exchange the 38,500 men in France and Salonika for the 20,000 Czechs, who as a force were later to become so famous, and 6,000 Polish volunteers who were somewhere in Russia. The plan to move all these men was a most elaborate one, involving the Americans' moving the Russians to Dalny, with the English and the Japanese transporting the Czechs and Poles through Port Said, Murmansk, and Archangel. It was a rewarmed version of the plan the Americans, the British, and the Japanese had rejected the previous fall.[42]

Late in March the *Huntsend*, making its usual run for Murmansk, reserved 700 places in third class for wounded and discharged Russians. There was to be no room for officers, and any departing soldiers had to be at Le Havre on Tuesday, April 2, at noon to be sent the same evening to Southampton. The British also asked that two interpreters travel with them overland to Newcastle, the port of embarkation. Eventually 700 Russians left St. Malo for Le Havre on March 31, and a few joined them at Rennes, to make a total of 711. This group departed from France on April 1 for Southampton, and on April 10 they left from Newcastle for Murmansk. Some passed through Sweden. The French government gave each man a final salary allocation as they were leaving.[43] With these small dribbles, the Russian Expeditionary Force that had come to France two years before took its first steps on its journey home.

These numbers, however, were only the proverbial drop in the bucket. A report to the prime minister in mid-February lists 14,500 Russians still in France (a later report cites 14,600) and 9,000 in North Africa (another report lists 9,500). The 14,000 includes those in work units, those in Île d'Aix and other prisons, and 2,424 that were hospitalized.[44] As usual, everyone had the plan how to move them, but no one could solve the problem of transport, the most crucial matter delaying their return.

On May 12 another small group of unidentified officers with their families departed. The next day 1,200 who had been wounded were scheduled to leave as well, although the boat designated to take them was given another assignment.[45] They were able to leave the next day, and with their departure, roughly 10 percent of those entering France in 1916 had gone home.[46] The reports give the impression that Lokhvitsky and the French screened these early deportees. Of the 1,200 just mentioned, the French reported that they were "mostly Maximalists [Bolsheviks]." Several other reports indicate that Lokhvitsky made several recommendations to return or not to return certain individuals, based on their patterns of behavior.[47] It is logical that when the chance came to be rid of some Russians, those who were the greatest problems—that is, the sick, the wounded, the political troublemakers—would be sent first. Until the flow became facile, the French government singled out those who were the largest burden for the earliest departure.

On March 7 Jusserand informed his government that the Americans would be willing to transport 20,000 Russians to Panama if the Japanese could be persuaded to take them from there,[48] but they had absolutely refused to carry these men across the North American continent. Secretary of State Robert Lansing told Jusserand that crossing France, a smaller, more densely populated country, is not to be compared with crossing the United States with its wide open spaces.[49] The incredible scheme that could have been devised only by desperate people called for the Japanese to transport the Czechs in Siberia to America and for the French to transport them from America to France. Meanwhile, the French would bring the Russians to the Western Hemisphere, where the empty Japanese boats would board them, taking them to Vladivostok. The Japanese put a final nail in the coffin in April when the Japanese Empire informed the French ambassador, Eugène Regnault, that it could not move the Russians across the Pacific because it had made a commitment to place 150,000 tons of shipping at the Allies' disposal to create a line of navigation among France, Japan, and the French colonies.[50]

The French, therefore, once again faced a dead end. No additional stratagems were forthcoming, however, probably because the major German offensives of 1918 had begun, and Clemenceau had more urgent matters on his plate. From March until August, the military situation again became parlous as the now numerically superior Germans drove the Allies back once again to within sight of the Eiffel Tower. The only avenue left to evacuate the Russians was the trickle approach, which would hardly ever be satisfactory. Soon even the Swedish route was closed when, in March 1918, Sweden recognized the Soviet government and began requiring Soviet passports of all transient Russian citizens. Since the repatriates had no way of obtaining them, this avenue of repatriation ended. Moreover, not only had the repatriation ceased, but those who had arrived on Russian soil were providing first-rate ammunition for the Bolshevik propaganda mill.

The head of the French mission in Murmansk quickly wired Paris that the "extremely violent anti-French propaganda" of these men on landing had produced "disastrous effects" and "destroyed in part work that [had been done] over several months." The soldiers had been agitated en route by *agents provocateurs* and "anti-French Jews" and had on landing "made here a tableau as false as it is sinister of their treatment in France and of the situation in that country." He strongly urged that special preventive measures and some surveillance be taken if new transports were to be created.[51] Those first repatriates left Murmansk immediately by train, after having had time to sell everything from their shoes to their ragged uniforms, reducing themselves to veritable nudity and making it so much the better to complain of the miserable conditions forced on them by the French and the English. To add to their discomfort, the first train to leave collided with another a short distance away.[52]

Numerous other versions tell of the hostility and bitterness of the soldiers returning home, yet it is a pity that we do not have any record of their reactions to what they found in Russia. The Bolsheviks, in the interest of appearing egalitarian, had destroyed in Murmansk all passenger cars save one, leaving only freight and cattle cars to transport these men southward. Most certainly they had no heat. The one good car that was left was a magnificent salon car inhabited by an agent of Trotsky, thus establishing early a precedent of the luxurious perks that were to accompany being a Communist bigwig from that time until the 1991 collapse of the party. They also returned to homes in which there was no food or heat. Many of them quickly found themselves drafted into the Red Army, where there were no soldiers' committees to protect their rights and discipline was enforced by the firing squad.

For all of the anti-French anger among the Russian community in France, the winter of 1917-1918 did see the flowering of a number of Russian organizations in France that were loyal to the Allies and expressed a wish to fight for them. Many were born as a reaction to the October Revolution. These groups, however, were constantly under the vigilant eye of the French secret police, whose records give us most of our information on them. Count Nesselrode, a French citizen of Russian origin, helped form and became the president of the League for the Defense of the Revolution, and he also assumed the presidency of another organization to aid Russians fighting under the French flag. Both bodies were made of politically disparate groups held together only because of their opposition to Lenin and their pro-Allied stance. There also emerged an association called the Russian Anti-defeatist Committee with headquarters in Paris. This organization produced the paper *Rossiia*, edited by M. Ashaourow and Admiral Vladimir Lebedev, with its headquarters at the ever-popular Parisian address, 46 Boulevard St. Jacques.[53] Even the impotent Zankevich tried to rally the few remaining loyal Russian troops with orders of the day blasting the Bolsheviks and calling on troops "to refuse to recognize a group of persons who seize governmental institutions without having the authority of state power." Lokhvitsky, on the other hand, called on Russians to join the French army. Meetings and rallies were held to protest the Communist seizure of power. At one, on rue Danton on December 6, police observers reported that 900 people were in attendance. The featured speaker was Ambassador Maklakov, who was still recognized by the French government as Russia's ambassador to Paris.[54] In March 1918, General Vasilii Gurko formed and became president of yet another patriotic group called Russians Loyal to the Entente in Order to Save Russian Honor.[55] An organization with a similar name (and probably the same organization) was the Committee of the League of Russians Loyal to the Country and to the

Alliance, which included Izvolsky, Lokhvitsky, the diplomat A. V. Nekliu-
dov, and several former Duma members. Moreover, in 1919 a select group
of Russian ambassadors and diplomats to Western governments formed in
Paris a sort of shadow government consisting equally of those who represented "Old Russia" and those who accepted the changes of the February
Revolution, both groups hopelessly ignorant of the fact that their respective
Russias had been long since swept into Trotsky's dustbin of history. They
hoped to protect Russian interests at Versailles and represent to the Allies
"the opinion of Russia."[56]

None of these societies seems to have made much difference in the
rallying of opinion outside their membership and merely contributed paper
to the already bulging files of the paranoid French security police, but they
demonstrated some Russian loyalty to the Allies. In almost all cases, these
organizations were created by those who opposed Bolshevism, and often
they were so out of touch with political reality that they were still in effect
trying to prevent the *February* Revolution. They had little understanding of
what the average Russian thought or felt, and this lack of perception would
be the major shoal that was to destroy the White movement in the Russian
Civil War. Their greatest concession to mass opinion was to cloak their anti-
Left activity under a guise that they were saving the revolution, when in
reality most of them would like to have prevented it.

In league with these antidefeatists were those former members of the REF
who offered to return to the front. By their actions, the Russian Legion,
Lokhvitsky's Third Category, was born. Exactly with whom the idea
originated is impossible to say, although it was probably Zankevich.
General Yuri Danilov, who later wrote a book about the REF, did suggest
the idea at some point as well. Possibly he raised it with Zankevich. After
the suppression of the La Courtine affair, however, Danilov reported to
the Provisional Government that although the force had disintegrated in
France, it could be resurrected. Despite their desire to return to Russia,
among these troops remained a certain element that wanted to reestablish
a unit and take a sector of the front.[57] Within a week of the Battle of La
Courtine, Zankevich suggested to General Foch that a Russian legion
from among the reliable soldiers be formed. He felt that among the officers
and soldiers in France there was "a considerable number who asked to
fight to the end of hostilities on the French front," and he found it
reasonable to create "several units," choosing them from the "better
elements." Before suggesting this plan to the Provisional Government, he
wanted Foch's opinion. The request passed over the desk of Clemenceau,
who was at that time on the eve of becoming prime minister. The Tiger of

France must have thought favorably of it because he forwarded it to Foch, asking him to let him know what he thought as well.[58] The French general's opinion also must have been favorable, for on October 5, 1917, after talking to Pétain, Zankevich wired Petrograd for formal permission to create a Russian legion.[59] Petrograd approved, and, on October 15, Russian units held a meeting to discuss the organization of a Russian force from the fragments of the old.

Surprisingly, it was a mass meeting, open not only to Russian officers but noncommissioned officers and soldiers as well, and it was chaired by Lokhvitsky. Rapp was also there. Having just returned from Paris seeking permission on the matter, Lokhvitsky told the men that the meeting had been called for the purpose of exploring the possibility of forming a unit of Russians to assume a sector of the French front. At this gathering, a contingent of stranded Russians who refused to accept the treaty of Brest-Litovsk formed a new fighting force in the West. They called it the Russian Legion.

One issue that quickly arose was the question of soldiers' committees. Representatives from Courneau, probably mostly officers, felt that there should be none, but some soldiers from Salonika protested vigorously at the removal of these guardians of soldiers' rights. Some spoke for at least the creation of an elected central committee to coordinate all activities. At the opening session, nothing was concluded on the subject, however, and the report of a Colonel Fonssagrives ended with the observation that "all had taken place in the greatest calm."[60] This question of soldiers' committees, conceived in the Russian Revolution, was to be shortly, and decisively, settled, however, by the French government.

In the midst of these developments, General Pershing and Major General James Harbord, after having just inspected the camp at Courneau, were having lunch in the seaside resort of Archachon and encountered two highly decorated Russian colonels who said that their general, presumably Lokhvitsky, had gone to Paris to see whether Russian soldiers could go to the front. Pershing asked if they felt that such a poorly disciplined bunch of men could hold a sector, and receiving a reply in the affirmative, he told the two Russian officers about the deplorable state at Courneau. The officers replied that it was that way when they had occupied it from the French, never explaining that if that was true, why they themselves did not clean it. Pershing and Harbord expressed the view to each other that any force formed could not be of much value at the front, and he concluded that the Russian soldiers were "drunk, absolutely drunk with liberty!"[61]

Intoxicated with liberty or not, at 6:00 P.M. on December 10, 1917, the Russian soldier in France got the beginnings of a unit in which he could fight for the Allies if he chose to do so. At French army headquarters, a committee under the chairmanship of General Alby outlined a detailed plan to create a Russian legion and decided to form a Russian base at the town of Laval as soon as possible to organize such a force. Colonel Kotovich was made local commandant. It was to have French administration, but the Russians would provide the official leadership. The Russian recruits for this force would generally be treated as French soldiers, receiving French rations and salaries.[62] The recruitment of the new unit was to come originally from volunteers at Courneau and Russian elements living around France. It would be constituted with a battalion and a *compagnie de dépôt* and would be attached to a large French unit. Each company would have a commandant and three officers, one of whom would be French, with two interpreters.

This first section of the reborn legion was comprised of 7 officers, 2 doctors, a priest and 374 soldiers and noncommissioned officers. It appears that it had begun organizing on its own under Colonel Gotua before the French and Russian military leaders decided on forming one. A French officer who could speak Russian was made adjutant. In this first group of Russians to return to the fight, by the way, was Private First Class Rodion Malinovsky, assuming his old place in a machine-gun company.[63]

As this first battalion of the Russian Legion marched to the station, all along the road were crowds of silent Frenchmen who emitted "not one cry, not one whistle." The men marched with rifles on their shoulders singing Russian songs in cadence with each step. Gotua went at the head on his steed in his Caucasian hat, a *papakh*, displaying on his chest the white Cross of St. George, and the silent crowd, however, burst into applause at this majestic sight. The bear mascot Misha was with him and growled at the crowd. They loved it.[64]

At the station, the cars designated to transport these men carried the label Russian Voluntary Units. On January 5, 1918, they joined Colonel Obertin's force, the 4th Moroccan Infantry, which with the 8th Zouaves, the 7th Moroccan infantry, and the 12th battalion of Malagesh Infantry, comprised a Moroccan Shock Division and a unit of the Foreign Legion.[65] In the beginning of February, Gotua's force was transferred to the 8th Zouaves as the unit's 4th battalion. Impressed by these soldiers, Obertin wrote, "They keep the love of their country and the faith that Russia will rise again. . . . It is necessary to them to free Russia and her glorious past from the gang of Bolsheviks. . . ."[66] With the activation of these men, the Russian Empire formally reentered the Great War.

By being first to organize, Gotua's force became the first battalion of the reconstituted Russian Expeditionary Force. Regardless of the appellation, however, the Russian command was to be fully under French control; the change formally took place on January 14, 1918.[67] Thereafter the soldiers had to recognize and accept French rules of order and discipline, and this change meant no committees.[68] The oath that each soldier took reflected the change: "I swear . . . to agree to serve in the ranks of the Russian Legion in France and submit myself to the rules of discipline which are observed there, that is to say, the French Military Rules without the intervention of any soviet."[69] It was stressed ad nauseam in memos and directives that the Russian soldiers would in all cases have to submit to *French* military regulations and authority.[70] There would not, therefore, be any of the committees, commissars, delegates, votes, or mass meetings that had wrecked the old Russian army. With the creation of the new Russian Legion under those stipulations, the Russian army in France had been dissolved and a new peculiarly hybrid organism had replaced it.

To form the other units, Lokhvitsky issued throughout France on December 19 a ringing call to arms for a Russian *levée-en-masse*. In an article entitled "An Appeal to the Russians of France," he summoned all Russians of military age to join the new force: "We, it is said, who were so fierce in carrying the Russian name, we Russians of France who love so our unfortunate country . . . will make the French confident in the forces of Russia." He continued in this heroic style with thundering appeals to action under the Russian flag, summoning his fellow nationals with the rather unappealing call, "Let us run to the trenches to mix our blood with that of the glorious French."[71] Lokhvitsky of course stretched the point that in fighting for France they were fighting for their own country and for "the eternal ideals of civilization," but under this reasoning he called on all those "who have the good fortune to be Russian, without distinctions of party, of class," to enlist. The sick and wounded could volunteer for the services in the rear, he suggested, with all others who are still able to carry a rifle to act as combatants.[72] The Soviet historian Ioffe, without giving his source, wrote that in January 1918 there were over 19,000 Russian soldiers in France or in its colonies.[73] From this bolt of Russian national cloth was drawn the majority of those who eventually would form the Russian Legion, and it would come to include representatives from virtually every ethnic group in the now-defunct Russian Empire. Clemenceau had insisted that all joining be volunteers,[74] so recruitment was based on persuasion. Its diversity is strong testimony to its appeal.

From this one summons, by March 1918 volunteers from all backgrounds were arriving even from beyond France's borders. Galician prisoners of war in Italy volunteered. There was even one Canadian of Russian background who asked to join. One Peter Bogalsky, who had been dragoman of the Russian consul general in Calcutta, came to Laval from Rome. The general head of the Franco-Polish military mission told the prime minister that a number of Russians in Holland wanted to join, as well as some Poles.[75] From as far away as Archangel, several Russians expressed interest in fighting in France.[76] They came from North Africa as well, with some 303 volunteers arriving late in March, although there was some attrition before the arrival at Laval. Four joined the Legion Armenia in Marseille, where five also had been jailed for causing trouble. One joined the Foreign Legion in Lyon, and three disappeared en route.[77] In October the French ministry of war also allowed the Russians currently serving in the Foreign Legion to transfer to the Russian Legion if they wished to do so. About 150 of them did.[78] Another large source of recruitment for the Legion was the Russian brigades at Salonika, which at this point had yet to revolt openly, and as late as June 1918, Russian soldiers from there continued to join. That month 200 landed in Marseille. Meanwhile, the Russian Legion also obtained an air squadron when 40 Russian aviators joined the unit.[79]

In 1918 Lokhvitsky issued his general appeal in Great Britain, where there had always been a Russian community. The British government gave formal permission for recruitment there in March, and the call appeared in *The Times* in the edition of April 4. The summons begged all Russians residing in England to join the Russian Legion "to continue the war against the Central Powers and fight on the French front." It listed the conditions of service just given.[80]

In mid-February enrollment in the Russian Legion temporarily slumped, and Lokhvitsky felt that it had done about all that it would do. He informed the ministry of foreign affairs on February 18, incorrectly as it turned out, that the number of effectives in the force "will no longer increase appreciably."[81] Moreover, a form of attrition had begun to occur from means other than battle casualties. In June soldiers Skril, Timorov, Zous, Gusev, and Kripunov were returned from the unit to Africa because of unacceptable behavior.[82] Others followed. All of these losses, however, did not prevent the French propaganda organ *La Victoire* from announcing mendaciously, and probably for German consumption, that there were now 22,000 Russians fighting in France,[83] a figure that was as unrealistic as it was bogus. While the figure never reached 22,000, however, the men did continue coming until the end of the war. Enough dribbled in and signed the oath that by early March, the French were considering the creation of a third battalion. Almost 400 new recruits at Laval were unassigned, and after 30 were sent to Gotua's battalion on March 7 and 216 constituted a Battalion under Lieutenant Colonel Ieske, there were

149 left. About 30 could be divided between the two existing battalions, leaving around 120 who could be the kernel of a third unit. By April, however, there were even enough men to form yet a fourth.[84]

Ultimately Lokhvitsky formed four complete battalions. By April 21, Gotua's battalion became the first of the Russian Legion, with 396 men and 10 officers with a depot of 3 officers and 94 men. The Second, of 11 officers and 374 men with a depot of 50 men and no officers, was commanded by Ieske, who had fought for France from 1914 until the Russians arrived. It went to the front in March 10 and joined the 178th division of the French army. After Ieske rejoined the French army in June, Colonel Kotovich replaced him as battalion leader.[85] Colonel Gregorii Simenov commanded the Third with 3 officers and the surprisingly small number of 122 men, with an attached depot of 3 officers. The Fourth and last battalion, commanded by Colonel Valerian Balbashevsky, consisted of 21 officers leading 504 men, with a depot of 8 officers and 334 men. The entire Russian Legion by April 1918 therefore consisted of 59 officers and 1,959 men.[86] General Danilov, whose numbers vary somewhat, wrote that 1,447 of these men were recipients of the Cross of St. George.[87] A report seven months later, just before the armistice, however, shows a total of only 524 men divided among three companies,[88] a chilling testament to the savagery of the fighting of the last year of the war and to the bravery of the Russian men in the Legion.

The rendezvous point for these troops was the base at the French city of Laval, given over to the Russians for coordination of the work units and now the Russian Legion.[89] The organizational structure of the Russian base, however, left no doubt that the French were in charge. While Lokhvitsky was formally the commandant of the base headquarters, General Jean Brulard, a French general who could speak Russian, was very much in evidence. He was to reside at the base and would have as his adjutants both a French and a Russian officer. The headquarters staff was to be comprised of three or four French officers and the necessary secretaries for clerical work. There would also be supply, health, and postal services, and a department of the bursar.

French authority, however, ran deeper. The second-in-command under Brulard was Colonel Barjonet, his adjutant. There was also to be a detachment of French military police under a sergeant or corporal of the cavalry. The highest-ranking Russian in the overall structure was initially to be the adjutant to the commandant, his main function being to provide a liaison between the top administration and the Russian troops. Shortly he was to be replaced by Barjonet. He was to report constantly to the base commandant on the morale of the personnel of the Russian units and handle any administrative problems dealing with them. He also was to serve as the intermediary between the French commandant and the Russian military attaché in Paris.[90] The most amazing feature of this chain of command, and one that must have sorely rankled the Russians, was that such a structure would place a colonel over higher-ranking officers who would be directly in touch with the men.

Immediately over the Russian forces, Clemenceau appointed General Lokhvitsky. In January 1918 the French prime minister wrote to inform Zankevich of his choice and to ask if he had any objections. Barjonet was to be the liaison to the Russian base.[91] With Lokhvitsky would be Generals Brulard, Antoine Dessort (after August 1919), and Colonel Barjonet. Under General Lokhvitsky were an assortment of officers in various positions, and the four battalions were headed by those just mentioned. Lokhvitsky raised many objections in mid-March to the removal of Russian officers and the predominance of French ones but got nowhere with the French High Command.[92] Moreover, he generally found displeasing the absence of any real power for himself and wrote to the minister of war of this situation.[93]

Lobanov-Rostovsky, who fought with the unit, felt that Laval was the worst possible place that could have been assigned them. Although the headquarters of the Russian Legion in France, it was full of demoralized Russian troops who were being drafted into labor units, and the mixing of the Russian soldiers with their former comrades-in-arms who had refused to fight proved "disastrous." Moreover, Laval's proximity to Paris meant that the deadly bacillus spread by the Russian-German provocateurs could easily reach the camp. When the news of the treaty of Brest-Litovsk arrived in France in March, agitators were quick to rush to the camp with the news, stressing the fact that the soldiers in the Russian Legion were the only Russians left in the war who were dying.[94] This argument was hard to refute, and after a month some unrest, as we shall see, reared its head at Laval.

Of more immediate importance to the soldiers in the Legion was the question of the legality of Russians' continuing to fight in France after the Brest-Litovsk treaty,[95] for a major concern was the Russian soldiers' status if captured. Would the Germans give them the same rights as other French prisoners of war? The French did give the question some thought, and the ministry of justice decided that the Hague Convention of 1907 indicated that Russians in Russian uniforms, fighting voluntarily under the French flag "does not by itself constitute a violation by the French government of the rules of international law."[96] Barjonet suggested that in case the Russians were not "legal," they could always be transferred into the Foreign Legion, where they would be. They could then also be due pensions and benefits of French veterans and would wear French uniforms.[97]

By July 1918 the German government was pressuring the Soviets to recall the Russians in France. In response, they received a reply that demonstrated the adroit footwork for which Chicherin was so skilled. The aristocrat turned Communist expressed surprise that the diplomatic representative of Germany had "returned to this long-ago resolved question" to which Chicherin had "repeatedly given thorough explanations of this problem." Not only that, the astonished Russian foreign commissar reminded them that he had even sent the Germans newspaper clippings. He reiterated that soldiers "remaining loyal to Soviet Russia" had not only refused to join "some sort of French force or legion" but had undergone "cruel treatment, even including forced African labor for refusal to participate in the war." Moreover, Chicherin, waxing righteously indignant, informed the Germans that this new Russian corps consisted of "traitors, enemies of the Russian government, Lokhvitskies and Maklakovs . . . , our implacable enemies." He then went on to lay blame for all of this perfidious behavior on the doorstep of the insidious French, who had refused to return these soldiers and not kept promises in regard to them.[98] The Germans were probably not satisfied, but with the war ending, they had other pressing concerns.

For the Russian soldiers the most difficult requirement to accept was the order in the spring of 1918 to wear French uniforms. The French feared that if the Russians were captured dressed as Russian soldiers, the Germans would treat them as citizens of a neutral country or hand them over to the Bolsheviks. French uniforms would at least make them part of the Foreign Legion and therefore entitled to be treated as French prisoners of war. Lokhvitsky, however, argued vigorously against the adoption of the *horizon bleu* uniform, pointing out that the Russian Legion was composed of men who had never accepted Bolshevism or the Brest-Litovsk treaty, so in their minds Russia was still at war with Germany. In a letter to the French prime minister, Lokhvitsky wrote that in denying them their Russian uniforms, "the very existence of the Russian Legion will be deprived of its essential base and will be badly taken by the soldiers." He went on to say that if the soldiers were not to be permitted their uniforms, it would be better to give them the uniforms of the French colonial troops, that is, the khaki, with the right to wear the brassard with the Russian tricolor flag on the left arm.[99] The khaki was allowed, but until after the armistice eight months later the Russian soldiers had to be content with painting the Russian colors (red, white, and blue) on the flagpole supporting the flag of the French Republic.[100]

French control of the Russian Legion early produced a major casualty—General Zankevich. He had challenged the subservience to French officers in a letter to the French prime minister dated January 10, 1918. Noting that in a number of cases his authority over the Russian troops in France and Macedonia had been confirmed, he insisted that the French government did not have the authority to take his powers from him. He pointed out that he must conserve all his rights and jurisdiction, and he could not tolerate the fact that the commandant over the Russian base was contacted directly without going through him. He even considered "inadmissible that Russian military workers be employed in some private concerns."[101] Not receiving satisfaction on the question, he resigned his position of commander of the Russian forces in France and Macedonia on January 30. "I can no longer by consequence assume any personal responsibility for these troops in the future," he wrote to the French government. "I see myself then obliged to resign my present function."[102] He passed his authority over the troops in France to Lokhvitsky and the command over the troops in Macedonia to General Taranovsky, who had been with them since they had arrived there. He made General Ignatiev the director of his personal chancellery as well as the director of the Rear, the latter scheduled for liquidation.[103] He shortly left France and entered Russia through Siberia, where he joined the forces of the anti-Communists.

As the highest-ranking officer of the Russian base, Lokhvitsky tried to gain for himself some measure of autonomy that had eluded Zankevich. In a lengthy memo to the French prime minister late in February, Lokhvitsky complained about the absence of authority he had even over his own troops and the lack of his power in general. He seemed especially annoyed by the fact that the chief of the French headquarters at the base at Laval was not his subordinate. Moreover, all reports of the base commandant to the minister of war had to be countersigned by the commandant of the French headquarters.[104] In a response dated March 7, the French government replied, effectively refuting all of Lokhvitsky's arguments and refusing to make any adjustments to what Lokhvitsky felt was necessary.[105] It is clear that the government considered the Russian Legion of little consequence and had no intention of according it or its officers the respect it had given them when Russia was still a powerful ally. One of Lokhvitsky's complaints had been the absence of any help for the Russian officers' families living in Paris, and the prime minister's response did not even show sympathy, much less give any succor.[106]

American troops were by now pouring into France by the thousands, making the help of the few hundred Russian soldiers there increasingly superfluous.

A final slap in the face came in July 1918 when the Russians were not allowed to participate in the festivities on Bastille Day, even after the French government had at first extended an invitation. All Allied troops had been asked to participate in the usual military parades with representative units, but the night before the event, the French authorities formally withdrew the offer to the Russians. The official sent to retrieve the invitation explained that it had been dispatched "through a misunderstanding." Sevastopoulo and Ignatiev then discovered that Lokhvitsky had not been asked to send even a Russian platoon, and they immediately went to the French chief of staff to ask why. They were summarily informed that the Russians, who were by this time sustaining heavy losses defending French soil, were being excluded because Russia had become a neutral country and had concluded peace with France's enemies. "The friends of our enemies were our enemies,"[107] the French officer curtly told the Russians. Ignatiev then went to the Russian "embassy" to get Sevastopoulo to approach Stephan Pichon, the French foreign minister, to obtain from him a cancellation of the insulting reversal of orders. Sevastopoulo refused to intercede for some reason, and Ignatiev went to see Kerensky, exiled in Paris after the Bolshevik Revolution, to ask him to try to do something about it.

On July 15, just as the Germans were launching their final assault on the Marne, where Russian soldiers were fighting, Kerensky went to Clemenceau's office to demand an explanation of the turnabout. The Tiger of France was in good spirits because word was coming in from all fronts that the German offensive was failing. Kerensky asked why the Russians had not been permitted to participate in the festivities of the French national holiday, and Clemenceau turned bright red. Pichon, who was present, became still and "nearly fell off his chair [?]," according to Kerensky. Clemenceau leaned back and repeated in French what had been told the former Russian prime minister the day before—the view that the *"amis de nos ennemis sont nos ennemis,"* concluding with the words "Those are my words and my orders."[108]

With Russians at that very moment dying for France, Kerensky, understandably, was hardly able to contain himself. Instead of replying to such a fatuous argument, he rose, closed his briefcase, and said to the premier, "In that case, Mr. Prime Minister, there is no point in my remaining in your office." He then bowed and walked out. Rumored accounts of the incident spread rapidly, giving rise to fears of potential trouble among the Russians at the front, and the next day Paul Deschanel, president of the French Chamber of Deputies, went to see Kerensky to try to soothe his ruffled feathers.

Making a rather prolix oration, he spoke of the strong ties between France and "national" Russia and its sacrifices in the war. He apologized for Clemenceau's behavior, saying that his words had resulted from an enormous strain that the premier had been under. A few days later Kerensky was invited to Poincaré's office where "in his own frigid way" the French president repeated what Deschanel had said, except he did it with fewer words. Kerensky described both apologies as "empty phrases."[109]

This second-rate status soon took its toll on the Russian officer corps, which had regained with the Legion some of its old vigor. Officer morale simply snapped, and the late spring and early summer saw a rash of resignations or forced firings of Russian officers with the Legion, a number of whom had been the best and most reliable. Its effect on the leadership was disastrous. Ignatiev himself went onto the French payroll in April, and that same month Lissovsky was removed as military procurator, having been told that the job was no longer necessary under the French reorganization.[110] The first to leave from the front was Gotua. Regarded by Barjonet as deserving the highest praise, Gotua nevertheless resigned, by one account, by another he was removed.[111] "Gotua is brave and his reputation proves it," General Albert Daugan, leader of the French Moroccan forces with whom the Russians served, reported to his commander-in-chief in June, "but he is of a rather primitive intelligence." The Russian account describes "his hot Caucasian nature," which led to his dismissal, not resignation. He was really of too high a rank to command a battalion, and his unit was under the 81st Zouaves, commanded by a lieutenant colonel. He complained at one point that the Zouave commander did not show him the proper respect. Probably this attitude led to some acts of insubordination. As enlisting in the French army was permanent, he was in reality probably dismissed, since he did depart. He was replaced by his assistant, Captain Lupanov, and after a few days' leave, Gotua was passed to a company of workers.[112] Colonel Ieske asked late in July to be allowed to pass once again into the French army.

By far the most important departure was that of General Lokhvitsky himself. On May 4, he asked to have an audience with the president of the republic,[113] which was denied. He then visited the Legion at the front on May 8 and May 10, and when with Balbashevsky's unit, he displayed an old tsarist army attitude that antagonized his troops. Apparently he had made it clear that he was a monarchist and was still loyal to the Old

Regime, and after he departed, General Gouraud noted a change in his men's behavior. Anonymous letters began to come to headquarters to the effect that the soldiers had not known that Russia had left the war. General Augustine Gerard wrote to Pétain that in the future, such behavior should be avoided "*at all costs* [his italics], for such incidents breed mutiny."[114] On May 15, Clemenceau wrote Lokhvitsky that he had learned that he had frequently been gone from the office of his command and warning that these absences were highly injurious to the good execution of Russian duties.[115] At about the same time his *laisser-passer* to the zone of the armies was suspended. Early in June Lokhvitsky asked the Convalescence Committee for a forty-five-day leave of absence from Laval to be taken at his wife's apartment in Paris. It was granted and he was slated to return to Laval on July 20. Meanwhile, Colonel Simenov, the oldest colonel there since Narbut was on leave at Bourbon, was to serve as acting commandant.[116]

Learning of his requested leave and apparently having had enough of what he perceived to be Lokhvitsky's weaknesses, Clemenceau dismissed him less than a week later. In a stinging letter that was signed by General Alby but had the claw marks of the Tiger himself, the French prime minister reminded Lokhvitsky of the warning about his earlier shortcomings and informed him that under "these conditions [?]" there could be no adequate direction of the Russian troops in France. Given all the problems, Clemenceau said that he had decided to release Lokhvitsky from his command and place him in a position of availability. General Brulard was made the real commandant of the Russian Legion, and Simenov, the most likely Russian to succeed Lokhvitsky, was swept aside.[117] Shortly afterward, even Lokhvitsky's horses were taken from him and sent to the depot of the 15 Hussars at Alençen.

Lokhvitsky's order of the day for June 15, 1918, was a farewell, but an upbeat one. He praised the valor of the Russian soldier, adding that "on the fields of battle of France, the Russian Legion proved gloriously to all that the honor of the name Russian is more dear than life." Waxing prophetic, he spoke of his conviction of Russia's "resurrection from the grave" in to which it had been laid by the Germans and the Bolsheviks, to take its place "at the side of the Allies." Leaving an opening for return, he made the point of bidding his men "Au revoir," not "Adieu."[118]

Lokhvitsky's departure caused a stir among the Russian officers at the Russian base and was most probably a major reason for the flurry of subsequent resignations that occurred over the summer. Ignatiev wrote to Colonel Ratkin at the Russian base a letter discussing Lokhvitsky's removal in a strong, anti-French tone. Intercepted by the French military, the letter was delayed while Brulard decided what to do with it. The French general sent a copy to the war ministry, pointing out that it contained "a number of inaccuracies which could be a source of misunderstanding which we wish to avoid."[119] Whether or not they relayed it, Clemenceau refuted its arguments point by point in a letter to Ignatiev on July 1, thus revealing that they screened his mail.[120]

In July Balbashevsky wrote General Lokhvitsky for the other colonels, wishing him well and expressing the hope that they would again serve under him.[121] It would never happen, of course, and Lokhvitsky's "*au revoir*" might have just as well been "*аðieu.*"

From the very formation of the Russian Legion, the morale of the individual soldier was always considerably less than what all had hoped — indeed had even been expected. The Russian officers in direct contact with the men spoke of good spirits, but French reports state repeatedly that the Russian officers were lying. Much of the old familiar accounts about discipline, casual behavior, refusal to clean camps, and so forth appear in reports. There was also some desertion and general disobedience even among the legionnaires. Lobanov-Rostovsky writes that the first overt sign of disorder had been directed at Lokhvitsky himself. An iron bolt was hurled at the general while he was reviewing troops at Laval in March.[122] No culprit was ever caught.

That same month Lobanov-Rostovsky himself had trouble. At drill one morning he learned that one of his platoons had refused to leave the barracks. Dismissing those who had assembled, he somehow managed to get the malcontents together, and he lectured them on the gravity of what they had done in regard to French discipline, to which each had agreed to submit. He then put them through exercises for an hour, running them across the field, then marching them for ten seconds, then rushing them again until they were utterly exhausted. Needless to say, under the existing conditions this punishment strained the leadership's relations with the men. One officer, Veshnovich, was fired on one night while inspecting the barracks, and another evening a private went to Lobanov-Rostovsky's hotel room to inform him that a plot was afoot to attack him that night. Lobanov-Rostovsky dismissed the soldier and then defiantly made an inspection tour about midnight only to discover that all was quiet and orderly.[123]

Not surprisingly, this misbehavior was especially bad among the soldiers who had volunteered from the units in North Africa. Most of these former incorrigibles had doubtless joined the Legion for the sole purpose of escaping the desert and had successfully hidden their insincerity from the officials there. Yet soon after returning to French soil, numerous incidents of disobedience and desertion took place. Lieutenant Mazurczak, who was with one group in which eight men vanished on arrival, described their spirit as *"assez médiocre."* Moreover, the French received word that some soldiers had joined with the idea of going over to the Germans, and three of them, Nadini, Klimov, and Moskalov, were returned to Africa for "being dangerous."[124]

A major discipline crisis occurred the first week of April, the day before the men were to embark on trains for the front. The men of Lobanov-Rostovsky's company met and decided to refuse to depart. That morning they did not report for drill. Not really certain of what to do, Lobanov-Rostovsky called the company out, and after some delay the 200 men did appear before him. Suspecting the cause of the unrest, he told them that their political views were their business but that they had sworn to fight for France to the end of the war, and it was his duty to keep his word. As long as he was in charge, both he and they would do so. He then asked if they would entrain for the front and received a resounding "No!" He waited a moment, asked a second time, and received the same answer. Then he said, "This is the last time I am going to ask you. Those of you who definitely refuse, step out of the ranks, but I warn you that I will fire at the first man who does so." He theatrically clutched his service revolver and stood there staring straight ahead. Knowing that he might be lynched, he felt that he had no choice but to shoot if challenged. No one came forward, fortunately, even when Lobanov-Rostovsky invited the ringleaders to do so. There was a meek silence and finally, at the command, "All those who will go, raise their hand," all hands went up. Lobanov-Rostovsky then dismissed the men and gave them leave for the rest of the day.[125] If this scenario demonstrates the state of the unit that was screened as loyal, one wonders at the behavior of the workers in Algeria.

In mid-May there was also a major incident in Balbashevsky's battalion the type that would happen over and over to the war's end. It occurred when replacement troops from Salonika claimed that when they volunteered, they did not know that peace had been made between Russia and Germany, and they argued that they no longer wanted to fight but wished to become workers.[126] Up until this time there had been only subliminal agitation under Balbashevsky; now there was open revolt that had to be, and was, suppressed.[127]

Late in May the French government dealt another blow to the Russian morale by demanding a new oath of allegiance and a general reorganization. On hearing of the trouble in Balbashevsky's unit, Pétain sent a memo to the minister of war calling for the voluntary dissolution of the battalions of the Russian Legion "where the political passions provoke between soldiers and officers . . . some too serious dissention thus compromising discipline," and the enlistment of these effectives in the Foreign Legion. He also suggested that all association between the units of the Legion fighting in the French army and General Lokhvitsky be severed completely. In conclusion, he added that all Russians who refused to serve either in the Foreign Legion or the reconstituted Russian Legion be sent to North Africa.[128]

The call for reorganization was poorly timed, for this new twist came when, to all accounts, the Russian soldiers' attitude was improving somewhat.[129] Lobanov-Rostovsky noted in his memoirs that matters had reverted "pretty much to normal." Exactly what the new pledge consisted has not been preserved, but it must have been stronger in its allegiance to the French government. To require this new enlistment oath seems pointless in the extreme, and it could only irritate further the Russian recruits. A new oath was not in itself going to result in improved discipline; in fact, most likely it would induce the contrary. Yet if the Russians did not sign it, they would not be allowed to serve in French ranks.[130]

The new oath, the departure of various officers, and weakening and losses at the front all led to a restructuring of the Legion in July. The Russian Legion was maintained despite Pétain's objections, but a number of its members entered the Foreign Legion and others entered work companies. In July Balbashevsky's battalion had to be dissolved, and the 113 men of his old unit that signed the new enlistment were submerged in a Moroccan division.[131] After July the French observers reported a further disintegration of the Russian soldiers' general attitude. One report speaks of "no cohesion."[132] The Russian Legion, although still existing, had become eviscerated by the fighting until it was virtually a hollow shell.

As an added irritant, the organization at Laval could not, or did not, prevent the politicizing of the soldiers. The men participated in political meetings where they aired their grievances. Wild sessions with speakers haranguing the soldiers occurred, and according to a French police bulletin, the soldiers at Laval even elected a soldiers' committee in direct defiance of the rules of French discipline. The report states that they chose two "Bolshevists," one Korsunsky and one Arkus, the former some sort of engineer, the latter an anti-French socialist who "hides his admiration for Lenin and Trotsky."

Much of this account does seem to be highly unlikely and overstated. We have seen that the French security police were very quick to label anyone who was not for *guerre à outrance* a Bolshevik, and that is probably the case here. Moreover, there is no other account of a soldiers' committee, so it could not have been too active, if indeed one had ever been elected.[133]

At this point, too, the French would have stopped overt defeatism and any behavior similar to that which had occurred at La Courtine. Yet there were some disturbances clearly, which the security police must have quickly labeled bolshevist. Whether the government in Paris felt that they were radically Leftist or not, it was highly suspicious of it. Quite likely that is the reason for the new oath to the French government that forced upon the Russians in the summer of 1918.

Furthermore, by July many were wearing French uniforms, probably since their Russian ones had finally worn out. The units had lost much of their identity, and when General Brulard assumed full command on Lokhvitsky's departure, the soldiers sent him a most pitiful letter. In the most hat-in-hand manner, they referred to Brulard as a father, and added that like all children, they sometimes requested things of their parents. They then asked to be allowed to wear the Russian uniform. "In this uniform," they wrote Brulard, "we are covered in glory and we will show to the Germans that the true heart of Russia still beats."[134]

The request was denied, for the good reasons that the French had given earlier, but on November 10, the day before the fighting stopped, Mikhailov finally gained permission to be allowed to have a flag with the Russian national colors, and the legionnaires were allowed to use it in the same conditions as the flag of the French Republic. Their flag was finally restored on November 29, 1918, over two weeks after the war had ended. Their uniforms never were.

TEN

Glory, Laud, and Honor

1918–1919

The Russian Legion was a reply to the Brest-Litovsk treaty, a living protest against the acts of the Russian Bolsheviks and also a precious symbol of the hope of the reconstitution of the Russian army.

—La Question des troupes russes en France[1]

Nothing to report. Their number [the survivors of the REF] has become, however, very reduced and their influence almost nothing.

—Extraits des rapports mensuels,[2]
October 1918

The Russians are barbarians and villains. Through them we are drawn into this war and through this treachery compelled to fight an extra year, bearing the whole of the German pressure and suffering innumerable losses . . . and now these same traitors expect, even demand our help. . . . I, as a soldier, obey the command of my government. But my heart is not in the enterprise. You must not stand on ceremony with the people. Shoot them without further ado if anything occurs, commencing with the muzhiks and ending with their highest representatives. I take full responsibility.

—General Louis Franchet d'Esperey[3]

The conduct of the French ships and their officers and crews was so amazing that no Allied government has yet dared to publish an account of it: theft, rapes, and all kinds of villainy were the order of the day. The French have become the most hated nation in Russia.

—C. E. Bechhofer[4]

"My God," he cried suddenly. *"I hope I live long enough to fight the French."*

— A Russian officer in France[5]

ALTHOUGH THE FIRST RUSSIANS TO RETURN to the front did so as a battalion led by Gotua in December 1917, the Russian Legion did not begin sending the other units there until March. Colonel Barjonet, the commandant of the French headquarters at Laval, reported to the war ministry on March 2 that on Tuesday, March 5, another contingent of 230 Russian volunteers would be going into service. Lokhvitsky asked that they not be placed near those men with Gotua since the 230 volunteers were recruited from the detritus of the *Courtinois*, while Gotua's men were taken from those at Courneau. The Russian general feared that if they were placed together, they might come into conflict.[6]

The second battalion was led by Lieutenant Colonel Ieske, and later by Colonel Kotovich, and consisted at first of 200 men.[7] On the way these troops stopped at Versailles-Chantiers for about three hours, and there they received gifts from Lokhvitsky, Maklakov, and several women of the Russian colony of Paris, financed by the French government.[8] About a week later, 2 officers and 32 men were sent to reinforce this unit, along with 122 men who joined Gotua's battalion.[9] On April 9 a battalion under Colonel Balbashevsky left Laval for the front. At three minutes after midnight the unit departed with 22 officers, 1 doctor, 58 noncommissioned officers, and 416 men. They also had 3 interpreters. Their leaving was without incident except for the refusal of two men, both originally from among the troops at Salonika, to entrain. They were promptly sent to Île d'Aix.[10] Shortly afterward yet another battalion under Colonel Grigorii Simenov joined their comrades. From this point to the end of the war, most of the Russian legionnaires fought in the VIII Army under General Henri Gouraud. Of the men who went, roughly one third had received the Cross of St. George.

Yet, even in these select units, discipline was still unstable.[11] When Lobanov-Rostovsky's men were due to depart for the front, he feared that they would not entrain despite their promise to do so. He decided that after the customary inspection, all officers would assemble and only then would the order to depart be given, so that there would be at least a group of fifteen to face whatever misbehavior the troops might display. Inwardly trembling, Lobanov-Rostovsky gave the command to march and the company followed without difficulty, although along the way to the station three "ringleaders" deserted. This tense situation must have continued, because Lobanov-Rostovsky later wrote in his memoirs, "Consequently during the period my participation in the war consisted [largely] in fighting against my own men. . . ."[12]

The first Russians to be engaged in any fighting were Gotua's battalion at Villers-Bretonneux, near Amiens, when the Germans launched their spring assault on that sector. The Russians marched at night to the region around Beauvais, where they were held in reserve. During the night of April 25-26, they took the forward position at Villers-Bretonneux and went into a counterattack on April 26. The two companies that participated were the 1st under Captain Lupanov and a company of machine gunners under Captain Valerian Razumov. They pushed ahead of their comrades in other units and took the first line of enemy trenches. Their losses were great, with their wounded including a priest. Thirty-four men were killed with seventy-six wounded and four missing.[13] Their bravery engendered extensive admiration. All officers received the Military Cross. Captain Lupanov received the Croix de la Legion d'Honneur on the field of battle and two noncommissioned officers the *médaille militaire*.[14] In his General Order No. 96, General Daugan noted that the Russian legionnaires "went to attack with an impetuous dash and a superb disdain for death. They held onto their positions despite furious counterattacks and continuous bombardment." He reported that they fought "with a spirit and bravery without equal," adding that they had won the admiration of all especially the Zouaves, with whom they fought.[15] On May 7 they were still in the line thwarting repeated German attacks. The Moroccan unit suffered terrible losses of around 4,000 casualties, but the road to Amiens remained blocked to the Germans. After the April fighting, they were pulled from the line for rest and regrouping. To the Russians among them, this first engagement obliterated the shame of the treaty of Brest-Litovsk.

On May 27, in less than four hours of furious shelling, 3,700 German guns hurled more than 700,000 shells and bombs on the unsuspecting French Sixth Army and some exhausted British units stationed in Champagne in the sector of the *Chemin des Dames*, where the ill-fated Nivelle offensive had failed the year before. The bombardment allowed the German army to advance thirteen miles in one day into the space between Reims and Soissons, the largest single one-day forward push by either side since 1914. By May 30 the French were in disorderly retreat, and the Germans had captured Soissons and much Allied war matériel there. By the last day of May, German troops once again stood on the banks of the Marne. It seemed to many on both sides that this attack might be the beginning of the end for the Allies.

Daugan's Moroccan-Russian force was stretched over six or seven miles astride the Soissons-Paris road on the side of the salient. The 1st battalion under Gotua again went into action on May 30, attacking in the direction of Soissons in union with the 3rd under Colonel Simenov. Despite murderous fire and the powerful enemy forces facing them, the Russian Legion fought with great valor and held the line during a German counterattack. *Le Soldat-Citoyen Russe* described the men as having "fought like lions." The proof of their performance lies in the enormous number of medals and decorations awarded them by the French command.[16] When all seemed lost, the Russian legionnaires counterattacked under the command of Captain Lupanov. When Lieutenant Ornatsky, an excellent singer who had often entertained the troops, was killed, the Russians were inspired even further. With a loud "Hurrah" they hurled themselves at the enemy. Even Dr. Zilbershtein, a battalion physician, took a rifle and joined the attack. Ultimately the core of the Russian troops was surrounded as it pushed ahead. Seriously wounded, 2nd Lieutenant Diakonov single-handedly held the Germans back while the remainder of the core fought its way out of the encirclement. He died covering them. Other German attacks were halted by Russian machine gun fire until it was silenced by German artillery.[17]

The 3rd company of the legion had been transferred from the 7th to the 8th Moroccan infantry before the battle began, and during the fighting it was sent to rescue the 1st Zouave battalion. The company advanced into murderous German discharge and helped the Zouaves hold their position. In the operation the 3rd lost three-quarters of its officers and 290 men in the fighting on the heights above Soissons. That city did not forget the Russian effort. In 1923 at a commemoration of the Memorial of Victory, a delegation from the Russian Legion was invited to be present. During the service, from the crowds came cries of "*Vive la Légion russe!*" The French press reporting the events began calling the Russian force "the Russian Legion of Honor." The name stuck.[18]

Throughout the summer of 1918, Russians continued to die for the Allies. In June Russians fought in the forests at Villers-Cotterêts and later near Compiègne. In July they were again in Villers-Cotterêts. The archives yield many death lists.[19] Even the Americans took in Russian wounded, and Russians, like 2nd Lieutenant Alexander Kostin, succumbed to wounds in an American hospital at Neufchâteau late in August.[20] Illness too took its toll. By the end of May almost a 1,000 legionnaires were reported sick from various nonmilitary-related health problems.[21]

With each account, however, came commendations and the praise of their fighting qualities. Communications are replete with phrases such as "sang-froid" and "oblivious to death." Time after time the reports speak of the tenacity that has so often in history been the trademark of the Russian soldier. They were "relentless in counter-attack," "calm under fire," and "oblivious to the dangers imposed by the awesome enemy," and so forth. Sergeant Basil Marchenko, who was in a group that was disengaging from the enemy that was mounting a heavy assault, not only led his men back in good order, but he brought with him a German prisoner.[22] Once again they distinguished themselves in the fighting early in September at Soing, and on September 10 one battalion received a citation from General Daugan, who praised their fighting all along the front from Amiens to the Somme. "The battalions of which the implacable hatred of the enemy enlivens all their actions, possess a complete scorn of death to the most beautiful enthusiasm for a sacred cause."[23] These paeans of praise and reports of heroism and bravery continue unabated in the reports on the men until the end of the war. The Russian Legion showed a courage unknown in many areas of the front at that point of the struggle.

While fighting a defensive battle on the Marne in mid-July, Foch and Pétain planned a counteroffensive into the increasingly exposed right flank of the German salient that had reached the famous river for the second time in the war. On July 18 at 4:35 A.M., General Charles Mangin's X Army, in which the Moroccan-Russian units were serving, attacked and drove to the Château Thierry road attempting to close the sac full of German soldiers still standing on the banks of the Marne. Most of the Germans were able to escape, but the French still bagged 30,000 prisoners and much war matériel, neither of which could the German army easily replace.

Yet there continued to be problems with morale — not sufficient to cause the fighting ability of the units to collapse, but enough to be troublesome. Early in April, some disturbance erupted among replacements sent to Ieske's battalion. A sergeant, a corporal, and a private, all of whom were drunk, stabbed three of their comrades, two very seriously. They were imprisoned, but the only punishment that the Russian commandant placed on them was incarceration. At about the same time some thirty-five men refused to board trains at Laval for the front. Voicing the now-familiar argument that Russia was not now at war with Germany, they expressed the opinion that Russians should therefore not be fighting Germans. All of these men were from the North African camps and had probably joined simply to escape the rigors of the deserts. They were all immediately arrested and isolated, and Barjonet recommended that they should be sent to Île d'Aix.[24]

These incidents, however, did not seem to hinder the units' fighting ability, possibly because when trouble occurred, the French and Russian leaders moved very quickly to defuse it. Early in May General Daugan even reported Russian morale among the Moroccans to be "excellent,"[25] and had it generally been otherwise, the Russian Legion could not have fought as well as it did to the end of the war. In August *Le Temps* sang the praises of the Russian Legion, extolling its performance in the fighting on April 26. "In the combat . . . , the legion has fulfilled an extremely difficult role. The Russian losses were very heavy, but those who survive are covered with pride when they have read the order of the day of the commandant of the division that tells how they have been appreciated: 'By their devotion and their unawareness of death, the Russians have struck the Zouaves with admiration.'"[26]

In August the Moroccan unit was dispatched to Breté to rest and reorganize, and the Russian Legion was placed wholly in the 8th Zouave regiment of the first Moroccan brigade. Their leader was a French Major Tramouser, new to the units. In his first review, he ordered them to present arms with the French order "Arms right!" Russians traditionally carried their rifles on their left shoulders, so they all obeyed the command by placing their weapons on their left, to the great consternation of Tramouser, until he learned the reason.[27]

In September 1918 the Russians resumed a place at the front near Soissons between the Aisne and the plateau Saint Gobin near Laon. In this sector it had been given the assignment to attack in the second wave behind the 12th battalion of Chausseurs Malgaches, who were deployed on the route from Soissons-Béthune, to take the village of Terny-Sorny. The advance took place on September 2 in the face of violent machine-gun fire from the enemy. Leaving from the northern edge of the Beaumont wood and from Côte 172, the troops advanced behind a rolling artillery barrage. As usual the Russian Legion was farther out front than its French-Moroccan comrades.

The units to the right of the 12th battalion of Chasseurs Malgaches were particularly stricken while the units to the left arrived at the edge of the western part of Terny-Sorny, where they began receiving enemy fire. At this point, the commandant of this battalion of the Russian Legion, also in the second wave, suddenly decided to push toward the east to make a flanking attack on the village with the idea of coming around it by the north, then to shift and execute an enveloping movement of attack from both the north and the south. Very cleverly under the violent hail of machine-gun bullets and artillery barrages, while all of the first line before it was immobilized, the Russian Legion made its move. With a remarkable zeal, the Russian battalion, with the officers in the lead, struck the village. The struggle was brutal. The enemy, solidly entrenched in the rubble, was determined to hold at all costs, and they defended themselves with the energy of desperation throughout the night. When the first morning light broke, the village was in Russian hands and was held until September 5 despite strong German counterattacks and intense bombardment with gas and all calibers of shells. In this maneuver the Russian battalion took 160 prisoners and considerable matériel. This daring action won the battalion of the Russian Legion a military citation, which was accorded them on September 30, 1918. It praised the Russians for their "heroic actions" since April 1918, culminating with their "magnificent act of arms" from September 2 onward. "Performing with a complete disregard for death," the Russian battalion had done its duty "with the most beautiful enthusiasm for a sacred cause."[28] Yet in the struggle, the Russians by one report lost their most famous soldier, the priest Andrei Bogoslovsky. Without a helmet, he had grabbed a rifle and joined the troops on the first day of the attack and had been killed by a German shell while fighting in the first line of German trenches taken in the assault.[29] Despite their losses, the Russians held their taken territory despite repeated German counterattacks.

After the fighting stopped on September 2, they were placed in reserve, but on September 14 this battalion of the Russian Legion returned to battle in an assault on the Hindenburg Line to the northeast of the plateau of Laffaux. On the night of September 13-14, they left their bivouac emplacements and were placed in the first line between the Foreign Legion on the left and the 12th battalion of Chasseurs Malgaches on the right. Their ordered objectives were to assist in the destruction of a very powerful pocket of enemy resistance, called the Rossignol trench; after accomplishing this feat, they were to take the Château de la Motte and put it in a state of defense.

At the designated hour the first company advanced, followed at 175 yards by the second. With what the French reporter called "*un élan impetueux,*" the 1st company fell on the trenches before them, taking the advance and two intermediary trenches with bayonet and grenade assaults. In their place of attack was a mine field and a German concrete blockhouse, which resisted desperately with all its machine guns, and the Russians were given most of the credit for reducing this obstacle that had stopped Allied progress for several days. From this point, the battalion advanced to take the Château de la Motte, its last objective. The ardor of the attack caught the Germans by surprise, and the Russians captured numerous prisoners and supplies. The action was so perfectly executed that the château fell with only nine Russian dead and twenty-five wounded.[30] The Russians had proceeded so fast that they fell under friendly fire from the French artillery and had to fire flares saying "We are already here, stop firing!"[31]

After a rest at Meaux, the Moroccan division was sent to occupy a sector in Lorraine near Lanneaucourt. It seems to have had to do little fighting, as most of the Allied pressure on the Germans war machine naturally fell farther to the west. In the night of November 10 the 8th Zouaves were planning a *coup de main* in the direction of Rosières-en-Blois when a cry arose from the German trenches, followed by a barrage of German signal rockets illuminating the sky. Shortly afterward came orders from the command to "hold all military operations" and "Fire only in reply to enemy fire." It was obvious that events were developing rapidly. At 5:45 A.M. on November 11, the unit received a radiogram ordering them to cease all military activity. "The enemy has accepted the conditions of Marshal Foch. End."[32] The Germans were to retire behind the Rhine, yielding all of the territory in between to the Allies. The Great War had finally ended.

The Russian Legion participated in the occupation of Germany. With the Moroccans, the Russian Legion of Honor passed through Lorraine, Alsace, the Saar, and into Germany up to the Rhine opposite Mannheim, eventually being dispatched to Friedrickshafen. The local population was shocked to find Russians in the occupying force.[33]

Despite its valor, there is ample evidence that all had not been rosy for the Legion. One point was its devastating number of casualties. It is difficult to tell exactly of what units the Legion consisted by this time, quite possibly because its numbers were so few and the imminent end of the war made their actions less and less important. One account to the war ministry reports grave losses and indicated that there was only one battalion still in the line by late September, probably explaining why the terms "battalion" and "legion" came to be used interchangeably in the reports on Russian activities toward the end of the fighting. A report on October 3 states that the Legion had only 272 men, two companies of effectives reduced to about 80 each and a company of machine gunners in three sections.[34] Furthermore, the depot at Laval sent to the front its last men, some 80 taken in all, on October 9. Reports note their engagements become rarer and rarer, yet the prime minister wanted a detailed account of the last actions of the force since "it can be used as propaganda." The Kotovich battalion, obviously decimated in the fighting, was dissolved into the 3rd Algerian sharpshooters. One historian wrote that of 24 officers (probably a low number) who went into the original Legion, 16 had been killed or wounded by the end of the war. Of the 3 doctors who entered the unit, all were casualties by November 11. Of the 7 interpreters, only 1 was unhurt when the Germans stopped fighting. Of the 994 soldiers and noncommissioned officers who answered Lokhvitsky's call, 523 were either dead or wounded when the fighting stopped.[35] A handful of men, therefore, was all that remained of the 20,000 effectives who had been "sold for shells" almost three years before. Moreover, one report to the war ministry written several weeks earlier speaks of Russian troops not having held under fire,[36] a final, but understandable, blot on the Russian banner.

Late in the morning of November 11, 1918, the guns on the Western Front fell silent for the first time in over four years. God alone knows the exact number on the list of the dead. The official figure for combatants is over 8 million, but this number could not possibly be accurate since it includes only 1,700,000 Russian dead, and that number could never begin to be correct. Added to that unknown total are those men who died prematurely in the 1920s and 1930s, decades before their time, from battle wounds inflicted or gas inhaled on the battlefields. The civilian toll likewise cannot be tabulated, nor can anyone accurately calculate the total loss of property. Hundreds of French villages disappeared never to be rebuilt. At this writing there still are dangerous areas around Verdun into which the French government does not allow the curious, and shells still explode to this day under farmers' plows along the hundreds of miles of scarred landscape of what had been the front.[37] Sadly, this death and destruction did not settle all the problems that had caused the gigantic struggle, and even worse, it created new ones that would sprout two decades later into another world war more horrible and destructive than the first. Marshal Foch realized it at the time, for he said of the Versailles treaty, "This is not peace; it is an armistice for twenty years."[38]

One of the many problems that the end of the war did not solve for the French government was the continued presence, both free and in captivity, of those Russian soldiers who had been so welcomed in 1916. After the fighting in September, what was left of the brigades was taken from the line, and General Brulard advised that these remnants be sent to Morocco and be reorganized as a unit in the Foreign Legion. He suggested that they finally be allowed to wear Russian uniforms to counter the German propaganda that the Russian force had disappeared. "It would show them," Brulard wrote, "that there is still a Russian army fighting with us."[39] A week later Brulard went to North Africa to plan for the Russian transfer, but within a few days of the November 11 armistice the plan was abandoned for unknown reasons.[40] The Russian base was slated for dissolution on April 1, 1920. A reduced central committee in Paris remained, however, to be kept until the final dissolution.[41]

The Russian Legion itself by December had still listed a 560-man membership with 22 officers. In the zone of the armies there were 4,569 men listed as workers and 9,379 men designated as workers in the interior. There were still 200 detainees on the Île d'Aix, and there was some sort of special formation of 240 men and 36 officers, the location and function of which is unclear. In Don Alger, Constantine, and Oran in North Africa, there were 8,736 Russians plus 40 officers without command who were also living there.[42] All of these numbers had been augmented by Russian soldiers who had joined the Russian community, having come into France from various places, including 30,000 from German prisoner-of-war camps. The lines of the original Russian Expeditionary Force had long since blurred.

Feeding and housing this large a number of men would most certainly be a nuisance, yet for the French there was one even larger than that: The Germans had indoctrinated the prisoners with liberal doses of anti-French propaganda. After the armistice, therefore, the Russian question assumed a more intense quality, and from this point onward, it becomes difficult to distinguish which difficulties were caused by the prisoners and which by the REF veterans.

To make matters worse, after the armistice discipline deteriorated each day, and some military and work units that had maintained some semblance of order lost it completely when the war was over. All the men could think of was repatriation, and no explanation, however rational, could calm them. Reports from North Africa describe the situation as "critical," and one recommended that there could be a calming of spirits if progressive repatriation could at least begin.[43] Especially unsound were those men who had been in work units, because they had not been under military discipline for over a year, and their leaders no longer possessed the authority necessary to make the men obey.[44] The year 1919 saw a continuous stream of Russian misdeeds. Reports show numerous incidents of refusal to work, desertions, anti-French activities, and other "Bolshevist" behavior. There were many accusations of the soldiers' spreading Bolshevik propaganda, much of which was probably not true. It is indicative, however, of the disorder that plagued the units.

The war's end saw a change of status for all grades of Russian soldiers in France, especially for the "incorrigibles" in Aix. Reports as early as 1918 begin appearing in the archives with lists of Category B members recommended for transfer to work units because of their good behavior. It has been noted that many people seemed to have passed through the gates of Aix into the dank cells, only to be released quickly to work battalions. In some cases it was easy to be transferred to the labor details, given the number that did so, and apparently little more than some sort of casual admission of guilt and declaration of reform was needed to be released. The archives for 1918 and 1919 contain numerous lists of men being recommended for transferal to work. No names are familiar, since at first at least the hardcore did not give in. Many of the lesser figures did. The last prisoners to leave Aix did so on January 8, 1920, to be incarcerated at Fort St. Jean near Marseille. They were probably about to be repatriated to Russia. The report stresses that these men seemed to be full of revolutionary spirit and describes them as "the most dangerous Russians." None of the names of prominent figures appear on the lists, however.[45] For the most part they had all joined work units, having "sold out" to the French bourgeoisie.

At Île d'Aix we hear for the last time of both Globa and Baltais. On February 4, 1919, some money was sent there by *Soldat-Citoyen Russe,* and Madame Nadine Stchofan, who wrote for the journal, put in a good word for Globa, saying "They [?] have told us of the soldier Globa as a man worthy of confidence."[46] Later that month Globa petitioned to be repatriated in the only letter we have that may be in his handwriting. In a note written in French in a very neat penmanship, he claimed that the "state of health" made him "*incapable* [his italics] of service," adding that he should be permitted to return home "like all Russian invalids." Until this point there is no account of his having been hurt or ill in any way, so he must have received a wound or become ill after his capture. A later report informs us that he claimed that he had received a severe injury with "compounding lacerations of tissue to the interior part of the right shoulder muscle rendering him incapable of service."[47] In his letter he asserted, as have many throughout the ages who had been incarcerated, that he was being held "prisoner without any charge against me for already two years, and I personally have not committed any crime. . . . " This bewildered innocent ringleader of the mutiny who had made so much anti-French rhetoric also claimed that he had "always wanted a strict liaison with the Allies."[48] In March Brulard, amazingly, recommended to the French ministry of war that Globa be released, stating that his behavior "has always been correct" and that "he has given no complaint since his arrival,"[49] which is more than can be said about some of those he influenced. To this report Brulard added in handwriting, "He will be taken in the first departure." Later lists of those on Île d'Aix do not contain Globa's name, and with Brulard's report of March 1919, this charismatic leader of the mutiny of La Courtine exits forever from our story.

At about the same time that Globa was professing his great innocence and was being given permission to leave France, M. Zitrone, a lawyer hired by the prisoners at Aix, wrote the French government that the Russian Council of War, whatever that was, supported Baltais's release, and in February 1919 the lawyer was awaiting a response from the French in order to continue with his case. The French minister of war, at first ignoring Zitrone, did reply to Ignatiev that Baltais's good conduct "would better his situation," and scattered reports state that he had been behaving well, again unlike those he incited, and this renewed discipline would enable him to join a work detail. Zitrone also sent Baltais 50 francs and promised to gain him a place on one of the early boats returning to Russia.[50] Zitrone must have succeeded, for we never have any word of this ringleader again.

One soldier who was not an incorrigible but was giving trouble early in 1919 was Rodion Malinovsky. He was scheduled in April 1919 to be repatriated from Marseille and had even drawn the departure indemnity given every Russian soldier when suddenly he refused to board the ship and returned to Laval, where he announced that he wanted unlimited leave without pay in order to become a chauffeur. He declared that he had means to support himself and would not return to Marseille.[51] Exactly what game he was playing is unknown. Had he been recruited to work for the Bolsheviks already, or was the future defense minister of the Soviet Union planning to defect to bourgeois France?

The late summer of 1918 witnessed the beginning of a curious diplomatic dance between France and the new Bolshevik state that in effect initiated relations between the two powers. The interaction, however, more nearly resembles the present-day negotiations between governments of civilized countries and radical terrorist groups than it does diplomatic intercourse. For France, it was the material of political nightmares; for the new Russia, it became a delicious opportunity to frustrate and annoy the nation that symbolized capitalistic imperialism to its Marxist ideological leaders. France frequently found itself moving like a puppet to the jerking of the strings by the Soviet diplomats, and to make matters worse for the French, much of the affair was carried out in the open, where any person with a radio could witness the helpless state of the exasperated French government. It was, however, the last headache over the Russian question that the French nation would have to endure.

At the core of this peculiar imbroglio were the remnants of the Russian Expeditionary Force, whose return to Russia, as we have seen, the Soviets demanded and which the French would have been only too glad to have granted. The Soviet government, hardly unaware of the French difficulties, made as much propaganda value of the French plight as it could, while doubtless some of the ideologues hoped that the rebel-

lious Russian soldiers might become the spark that would ignite the
predicted World Revolution in France. That frightful possibility had also
crossed the minds of the French.

On February 28, 1918, the French ambassador left Petrograd, as
other diplomats did, because the Germans were approaching it during the
breakdown of the Brest-Litovsk peace negotiations. From that point until
1924, there were no normal diplomatic relations between Russia and
France, a fact that enormously aggravated the already difficult situation.
The Russian government continued to wax indignant by every means
possible at the French "detention" of their nationals, using the lie to the
full extent of its potential. Using the public forum of the Fifth All-Russian
Congress of Soviets in July 1918, Iakov Sverdlov, a prominent inner-
circle Bolshevik, sent greetings to the Russian soldiers in France,[52] thus
receiving high visibility within Russia for the "imprisoned troops." With
this salvo, a Franco-Russian "cold war" began.

In August, however, the struggle turned nasty. The civil war was
intensifying, and in July there had been an attempt on Lenin's life.
Already detaining several consular officials, the Soviet government
ordered on August 6 the arrest of the French military notables in Moscow,
among them General Alphonse Lavergne, and two days later the French
consul general in Moscow, Joseph Grenard. The following day the
French government, using the Swedes as intermediaries, sent a note to
the Soviet Russians expressing French willingness to return all Russian
soldiers in France with the help of the International Red Cross, if the
Russian government would guarantee the exit from Russia of officers and
soldiers of the French military mission.[53] At that point Maxim Litvinov,
who was the second-in-command in the Soviet foreign commissariat and
would later be the Soviet minister of foreign affairs, was being held in
England, and the Russian response made release of the consular officials
contingent upon the release of Litvinov, knowing that his detention was
in no way under the control of the French.

Speaking to the French request of August 9, Chicherin replied that
the detainees could leave "under the condition . . . that the French
government will not oppose the return to Russia of the Russian soldiers
which are in France" (something the French had already in their
suggestion agreed to do), but adding the demand that the French accept
the visit of delegates of the Russian Red Cross to direct their repatriation.[54] Chicherin also requested that the Swedes permit all Russians to
return via Sweden. On this part of the response the Soviets received
only silence from Stockholm until September 24, when the Swedes
agreed to permit their passage after the Soviets had asked again, this
time dangling before the Swedes the carrot of trade.[55]

Eugène Thiébaut, the French consul in Stockholm, reported this proposition to Paris with the bizarre advice that the troops' release would produce a good impression "on the masses."[56] Foreign minister Pichon readily agreed that the French would not hinder the troops' return, since they had suggested it in the first place, but he made no mention of the admission of the Russian Red Cross into France. He also strongly urged that the arrested General Lavergne and M. Grenard not give the appearance of negotiating with the Russians.[57] Tensions eased somewhat when, as a gesture of goodwill, the Soviets shortly released Lavergne and Grenard but did not allow them to leave Moscow.

Thiébaut then raised the question of allowing the departure by Vologda, Kotlas, and Archangel of all French civilian personnel, with the French military personnel leaving through Astrakhan and Persia for some reason. Chicherin seemed to be in agreement, but then word reached the French that other French nationals in Russia were being persecuted, and they demanded immunity for these people as well. The situation worsened when at 4:30 P.M. on August 19, a detachment of Russian soldiers invaded the French consulate in Moscow threatening the staff with revolvers and holding them prisoners. Within an hour and a half the Danish government issued a strong protest, but it took the additional complaints from the American, Japanese, and Swedish consuls to bring about their release by three o'clock in the morning. Yet on August 22 the French learned that although their consular staff had been freed, twenty-five other French nationals had been arrested, and Eugène Conty, the French consul in Copenhagen, advised the French government that all French nationals in Russia were in danger since the Bolsheviks "have sensed the arrival of their final hour, they have become like ferocious beasts."[58]

Whatever the catalyst, the Soviets suddenly became more difficult. Before the end of August, they told the Danish minister that the French military would not be allowed to leave Russia until the representatives of the Russian Red Cross had organized the return of the Russian troops in France, and on August 29 the Soviet government issued a directive to detain all French nationals in Russia between the ages of eighteen and forty and certain British nationals as well. They likewise seized the French diplomatic and military missions in Moscow, and the consulate itself was placed into the hands of the Danish government.[59] Denouncing this action as "inadmissible," Conty noted that the Russians were suddenly formulating "new conditions" when they were "scarcely in a position to dictate them."[60] The Russian action soon became clear: They had merely put some money into their account. On September 2, Chicherin proposed exchanging the troops in the West and Litvinov, who by that time was free, for the French hostages that they held.[61]

The British retaliated by rearresting Litvinov, and the Russians then countered by sacking the British legation in St. Petersburg during which they killed a British captain. By September 10 twenty-eight Frenchmen and eleven Englishmen, among them R. N. Bruce Lockhart, the British government's special agent, were incarcerated in terrible conditions in the Petropavlovsky fortress in Petrograd. Lockhart was condemned to death.[62]

In dispatches in the days that followed, there is an often contradictory flow of evidence of when and who was still detained. By mid-September apparently many had been released, although those in the eighteen-to-forty age group remained in detention "under intolerable conditions." The British soon exchanged Litvinov for Lockhart,[63] and a number of lesser figures, including 90 British, 50 French, and 10 Americans, were allowed to leave. No note indicates who, but probably they were the very old and the very young. Conditions were set for the departure of the remainder. The diplomatic and consular personnel would be permitted to leave only after Litvinov's arrival in Bergen had been confirmed, and the military mission in Russia could depart only after the first trains of Russian soldiers under the control of the Russian Red Cross had arrived in Switzerland, a location that at this point had not been suggested or cleared with the Swiss government.[64] A convoy of 176 French and 87 British citizens were allowed to leave Moscow early in October and exited through Kokala, Finland, where they were briefly detained at the border.[65] With this group, however, any further exodus stopped.

Mid-October witnessed frenetic diplomatic activity with Harald Scavenius, the Swedish consul general in Moscow, playing go-between. He arranged the departure of two Russian Red Cross delegates to Switzerland, with one going for some reason through Stockholm, the other through Germany. Meanwhile, Pichon, who had to have realized that France was negotiating from the weakest of positions, tried to assume a brave front and sent word to the Russians that release of the thousands of soldiers in the REF was dependent on the release of the hostages. As an additional bargaining chip, he asked the Norwegian government to hold Litvinov until specifically Pierre Darcy and two other consular detainees, Mazon and Ducastel, were also released. Probably the hesitancy of the Norwegian government to become involved in the affair led Pichon to agree to Litvinov's early release. He called, however, for the holding of three of his traveling companions, French consular officials less destined than he for the spotlight of history, held in Moscow.[66] Litvinov left Bergen for Stockholm on October 18, leaving behind three members of his entourage, but the Norwegian government warned the French that they could not hold these men indefinitely.[67] On October 22 three Russian Red Cross delegates left for France. Isaac Orlov and Joseph Savitsky started across Germany to the Swiss border, while the other, whose name and identity is unknown, for some reason went in the direction of Stockholm.[68] The tense situation was quickly aggravated, however, by the affair that developed around one of the French detainees whom the Soviets called "the Judas Darcy."

Darcy was one of the most respected members of the French colony in Russia. He had been at one time or another president of the French Society of Beneficence, president of the French hospital, vice president of the Alliance Française, and president of the French Community in Petrograd. The French government designated him in July 1918 to fulfill the position of commercial attaché in the Moscow consulate, and he was arrested like the others in August. He was slated to depart with the October release, but at the last minute the Soviet government accused him of complicity in the escape of French officers in Petrograd and threw him into prison, claiming that he was not really the attaché. The Russians then told the Danish consul that if someone could bring proof that he was indeed the commercial attaché, he would be freed. There followed a Catch-22 situation whereby the proof had been in the consular archives but had been removed by Darcy himself and given to Consul General Gustave Engelhardt, who supposedly never knew that the papers were being sought.[69] The French suspected that the whole confusion was created by the Russians as a pretext to hold Darcy, and it may indeed have been, but whatever the case, Darcy's imprisonment was to have dire consequences for Franco-Soviet relations, and especially for Darcy.

On November 7 the French received word that Darcy had been beaten in prison and was suffering from a cerebral hemorrhage, which was going untreated by the Soviet prison officials. Bypassing the Swedish route, Pichon sent an open radio message to Chicherin on November 10 denouncing the "revolting inhumane acts" committed by the Bolsheviks, whom they accused of not living up to their supposed principles.[70]

November saw a confusing change of events. First, Mazon was for some reason released by the Bolsheviks, probably to appease the general international anger at Darcy's treatment. Second, Russian subversive activity in Switzerland led that government to the aforementioned closing of the Swiss door to the two Russian Red Cross delegates who had just arrived there. Shortly afterward, the Danes, the Swedes, and the Norwegians recalled their delegations from Moscow, thus severing relations and ending the line of contact for the French. In their one last message through the vanishing Swedish connection, the French suggested that they would transfer a convoy of Russian soldiers to any Baltic port that the Russians designated if they would be prepared to have Ducastel, Mazon, and Darcy there for exchange.[71] The French officers and hostages would return to France on the same ships that had delivered the Russians. As an additional carrot, the French offered to return at the same time "certain Russian civilians," presumably Bolsheviks, whom the Russians might wish to see repatriated. In the meantime, they would be held for the protection of the French hostages, two Russians guaranteeing the safety of every French subject.[72]

With the Scandinavian connection having closed, the French permanently opened their radio diplomacy with the Russians for all the world to listen, including the Germans who recorded in their archives verbatim many of the Franco-Russian exchanges.[73] Dispatches were sent from a transmitter in the Eiffel Tower to a receiver at Tsarskoe Selo outside Petrograd and then wired to Moscow. Replies came the same route. In their December 9 broadcast, the French warned that the Soviet Russian leadership would be held personally responsible and threatened "to take immediate, justifiable measures against the Russian Bolsheviks which are on [our] territory."[74] Chicherin's response, which is undated, must have come several days later, likewise by radio; responding to French "calumnies," he branded the French as being "insincere" and accused them of "stonewalling." He stressed that the imprisoned French were all comfortable and charged that those who were pro-Bolshevik in France were the ones being mistreated by the Allies. He concluded with the promise that the French proletariat would shortly take care of the bourgeois French government.[75]

In a responding radiogram on December 20, the French again condemned the Russians for mistreating French nationals in such "a manner dangerous to their health." Their indignant response did leave open the door for the earlier plan by adding that the French admiralty could have a boat at any Baltic port between the sixth and the tenth of January.[76] The navy offered on December 18 the use of the ships *Mégally Hellas*, *Oran*, and *Dunkerque*, and suggested instead a Swedish port for the exchange because of the danger of unswept German mines scattered along the shore of the eastern Baltic. The hostages could go overland by Finland.[77]

Chicherin, likewise by radio from Tsarskoe Selo, responded rather warmly to this idea, informing the French, "We are absolutely in accord to go with the execution of the plan." He suggested that the Russian Red Cross go by sea, since crossing war-ravaged Europe would be difficult. He also stated that he would provide the French with a list of Russians to be repatriated, adding that "other details will be decided eventually."[78]

To arrive at some agreement was suddenly made more urgent from the French point of view when word somehow reached them on December 28 through the Danish consulate in Helsinki, Finland, that Darcy had died on December 23 in a private clinic in Moscow to which he had been taken on the twenty-first, thanks to Danish intervention by their departing consular staff. This development was complicated by the fact that the French had now decided that they did not want a Russian Red Cross delegation on French soil since the Russian Red Cross in Switzerland had engaged in espionage. Yet Darcy's murder placed the French in a serious predicament because the Bolsheviks also had threatened to execute French hostages by firing squad. Clearly they were not opposed to abusing French prisoners regardless of world opinion.[79]

As Pichon saw it, France had two unpleasant options: It could either refuse the entry of the Russian Red Cross delegates and risk reprisals against the French hostages à la M. Darcy, or it could admit the Red Cross and risk the dangers of revolutionary propaganda that its representatives would most certainly sow on the fertile ground of war-bitter France or among the homesick Russians. If they were allowed to enter France, common sense dictated that they must be told that if they import any propaganda, they would be punished by immediate expulsion. Yet Pichon wondered how much freedom the delegates should be permitted. Should they be allowed unsupervised exposure to the Russians in the camps? Should they be allowed to circulate freely in France?[80] The French faced a dilemma indeed.

At least temporarily, the French handled the problem by ignoring it. In his radiogram from the Eiffel Tower on December 27, Pichon proposed the swap. He gave a suggested time, around mid-January, and even asked if the Russians would find that enough time to bring the French hostages, especially military figures, to a Swedish or Danish port. A list was provided of the individuals the French especially wished to have freed.[81] Nowhere, however, did Pichon mention the Red Cross mission. The Soviets responded positively the same day, acknowledging the receipt of the message, but Chicherin added, "We are totally surprised that we did not receive an answer for our request concerning the arrival in France of the mission of the Russian Red Cross." He then asked not whether the Red Cross would be permitted but by what means it "must enter France, so as not to expose it to danger."[82]

Probably fearful that if they denied the Russian Red Cross entry into France, the Russians would refuse to return the hostages, the French grudgingly radioed at 4:30 A.M. on January 1, 1919, that the Russian Red Cross delegates would be admitted, but the French government sternly warned the Soviets that the delegation must not carry, as it had into Switzerland, any propaganda "under the cover of their humanitarian task." The French made it clear that if the Russians did not obey this condition, the delegation would be expelled immediately. The French then gave the name of the ship ⁺hat would make the exchange, the *Mégally Hellas*, which would be sent to whatever port the Russians designated with 1,157 arbitrarily chosen military personnel and 57 civilians.[83]

The Russians accepted the conditions on January 4, and Pichon immediately notified the French consulates in Copenhagen, Stockholm, Christiania, and Archangel. The Russians had added the ominous caveat that until all the Russian Red Cross delegates had arrived in France, they would continue to hold "a certain number of Frenchmen," and Pichon informed Clemenceau on January 11 that quite probably all of the detainees would not be released at once and a second convoy would have to bring the remainder. Mindful of the potential Red Cross menace, Pichon felt that it would be necessary to take control of them as soon as they arrived and totally channel their activity. To perform this task, a governmental delegate should be sent "as quickly as possible" to Dunkerque, since apparently the Russian Red Cross delegation would be departing from Russia on January 22.[84]

On January 7 the French supplied the Russians with a list of the personnel that they wanted, most of whom were military but included Edmund Duchesne, the French consul general in Petrograd, and Mazon. The French added that without these men, the soldiers would not be returned nor the Red Cross delegates admitted into France. The *Mégally Hellas* was to leave French waters on January 15 for the Baltic port of Nynäsham, which the French had chosen for a rendezvous to take place on January 20. If the Russian boat was not there, the *Mégally Hellas* would be recalled.[85] On January 7 the Soviet-designated Russians arrived at Dunkerque from destinations all over France and began embarkation at 4:00 P.M.

The French were trapped in an unenviable situation and were at the mercy of the Soviet regime. They could not for a moment permit the Red Cross to play any subversive games, yet any interference might result in the Soviets' abuse of the hostages. In a democratic nation with a free press, the torture and murder of its nationals by foreigners places an obligation on its government that is not a problem in a dictatorship with state-controlled journalism. The administration of President Jimmy Carter was to learn this lesson over half a century later from revolutionary Iran. Moreover, the care and maintenance of thousands of soldiers was a much greater problem for France than the detention of a few hostages would be for Russia.

On January 10 the incarcerated Duchesne was allowed to send a dispatch, in which he suggested an exchange under Danish control in Reval (modern Talinn) or some other Baltic port. He also announced the selected Red Cross delegates: Dmitri Manouilsky, Inessa Armand, and Jacques Davchian. Since the latter was ill, the French diplomat added that he might be replaced by Jean Beraud, a Russian native of French descent. Both Manouilsky and Armand are stellar figures in the galaxy of Soviet saints. Manouilsky, a Ukrainian Bolshevik turned Menshevik turned Bolshevik again, has the distinction of being one of the few old Bolsheviks to survive Stalin. He also headed the Ukrainian delegation to the founding meeting of the United Nations in San Francisco in 1945, and he personally attended four general assembly meetings over the next five years. Inessa Armand, *née* Elizabeth d'Herbenville, was herself French and had been born in Paris. She had gone to Russia to live with her aunt and her grandmother, who were tutors to the Armands, a wealthy Russian family of French ancestry. She eventually married one of the sons, later divorcing him to live conjugally with his younger brother. While residing in Stockholm, she became a Bolshevik after reading some of Lenin's works. She is reputed to have later become his lover, but there is no real evidence that such an affair took place. Both her political and her French connections secured her a place on the delegation.

The French deemed Revel and Libau to be the best of the Baltic ports for the transfer. Riga was eliminated because of both ice and unswept mines. On January 13, 1919, the two powers agreed to make the trade in Revel, and Russia requested that the Danes place a representative aboard their boat when it passed through Copenhagen. The French wired their acceptance that same day, and all agreed that the Danish representative would be a Colonel Philippsen of the Danish Red Cross.[86]

Late in January 1919 the *Mégally Hellas* left France with about 1,200 men on board, and on January 24 it arrived in Danish waters, where it was escorted to Copenhagen by the Danish ship *Ancre*. The French minister to Denmark, Charles Brugère, was to have contact with them while they were under Danish authority. The Russian soldiers aboard were mostly war invalids.

Yet just as the agreement seems to have been going according to plan, the Russian food situation began to cause a problem. There simply

was not much foodstuff available in Moscow, and the Russian government was not likely to lavish what it had on the French community there.
By mid-January Pierre Delavaud in the French consulate in Stockholm
wired the French ministry of foreign affairs that the French community
would starve within a month unless some food was obtained. He even
suggested that the departing Swedish consulate be asked to help.[87]

There is no direct proof that this plea created the Russian reaction
the next day, but it is quite likely that it somehow did. Probably thinking
that the French would assume that they were intentionally starving
French nationals, Chicherin blasted the French government on January
17, believing that the best defense was an offense. Accusing the French
of treating the Russians in France like prisoners of war "or worse," he
attacked the French government for forcing the Russians to fight against
Bolshevik Russia. It is true that the French were enlisting volunteers
among the Russians in France to fight on the side of the Whites in the
intensifying Russian Civil War, but there was no coercion whatsoever,
and Chicherin must have known this fact. Yet the charge itself would give
him bargaining power, and with his usual eloquence, he waxed hot against
alleged French duplicity: "Such acts of violence outraging universal
human sentiments transports us to the most barbarian epochs," he
stormed at the innocent French, whom he accused of forcing the Russians
in France "to raise their hands against their fathers and their brothers."
Referring to deportation to Africa, he charged that they were forcing these
soldiers "to submit to cruel torments and persecution." He concluded that
the Russian government would hold the French responsible not only for
the forces in France but those in Salonika as well.[88]

This blast was the first of Chicherin's righteously indignant attacks
on French behavior that he would use with consummate skill to torment
the French over the next year and a half. He would take great delight in
jerking their chain. His indignation in no way deterred him from calmly
suggesting on January 21 that Riga would be a good port of exchange,[89]
as if there was no bone of contention between the two nations. He certainly
ignored the fact that the Russians had beaten to death one of the French
hostages. The French, probably realizing the note for what it was, did not
even reply. The point, however, had been made.

On January 27 the Russians raised once again the question of the
admission of the Russian Red Cross into France and additionally requested
that these delegates be allowed free access to a private means of communication with the Soviet government and the right to send and receive inviolable
couriers. The Russians also requested that these three delegates be given a
number of aides and assistants, such as secretaries and other support staff.[90]

Permitting limited support staff, the next day the French nevertheless stressed once again that the Red Cross deputation must behave itself
and that if it did not, it would be expelled from the country. On the point
of closed correspondence, the French flatly refused. The French foreign
ministry informed the Soviets that they could not give the Russian Red
Cross rights that they did not give the International Red Cross in Geneva.
Pichon pointed out that these deputies were not ever granted any particular immunity, such as the status given diplomats, and they always had to
accept rules applicable to the citizens of any foreign power. The French
then plaintively asked the Russians to give assurances that these Red
Cross deputies would not busy themselves with political questions when
in their country.[91]

Meanwhile, various events led to the rejection of the Baltic states as
a point of exchange. First, the Baltic republics were less than enthusiastic
about Russian soldiers crossing their borders, but also the Germans, on
evacuating from these states after the armistice, had stripped their railroads of all rolling stock, so that getting sufficient cars to transport the
men would have been very difficult. Finally they began negotiating on a
Finnish port, and by January 28 the choice had been narrowed to either
Abo or Hangö.[92] By the end of January, Brugère had completed the
details of the first troops-hostage exchange, which was to occur at the
Russo-Finnish border town of Rayayoki on Thursday, February 6, 1919,
at 10:00 A.M. On February 4 the Red Cross delegation left Moscow for
Petrograd, and suddenly the diplomatic conversations by the Russians
became very friendly, with such phrases as "expression of our gratitude
for the amicable concourse to the procedure of the exchange" gracing their
language.[93] The Russians were at this time calling for a truce in the Civil
War, and their sugared tones were probably due to the fact that they
needed a good diplomatic climate to gain a cease fire. This attitude would
change once more.

The *Mégally Hellas* did not complete the journey. Its size did not
permit it to pass through the Danish straits, and the navigation of these
waters presented serious risks because of still-active German mines, so
the French government commissioned the Danish boat *Russ* to complete
the voyage. The 1,200 passengers were transferred to it, with the switch
being completed on January 27. They were then joined by the newly freed
Duchesne, who had been allowed to exit into Finland on January 23.[94]
All aboard, the repatriates departed from Copenhagen on February 1 and
wended their way through the Baltic, sailing close to the Swedish coast,
crossing the Gulf of Bothnia to the Aland Islands and the safety of the
Finnish coastal islands. Ice made travel slow, but on February 6 at 4:00

P.M. the *Russ* finally arrived at Hangö, the agreed port of exchange. Extended to the French officers was an invitation to visit Marshal Carl Mannerheim, the regent of the new Finnish republic, with whom they passed the time as the exchange moved forward. The next day, February 7, Duchesne and a Colonel Philippsen with the Danish Red Cross left for the Finnish border to collect their charges, and they received them the next day at Rayayoki at 8:00 P.M. A train returned the hostages and the Russian Red Cross delegates to Hangö on the night of February 9-10, and at 10:00 A.M. the next day the Russians and the designated French repatriates were transported to the *Russ*, which was escorted by the French torpedo boats *Intrepide* and *Temeraire*, some French police, and 100 Algerian infantrymen, who must have looked and felt out of place on the frigid Baltic Sea.

The Finnish government had closely watched the Red Cross delegation after it had crossed their borders, even to the point of guarding their train compartment. The French isolated them as well. They were permitted to travel in first-class accommodations and were treated correctly, but they were under close surveillance by French officers. Three days after they had left Hangö, they sent the Soviet government a radiogram telling of the exchange, their proper departure, and their good treatment so that those Frenchmen in Moscow who had still been detained could be freed. Since there was no direct telegraphic link with the Soviet state, the original of this telegram was given to Duchesne, who in turn sent it to Paris, from where it was dispatched via the Eiffel Tower to Tsarskoe Selo. The code name used was Montcalm.

After they were on board the *Russ*, however, the Red Cross delegates were not allowed any French contact, and the Danes also quarantined them as if they were infected with some terrible bacillus.[95] When they tried to disembark, they were stopped, and when Manouilsky tried to contact a Danish Red Cross nurse to send a telegram for him, he was prevented from doing so.[96] To add insult to injury, the whole time they were on board, they were watched by two noncommissioned officers, and the Danish police on board controlled all movements in and out of their compartment.[97] The *Russ* stopped in Copenhagen and boarded some additional passengers, and on February 18 it departed for Kiel, accompanied by the *Ancre*. This curious collection of argonauts arrived at Dunkerque on the afternoon of February 22.[98] While the first part of the exchange was over, the affair itself was far from ending.

The French remained doubtful about the Red Cross delegates. Pichon wired both Delavaud and Brugère his suspicions when he informed them that the Russians had accepted all the conditions.

Somehow seeing the ready acquiescence of only the support personnel as proof that Russia's principal goal for its Red Cross mission was "to penetrate into France some propaganda agents," he instructed the ministers in Stockholm and Copenhagen to be wary. Pichon had felt that admitting the Russians was an "extreme concession" and was made only because it was a sine qua non for the exchange.[99]

Moreover, the French learned that Manouilsky had in his possession 49,000 Swiss francs and 1.5 million Russian roubles, quite a large sum for so small a mission, and they were certain that the money was designated for subversive purposes. Pichon, observing that the delegates had no diplomatic immunity, recommended to Clemenceau that the money be confiscated and placed on deposit in a French bank, allowing the Russians to withdraw only small sums for recognized functions.[100]

France had conscientiously traveled the extra mile to reach an accord with the Soviet regime solely for the welfare of its hostages. Note after note to the various French diplomats involved emphasize that all care must be taken to preserve the tie to the Soviets for the sake of the French nationals whose lives and security were in danger. Pichon, in giving Burgère and Delavaud instructions on how to handle the exchange, constantly stressed this fact. The Russians were scarcely unaware that there was more pressure on the French than was on their government to settle the matter, and whatever bad publicity the French might try to utilize about Russian treatment of French nationals, it would never have the value that France's holding over 20,000 Russians would have for the Bolsheviks as a propaganda tool at home. Moreover, the Russians well knew that the French were most eager to be rid of this unwanted burden and that any delays in their repatriation would be logistical in nature. The Soviet government also was aware that these soldiers would be treated well, despite their accusations to the contrary, and were fed better than they would be in the chaos of their homeland. Unlike the French, however, they had no reason to end the matter speedily. The Soviets were holding all the cards in this first diplomatic poker game they were to play with the West, and they played them with consummate skill.

On arriving at Dunkerque, the Red Cross delegates were immediately taken to a hotel in nearby Malo-les-Bains for debriefing and what was in reality their detention. Manouilsky demanded a "fixed, well-known residence" as headquarters in Paris where all Russians who wished to return could find him. What he was requesting sounded to the French government like an embassy, and Pichon termed the request "inadmissible," adding that he had "no intention of entering into [diplomatic] relations with these delegates."[101] The French did permit Manouilsky to send another wireless message via the Eiffel Tower to his government stating that all of them were safe and calling on Chicherin to release additional French hostages per the agreement, but no secret channel was afforded them. The message generated only silence from Moscow.[102]

The French hostages who accompanied the Red Cross deputation were somewhat the worse for wear. One man had a very bad case of flu with high fever. He was taken immediately to the Rosendal Hospital in Dunkerque. The rest were sent on to Paris, where they arrived at the Gare du Nord on the night of February 23, exactly six months to the day after they had been arrested. Reporters from *Le Petit Parisien* were the first to interview them and reported to their readers that conditions in Russia had been horrible. Their food had been "terrible" (*épouvantable*) and sleep had been "impossible."[103]

Chicherin, who did not rush to reply to his only emissaries in France, did not hesitate to wire the French. By March, the first Russians returning from France had had time to be debriefed by Moscow of their adventures there, and in a radiogram on March 11, the people's commissar of foreign affairs ripped into the French government for its "inhuman treatment" of the Russian soldiers that had resulted in "illness and infirmities." He accused the French of mistreating these Russians simply because they would not fight and wanted to return home. He ticked off a litany of alleged French sins, even mentioning the various prisons and places of detention, and demanded that the French free the Russians and "live up to the agreement."[104] It is, of course, possible that Chicherin was truly concerned about what he believed to be French abuses and that his information came from returnees who embellished the gravity of their conditions in France. We have seen that the French had been rather circumspect with the rebellious Russians. It is far more likely, however, that Chicherin saw a chance to acquire additional high cards in his diplomatic game for any future conflict with the French.

The French do not seem to have replied to this latest tirade but instead informed the Russians the next day, March 12, that the *Dumont d'Urville* had been designated for the next exchange, which they hoped would be around the first of April. There followed the usual jockeying about which Baltic port would be used for the exchange.[105] Yet now with the Red Cross delegation in France itself, the negotiations could take place on two fronts, and not to the advantage of the French. On March 13 several French officials met with the delegation and were immediately attacked by Davchian and Manouilsky for encouraging the Russians in France to join General Anton Denikin's anti-Red forces.[106] Armand criticized the choice of detention camps, which she felt depended less on distance and more on the utility of inmates.[107] In a second meeting that same day, they told the French officials that since some in prisons were there for desertion, they were therefore political prisoners, and the delegation demanded all dossiers on their trials and a lawyer for them of their own choosing.[108]

The archives do not yield the French response, but the next day the delegation sent Chicherin a radio message indicating that the French were completely restricting their movement and keeping them isolated from French citizens. In words that were intended more for French than Soviet consumption, they complained that there was "no possibility of being convinced that there are not Russian citizens incarcerated for political reasons in prisons and concentration camps." They likewise told Chicherin that their own detention made it impossible for them to fulfill their mission, and they wanted instructions from him.[109]

A reply to the delegates' earlier radiogram finally arrived on April 1, and it has the same familiar ring to it of those from the Provisional Government to the officers of the REF. It was not signed by Chicherin but by a Benjamin Sverdlov, an unknown in the foreign commissariat. The missive told the delegates to continue despite the difficulties and ordered them to obtain the immediate freedom of all Russians detained by the French, no matter what, especially those accused of political crimes. Sverdlov especially emphasized that the delegation demand the cessation of recruitment for the armies of General Denikin.[110] Not only was the delegation powerless, however, to stop anything the French might have been doing to the Russians, the French were now becoming openly hostile to the delegation itself. Word had reached them through Switzerland on March 26 that Manouilsky had led one of the Bolshevik takeovers in Kiev, information that would hardly endear him to the French. Meanwhile, Chicherin continued his anti-French bombasts with the usual accusations about the barbaric mistreatment of Russians in France and the hindering of Manouilsky in his work. On April 6 the French bluntly countered these false charges and pointed out that they had never agreed to handle the Russian expatriates in the manner desired by the delegation. They also stressed that the French had never beaten to death a helpless Russian national in prison as the Russians had Darcy.[111] Chicherin replied three days later with yet another lengthy polemic accusing the French of all sorts of supposed misdeeds without refuting the French charges.[112]

At this point French patience finally snapped. The French exploded about the numerous delays, the false accusations about "political prisoners," and the mistreatment of Russians. On April 11 they simply dismissed the Russian complaints by saying that it was useless to recount the "inaccuracies and false accusations" that the Soviet government had made, and they bluntly stated that either the Russians allow the departure of the French citizens in Moscow or the French would return Manouilsky and company on the *Dumont d'Urville*. While allowing the Russian Red Cross delegation relations with Russian military personnel in France, the French government stated firmly that any contact with Russian civilians would be made only through the French Red Cross. They demanded a reply by April 14; any delays after that date would be "considered as a sign that the Soviets wanted to break off negotiations." They concluded by demonstrating the vulnerability of their position by informing the Russians that they would continue to return Russian soldiers home regardless of the absence of a formal agreement.[113]

On the day that the French demanded a reply, they learned something even more disturbing about a plot concerning the Russian Red Cross mission. Two men, posing as Belgians, had offered a bribe to a chauffeur in Dunkerque to take Inessa Armand from the beach at Malo-les-Bains to Paris, where she would have been hidden, presumably by some Bolshevik sympathizers there. Armand probably was chosen because she was native French, and since she had spoken French from childhood, she could vanish more easily into the French population. The French even learned the exact route to Paris that the car was to take and that the driver was to be paid 100,000 francs up front and 100,000 francs on the successful completion of the mission.[114] On hearing of this scheme, the French ordered a clampdown on the delegation and informed the members that the *Dumont d'Urville* would take the entire group back to Russia when it departed on April 17.[115] Manouilsky received the news "with evident bad grace." Armand took the news more calmly. Described as being "prodigiously cunning," she had been making outside contact during her strolls on the beach, in movie houses, and on visits to the toilet. Despite bad weather, she would remain for a long time at an open window, and the French believed that she was somehow obtaining or sending messages to confederates through it. When she was informed that she would be departing, she replied casually that she could not leave just yet as she had some errands to run (one being the buying of a hat).[116]

Not taking any chances or allowing Armand to make her purchase, the French authorities moved them all onto the *Dumont d'Urville* for safekeeping; the dock was cordoned off, and sentinels were placed around their cabins.[117] The next day Manouilsky staged a desperate effort to stay, and he had a long talk with his captors and dangled "Russia's immense riches" before the French, as well as Russia's good faith in wanting to come to terms with its erstwhile ally. He even made the ridiculous offer to repay all of Russia's debts to France, something he had no authority to proffer,[118] as well as an agreement to stop all official anti-French propaganda. Nothing worked. The French had had enough. Yet his overtures were a clear indication to the French that their suspicions about the Red Cross mission were correct and that Russia had pinned on it great hopes for some action beneficial to Russia and detrimental to France. Chicherin himself chimed in the next day in a rather soft note to the French unlike his previous blasts. He wired that he regretted the forced departure of the Manouilsky mission as "an act not confirming with the agreed-upon accord" and noted that it was unfortunate for future attempts at agreement. He added that his government would do anything to see that the thousand or so men on the *Dumont* would be admitted into Russia, and he suggested a Black Sea route as the most favorable.[119]

Through with being diplomatic and eager to be rid of their two-year-old problem, the French began scouring the seas for bottoms in which they could return the thousands of Russians under their care. Meanwhile, the government resumed their negotiations through Colonel Philippsen. They informed the colonel through their minister in Copenhagen that despite the fact that they were unilaterally returning Russians, they would retain some as long as there were French detained in Russia.[120] With Manouilsky shouting "with extreme violence," the *Dumont* left Dunkerque on Thursday, April 17, with 1,000 Russians: 110 civilians, 947 soldiers, and the Manouilsky mission. Their destination was Hangö, which they expected to reach by about April 25.[121]

On May 9, Chicherin blasted both the Danish and French Red Cross, and in retaliation for the French expulsion of the Red Cross delegation, the Soviets rearrested the fragment of the French military mission in Moscow to hold them "until the day when the Russians would be at liberty to move about." Chicherin went on to threaten the French: "In the event that the Russian citizens . . . mentioned above have not arrived on Soviet soil in five days," the Soviet government will be obliged "with regret and against its will" to take "the most energetic repressive measures against the French mission and the other French citizens in Russia."[122]

The *Dumont* arrived at Hangö on April 29, but by May 3, the French still had not disembarked the Russians because for some reason the Russians had decided to delay the exchange again. Chicherin had struck once more with one of his diplomatic *pas de deux*. Some Red Finnish soldiers opposed to the exchange for some reason had closed the Soviet-Finnish border, and the Soviet commissar of foreign affairs informed the French that the Soviet government "energetically protests against the detention of the mission in Finland," knowing full well that the French were in no way detaining it. He went on to threaten the French with reprisals if these repatriates did not return to Russian territory.[123] Under this renewed flare-up, Philippsen resumed his difficult mediation. Despite the difficulties raised by the Russians, however, the French continued repatriation unilaterally, thus underscoring once again their desperation to get the soldiers off their hands. The Russians could not fail to notice that the French sent Russians home despite the continued Russian detention of Frenchmen, nor could they ignore its significance.

Yet the diplomatic ice seemed to be breaking. The Danish minister of war wired Philippsen at his post at the Finnish-Russian frontier on May 15 that there was a possibility the Russians would return the French hostages immediately in exchange for the release of the Russian Expeditionary Force.[124] Since this position already had essentially been accepted, it was hardly news. Pichon seized on it, however, and suggested the Russian naval base of Kronstadt in the Gulf of Finland as a place of exchange,[125] once again underscoring for the Russians the degree of French desperation.

On May 20 Conty reported to his government that Philippsen had worked out an arrangement whereby the Russians on the *Dumont* would cross the Russo-Finnish border before the end of the month and that the delays had been the result of Finnish railway problems, not pro-communist Finnish soldiers as had been supposed. He also stated that the Russians were ready to evacuate the French hostages because they had begun to realize that to hold out "for the complete evacuation of their compatriots detained in France is not reasonable."[126] The Russians contacted the French on May 29, their first response to French overtures in a while, asking them to press the Finns to allow the Russians to pass through their territory into Soviet Russia and insisting that they had asked the French on May 14 to send the *Dumont* on to Petrograd but had gotten no response.[127] The French replied that the Russians themselves were guilty of having made no démarches to the government of Finland and claimed that the Russians had never replied to their question of where in Russia to land these people if passage through Finland became impractical. They also were critical of Moscow's not having responded to French radiograms on May 5, 9, 14, 19, and 26 until May 29.[128]

Lack of Russian replies and the seeming contradictions in many of the notes most probably were caused by the method of transmission and a general chaos in Russia and in the Russian commissariat of foreign affairs in particular. Furthermore, at this point Admiral A. V. Kolchak was reaching the high-water mark of his drive on Moscow, and the Soviet government was probably too busy planning its evacuation from the capital to reply to the French diplomatic moves. Moreover, given the indirect method of transmitting messages, some must have been lost, if they were ever sent. One dispatch broadcast on May 4, 1919, to Tsarskoe Selo was not wired to Moscow until May 26.[129] Yet it became obvious that suddenly the Russians were willing to deal. The *Dumont* was able to discharge passengers in Finland, and on June 2 she began her return trip to Copenhagen, where she arrived on June 4, having spent twenty-nine days in Hangö. She had as passengers three Frenchmen of the military mission whom a Russian doctor had deemed too ill to be kept.[130] In this way another small step had been taken.

New information coming out of Soviet Russia, however, gave the French fresh cause to worry. During the first two weeks of June, the Soviets confiscated the passports of all foreigners in Petrograd in order to use them as hostages to force their nationals to give Russians in their countries free movement.[131] At about the same time Chicherin publicly declared that he would execute all English and French spies, whom he likened to bandits.[132] The threat was of course directed against all nationals of English or France, any of whom could be arrested as "spies," should the Soviet government need to find a few. As many French nationals still were in Russia, this menace was very real to Pichon. To counter this danger, the French government offered on June 7 to liberate any of the Russians imprisoned in France for criminal or political reasons, essentially a list that had been supplied by Manouilsky, if the Soviets would allow all French nationals to depart.[133] Noting that over 2,000 Russians, both civilian and military, would shortly be leaving Marseille for southern Russia, Pichon asked the Soviets to release the remaining French hostages. Since the Russians would be arriving in a few weeks, the French government informed the Soviets that its government "hopes that the people's commissariat will profit from the presence of the French boat" to repatriate the civilian and military personnel held in Moscow. The French were once again admitting their weak position and underscoring it by adding "as I have already indicated the repatriation of the Russians will continue and will be able to be ended in about a year." The French did stress that if the Soviets continued holding the French, the French would detain some Russians.[134]

Perhaps due to a serious lag time between messages and responses, the Soviets ignored this suggestion and asked the French to allow the Russian Red Cross to go to Salonika to the 8,000 Russians still there. The French quickly refused. On July 1 the Soviets seem to have replied at once to all of the month's offers that had come through the pipeline.

The Soviet government called the conditions of exchange through the medium of the Danish Red Cross "unacceptable,"[135] rejecting the conditions of total exchange of all French nationals for all Russians. The note did express pleasure that Russians would be unilaterally returned home, but the denied Russian request on June 27 that a member of the Russian Red Cross be allowed to go to Salonika was grounds for the new rupture in the negotiations. The Soviets went on to say, however, that they were willing to continue accepting repatriated Russians in the south of Russia.[136]

About a week later the Soviets escalated the tension by arresting all free Frenchmen, especially those in Petrograd, who had, except for Duchesne, somehow heretofore escaped most Soviet persecution thus far. The French exploded over the matter since they were clearly doing everything possible to speed the process of repatriation. They expressed "the greatest astonishment" at the fact that the continued energetic efforts to repatriate Russians had not stopped the arrest of French citizens in Moscow and notably Petrograd. The French radiogram "invited" the people's commissariat to free the French nationals "in the briefest delay possible in order to prevent reprisals against Russians in France, especially Russian civilians, meaning of course, those of a certain political nature."[137] To pressure them, civilian repatriation would cease immediately. At the very least the "acceleration of repatriation" would continue only if the detainees were released.[138] Meanwhile, the repatriation continued as quickly as was possible, with the *Buenos Aires* departing with 2,000 on July 25 and the *Euphrates* leaving on July 18 with 750.[139]

Chicherin's response was conciliatory. He asked for verification that repatriation was indeed occurring "with the greatest celerity possible," for given the lack of Bolshevik control of much of the South, he could not have known whether it was taking place. He then castigated the French for their expulsion of the Red Cross delegation, reminding them that verification of repatriation "was why we sent Manouilsky, whom you kept under house arrest for three months." He then enumerated the numbers of Russians in camps in France and Algeria (he puts the number at a grossly exaggerated 50,000) and noted that 500 (a more realistic figure) had been sent to Denikin "to fight their brothers, peasants and workers." In view of this mistreatment, he opined that the French government had no right "to speak in an indignant tone." He denied that there had been mass arrests of French citizens in Russia but did admit that some had been detained, along with Russians, when a military plot had been discovered. He then suggested that each government should send a delegation to a neutral country to thrash this question out.[140]

The new French foreign minister, Philippe Berthelot, replied on July 23 that France would not participate in any such meeting since the Soviets would use any delegation for propaganda purposes.[141] During August and September there followed a diplomatic tit-for-tat in which the French threatened to halt repatriation since the April 7 statement was a declaration and not an agreement, so it could be rescinded whenever they wished.[142]

Despite the absence of an agreement, however, the boatloads of Russians continued to flow homeward. To gain a little extra leverage, the French asked both Denikin and the government of northern Russia in Archangel for any prominent Bolsheviks they might have to be used as hostages. On October 6 ten Bolshevik prisoners arrived at Brest from Archangel to be employed as "*monnaie d'échange*" with the Bolsheviks, and they were "banked" in a prison at Rennes.[143] In November Denikin agreed to send any Bolshevik notables he might have had, but he added that he had none, since his soldiers immediately shot any as soon as they caught them.[144]

The firming of French attitude from the summer onward began bearing fruit, assisted by Denikin's successes early in the fall of 1919. On September 25, French embassy personnel were embarked on the *Condé* at Archangel, and they arrived at Brest early in October. The Russians eased their restrictions all over, for after this time the French began trickling in from Russia in many places, including Maxim Gorky's mistress, a Madame Rogger. Now more confident and playing Chicherin's own game, the French informed the Soviets on November 11 that they had "a certain number of Bolshevik agents" and proposed their exchange for any French citizens still held in Russia. Having stated their blackmail, they suggested to the Soviets that they consider "an exchange based on the principles of universally adopted humanity."[145]

Not bothering to respond to the French exchange suggestion, the Soviets replied on November 20 with the usual complaints of French perfidy. Contending that they were defending the Russian people against "tsarist officials," they condemned the French for sending Russians stranded in France to Denikin's armies, an action that they were indeed doing, as we shall see. They restated that they had always insisted that it was the French government's duty to "guarantee the safety of these men up to Soviet territory," in other words, they were not to be dispatched to Denikin.[146]

As matters developed, at this time the Bolsheviks gained an unexpected ally in General Denikin himself. He had never been pleased with using these men, who he felt had been infected with indiscipline and Left-wing political sentiments, and on January 4, 1920, he formally asked the French government, after having suggested it many times before, to cease sending him troops from France. He pointed out in his communiqué that these men were without means and therefore constituted a danger. Five thousand of them had run amok in Odessa, and another contingent of them in Novorossiisk had joined a band of Greens, an anarchist movement that fought both the Reds and Whites.[147]

The French continued to return Russians wherever they could, however, and there are numerous reports of small groups of French citizens leaving Russia through this or that port, so the exchange was taking place without a formal agreement. Occasionally the French would radio the Russians that a group of their nationals would be disembarked at a certain point, as they did on March 1, 1920, about Odessa, as always suggesting that the empty ship could return French nationals.[148]

Although repatriation continued from both sides without an agreement, each side knew that at some point it would have to stop. Neither side would play its last cards without the other doing so. This realization more than anything gave birth to the formal understanding. After a month and a half of diplomatic jockeying, on April 20, 1920, Duchesne and Litvinov finally signed in Denmark an accord, which is called for historical purposes the Accord of Copenhagen, the de facto opening of Franco-Soviet relations. After all of the bitter words and accusations, French premier Alexandre Millerand and Chicherin exchanged amicable notes.

In the agreement, France obligated itself to repatriate into *Soviet* Russia all troops from Macedonia and France, including presumably Algeria, which amazingly was not specified. Article 1 of the accord stated, "The French government will repatriate into Soviet Russia and the Soviet Ukraine all the Russian soldiers consigned there, especially those who had taken part in the Russian Expeditionary Corps in France. . . ." Also to be returned would be the civilians who wanted to be repatriated. They were to be returned according to rolls given to the French government, and when each boatload arrived, the French representative was to present the list for checking. To these ports of exchange, the Soviet government would be responsible for delivering the French hostages. Article 5 designated a ratio of return of 100 Frenchmen for every 2,500 Russians. The determined exit point was to be Odessa, which at that time took an incredible twelve days to reach by train from Moscow.[149] On the basis of this agreement, the exchange of the remainder was started. By late 1920 the last of the Russians who wanted to return had done so,[150] and this sordid diplomatic beginning of France's relations with the Soviet state came to an end.

Late in December, while the Soviets were still being perverse, the French minister of war wrote a letter to the minister of the interior that he wished to proceed with repatriation "with as brief a delay as possible." The minister of war did make the exception that he wanted the repatriation only of those "who want to return" and called on the minister of the interior "to invite them to form clearly their intentions."[151] Indeed most now did wish to return, yet in April several soldiers refused to board ships at Dunkerque to leave for Russia,[152] indicating a realization at least to some that the workers' paradise might not be all that they had believed it to be. In time many others would choose to remain rather than chance the uncertainty at home.

On January 14, 1919, at 5:00 P.M. at the ministry of war, a meeting was held to discuss the general question of broad repatriation, and some sort of organization and plan was formulated. Early in February, Clemenceau ordered Brulard to organize a camp near the points of embarkation; from these locations the repatriates would be fed into the transports to take them home. There should be a definite organization so that everything would function smoothly and quickly with absolutely no pressure put on any Russian soldier not wanting to leave. The older and the married men would be dispatched first, then the prisoners of war and the workers, but the two groups would not be allowed to leave in the same boats for fear of trouble.[153]

In the early days of repatriation an old problem resurfaced—the Courneau-Courtine schism. Soldiers from the different groups fought and threatened one another. A soldier Paul Ipatov, who was designated to be repatriated in April, asked not to go at that time because he was slated to be placed among soldiers from the La Courtine rebels, and they had already threatened him.[154] This incident was a clear indication that the rift still existed, although soon it would no longer be a French problem.

With the end of the war, the seas were no longer in danger of German U-boats, and with the collapse of Turkey in October 1918, there was no reason that the Straits at Constantinople could not be passed. Moreover, transports were no longer in short supply,, and with that the major obstacles to repatriation were removed. By late 1919 the Russian Expeditionary Force, along with the prisoners of war and all other Russian citizens, started to go home in great numbers.

By June 1919 only 4,500 or so Russians had returned from all points, leaving 45,000 in the West, 33,000 of whom were German prisoners of war. At that time there were still 8,500 Russians in Algeria and 8,000 in Salonika. Throughout the year governmental documents expressed the same urgency to return these men as they had before the war ended, and by June, when the Allied blockade was lifted from Germany, the trickles here and there became a veritable flood. When all of the boats that they hoped to utilize were sent into service, the French would be able to repatriate 7,000 men a month. There had been some talk of sending them across Germany and Poland, but that idea had to be shelved because the Polish government refused to allow it. It was argued that the 33,000 prisoners of war be returned to the Germans for repatriation. If the Germans should refuse to accept them, someone suggested that these Russians be deposited on the right bank of the Rhine under an interdict to return to France.[155]

Yet from the beginning a certain group was sorted from the returnees, those whom the French government felt would fight on the side of the Whites. Exactly who in the French government formulated this plan is anyone's guess, but it is not surprising that someone did. The government decided that those who were thought dependable would be sent to the French occupation zone in Russia or some White-controlled area. Detachments of workers or prisoners of war who must have been thought unreliable were simply to be taken to Russian territory and dumped.[156] Report after report in the archives show Russians leaving Dunkerque, Cherbourg, and Marseille all throughout 1919 for Murmansk in the north and Sevastopol and Novorosiisk in the south. A mixture of boats was assigned to the task, including one named *Imperator Nicholas I,* obviously of Russian origin, and the *Dumont d'Urville,* which had ferried Russians to France in the first place.

The candidates for repatriation seem to have been gathered rather haphazardly, with whoever happened to be present or handy being taken. For example, 600 Russians were embarked at Dunkerque in April, 1919, and they seem to have been collected from the vicinity by some French soldiers.[157] That same month the soldier destined to be the most famous from the REF, Rodion Malinovsky, returned to Russia, having for some reason abandoned his goal to become a chauffeur.[158]

Of special significance was the return of the officers, for they for the most part were interested in joining the White movement. An encouragement for joining, however, was the French termination of their salaries in September 1919. Like the soldiers, they were sent to different places, the Baltic, the Ukraine, the Caucasus, and Siberia, and by late November, only around 1,200 were left in France.[159] They never seem to have lost their sense of old regime status. When the British tried to send some 400 officers in third class in October 1919, they balked because of the accommodations. Only the arguments that they were urgently needed by General Nicholas Yudenich and the only alternative to third class was to send them at a later time pacified them. Yet efforts were made to improve their food and to segregate them from the other third-class passengers.[160] This mentality was the political material that doomed the White cause.

On the whole, the repatriation must have gone smoothly for by December 1919, despite the fact that the base at Laval still administered almost 25,000 Russians (20,000 in France and 4,000 in Algeria), the French began liquidating it, the completion of which was formally to be on April 1, 1920. A committee of three officers, however, would remain in Paris for whatever functions might be necessary. There would hardly have been plans to close the post by January unless the French were fairly certain to be rid of these men soon. By January 1920, 2,000 more had departed from France and about 5,000 had left Salonika for southern Russia, leaving only 2,400 still there.[161] At some point in the year 1920, the Commission of Russian Liquidation was established to execute the last of the Russian matters. By mid-June 1920, a total of 47,289 REF soldiers and prisoners of war, counting from the beginning, had been repatriated, leaving 25,711, of whom 8,000 are unaccounted for. These must have included those who had died as well as the 3,500 who chose to remain in France; about 1,500 asked to be repatriated to the Baltic countries, which had newly won their independence from Russia. That left almost 18,000 to be sent back at that point.[162] Repatriation moved at a brisk pace because by August 3, 1920, only 7,000 Russians in France and 3,600 in Algeria were waiting to return.[163]

On October 3 the last of the French hostages exited through Finland. M. Rosset of the embassy staff wired Millerand, "Prisoners Moscow arrived Finland today addresses to M. Millerand the expression of their most lively gratitude at the occasion of their liberation."[164] On October 5 the Russian government radioed Paris that all of the French who wanted to leave were now out. Shortly afterward, the last Russians departed from French ports.[165] The French, and probably to some degree the Soviets, breathed a collective sigh of relief. The Russian soldiers who had gone to France four years before had done what men in all armies from the beginning of recorded time have longed to do: They went home. For some, however, their departure was not the end of the story.

ELEVEN

The Last Mile Home:
The Crucible of Civil War

1918–1920

Do not interfere with an army that is returning home because a man whose heart is set on returning home will fight to the death against any attempt to bar his way, and is therefore too dangerous an opponent to be tackled.

—Sun Tzu[1]

But it is not as soldiers that the great majority want to go home: they consider in effect that the war as over, their Russian comrades have been demobilized and they have long ago returned to their homes and they do not generally believe in the disorder and the troubles of which all dispatches speak. . . . There must be a new propaganda campaign to inform them of what has gone on, that they must intervene on the side of the Allies.

—General Jean Brulard[2]

Have there been indeed officers in Russia? As far as is known there have been none, . . . but there have been drunkards, indefatigable debauchees, who prepared this punishment for themselves. For many years they abused the soldiers, like beasts and worse than that. And [now] the Russian soldier wants for the moment revenge upon the officer. . . .

—*Russkoe slovo,* 31 December 1918[3]

In a civil war, more than any other, the moral element is paramount.

—General Anton Denikin[4]

ONE OF THE SADDEST EPISODES of the Russian Civil War was the attempt by the Allies to intervene on the side of the Whites. Before the war ended and the Bolsheviks emerged victorious, Americans, Frenchmen, Englishmen, Canadians, Japanese, and Italians fought and died supporting a movement that was doomed to fail. In fact, their halfhearted support of the anti-Bolshevik movement did more damage than any benefit derived from the lackluster performance of any of the troops that were sent or from the generally inferior military hardware they gave the anti-Communist forces. The soldiers the Allies dispatched were often not their best, and the arms and supplies were given with little consideration to their value or quality. Shells did not fit the guns, or rifles were sent without bullets. One veteran of the Russian Civil War complained to the author that all he ever got from the British was two pairs of Bermuda shorts.[5] The fact that the Allies helped the Whites or sent them anything at all gave the Reds an invaluable propaganda weapon to use to influence the generally xenophobic Russian masses. The Whites with their foreign support, poor though it was, could be painted by the Bolsheviks as traitors and dupes of foreign imperialists who wished to enslave their native land. Paul Miliukov, the great prerevolutionary liberal leader, observed, "The Allies should have either given the Whites a great deal more help or none at all."

Initially the intervention came about for the dual purposes of protecting the gigantic amount of war matériel that the Allies had shipped to Russia and to open a second front against the Germans. After the November armistice in 1918, however, the purpose given for the intervention changed "to the reestablishing of order," a code phrase for defeating the Bolsheviks. In October 1918, General Lavergne, in a report written while he was passing through Stockholm on returning to Russia, called for rapid intervention to thwart the increasing strength of the new Bolshevik regime. He warned it was preparing to export revolution and its ever-increasing strength required immediate action. Its success could mean exposing Europe to the "virus of revolution." Noting that the anti-Bolshevik elements could not win on their own, Lavergne advocated the sending into Russia a half million men to defeat the Bolshevik menace.[6]

The French were the most verbally insistent Allied supporter of the White movement because they were the largest creditors of the old governments. France had gone from being a creditor to a debtor nation between 1914 and 1919 and desperately needed the repayment of the loans made to former Russian governments.[7] In February 1918 *Pravda* cleverly stated the French position when it told its readers, "The petty bourgeois Frenchman will pardon the millions of victims on the field of battle, but he will not forgive his material ruin."[8] As the Bolsheviks had declared that they would not repay the old debts, France had a strong vested interest in seeing their replacement with another Russian government that would.

To aggravate future developments further, French behavior in the parts of Russia they occupied was less than laudatory. In Odessa, Lobanov-Rostovsky, who had been one of the early repatriates in December 1918, described their actions as being like troops occupying a conquered country.[9] Moreover, the French sent a large number of Algerian and Moroccan units whose actions were even more abusive than those of native French soldiers. The overall performance of France's interventionist forces was, therefore, of little help to the Whites. General Franchet d'Esperey had always predicted that the French soldiers would not perform well "in vast cold Russia" and wrote the French prime minister, "Those who willingly advance into Hungary as a foretaste of their triumphant entry into Germany, will hardly consent to take part in operations leading to the occupation of Russia."[10] French mutinies in Odessa in April 1919 came as little surprise to him.

Furthermore, from the beginning there was also unhelpful tension between the French and their White allies. The French immediately refused the Volunteer Army, the anti-Bolshevik force in southern Russia, supplies on credit,[11] and later, after General Baron Peter Wrangel surrendered to the French all Russian ships and 100 million French francs as a pledge for war matériel, the French refused to return the money.[12] At another point the French refused to give Denikin 320 billion gold roubles held under French control for the imperial army.[13] These actions naturally bred strong hostility. After the French troops' mutiny in Odessa and the subsequent French evacuation from the south of Russia, the White generals could have felt little love for the arrogant French military.[14] In May White General A. N. Grishin-Almazov was taken prisoner by the Bolsheviks. On his person his captors discovered a letter from Denikin to Kolchak bitterly criticizing the French and stating that while the British gave them "ample assistance," they were receiving "ample opposition" from the French. The Bolsheviks published the letter in *Pravda*, and it was of course read by the French government. When Clemenceau met General A. M. Dragomirov in the summer of 1919, the French prime minister strongly protested, and the whole incident led to additional tension between the Whites and their French "allies."[15]

Since the French themselves were not willing to fight in the Russian Civil War, it is not surprising that they quickly thought of sending in their place the remainder of all Russian troops still in France. It also logically made good politics to include as many Russians as possible to assist any Allied interventionist elements. The Russians would be fighting in their homeland, for their homeland, and would not, presumably, have the same discipline problems.[16] The use of Russians also would not give the impression, the French felt, that they were intervening in Russian internal politics, an impression that would indeed be hard to avoid. At any rate, such was the reasoning.

The idea to use all of the Russians in France had begun germinating in French minds as early as January 1918, and it developed apace after that. In the mid-summer of 1918, the Slavic Bureau of the French Army formally recommended the use of "judiciously chosen troops" in the Russian Civil War,[17] and a similar note from other departments suggested the same in August, observing that such a force could become "a kernel of the future Russian army."[18] It is not surprising that the notion also was given life among some of the White Russian generals. The first seems to have been the REF's own Colonel Nechvolodov. In April 1918 he sent the French war ministry a memo on the possibility of some action near the port of Archangel using Russian elements currently in France "in favor of the Russian national renovation and the Allied intervention in Russia." Having been besieged in China in the Russian embassy during the Boxer Rebellion, Nechvolodov was a bitter enemy of revolution and a staunch monarchist to boot, referring repeatedly to Nicholas II in his twenty-five-page memo as "our legitimate sovereign."[19] He had even begun to do some recruiting on his own. France gave him permission to organize a unit with the idea that it would supply "sufficient" artillery, airplanes, "and if possible several tanks."[20] Clemenceau, however, was not totally pleased with either the scheme or with Nechvolodov. Until April 1917 the Russian general had been the commandant of the 1st Special Regiment, and although he had the reputation of being a brave soldier, he also had a well-known taste for the easy life. Not only did his intransigent monarchism rub the arch-republican Clemenceau the wrong way; it also made him unacceptable to command Russian troops in the existing political climate. Moreover, Nechvolodov had left his command without orders during the May mutiny, resulting in removal from his post and his recall to Russia. For some reason he had gotten no farther than Paris, where he was living at the time he offered his services to the French government. Agreeing to utilize him, the cynical Clemenceau noted that this resurrected Russian colonel had begun "to show signs of life" only after the trouble was past.[21]

A Russian general, one Belosersky, asked the French military attaché in Stockholm in June 1918 to forward a similar request for the utilization of officers, noncommissioned officers, and soldiers of Russian contingents (again "judiciously chosen") to serve as agents of recruitment and propaganda to create units that would be used all over Russia.[22]

The most important figure, however, to call for such a force was General Lokhvitsky himself. In a conversation with President Poincaré on Wednesday, May 17, he suggested sending Russians to fight in Siberia, adding that in his opinion "one would find among these officers and these men several very resolute elements to assist the action of the Allies in Russia. . . ."[23] Poincaré must have encouraged him to contact Clemenceau on the matter, for, on May 22, Lokhvitsky wrote suggesting the creation of a Russian force to fight on the side of the Allies in the intervention. Denouncing the revolutionary anarchy in Russia, Lokhvitsky predicted to the French premier that if something were not done about it, the country would become "a cemetery, a pile of ruins to the greatest detriment of civilization and of humanity and a backwash for Germany." Noting that it was time to establish order within the country, Lokhvitsky suggested that Russian patriots would rally to a call to assist Allied intervention; he added that the inclusion of Russians in such a venture was the "essential condition for success." Not surprisingly, he charged himself with organizing the Russian portion of an interallied mission. Observing that only the Germans had restored order in Russia, Lokhvitsky added that it was essential to show to the Russian people that the Allies could recreate stability better. Stressing that the German enemy was penetrating into the interior of the country, Lokhvitsky demanded quick action "since there was not a moment to be lost."[24] In an additional memo written after the armistice he suggested another source of manpower, prisoners of war who had been captured in 1914-1915, because they would not have been infected with the bacillus of revolution and therefore would be more politically reliable.[25]

It was late in July 1918, however, before Clemenceau began formulating a plan for the utilization of the Russians on hand, especially those in the Russian Legion. In a memo responding to Lokhvitsky's suggestion, Clemenceau noted that "this question has already come to my attention," referring to Nechvolodov's April letter. He suggested to Foch a scheme to form two companies of volunteers, adding that if it brought good results, the French government might consider creating others. He advised against the idea of forming Russian battalions in France under Russian officers, given their poor performance to date, as well as the fact that many of them did not want to command Russian troops.[26]

On July 31, Clemenceau wrote the minister of foreign affairs suggesting the use of Russian troops in the intervention movement, but he recommended appealing only to officers who had been in the REF in France, since a "good number have passed our centers of instruction." He urged the Allies to move forward to get officers to raise troops for service in Siberia, including noncommissioned officers only "after serious consideration."[27]

With Ignatiev's help, the French government outlined a plan to form such a force. The memorandum stressed the volunteer nature of such a unit and the need to be discriminating in choosing the men. Its destination would be Siberia. They would be mixed with the Japanese there to "prove" to the Russians of the interior that the Allied intervention had no ulterior motive. Somehow the authors of the scheme thought this action would derail any German attempts to mobilize Russian prisoners of war against the Allies. In a more realistic vein, however, the memo noted that in addition to presenting "the most radical solution" to the problem of the Russian contingents in France, the plan gives at the same time the "possibility of lightening the burden that it creates for the French government and to eliminate a source of friction between the Russians and the French."[28] The officers were not a problem, despite the fact that they were demoralized, but Ignatiev suggested that a center of instruction for them be organized and that the French government create a means by which the noncommissioned officers could become regular officers, as in the French army. As for the infantry, it was described as "excellent human material" but imbued with the ideas of Bolshevism; Ignatiev felt that the solution would be to use elements of the REF as a core for the formation of better units. He likewise suggested opening a center to permit soldiers to become noncommissioned officers and generating a new spirit in each detachment by incorporating weaker groups into stronger ones.[29]

Late in August 1918, Ignatiev drafted an appeal. In the usual style of ringing patriotic oratory, the Russian general wrote a clarion call to arms to all Russians in the West to join the force to expel the "band of vagabonds" who had "under false pretenses usurped power in Petrograd." Accusing these blackguards of "provoking the common vicious instincts to all the popular masses," the summons condemned them for dishonoring the immortal glory of the Russian soldier and the "honest Russian people" by a separate, treasonous peace and having brought "famine, epidemic, and ruin" to the country itself. Ignatiev called for solidarity and unity, blaming the lack of it for the problems of the country. Like the author of "The Lay of Igor's Host," he stressed the need for the unity of the Russian detachments and a Russian committee of all political organizations in

France. He wished this committee to be drawn from across all social classes to fight for a Russian government "*based on the will of all the people* [his italics]." Affirming that the "democracies" were behind them, the author stated that the Allies would transport, feed, and finance the unit. He likewise made it plain that the old discipline would be restored in the unit formed, adding that no one was required to enter the detachment, but anyone who did so and betrayed the enterprise would be treated "without pity." He ended with a plea for Russian honor: "We must return to our native land with our head high . . . to save with the aid of our allies our country from the clutches of a disloyal enemy."[30] This summons, however, was not issued at this time, probably because Clemenceau still had reservations about the Russian leadership, and the Russian Legion also needed replacements. In a letter to General Belin four days later, the French premier expressed doubt that the Superior Council of War should go along with Ignatiev's proposal because it would return to the Russian command control over the Russian contingents that the French government had had to take from them that very year due to their "incompetence and lack of authority." Clemenceau did think that they could be used in Russia, but exactly how would have to be decided later.[31]

After the November armistice ending the world war, the talk increased about sending Russian forces to fight against the Bolsheviks either under the Allies or under Denikin in the south, and by early December a marching battalion of about 600 men and 19 officers, all of whom were volunteers from those who had fought effectively in French ranks in the Russian Legion or the French Foreign Legion, was organized for assignment to Denikin. A Colonel Bouchez wrote an appraisal of the group for the French army but recommended a different group of officers, stating, without giving his reasons, that there were better officers to be found at Laval. He also questioned their morale, saying that the only thing holding them together was that they were among elite troops composing a Moroccan division. Several Russian officers had expressed these same concerns.[32] Despite doubts, however, on December 9, 1918, Russian troops started moving to Chaussin, France, in the department Jura, to begin encadrement of units to be shipped to Denikin. On December 18 the order of the day was a formal call to arms. Noting that Russians finally had been allowed their individual banner, the author called for all Russian nationals in France and Algeria "to unite with honor" to the Russian Legion and expressed the belief that "each and every heart will join under the standard to participate in freeing the native land."[33] As in the formation of the Russian Legion, Russian soldiers all over France answered the call in twos and threes.

The French took great care to screen the officers to fight for the Whites, and one report of the sifting process has some names crossed out while others are labeled with such descriptions as "intelligent" or "opinion totally favorable."[34] Throughout the year they trickled into distribution points and along with the other repatriates headed east to fight Bolshevism. The lists do not contain many familiar names, although a roll of departees in June includes that of Lissovsky.

The French determined a set of rules and privileges for all who joined. All officers who were repatriated to the White areas had to ask in writing to be sent there. The French gave free repatriation, a salary advance, and a half-bonus if they enlisted.[35] Admiral Sergei Pogulaev felt by June that since the Allies had recognized Kolchak as the unifying leader of the anti-Bolshevik government Russia, it would be easy to organize volunteers. So optimistic was he that he asked the French to establish more camps to house them, estimating that the unrealistic figure of 50,000 men could be gotten.[36] Nothing near this number ever appeared, of course, as it would have had to include almost every Russian in the REF as well as all of the prisoners of war who filtered into France. In reality the numbers sent were much smaller.

Even the quality of the select force must have been questionable, and most certainly some people must have joined simply for the money and the better living conditions with every intention of deserting at the first good opportunity. Dr. Stanislas Lazovert, a Russian émigré who appeared in France in 1918 and who was possibly the same man who supplied the poison that was fed to Rasputin, had several friends among those in the Legion; they told him that the state of morale was very bad and that the soldiers were becoming anti-French. Lazovert questioned the value such a force might be to the White cause in Russia,[37] but by March 1919 a police report described the Russian soldier in France as having mellowed. "The excitement which manifested itself last year in the Russian military bases seems to have *entirely ceased* [their italics]," it reported, and attributed this change to the fact that Mikhailov had played no part in the organization process.[38] These statements are the only available indication of the morale of the new Russian forces. Their morale must have been reasonably good at this point because they were all volunteers, and only a small minority of the total Russian military effectives in France, who at this point numbered in the tens of thousands. At any rate, once these first units left, Russians would again find themselves fighting for French interests. There were basically three areas to which any Russians willing to fight for the Allies in their homeland were sent. One was to the north around Murmansk and the White Sea port of Archangel. There a strange conglomeration of units under Allied auspices had assembled. British General F. C. Pool was in Archangel to coordinate all British military efforts in the vicinity. Americans were also there in force and even fought a furious battle with the Bolsheviks on Armistice Day. The Russian General Evgenyi Miller, from his home in Rome, Italy, organized some disparate forces for the north, and the venerable old antique of Russian populism of the 1870s, Nikolai Chaikovsky, was positioned there as head of the Allied puppet Government of Northern Russia. Into this mishmash of troops, nationalities, ideologies, and interests came some of the Russians from France.

General Pool had told his government in August 1918 that he needed only junior Russian officers for an officers' training corps that he had formed. He cautioned that only a select number of officers, "those thoroughly vouched for," could be accepted.[39] That same month in Rome, General Miller listed the classes of Russian officers in France from which they might draw. The first group, and easily the most numerous, were those who had gone with the Russian Expeditionary Force, and he placed that number at a rather high 818 men. The second category was those who were in some service or other in France, as military attachés to the diplomatic service or to some French unit. Most of these had since been placed on permanent leave. The third group, as Miller saw it, were those living in Paris purely in a private capacity who had left Russia because of the present crisis. He felt that there was some use for the second and third group, but "at the present moment" he exposed doubts about the REF.[40] Miller did not give, or else the attaché did not report, the reason for the hesitancy to use REF officers, but it is obvious that he did not feel confident that they would be reliable. Their inability to control their men was not entirely their fault, but it is easy to see why Miller would be hesitant to use the very officers who had presided helplessly over a rebellion. He must have heard how they had avoided their men in the height of the La Courtine crisis, and this behavior probably stigmatized them.

In November Miller formally presented a plan with options for formulating a corps to fight in Russia; his scheme called for the rapid shaping of these units "*under a Russian command* [italics in original]." Miller believed the officers were willing to serve Russia in some capacity, but a major problem was whether to create obligatory service based on the authority of the Provisional Government, which had recently been overthrown by the Bolsheviks, or to make the unit entirely voluntary. Miller felt that a voluntary force would be small and weak, whereas a uniquely Russian unit under Russian leadership created by the now-defunct Provisional Government would somehow be better.[41] Some of the Russian leaders wanted to restore the authority that they had lost. The French for their part had doubts that an order of the Provisional Government would carry any weight with Russian soldiers in the West. Composed of dubious elements, this warmed-over unit might need to appeal to a French force to maintain order, thus risking a second La Courtine affair. From the French point of view, the only way to constitute any military unit from the Russian remnants in France was to make it voluntary.[42] General Miller was simply out of touch with reality to assume that these troops, who had been reluctant to obey orders of the Provisional Government in better times, would do so now that that government had ceased to exist.

Nothing more seems to have been done about Miller's suggestion, and since the general was still in Italy, Noulens pressed Marushevsky, who surfaced in Archangel in the fall of 1918, to assume command.[43] Marushevsky agreed and requested thirty company commanders and two or three good battalion chiefs.[44] By June 1919, 22,000 Russians had been collected in the north of Russia, to be augmented by 1,200 officers from Britain who would be sent as soon as travel conditions permitted.[45] All of these had not, of course, come from those units that had fought in France, but those who did were incorporated into the groups from many places that planned to fight against Bolshevism. For the most part any distinguishing trail of them vanishes here.

The next area to which the Russian volunteers were sent was in the south of Russia, the Whites' most solid stronghold. It was certainly the most accessible to the French. The territory along the Black Sea littoral and the regions of the southern Ukraine and northern Caucasus drew the anti-Bolsheviks like a magnet. General Lavr Kornilov, the leader of the White forces until his untimely death, formed an organization there, followed by General Denikin and later General Peter Wrangel. The White movement in Siberia technically controlled much more territory, but its authority there was very tenuous, as the rapid collapse of the regime of the self-styled Supreme Overlord of Siberia demonstrates. Anti-Bolshevik efforts in south Russia enjoyed the greatest successes, possibly because it was more easily supplied, and it was the last major region to fall to the Bolsheviks. At one point all Black Sea ports were in White hands. Perhaps because of this situation, coupled with the relatively easy access by Mediterranean and Black Sea sea lanes, most Russians assembled there. The French government as early as February 1919 composed a plan to dump all of their Russian problems there,[46] the most logical and easiest location for them.

The armistice had been signed scarcely a month when the first contingent of officers was corralled for dispatch to Denikin.[47] One man involved with the organization of forces for Denikin was well known, Colonel Gotua, who played from the beginning a prominent leadership role in the intervention. On December 9 he was summoned to organize a battalion to join Denikin. He was picked, as he had been for past assignments, because he was known for his energy and as a superior officer. Gotua had accepted this assignment gladly, but he had particularly requested the right to choose the officers and soldiers under him from volunteers in order to form a force that would perform well. The convocation point of the new unit would be Châlons.[48] Brulard thought that Gotua's ideas were good but pointed out that it was contrary to French military practice to permit a commander to choose officers and men. From what can be determined, Gotua's wishes were not granted. Another development that probably was most displeasing to him was the fact that these troops would be under French control, not under the command of the Volunteer Army.

Meanwhile, a second battalion of 500 men under Colonel Ieske was slated to be embarked at Marseille early in February; to it were to be added 323 men remaining at Pleurs. These would be reinforced from 125 volunteers then at Laval. In addition, four companies from the 7th region would be augmented with a company from Montaigu to constitute a second battalion.

In January and February 1919 the French and the Russian leaders busied themselves with the formation of the Russian Legion of the Orient to fight with Denikin. The same care and enthusiasm was involved in the organization, plans for payment, victualing, and all other needs of an army that the French had shown in the birth of the Russian Legion over a year before. All of the proper committees, bureaus, and administrative offices were formed. The French memos and directives carry with them a certain optimism and enthusiasm for the project,[49] probably fueled by the idea that they would be able to encourage Russians to assume the leadership role of toppling the Bolsheviks. The destination of these troops was to be Novorossiisk on the eastern Black Sea coast, Sevastopol in the Crimea, and Odessa on the western Ukrainian Black Sea littoral. In the midst of all the planning for the creation of these units, no one seems to have asked Denikin if he wanted them. At the beginning he was at best lukewarm toward the idea. He was favorable to the suggestion of recruiting some Russian prisoners of war,[50] yet when some units arrived at Novorossiisk, Denikin refused to accept them.[51] Exactly why is not clear, but he strongly resented the French role in the leadership of the Russian Legion of the Orient, and the fact that these men were not under his command was probably a major factor.[52] The French naturally felt it necessary to change the Russian general's mind. If they could not, the nearest place where the troops could be used was Archangel.

This stream of Russians in France into the White Army, however, continued throughout 1919. Colonel Rytov, commandant of the 1st battalion, left after Ieske in March, and in May the *Buenos Aires*, no stranger to Russian waters, took 2,100 Russians (1,900 of them soldiers) into the Black Sea theater. Most of the recruits were from the Russian Legion that had fought in France, and before departure they were given good clothing, underwear, and four days' worth of food. Weapons and horses were to be distributed to them on arrival. Yet despite the care with which they had been chosen, they were watched as if they were not to be trusted. The French called it a "discreet surveillance" and tried to avoid appearing to be guarding them against discipline problems, pretending instead that the aim was simply to make the recruits observe "strict rules."[53] Few could have been fooled.

Still leery of Russian leadership, Brulard expected that when these units passed from French to Russian authority, there would be some defections. His fears proved well founded. On February 7, just before the first units left Marseille on the boat *Chichikov*, twelve men already had left the vessel rather than "go fight in Russia." Two days later the ship had to return to port because of an engine breakdown, and another seventy deserted while in Camp Mirabeau, declaring that they wanted to remain in France indefinitely. A frequently voiced complaint seems to have been the food the French gave them, which Brulard merely dismissed as a fresh example of indiscipline and advised the French authorities not to tolerate this breech of behavior as it would set an example for Russians in other units and for those whom they were trying to repatriate.[54]

Early in June 1919 a convoy of 2,000 repatriating Russians was to leave from Marseille. Of these only 54 were volunteers bound for Odessa, and certain ones who had enlisted now decided that they did not wish to depart. The sudden change of mind had been caused by the newspapers *Journal of the People* and *Populaire*, which had been telling their readers that the Bureau of Russian Civil Repatriation in Paris was using the choice as a trap for discovering which Russians were pro-Bolshevik. The *Buenos Aires* was to leave for Odessa on June 1; but its departure was delayed for a week. The report does not state if all of the 54 finally departed. Their hesitation also might have been encouraged by an article in *Humanité* entitled "*La Legion Russe Assassinée par Denikin.*" The article, circulated among the soldiers in a journal called *La République russe*, reported that the first troops sent under Ieske were "made" to fight under Denikin. When they refused, there had been trouble, and Ieske himself was killed by his own men.[55] Although *Humanité* admitted that the story could not be confirmed, it went on to state that the soldiers who refused to join Denikin's corps were surrounded and "were killed to the last one." Again acknowledging that it could not confirm the tale, *Humanité* asserted that if and when the story was verified, the journal would encourage the French proletariat to protest and call on French troops to mutiny.[56]

Anti-French sentiment, homesickness, and Leftist propaganda had, therefore, by mid-1919 created a strong anti-White sentiment among these men. One letter circulated among the Russians soldiers of the 5th region warned them that repatriation was a trap: "Repatriation had begun . . . ," it noted but asked rhetorically, "Do we have the possibility of seeing our families, to return home, to throw off the 'gray skin' of Nicholas? I fear not." The author then went on to declare that all repatriates were being sent to Denikin. He called on all readers to resist both work and repatriation and concluded by predicting that the French socialists would be on their side.[57] As late as June 1919, however, the French were still sending some Russian troops to the general. One of the last shipments were some soldiers aboard *Emperor Nicholas I*, which the French thought imperative to be sent to "the region occupied by the armies of Denikin."[58]

These men sent to the south seem, however, to have been of questionable value, and the British complained bitterly about the "exasperating Russians" there, who "did not care for their weapons, usually neglecting to oil their guns." Russian officers had sent expensive artillery pieces to the front without showing the men how to operate them, and those who used them guessed the angle of artillery trajectory instead of calculating it, thus needlessly wasting ammunition. Most disturbing was the fact that Russian officers insisted on taking afternoon naps, regardless of the military situation.[59] The British also reported that when 2,000 of these Russian soldiers disembarked at Odessa, they immediately raised a red flag to great applause from some of the population. Witnessing this disturbing event, the British called on the French to cease repatriation because of the "grave danger which could result for the Volunteer Army . . . if the French government continues to repatriate 50,000 [?] . . . Russians with Bolshevist tendencies."[60] One returnee told *Pravda* after the Civil War that his group had been taken to Sevastopol, where they were told by "the general," "Rest here a month and a half and then you will go save Russia from the Bolshevists." The men did not rest, however; instead they scattered and filtered into the new Soviet republic.[61]

It was not long, however, before all leaders fighting on the side of the Whites were calling for a halt to the repatriation of any Russians at all. In October Denikin was reaching Orel, the high-water mark of his drive on Moscow, and where his defeat took place. The White general feared that the continued repatriation of any Russians would result in the loss in his rear of the Crimea and the Black Sea littoral.[62] The ubiquitous General Mangin, now in the Crimea, also called for the suspension of all repatriation. In December he wrote to the minister of war that Denikin's position was most serious and that the French government should not take any measures that could aggravate his situation, especially the repatriation of Russian prisoners, "all [of whom are] Bolshevik." He suggested sending these men to Serbia perhaps, but added, "I have the *duty to insist that all repatriation be suspended until a new order* [underscored by hand in the original] is restored."[63] As a result, in November 1919 authorities in Odessa and Novorossiisk stopped the disembarkation of over 1,000 men on the *Dumont d'Urville*, and the boat had to return to Constantinople.[64] At the end of December, the *Itu* managed to deposit 600 Russians on the right bank of the Dnieper River and 1,300 "for central Russia [?]," but in January 1920 the French halted all repatriation of White reinforcements "until further notice." Locations were sought for the "temporary transit" of these units, obviating their return to Russia, where they might help the Reds more than the Whites, "while a definitive decision on the subject of their disembarkation on the Black Sea" could be made.[65]

Exactly how long repatriation stopped is not clear, but in August, General Wrangel, who had taken over Denikin's shattered armies, was begging the French to send the repatriates to the Balkans, repeating the warning that if they were deposited at Odessa, "they are just going into the Red Army."[66] The attempt to send Russians to fight for Denikin had failed to help that general's cause and probably aided his enemies. Historically speaking, those units that were dispatched vanished into the maelstrom of the Russian Civil War. At any rate, the numbers who volunteered were too small to have done the White movement much good, even if they had performed well, and the repatriation of the general members of the former brigades clearly did the White cause some harm.

The last major area of focus for the White movement in the Russian Civil War was under Admiral Kolchak in Siberia. The recognized leader of all White forces, he was technically the dictator of all the territory of the Russian state from the Pacific Ocean to within a few hundred miles of Moscow. It was into this part of the White movement that some of the remnants of the REF went, including General Lokhvitsky. Lokhvitsky had envisioned a unit sent to Siberia, and after his removal he had made energetic attempts to be named head of the

Russian Mission for Vladivostok.[67] It was natural, therefore, that he go with an army to Siberia.

Late in August, General Ignatiev submitted a plan for a Russian force to be established in Siberia as the core of a Russian army for the Allies there. His plan called for its creation in France "on a democratic basis." Like others, he felt that it would indicate to the Russians at home whose revolutionary government had removed the nation from the war that the Allied intervention had no ulterior motives. It was to be open to all people of Russian nationality in France, and its stated objective was to fight against the Austro-Germans and "against those who made common cause with them in Russia," a thinly veiled reference to the Bolsheviks. Ignatiev stressed that the "human resources" were excellent but that the men were imbued with the ideas of Bolshevism. He suspected that all would respond to the call but many would do so only as a means of returning home.[68]

It was almost a year, however, before the Siberian front received much attention from Admiral Pogulaev. In the lists of officers slated to be sent to Kolchak in 1919, many familiar names appear, such as Colonels Balbashevsky, Narbut, Kotovich, Rakitin, and Gotua.[69] In August 1919, General Zankevich and Colonel Kotovich left for Siberia via the United States and Japan to join Kolchak.[70] Some who volunteered were not allowed to go. Lists often have certain names deleted with notes such as "undesirable — has been relieved of his command by the French authorities" written by them. One doctor who volunteered was scratched for being a "demagogue."[71] By mid-October 1918 the roll of the men who would go the next year was complete, and after the first of the year the exodus began.

By May 1919, Lokhvitsky was in Siberia in command of the second of five army troops of the Army of Siberia under General Mikhail Diterikhs. It is unclear exactly when Lokhvitsky departed from France, but he arrived in Vladivostok, Siberia, on February 28, 1919, with General Lavergne. The British reported that the French General Staff had informed them that a detachment to reinforce the Siberian battalion would leave Marseille about February 25 and would consist of 6 officers, 16 corporals, 12 other noncommissioned officers and 400 men.[72] Lokhvitsky arrived with a group of officers carefully chosen for their francophilic tendencies; the idea was for these men to provide some French control over Kolchak, since direct French efforts to influence him had failed. Clemenceau wrote to General Janin that Lokhvitsky was "in our pay and had gone into the service of Kolchak."[73] The I Army under General Anatole Pepelaev was already stationed north and a little to the east of Ekaterinburg. The II Army under Lokhvitsky arrived at Zlatusk on May 12, 1919, and by the fourteenth it was eighteen miles east of Ekaterinburg.

When the Bolsheviks attacked all along the front, all of these White forces fought badly.[74] One by one, like dominoes, the cities under Kolchak's nominal control fell to the Reds in the summer of 1919, and Kolchak's entire front disintegrated into a rout. Ufa fell on June 11, as did Perm on July 3. The Bolsheviks crossed the Bisert River two days later, and they captured Ekaterinburg, the city where the tsar had been murdered, on July 17, almost a year to the day after his execution. Cheliabinsk succumbed to the Red tide within a week. By August Kolchak was planning to move his government from Omsk to Irkutsk; he was spared total defeat only by the beginnings of Denikin's advance in the south, as the Bolsheviks had to transfer troops to the Ukraine to stop him. In the lull the Whites reconstituted three additional paper armies assigned to hold the line on the Tobol River about 300 miles from Omsk under the command of General Diterikhs. The I, supposedly composed of 20,000 men, was to stand to the right flank, Lokhvitsky commanding the II with 31,000 in the center, and General N. P. Sakharov with supposedly 50,000 to hold the left flank. These figures most assuredly were largely fictional, or at least exaggerated. Certainly their defense was, since all along the line soldiers and officers were discarding their gear and making hastily for the rear. The sick and wounded were often left unattended and died later where they fell. The retreating soldiers were joined by refugees, and the withdrawal turned into a total debacle.[75] According to Janin, the assassination of officers was "very frequent," and regiments and in some cases entire battalions passed over to the Reds.[76]

By late July, Lokhvitsky's "army" was east of Chedrinsk, which is itself directly east of Ekaterinburg on the Isset River. Essentially no front existed, only several rearguard actions and several elements designated to protect the railroad. To the northwest of Lokhvitsky was whatever force remained under General Pepelaev before Tiumen/Irbit rivers on the railroad between Ekaterinburg and Tobolsk. By late August, Lokhvitsky was basically in the same place, although his position was not due to renewed resilience but rather to the fact that the Bolsheviks were being pressed in the south by Denikin. When his armies reached their apogee in October 1919, Lokhvitsky was essentially still on the Tobol River.[77]

Also surfacing in Siberia was General Zankevich, who had been given the rather important post of quartermaster, despite the fact, Janin reports, he had since his arrival in Siberia said "the worst things" about Kolchak.[78] As Kolchak retreated, Zankevich had the difficult job of getting the "Supreme Overlord" to safety. The famous Czech Legion had control of the main lines of the Trans-Siberian Railroad and forced the retreating general onto a congested line, giving his train insufficient coal on orders from some certain elements in Irkutsk. On December 13, 1919, Zankevich protested by wire to Janin in Irkutsk that there had never been a Czech liaison officer attached to Kolchak's train and that this omission had led to the current difficulties. As a result of Czech ill will and hostility, they had traveled only ninety miles in four days.[79] By the end Zankevich was relying on a miracle in the form of bad weather more than any military action to save the admiral and himself.[80]

As Kolchak approached Irkutsk, the admiral sent Lokhvitsky there to prepare for his arrival, ard at one o'clock in the morning Lokhvitsky burst into Janin's car. No one knew exactly where Kolchak was because of a general communications breakdown and the dispersal of his entourage, which seems to have consisted of seven separate trains. Janin and Lokhvitsky sent a telegram through the Czech leader to try to locate the admiral, and after the dispatch was sent, Lokhvitsky remained in Janin's car. Lokhvitsky was especially fearful that Kolchak would arrive in Irkutsk amid some sort of uprising and asked the impotent French general to suppress some disturbances already in progress.[81]

When Kolchak finally did appear in Irkutsk, the French were pressured to hand him over to the Social Revolutionaries, his erstwhile Leftist allies whom he had seen fit to start shooting in the heyday of late spring when he had visions of taking Moscow. They returned the favor by executing him and throwing his body into a hole in the ice of a tributary of the Angara River. After Kolchak's death, Lokhvitsky commanded the detritus of the Army of Siberia, which he led until the fall of 1922, where it was finally crushed after, in the general's words, "a thousand dangers." As for Zankevich, in January 1920 he made some sort of declaration against "reaction" and called for an end of war with the Soviets. Yet he stated emphatically that he would never serve the Red government, although he was disposed to serve "the people." Whatever was left of the Omsk government hiding out in Vladivostok placed confidence in Zankevich and charged him with the necessary forces "to end anarchy and disorder, fight reaction and conserve national property." As always, the instructions called quixotically for the reestablishment of order.[82] Lokhvitsky's last démarche was an abortive coup against the fragments of the government in Vladivostok on March 30-31, 1921, which even with Japanese help was too weak to succeed.[83]

In the last days of this dying regime, there was one small bright, if sad and sentimental, spot. In November 1919, when only the most optimistic or foolhardy White leader could possibly expect a chance of victory, the Russian Legion sent from France to Siberia asked, in the chaos of Kolchak's defeat, that they be allowed to remain grouped as a unit and to retain their uniforms. The Vladivostok French commander, who had always really been their leader, apparently approved and wired the French government at the end of November to forage about and find him 300 *croix de guerre* to award the little unit, all that was left of the spirit of Old Russia that had gone to France to such acclaim three long years before.[84] We have no way of knowing for certain, but this brave force probably never received its decorations.

EPILOGUE

Where Is the Border?

*What is going on, what is going on? The French hold up their hands
and gaze with apprehension at the Eiffel Tower. It is the only thing
left that has not been captured by the Russians.*

—Don Aminado[1]

*Enfants de France! Quand l'ennemi sera vaincu et quand vous
pourrez librement cueillir des fleurs sur ces champs, souvenez-vous
de nous et apportez-nous des fleurs.*

—Father Andrei Bogoslovsky[2]

*Russia entered the struggle the same time as us. For this act of
loyal confraternité . . . the army of the tsar has the right to the
gratitude of France.*

—Marshal Joffre[3]

Dirty Russian, why don't you go back where you came from?
—Students to Vladimir Volkoff[4]

AFTER THE WAR HAD ENDED, the flow of Russians eastward continued, not just those who had been members of the REF, but those who
had been prisoners in Germany or those who had initially fled the
Bolshevik takeover and had now decided that Russia under any regime
was better than life in a foreign land. France had begged again for Allied
help in repatriation as late as June 1919, yet still not much was
forthcoming. From the beginning to the end, the Russian soldiers were
a French problem and France essentially handled it alone. Marseille

remained the major base of repatriation and was still functioning as such in 1920. Over a year later a Base of the Levant near Marseille still contained over 100,000 Russians from different places, some arriving from the horror at home, others waiting to return to experience that nightmare.[5] In July 1920 alone, 8,000 returned as the *Bataria, Imperator Aleksandr Tretii, Imperator Nicholas I, Austria*, and *Allegrette* made the shuttles between Marseille and points on the Russian Black Sea coast.[6] By March 1920 there were by one report 21,400 Russians still in France, Algeria, and the Orient, with most of those in France the prisoners of war who had filtered in from Germany. Of these, only 1,077 were from the 20,000 soldiers of the former REF.[7] As early as the fall of 1919 Clemenceau notified Colonel Narbut that families would not be able to return even on reduced fares. The premier explained that this right was not accorded to French families who found themselves trapped in Russia, so free passage could not be extended to Russian families of soldiers in France. As for the Soviet government, it continued to utilize as propaganda the troops in France.[8] One deputation returning home at the end of 1918 was personally greeted in Moscow by Lenin.[9]

About 3,500 had remained in France, as well as about 1,300 deserters who also stayed because they had fled and could not be found for repatriation. There were an additional 100 or so in hospitals too sick to leave. Some of these did wander into the Russian base at Laval later to ask repatriation, and Captain Perlier of the skeleton staff there wrote in August 1922 that "daily some Russians *(congé sans solde)* come to me to seek repatriation" long after the French stopped sending them. These were lucky ones, since by then repatriation would most likely mean starvation, to say nothing of victimization by the political terror that was then in progress. Some did go to the French colonies to work, with 600 or 700 departing for various colonies in Africa as paid laborers as late as December 1922.[10]

The plight of those who remained in France was a grim one. The French government stopped salaries to the Russians and rejected a French war ministry's request for continued remuneration, adding the unhelpful note that these supplicants could return to Russia if they did so in Russian ships.[11] On June 2, 1921, a Russian soldier in the hospital at Rennes was informed that after the maneuvers of 1920, there would no longer be any credits in the budget to pay for the attention of the Russian soldiers. Any future help given them would be accorded only from "Russian funds,"[12] whatever that might have meant. Various French archives hold numerous Russian requests for assistance sent after 1920, none of which received a positive reply. There was for years a trickle of Russians homeward after the last large shipments to Russia by the French, but only a trickle. For example, twenty returned on November 20 and another fifty or so on February 2, 1921, both groups being transported on the *Taдla*.[13] Sources do not indicate who paid their passage. By October 1921 the French government figures show that about 73,000 had been returned, stating the unlikely high figure of 40,000 from the brigades in France and Salonika and 33,000 prisoners of war, leaving about 7,000 to remain in France or the colonies. Ever mindful of the cost, the French government observed that the total bill for repatriation had come to 43,745,000 francs.

The last episode in the whole question of the REF occurred in 1924, when the French government finally decided to give diplomatic recognition to the Soviet regime. In the negotiations, the Soviets demanded that the archives of the Paris embassy be turned over to them, primarily so they could gain control of the records of the *Okhrana*, the tsarist secret police. The French government debated whether to send the Soviets the section of documents on the Russian Legion, since these papers would contain names of men, many of whom were in Russia, who had fought against the Germans after the treaty of Brest-Litovsk. Since they formally considered actions of the Legion illegal, the Soviets could prosecute the Russians involved. Due to the activities of Christian Herter, a member of the American diplomatic corps and later governor of Massachusetts and secretary of state under President Dwight D. Eisenhower, these documents were smuggled out of France without French knowledge; they are now on deposit at the Archive of the Hoover Institution at Stanford University in California.[14]

There were, of course, those among the REF and the Russian Legion who never wanted to return home. Perhaps they had no family there, perhaps they did not wish to resume the life they had had. Perhaps they feared political repercussions. Whatever the reason, there were those who felt that staying in France was at least for the present better than returning to Russia. A year after the war ended, Mikhailov asked the French premier to allow those who wished to live in France to remain. Making it clear that only *"those of our soldiers which express the desire* [his italics]*"* should be allowed to make their home in France, Mikhailov asked for formal permission for these men to resettle in France. He reminded Clemenceau that in "the hours of great peril in 1914," the Russian political exiles of 1905, of which Mikhailov was one, almost all joined the French army to defend "the Land of Liberty," and many had "fallen on the field of honor in France." Now in 1919 they no less wished to defend the honor of France. Such a deep love for France must be rewarded with permission to remain.[15] Whether Mikhailov's letter had any effect or not is unknown, but roughly 6,300 Russians from the REF and prisoners of war did remain in France. Their life was not easy. The few jobs that existed were reserved for Frenchmen, and a foreigner could work only if he had a work permit, and he could receive a work permit only if he had worked before. The familiar stories of former aristocrats performing janitorial labor are not fiction, and archival collections carry many letters of Russians pleading for help from French government officials, reminding them how they had fought for France and of the sacrifices they had made. Some ultimately chose to return to the uncertainty of famine-gripped Russia of the early 1920s, so bleak was their situation in France. By late 1921, 2,226 of the 6,300 asked to return home to what was certain political discrimination and possible death by starvation,[16] so desperate was their plight in France.

Various organizations gave some help. There was in Paris the *Fédération Générale des Invalides Mutilé de Guerre Russes à l'Etranngère*, whose stationery had at the top in bright red the words "Russia has lost during the Great War 6,000,000 men killed, dead, wounded and MIA for the Common Cause."[17] Another such organization sponsored by the French was the *Oeuvre des Mutilés Russes du Front Français*, created by yet another organization with the preposterous name of the National Union for the Exportation of French Products and the Importation of Necessary Materials for Industry. An earlier group that seems to have been short-lived was the Committee of Assistance for Russian Invalids, which changed its name in 1919 to Friends of Russian Prisoners of War. Its president was Count Nesselrode.[18]

To raise money fetes were given, such as a dinner dance held in March 1925, in the Salons George V in Paris for the benefit of widows and orphans of former Russian combatants. The entrance ticket informed the bearer that there would be a buffet at the additional price of 10 francs. Assistance took other forms as well. Mikhailov organized schools, libraries, and theaters for the remaining soldiers. He wrote to the war department in 1920 that he had taught a majority of those left to write Russian and even had them studying French.[19]

These efforts were meager at best because those who would be most interested in helping would have been Russian émigrés, and they had little money to give. After the war, especially after the loss of the Civil War, the French were at best insouciant, at worst hostile to the predicament of those Russians left in France, even to the soldiers who had fought in their country. There did exist some modest individual help, such as General Niessel's intervention, which obtained for Sergei Shchalva, a soldier who had been wounded in the assault on Brimont, an artificial limb. But for the most part, there was little. As for outright French hostility toward these unfortunate individuals, there can be little doubt, for the archives contain too many bitter, complaining letters for there not to have been a great deal of truth to it.[20] Maxim Gorky wrote a pamphlet entitled *Prekrasnaia Frantsiia* [Marvelous France], condemning French treatment of Russians. Published even in New York and sold there for a dime, it attacked France, "the fountain of Liberty," for its insensitivity toward the Russians stranded there.

The end of the Civil War resulted in the flood of émigrés fleeing the reprisals of the Communist regime. A large percentage were military evacuees, making the overall flow 69 percent male. One-seventh of them were university graduates and two-thirds had high school diplomas. Never in the history of humanity has an immigration been so well educated,[21] until the exodus from the Soviet Union that followed the Helsinki Accords of the 1970s. Many of them went to Germany because the collapse of the mark in the early 1920s made living less expensive, but when in 1923-24 France opened its doors, they flooded into Paris, which remained from that day to this the Russian émigré capital of the world. Eventually about 60,000 Russians ended up there, gravitating mainly in the 5th, 6th, 11th, 15th, and 16th arrondissements. In all nearly a quarter of a million finally settled throughout France.[22]

The Russians found work wherever they could, a number joining the Foreign Legion. Some entered the Polish army. There were those, however, like Captain A. Andreev, who found "a stable situation in industry" and came to love their new homeland. Yet there were also those like a Captain Komarov, who never could adapt and committed suicide.

In response to the soldiers' obvious needs, a number of Russian military organizations blossomed in France in the 1920s. The Union of the Knights of St. George had as its membership all of those who had been awarded the Cross of St. George. Smaller, more elite units were also formed, such as the Society of the Former Cadets of the Nicholas Calvary School. More broadly based were the Union of the Disabled Abroad for Russian War Invalids and the Union of Russian Officers Who Fought on the French Front, called at this writing *Association du Souvenir du Corps Expéditionnaire Russe en France*. Its membership is composed of Russians who were ever officers in any army inside or outside of Russia, since no known officers of the REF are still alive. Binding all of these military organizations together was the General Military Union, formed by General Wrangel and headquartered in Paris. The nominal head was Grand Duke Nicholas Nicholaevich, but he was succeeded on his death by General A. P. Kutepov, who had established a model camp for émigrés and soldiers at Gallipoli in Turkey. On January 26, 1920, however,

Kutepov went out on foot to run some errands, forgoing his usual taxi, which was provided for him free of charge by a Russian taxi driver, and never returned. He was succeeded by General Miller, who also vanished into a car one day while walking near the Arc de Triomphe.[23] We know now that Miller was kidnapped by the Soviet secret police because his second-in-command was supposedly one of their agents and probably would succeed him. We can assume that the same fate befell Kutepov.

As for the particular individuals, the trail ends in most cases somewhere short of death. Of minor figures, Zubov refused to leave France, appeared at Mailly before embarkation, and was ordered back to the collection point at Orange. As noted earlier, Zhilinsky returned to Russia just in time to encounter the Revolution. He made his way to the south in 1918 and died there that same year. Captain Valerien Razumov, son of General N. Razumov, went to France with the Third Brigade and was awarded the Cross of St. George. He fought in Champagne and joined the Russian Legion on December 21, 1917. He was wounded twice on January 5, 1918, and was decorated with the *Croix de guerre* and made a member of the *Légion d'Honneur* on July 26, 1918. He returned to Russia, fought with Wrangel, and was evacuated with him to Constantinople in October 1920.[24] He emigrated to France, where he did not receive any assistance from the French government. French military officials churlishly argued that since the records showed that he had been repatriated to Russia on the *Allegrette* on February 13, 1920, he had already "benefited from the advantages set aside to the Russian officers coming into France during the war." The French government, therefore, "could not act favorably on the request for help."[25] We have seen that father Andrei Bogoslavsky died in December 1918 of wounds he received a few days before the armistice. His inscription, "Children of France! When the enemy has been defeated and you are free to cut the flowers in your fields, remember us Russians and cut some for us," appears on the obelisk that is today the monument to the Russian dead at Mourmelon-le-Grand. His wife returned to Russia and last appears in 1921, when she wrote to General Miller about the possibilities of receiving her husband's 700 franc salary, which was being held at Laval.[26] Colonel Simenov, the adjutant to the commandant to the Russian base at Laval, worked through diplomatic and military channels to learn what had become of his wife, who had been left behind in Russia. He had heard nothing from her in ten months, and she had last lived in Odessa. As it turned out, his wife, who was French, had escaped and was stranded in Constantinople. She asked permission to enter France, and General Brulard opened all possible paths for her.[27] Presumably they were reunited. What became of the colonel himself is not known.

Zankevich's trail likewise ends in France. Yet on February 14, 1920, when still on Russian soil, he visited Janin on his way through Verkhni-Udinsk and asked to be allowed to return to France. He told Janin that he had in his possession about 30,000 francs. He somehow did get back to France, because his name later appears among members of a commission in France to examine military matters.[28] Rapp's trail ends in Paris in 1919, when he was living at 7 rue Champagne-Première. He had become active in yet another Russian émigré organization, the Russian Republican League. The French security police, who were still watching him, wondered if "when order is established in Russia, [would] he not be liable for a military justice trial?" since they blamed him for the whole La Courtine affair. At some point he might have married Madame Staal, whose name we have seen in police files.[29] Mikhailov continued his mysterious activities with his Russian schools after the war. In July 1920 he asked the French government for money for "Francophile propaganda," and in late 1920 he met with one Krassin in London to advise him on Bolshevik relations of some mission then in London. At about the same time he offered himself to the French government as *homme de confidence*. The French, however, were wary. Noting that he surrounded himself with "non-Bolshevik" Leftists and directed the Leftist journal *Luch* (The Ray), the officials advised avoiding using his services, describing him as "a gossip in which one is scarcely able to have confidence." He was likewise categorized as "ambitious, a consummate schemer, [of] mediocre intelligence, disorganized, and lacking in the use of French." The author of the note opined that Mikhailov's publicly voiced rightist political positions had been acquired "in order to procure money."[30] Another account calls him "a dedicated communist" who "contributed to *the breakup of the Russian contingents* [their italics] on the Western front." Although they claimed that he had become a Bolshevik only in 1918, he was nonetheless "dangerous."[31]

Boris Savinkov returned to Russia, was arrested in the Soviet Union in 1924, and was sentenced to be executed. His sentence was commuted to ten years of hard labor, but he died the next year, Soviet sources say, by his own hand.[32] Foreign minister Tereshchenko, whose wife Margarite was French, left St. Petersburg in April 1918. He had been released by the Bolsheviks the day after the October coup and lived the rest of his life in Paris, generally avoiding the émigré squabbles that sundered the Russian community there. He worked in banking and finance, amassing a modest fortune. He died in Monaco in 1956.

As for the famous mutineers, the trail for the most part ends at repatriation. We do not know exactly when Baltais or Globa were returned. Late in June 1920, the *Batavia* left Marseille with a group of

2,400 men and 100 civilians deemed *"indésirables."* Because of the cargo, the ship was sent under escort and remained constantly under surveillance, and Litvinov took enough interest in the boat to direct it personally to Novorossiisk.[33] It is quite probably that among the 2,400 were Volkov, Baltais, and Globa. The trail on all three vanishes completely at this point.

Vavilov, whose memoir is fundamental to the story of the REF, escaped from France through Switzerland. He and some comrades slipped off into the woods from a work detail and made it to the Swiss border, crossing it in the night of December 17, 1917. The first Swiss citizens they encountered were curious since they never had seen any Russians. He worked in a Swiss village until the end of June 1918 and then crossed Germany into Russia, arriving there on July 3, 1918.

Kozlov, whose memoir offers a good insight into the working of the Third Brigade, also exited through Switzerland, but in a much more dramatic way. Learning that the Swiss border was near where he was cutting wood, Kozlov began to plan his escape. One night while staying in a French home, he saw a child's geography textbook. Thumbing through it, he found a map of the region, and despite the fact that it was old, he knew he could rely on it. He tore it from the book, and from another home he stole a compass. On the day he decided to flee, he packed extra bread and tobacco. He and a comrade escaped in the dark of night and went eastward. After working their way through the forests and the mountains, they met a woman, who was at first frightened. Kozlov told her the truth about who he was, and she informed him that they were in Switzerland. He came upon a police station, where they were given soup, bread, and potatoes. He soon found about thirty of his former comrades, and after working and even doing a stint in jail, he made it back to Russia through Germany on a train with a German guarding each compartment. Ironically the guard in Kozlov's compartment had fought against the Russians at Reims, where he had been wounded. At Dvinsk he left the train and was warned that everyone was leaving Russia, not entering. He was told there was only hunger in his homeland, but he went anyway. He entered Petrograd, passing the Warsaw station and disembarking at the Finland station. Within a few months he was in the Red Army.[34]

The two members of the REF who do not figure prominently in these pages but who otherwise crossed the stage of history, are twenty-three-year-old Vadim Maslov and Rodion Malinovsky. Risking her life by coming into France to meet Masslov in 1917, Mata Hari was arrested for being a spy. Hoping to see him one last time at her trial, she was disappointed when he sent a deposition instead. In it he stated that he had made one last unsuccessful attempt to see her only for the purpose of ending the affair. With that wrenching disappointment, she fainted in the courtroom. Maslov, it is believed, went on to become a priest.[35] Malinovsky eventually became the defense minister of the Soviet Union under Nikita Khrushchev in the 1950s. Returning to Russia through Vladivostok after fighting in the Russian Legion, Malinovsky crossed Kolchak's Siberia to join the Red Army. Several times under Stalin's regime his association with the REF placed him under suspicion. In 1960 he went to Paris with Khrushchev for a meeting with President Eisenhower and other world leaders, but the downing of the U-2 spy plane over Soviet air space wrecked the conference. To utilize the now-vacant agenda, Malinovsky suggested that he and Khrushchev visit Champagne, where his old unit had been stationed. They went by car and Malinovsky easily found the old peasant's house where he had stayed at one point. The father had died but his wife and son, who now had children, still lived there and welcomed him graciously. A party spontaneously started, joined by the neighbors, and champagne flowed. Malinovsky asked about a bar he used to frequent, and the locals were amazed that he knew about it. He asked about a certain girl and learned that she had been dead for quite a while. Some of the denizens asked about their bear Misha. Malinovsky reminisced and said that he was sorry that the Revolution had occurred when he was away from home.[36]

A story circulates today in the émigré community in Paris that Malinovsky was present for a memorial service for the Russian war dead in France held at the Russian cemetery at Mourmelon-le-Grand (one is still conducted each year to this day). These émigrés naturally flew the flag of old tsarist Russia. When the flag passed in review, Malinovsky, the defense minister of the Soviet Union, snapped to attention and saluted it![37] Others who had fought in the force and returned home were not so lucky. In his mammoth study of the Russian slave labor system, Alexander Solzhenitsyn wrote that during the nightmare years of the Purges, simply having been in France with the REF was enough to make an individual vanish into the abyss of Stalin's terror.[38]

Of the major officers, the story is checkered. During the Russian Civil War, Marushevsky, as we have seen, commanded the Archangel front. In this capacity, he denied Mariia Bochkareva, the founding leader of the Russian Women's Battalion of Death, any further military role, expressing the opinion that allowing women to serve in the armed forces in the northern region "would be a heavy reproach and a heavy stain" on the whole population. In 1920 he became the official representative of the government of General Wrangel in Scandinavia and Central Europe and hereafter vanishes. In 1922 General Niessel wrote a recommendation for help for him to the French ministry of war praising "the attitude that he had always had in regard to France and the service that he had rendered in the struggle against Bolshevism."[39] What became of him after this time is unknown. Ieske returned to Russia with what was thought to be a "reliable" unit to fight with the Whites, but on the first day of Russian Easter, he and two captains were bayoneted to death by their own men who went over to the Reds.[40] The story in *L'Humanité* had been true. Lissovsky tried in May 1918 to move to Italy with his wife to join the Russian military mission there, but permission was denied early in June because the mission had been disbanded. He wrote his memoirs and vanished to history.[41]

General Palitsyn had returned to Petrograd but left at the time of the Bolshevik coup, ending up in Paris in November 1918. A group of Russians from the Provisional Government embassy organized a commission to study military and naval problems, and Palitsyn was asked to be its president. Other members included Zankevich, Ignatiev, Miller, and Admiral Populaev.[42] Palitsyn appears on a list of the members of the *Comité Historique Militaire* in 1920. He left France in October of the next year, however, moving to Berlin, where he and his wife thought life would be less expensive. The couple did not find it so. He died there on February 18, 1923, and was buried in the Russian cemetery Tegele in Berlin. The officers in Paris provided a fund to send his ashes into Russia when it might one day be possible.[43] Presumably now it is.

After the war General Ignatiev married the dancer Trukhanova, who had appeared in a ballet suite at one of the embassy parties. She convinced him to return to Soviet Russia, and he became an inspector of military schools training cadets for the Red Army. He was instrumental in securing for the Soviet government various monies of the old embassy deposited in French banks. He served in the Military Publishing house from 1937 until 1947. He wrote his memoirs, *Fifty Years in Service,* which have a rather leftist tone that was definitely not part of his politics when he was in France. His family disowned him, yet Hélène Izvolsky, daughter of the last tsarist ambassador to Paris, knew him well and felt that he had returned to Russia not because of any Communist affiliation but because of his deep love for his country.[44] He died in Moscow in November 1954.[45]

Lokhvitsky remained in France and fell on the same difficult times that came to so many. There is a letter in the files of the war ministry dated June 17, 1923, asking for work, making it very plain that he would do anything for employment. The reply from the minister of war stated that he had asked around but that nothing had turned up.[46] The Russian general died in Paris in 1933 ironically on the anniversary of the

Bolshevik Revolution. The next day a few short obituaries appeared buried in several of the larger French papers. In a short article *Figaro* reported that the general had refused to join the Bolshevik victors as others had and noted that he had died in *"une situation très modiste,"* refusing to the end to solicit any help. The piece ended with the words "He has a right to the recognition of France."[47]

Eventually a monument to Russian participation on the Western Front was built several miles outside of Mourmelon-le-Grand. B. A. Suvarin, editor of the Russian journal *Vechenee vremia*, first advanced the idea in his newspaper, and Lokhvitsky was made president of a committee to direct the project, which first suggested only a single monument, but then later added a cemetery and a Russian church. Most of the money came from French contributors. In 1934 the architect Albert Benoit drafted the plans for the church, and the first stone was laid on April 19, 1936, with the church being consecrated in May 1937.[48] Across the road from the church and the cemetery in the woods stands the granite pillar bearing Bogoslovsky's words.

Finally, we know part of the fate of Misha, the bear mascot of the Russian force who was born in Siberia in January 1916 and at the age of five months was bought by Captain Trachek and Captain Cerniak for forty-five rubles. Misha went to France from Archangel with the Third Brigade, was several times under fire, and even sustained a gas attack, which he survived only by sticking his snout into the snow. He convalesced three days in the infirmary with only a milk diet. Sometime in 1919 Colonel Gotua gave him to Adolphe Chérioux, vice president of the Paris City council, when the city paid tribute to the Russian army and the Russian people. He was put in the *Jardin d'Acclimatation*, one of the three major Parisian zoos near the Bois de Boulogne. Speaking for Misha, the Russian donors stated that he loved the Allies very much and "always France." "Give me some cut meat to prevent my becoming nasty," he was quoted as having said to the people of Paris, "and some honey when life will be less hard."[49] Mishka had spent his entire life uncaged and did not like the confines of the pen into which he was placed. It is reported that he cried pitifully at being left there.[50] Dmitri Varenov, a former caretaker of the Russian cemetery outside Mourmelon-le-Grand, wrote this author in 1986 that a French soldier Vsevelod Miller serving in the French army in 1939-40 saw in northeastern France a stuffed bear and was told that it was the mascot of the Russian Expeditionary Force. Later he could not remember where it was and advertised in several newspapers in northeastern France. He never received any answer. Most probably the mounted bear was not the REF's mascot.[51]

Some years after the Great War a Russian émigré living in Meudon, France, Ivan Kolomitsev, visited the Paris zoo to see Misha. In a pen there were two similar bears, and Kolomitsev did not know which of the two was the brigades' mascot. He called out "Misha," and one of the two bears turned and looked at him. Kolomitsev felt certain that this bear must have been the REF's beloved ursine comrade. When he died, Mishka was supposedly interred with his comrades in the Russian cemetery at Mourmelon-le-Grand.[52]

The military activities of the Russian Expeditionary Force had no discernible effect on the outcome of the Great War. Even the collapse of discipline played no role in the French mutinies of 1917, despite the fact that the French government at the time, and some historians since, have tried to link the two. Had the Russians remained true to their original obligation and dispatched the 400,000 promised effectives, they may have made a difference in the fighting in 1916 or in the Nivelle offensive the following year. To speculate on this matter, however, is not the job of the historian: The what-if form of historical writing quickly places the practitioner on thin ice. More certain is the fact that from the French perspective 400,000 Russians could have adversely altered the outcome of the war, for had an army of that size gone beserk in France in 1917, the French government could never have controlled it. What such a disaster would have done to the French defenses needs no Nostradamus to predict. Yet fortunately the longed-for Russian hordes never arrived, and those few who did come could be contained before they did any lasting harm. Because of their small numbers, the Russian Expeditionary Force did not alter the history of the Great War.

Yet the history of this small unit is significant. It provides both the historian and the political scientist an unusual aquarium view of a military revolt and a microcosm of revolution. It likewise shows the spread and resistance to revolution within differing social classes. The First Brigade, dominated by proletarian elements from Moscow's workers, led the mutiny, as urban elements have led every broad, successful social uprising in history. Few if any successful major revolution has ever had its origins in rural society. Many "revolts" have begun there, but they have either sputtered out or been crushed. They have, however, made urban revolutions complete by following their lead, as they did in France after 1789 or Russia in 1917. When they did not copy their urban countrymen, the revolutions have usually failed. The social revolutions of 1848 are a good example. All started in the capitals of Europe but died a slow death because the countryside did not continue them. Indeed, the resistance of rural forces was a major factor in the failure in 1848-1849 of the urban radicals to carry through their plans. In cases in Austria, Prussia, and to a degree Hungary, troops from the provinces suppressed revolutions in the cities. In France, the villages did it at the ballot box, when they overwhelmingly elected Louis Napoleon Bonaparte, who in time restored an absolute monarchy.

The rural elements within the Russian First Brigade and the entire Third, recruited from farms and villages, followed the radical lead for a time. Yet without the unifying hatred of the trenches, the peasant soldiers calmed down, creating a force that enabled the suppression of the isolated radicals. For a revolution to succeed, there must be a broad desire to end the status quo, for whatever motive the various parts are induced to unite. When the focus of their discontent, the detested object that is making matters unpleasant, is gone, then a struggle usually ensues among the victors because each now-ununified segment has a different agenda for the future. For the REF, it was needlessly dying in the war. When that danger had been removed in June 1917 by their transfer to La Courtine, the innate makeup of the units began to manifest itself. The more conservative parts calmed down, the revolt lost its unity, and it was doomed to defeat at the hands of Russian, not French, troops.

The French mutinies at the same time beg comparison. Whereas the French army essentially collapsed and endured widespread desertions in the late spring of 1917, by the end of the year it was making successful offensives once again. It fought well in 1918, at a time when only a fragment of the Russian troops had been willing to return to the front. The fact that the French soldier was defending his homeland was of course an important factor, but that could not tell the entire story. Even among the "loyal" troops who agreed to fight again there was open dissent from time to time, if not outright indiscipline. A major reason lay in the relationship between the Russian officer and the soldier he led.

In a recent study of the mutiny of the Fifth French Infantry Division,[53] author Leonard Smith makes many interesting points, but he demonstrates that in democratic France, the soldier came into the army with the basic civil rights of citizens of a free republic. Of course, no successful army can function democratically: There must always be someone to give orders and others to follow unquestioningly. Yet armies of a free society have a bridge between officers and men based on John Locke's natural rights. The French soldier had that tie in 1917; the Russian did not. Smith points out that the French mutineers did not see their officers as the enemy. In the French mutinies, the officers were not mistreated, even if they were ignored. In the Russian army, many officers had to flee to avoid being lynched.

Russian soldiers, almost all from the peasant classes, lived in a society without human rights. Pre-revolutionary peasants could still be arrested for such vague reasons as "the protection of state dignity." They still carried an internal passport. They still bowed to the master, whom they might hate, but to whom they looked for protection. Transferred to the army, peasants found themselves in the same relationship to superiors as they were to their civilian betters. They readily accepted the flogging that was still permitted in the tsarist army and the groveling respect they had to show those above them. To them, freedom and individual rights were not known entities. This built-in subservience is one explanation for the fact that the tsarist army held together as long as it did under such tragic suffering and privations. Yet when General Order No. 1 suddenly transformed Russian soldiers into human beings whose rights had to be respected, the transition was too much for both the officers and the men they led. The latter quickly became what General Pershing called "drunk with freedom." They were like schoolchildren who had seen their tyrannical teacher replaced with a powerless substitute. To them their new rights extended to the legitimacy of disobedience. As for the officers, who had never had their authority challenged, they could not cope with the defiance. The tsarist regime had in no way prepared them for an army in which the soldier had rights as an individual. No officer ever thought indiscipline was an evil that they might one day face. Not only were they deprived of their weapons of terror, they were now devoid of anyone to implement them. Russian officers did not know their men because in the past he had not had to know them. When the revolution broke the officers' control, they had no link or tie to restore it. Their French counterparts did.

Notes

Abbreviations

C-in-C.	Commander-in-chief
cmdt.	commandant
com.	*Commissaire*
CPAE.	*Commissaire du Peuple des Affaires Etrangères*
D.V.P. SSSR.	*Documenti vneshei politiki; soiuz soviet-icheskikh sotsiales ticheskikh respublik*
F. O.	Foreign Office
E-M de l'A.	*Etat-major de l'Armée*
E: R.	*Europe: Russie*
Gen. Cmdt.	General Commandant.
G: R.	*Guerre, 1914-1918: Russie*
K. A.	*Krasnyi arkhiv.*
Lég. rus.	*Légion Russe*
PM.	Prime Minister
Rap.	*Rapport*
MFA.	*Ministère des Affaires Etrangères*
M. Int.	*Ministère de l'Interieur*
Min. War. (or MW or War)	*Ministère de la Guerre*
W. O.	*War Office*

Chapter 1

1. Sun Tzu, *The Art of War* (New York: Delacorte Press, 1983), 9.
2. Leo Tolstoy, *Christianity and Patriotism* (London: J. Cape, 1922), iii.
3. This story was first told me by Professor Felix Markham of Hertford College, Oxford University, and I have since rarely found an Englishman who had not heard it. For the other rumors, see Rev. Andrew Clark, *Echoes of the Great War;*

The Diary of the Reverend Andrew Clark, 1914-1919 (Oxford: Oxford University Press, 1985), 9, 10, 13, 16, 21-22.

4. Ibid., 9; *Literary Digest* reported that the rumor had been caused by a telegram of a provision merchant ordering Easter eggs. "Russians in France," *Literary Digest*, 52 (June 3, 1916): 1624.

5. Ariadne Tyrkova-Williams, *Cheerful Giver: The Life of Harold Williams* (London: Peter Davies, 1935), 150, quotes the August 12, 1914, edition of the *Daily Chronicle*.

6. *Le Figaro*, September 20, 1914, quoted in Ioannis Sinanoglou, "France Looks Eastward: Perspectives and Policies in Russia, 1914-1918," Unpublished Ph.D. dissertation at Columbia University, 1974.

7. Carnet de Maréchal Foch, no. 3, entry 1 January 1916, carton 5, Foch Papers, 414AP, Archives Nationales. Paris, France.

8. Charles Rivet, *The Last of the Romanofs* (New York: Dutton, 1918), 294.

9. Ibid., 301.

10. John Anderson, *Britain's Discovery*, 112, cited in Keith Neilson's *Strategy and Supply: The Anglo-Russian Alliance, 1914-1917* (London: Allen and Unwin, 1984), 2.

11. Barbara Tuchman, *The Guns of August* (New York: Dell, 1971), 80.

12. Memorandum on the fighting in Galicia by Bernard Pares, p. 11, June 5, 1915, War Office [hereafter cited W. O.] 106/1136, Directory of Military Operations and Intelligence, Public Record Office, London, Great Britain.

13. Rivet, 287.

14. Cyril B. Falls, *The Great War* (New York: Putnam, 1957), 34.

15. Bruce Lincoln, *Passage Through Armageddon* (New York: Simon and Schuster, 1986), 60.

16. Leon Trotsky, *The History of the Russian Revolution* (New York: Simon and Schuster, 1937), 1: 252.

17. Ibid.

18. *Dnevnik byvshego Velikogo Kniazia Andreia Vladimirovicha za 1915 god*, ed. by V. P. Semmenikov, (Moscow, 1925), cited in Lincoln, 152-53.

19. Maurice Paléologue, *An Ambassador's Memoirs* . Tr. by F. A. Holt. (New York: Doran, 1924-25), 1: 226.

20. Ward Rutherford, *The Ally: The Russian Army in World War I* (London: Gorden Cremonesi, 1977), 24.

21. A. W. F. Knox, *With the Russian Army, 1914-1917* (London: Hutchinson, 1921), 2: 473, 484.

22. *The Times* (London), December 28, 1916, p. 5.

23. *New York Times*, April 22, 1916; Jusserand to Briand, April 23, 1916, 763: 159, Guerre, 1914-1918: Russie [hereafter cited G: R], Archives du Ministère des Affaires Etrangères, Paris, France.

24. Tyrkova-Williams, 146.

25. Prince Bernard von Bülow, *The Memoirs of Prince von Bülow* (Boston: Little, Brown, 1931), 3: 195.

26. Paléologue, 1: 106; French ed., 1: 102.

27. Knox, 1: 90.

28. Sir George Buchanan, *My Mission to Russia and Other Diplomatic Memoirs* (Boston: Little, Brown, 1923), 2: 195.

29. Marshal Joseph Jacques Joffre, *The Personal Memoirs of Joffre* (New York and London: Harper Bros., 1932), 1: 157; French ed., *Mémoirs du Maréchal Joffre (1910-1917)*, (Paris: Plon, 1932), 1: 265.

30. General Ferdinand Foch, *The Memoirs of Marshal Foch* (Garden City, N.Y.: Doubleday, Doran, 1931), 191-192; French ed., 1: 263.

31. Général de Goulevich, *Le Rôle de la Russie dans la Guerre Mondiale* (Paris: Revue Hebdomadaire, 1934), 8.

32. General Maxime Weygand, *Recalled to Service* (London: Heinemann, 1952), 11.

33. Journal de le 1917 Voyage, no date, p. 4 of an apppendixed speech after p. 65 of the report, carton 176, Papiers Albert Thomas, 94AP, Archives Nationales, Paris, France.

34. Foch, Eng. ed., 1: xliv-xlv; Fr. ed. 1: xvii-xxvix.

35. Knox, 1: 219; Paléologue to Delcassé, September 28, 1917, G: R, 641, cited in Sinanoglou, 27.

36. Albert Pingaud, "La Mission de M. Paul Doumer en Russie," *Revue des Deux Mondes*, 9 (1932): 866.

37. Buchanan, 1: 219.

38. Paléologue, Fr. ed., 1: 231-232.

39. *Padenie tsarskogo rezhima*, 4: 123, cited in Lincoln, 105.

40. Paléologue, Fr. ed., 1: 305; Eng. ed., 1:206.

41. Lincoln, 61, 90, 106; Knox, 1: 220; Norman Stone, *The Eastern Front, 1914-1917* (New York: Scribner's, 1975), 144-145; Buchanan, 1: 236.

42. A. A. Polivanov, "Iz dnevnikov," 184, cited in Lincoln, 145.

43. Abel Ferry, *Les Carnets Secrèts d'Abel Ferry, 1914-1918* (Paris: Grosset, 1957), 49, cited in Sinanoglou, 27; Joffre, Fr. ed., 2: 175; Eng. ed., 2: 419-420.

44. On the question of Russia and the Allies *in re* war matériel, see A. L. Sidorov, "Otnocheniia Rossii s soiuznikami i inostrannye postavki vo vremia pervoi mirovoi voiny," *Istoricheskie zapiski*, 15 (1945): 128-179; V. A. Emets, "O roli russkoi armii v pervyi period mirovoi voiny, 1914-1918 gg," *Istoricheskii zapiski*, 83 (1965): 57-84; for orders falling short of needs, see carton 174, d. "1er voyage," rapport A6 and folder "munitions" in carton 175, d. "Fourniture de la France à Russie," Papiers Thomas, Archives National, Paris, France.

45. Lincoln, 133-134.

46. Joffre, Eng. ed., 2: 603-4; this statement does not exist in the French edition.

47. Lincoln, 165; Stone, 212.

48. Lincoln, 166.

49. Dispatch LXXXIII, November 10, 1915, p. 10., W. O. 106/1006.

50. Neilson, 74 ff.

51. Dispatch LXXXIII, November 10, 1915, p. 10, W. O. 106/1006.

52. Convention attached to Ribot's letter to the minister of finance, 9 October 1915, carton 175, Thomas Papers.

53. Neilson, 129-130; 131.

54. Senate: Rapport fait à la commission d'Armée sur les fusils, mitrailleuses, et cartouches by Henri Cheron, 20 November 1915, carton 65, Papiers Paul Painlevé, 313AP, Archives Nationals, Paris, France.

55. Knox, 2: 422. His figures on the French numbers are roughly the same as those given in the Senate report; for details of all France provided, see Emets, "Petrogradskaia konferentsiia i Frantsiia, *Istoricheskii zapiski*, 83 (1969), 23-37.

56. Neilson, 117.

57. Interview with Prince Dmitri Romanov, the nephew of Tsar Nicholas II, in London, May, 1971; "The tsar spent it all for the cause," he told the author. "Believe me, I would know it if he hadn't."

58. Stone, 232.

59. E. Z. Barsukov, *Russkaia artilleriia v miroviu voiny* (Moscow, 1940), 2: 284 and 350, cited in Emets, "Petrogradskaia konferentsiia," 27.

60. Munitions d'artillerie de campagne, 18, n. d., carton 174, d. 1er voyage, rapport A6, Papiers Thomas.

61. Ts. G. V. I. A., f. 2003, op. 1, d 1151, 11.73-82, cited in Emets, "Petrogradskaia, 27.

62. See *The French Army in the First World War,* vol. 1, annexe 1, cited in Emets, ibid.

63. Winston Churchill, *The World Crisis* (New York: Scribner's, 1927), 1: 300.

64. Jean-Jacques Becker, *The Great War and the French People* (New York: St. Martin's Press, 1986), 47.

65. Ludendorff, German ed., 1: 240; Eng. ed., 1: 361.

66. Raymond Poincaré, *Au Service de la France* (Paris: Plon, 1926-74), 5: 301.

67. Sukhomlinov to foreign ministry, October 17/30, 1914, no. 8678, cited in N. Valentinov, "Russkie voiska vo Frantsii i Salonikakh," *Voenno-istoricheskii Sbornik,* 4 (1920): 3.

68. Tel/fpr Er,p; pv., 24 October/6 November 1914, no. 514, Valentinov, 3-4.

69. Poincaré, 5: 223.

70. Frank Pattyn, *La Russie en Guerre: Histories des unités russes sur le front occidental, 1914-1917* (Brussels: University of Bruxelles, 1979), 58.

71. Paléologue to MFA, September 29, 1915, 2: 111, Papiers Maurice Paléologue, Archives du Ministère des Affaires Etrangères, Paris, France.

72. Valentinov, 5.

73. Yanushkevich to Goremykin, January 24/February 6, 1915, in Valentinov, 6.

74. Chéradame to MW, December 15, 1915, 7N795, Etat-major de l'armée, 795, d. 3.

75. Joffre, Fr. ed., 2: 177; Eng. ed., 2: 421.

76. Rapport sur les Effectives by Noel and Albert Favre, no date except "1916," Papiers Painlevé.

77. Knox, 1: 354-355; 364-365.

78. Briand to French embassy, November 12, 1915, G: R, 763: 5.

79. F. O. Lindley for Buchanan to Edward Grey, January 10, 1916, 2745: 483, F. O. 371 General Correspondence: Political, PRO, London, Great Britain. In Poincaré's papers he notes that the exchange was to be guns for men to go to Salonika. Notes journalières, November 10, 1915, Papiers Raymond Poincaré, Bibliothèque Nationale, Paris, France.

80. Ibid., December 2, 1915, 2: 128-129; Paléologue to Briand, December 2, 1915, G: R, 763: 20.

81. Briand to Paléologue, December 3, 1915, ibid., 763: 22.

82. Ibid., 23.

83. Pingaud, 869.

84. Paléologue to Briand reporting for Doumer, December 7, 1915, G: R, 763: 24-25.

85. Paléologue to Briand, November 18, 1915, ibid., 763: 13.

86. Trotsky, *History,* 1: 252.

87. Paléologue, Fr. ed., 2: 135-136; Eng. ed., 2: 133.

88. Valentinov, 7.
89. *Oktiabr' za rubezhom,* no page given, cited in A. Vavilov, *Zapiski soldata Vavilov* (Moscow: Gos. Izd., 1927), 6.
90. Lindly for Buchanan to Edward Grey, January 10, 1916, 2745: 48, F. O. 371.
91. Sergei Sazonov, *Fateful Years, 1909-1916* (London: J. Cape, 1928).
92. *The Nicky-Sunny Letters; Correspondence of the Tsar and the Tsaritsa, 1914-1917* (Hattiesburg, Mississippi: Academic International Press, 1970), 115.
93. Paléologue to Briand, December 15, 1915, G: R, 763: 26-27; Pingaud, 871-872.
94. Paléologue to Briand, December 16, 1915, G: R, 763: 29-30; "Russkie soldaty po zapadnom fronte v mirovuiu voiny," *Krasnyi arkhiv,* 44 (1930-31): 153.
95. Paléologue to Marine, December 18, 1915, 7N795, d. 1.
96. Doumer to MFA, December 17, 1915, G: R, 763: 34.
97. Paléologue for naval attaché, December 18, 1915, ibid., 763: 38
98. Papiers Paléologue, September 30, 1915, 2: 112.
99. Ibid., December 18, 1915, 2: 146.
100. Alexeev to Beliaev, November 30/13 December 1915, no. 6255, cited in Valentinov, 8.
101. Alexeev to Zhilinsky, December 4/17 (sic), 1915, no. 6369, cited in Valentinov, 8.
102. Paléologue to MFA, December 23, 1915, 763: 40, G: R.; Papiers Paléologue, December 23, 1915, 2: 148.
103. Joffre, Fr. ed., 2: 177-78; Eng. ed., 2: 422.
104. Paléologue to MFA, December 23, 1915, 763: 41, G: R.
105. Poincaré, *Au Service,* 8: 7.
106. Dispatch M. 2: visit of M. Albert Thomas . . . , n. d., W. O. 106, 1077: 1.
107. Lincoln, 129.
108. Rossiia v mirovoi voine (v tsifrakh), table 9, cited in Lincoln, 179.
109. Emets, "Pet. Kon.," 27.
110. "L'URSS n'est pas la Russie," Papiers Général Nekrachewich, AP65, d. II, Archives Nationales, Paris, France.
111. Paul von Hindenburg, *Out of My Life* (New York: Cassell, 1920), 273.
112. Pau to MW, December 26, 1915, 763: 43-44, G: R.
113. Lindly for Buchanan to Grey, January 10, 1916, 2745: 483, F. O. 371.
114. Edward Grey to H. MacMahon (Cairo), March 31, 1916, 2745: 499, F. O. 371.
115. New York *Times,* April 21, 1916, 1.

Chapter 2

1. Princess Stephanie Dolgorouki, *Russia Before the Crash* (Paris: Herbert Clarke, 1926), 249.
2. Quoted from *Le Temps,* April 27, 1916, 3.
3. Youri (Iurii) Danilov, *Russkie otriady na frantsuzskom i makedonskom frontakh, 1916-1918* (Paris: Soiuz ofitserov uchastnikov voiny no frantsuzskom fronte, 1933), 47.
4. Beliaev to Laguiche, 19 January/1 February, 1916, 7N390, d. "Russie."

5. *Le Bonnet Rouge,* April 22, 1916; *The Times* (London), April 29, 1916, p. 8; Ernest Schultz, *La Vie des Soldats russes en France sur le front et à l'interieur, 1916-1918* (Paris (?): no publisher, 1918) n.p.

6. Vavilov, 1-23.

7. Schultz, *passim.*

8. Pierre Poitevin, *Une Bataille au Centre de la France* (Paris: Payot, 1938), 13.

9. Kolomitsev interview. For his background, see the folder "Obituaries," in box 11 in the papers of Alexandra Teffi, Bakhmetev Arkhive, Columbia University, New York.

10. P. 3865.u., October 30, 1919, Russia, 1919, F⁷13488, d. October 1919.

11. Danilov, 27.

12. See 7N609, d. 1 and Lt. Col. Riasansev to Capt. Duboin, January 1, 1918, 7N611, d. 3.

13. See pictures in Schultz, n.p.

14. Paléologue to MFA, February 17, 1916, G: R, 763: 73.

15. Joseph Noulens, *Souvenirs de ma mission en Russie* (Paris: Plon, 1933), 2: 137.

16. Ibid., 113.

17. Pau to Min. War, February 1, 1916, G: R, 763: 57.

18. Wladimir Rychlinski, "Souvenirs d'un officier du corps expéditionnaire russe en France," *Revue historique de l'Armée,* no. 1 (1965), 114.

19. The figures of troop numbers and departure dates vary somewhat, even within the French archival accounts. See G: R, 763: 71-104.

20. Gov. of Straits Settlements to Sec. State for Colonies, March 10, 1916, 2745: 494, F. O. 371.

21. "Russians in France," *Literary Digest,* 52 (June 3, 1916), 1623.

22. Rychlinski, 116.

23. See Schultz, *passim.*

24. New York *Times,* April 22, 1916, 4.

25. Sir H. MacMahon (Cairo) to Sir A. Nicolson, March 30, 1916, 2745: 497, F. O. 371.

26. MacMahon to Nicolson, March 30, 1916, 2745: 497, F. O. 371; Note to Ignatiev, March 15, 1916, 7N609, d. 2, folder "Tresor et Postes."

27. See various newspaper accounts in the New York *Times,* April 21, 1916; 1: 5; *La Libre Parole,* April 21, 1916, 1; *Le Matin,* April 21, 1916, 1; *The Times* (London), April 21, 1916, 4.

28. *The Times History of the War* (London: The Times, 1914-1920), 8: 504; New York *Times,* April 21, 1916, 1-2.

29. *Le Temps,* April 22, 1916, 2.

30. Joffre to Pau, April 18, 1916, G: R, 763: 141-142.

31. Vavilov, 25-26.

32. *Echo de Paris,* April 21, 1916, 1 & 4.

33. *Le Bonnet Rouge,* April 22, 1916, 1.

34. "Russians in France," *Literary Digest,* 52: 1623.

35. *Le Matin,* April 24, 1916, 2.

36. *Echo de Paris,* April 22, 1916, 1.

37. A. A. Ignat'ev, *50 let v stroiu* (Moscow: Gos. izd. khud. lit., 1948), 701.

38. Foch carnet, April 1916-August 1916, entries for April 20 and April 21, 1916, Papiers Ferdinand Foch.

39. *La Libre Parole,* April 22, 1916, 1; Vavilov, 25-26.

40. *La Libre Parole,* April 22, 1916, 1.
41. Lee Meriweather, *The War Diary of a Diplomat* (New York: Dodd, Mead, 1919), 78.
42. *The Times History of the War,* 8: 504.
43. *Le Matin,* April 26, 1916, 2.
44. *Vchernoe vremia,* September 10, 1916, quoted in Mission en Russie, Grand Press Russe, 13/25 September 1916, arrived in France October 9, 1916, p. 14, Papiers Albert Thomas.
45. Interview with Mikhail Kolomitsev in his home in Meudon, France, November 1985. I was accompanied by Inna Cantou and Igor Simorov
46. Pattyn, 58.
47. *Le Matin,* April 24, 1916, 1.
48. A. Kozlov, *Prodannye za sniady* (Moscow: Gos. Izdat., 1928), 13.
49. *The Times* (London), April 26, 1916, 5; "Russians in France," *Literary Digest,* 52: 1624.
50. *The Times* (London), April 26, 1916, 5.
51. New York *Times,* April 28, 1916, 2.
52. New York *Times,* April 21, 1916, 2.
53. Rapport fait à la Commission de l'armée sur les effectives by M. A. Gervais, July 21, 1916, Papiers Painlevé.
54. Activité des meneurs sur les contingents alliés, March 1917, F⁷12895, Révolutionnaires russes, 1917, Ministère de l'Intérieur. Police générale, Archives Nationales, Paris, France.
55. Paul Cambon, *Correspondence, 1870-1924* (Paris: Crasset, 1946), 3: 102-103.
56. Ibid., 3: 104.
57. Jusserand to MFA, April 8, 23, and 24, 1916, G: R, 763: 133, 150, 153-154.
58. Military attaché to MG and C-in-C, May 11, 1916, G: R, 763: 184-185.
59. Russie, *passim,* carton 130, Papiers Painlevé.
60. 6e rapport, Langlois, p. 38, no date, carton 130, d. 1, Russie, Papiers Painlevé.
61. *Rech',* September 8, 1916, arrived in France, October 9, 1916, p. 12, carton 174, d. "ler voyage en Russie, Papiers Thomas.
62. Mil. attaché to Min. War, April 25, 1916, G: R, 763: 164.
63. Engelhardt to Briand, April 17, 1916, G: R, 763: 140.
64. Senate Rapport fait à la Commission de l'armée sur les effectives," by M. A. Gervais, p. 27, n. d., carton 65, Papiers Painlevé.
65. PM to Paléologue April 23, 1916, G: R, 763: 152-53.
66. Vladimir Lazarevski, ed., *Archives Secrètes de l'empereur Nicholas II* (Paris: Payot, 1928), 97.
67. Z. A. B. Zeman, *A Diplomatic History of the First World War* (London: Weidenfeld and Nicolsen, 1971), 290.
68. Knox, 2: 418-419.
69. Frank Golder, ed. *Documents of Russian History, 1914-1918* (Gloucester, Mass.: Peter Smith, 1964), 109-110.
70. Knox, 2: 418-419.
71. Paléologue, Eng. ed., 2: 247-49; Fr. ed., 2: 258-260.
72. Paléologue to MFA, May 8, 1916, G: R, 763: 174.
73. Ibid.
74. Paléologue, Eng. ed., 2: 249-252; Fr. ed., 2: 261-263; Buchanan to F. O., May 9, 1916, 2745: 501-502, F. O. 371.

75. Pau to Min. War, April 20, 1916, G: R, 763: 142-143.
76. *Nicky-Sunny Letters*, 177.
77. Paléologue, Eng. ed., 2: 253-254; Fr. ed., 2: 265-266.
78. "Convention Franco-Russe," May 4/17, 1916, carton 174, d. ler voyage, rapport A6, Papiers Thomas.
79. Untitle typed copy of Thomas-Shuvaev-Believ agreement, May 7, 1916, carton 174, d. ler voyage, Papiers Thomas; Danilov, 36.
80. Adrien Rémond, "Quelques souvenirs de deux missions en Russie, 1916-1917," *Soc. Nivernaise des lettres, sciences et arts. Bull.*, 27 (1930): 540; Paléologue, Eng. ed., 2: 255; Fr. ed. 2: 268-269.
81. This facility was the only poison gas factory that the Russians had. Rémond, 540.
82. Ibid., 542-543.
83. Paléologue, Eng. ed., 2: 261; Fr. ed., 2: 274.
84. Dumesnil to Ignatiev (copy), August 29, 1916, carton 175, d. Russie, fourniture de munitions . . . 1915-1916, Papiers Thomas.
85. Paléologue to MFA, April 26 and May 8, 1916, G: R, 763: 166 and 173.
86. Ibid., 170.
87. Paléologue to Marine and War, July 28, 1916, G: R, 764: 104.
88. "Russkie soldaty na zapadnom fronte v mirovuiu voinu," *Krasnyi arkhiv* [hereafter cited as *K.A.*], 44 (1930-31): 154.
89. For the Russians in Salonika, see Alan Palmer *The Gardeners of Salonika* (New York: Simon and Schuster, 1965), and Youri (Iurii) Danilov *Russkie otriady na frantsuzskom i makedonskom frontakh, 1916-1918* (Paris: Soiuz ofitserov uchastnikov voiny na frantsuzskom fronte, 1933).
90. Kozlov, 14.
91. P. N. Vrangel Archive, Box 57, folder 229, Hoover Institution on War, Revolution, and Peace, Stanford, California.
92. Rychlinski, 111.
93. Ibid.
94. Ignat'ev, *50 let*, 705. All citations in this work are from this work of Ignatiev.
95. Kozlov, 9.
96. The author of this account apparently had done a little mental editing by the time of his writing almost a decade later, because at the time of embarkation, the Third Brigade was destined for Salonika.
97. Prikaz 26 July (o.s.), 1916, Ekaterinburg, Box 57, folder 229, Vrangel Archive.
98. Kozlov, 10.
99. Danilov, *Russkie otriady*, 50-51.
100. Pattyn, 60. Pattyn states that these men were destined for the First and Second brigades, but apparently he is mistaken.
101. Paléologue to MFA, August 31, 1916, G: R, 764: 132.
102. Kozlov, 11-12.
103. TsGVIA, f. 15304, op. 8, d. 76, 112, 6-7, f. 2003, op. 2, d. 1014, 11.6-9, in A. L. Sidorov, *Revoliutsionnoe dvizhenie v armii i na flote v gody pervoi mirovoi voiny; sbornik dokumentov* (Moscow: Nauka, 1966), 422, footnote 86; see also 197.
104. Ignat'ev, 706.
105. Ibid., 708.
106. Ibid., 710.
107. Ibid. They were actually executed in France. See chapter 3, pp. 88-89.

108.   See Sidorov, *Revoliutsionnoe dvizhenie*, 422, footnote 86; see also 197; Paléologue, Eng. ed., 3: 17; Fr. ed., 3: 8;Coquet to War, August 17, 1916, G: R, 764: 122.

109.   Joffre to Pau, September 17, 1916, G: R, 764: 158.

110.   *Nicky-Sunny Letters*, 204-205.

111.   Ioffe, 42.

112.   Joffre to Pau, September 17, 1916, G: R, 764: 138.

113.   Gen. Ct. 14th region to War, August 20, 1916, G: R, 764: 128.

114.   Paléologue to PM, November 27, 1916, 7N795, d. 3.

Chapter 3

1.   Note de Service Postale, 24 July 1916, 7N609, d. 1, E-M de l'A.

2.   Paléologue, Eng. ed., 3: 17; Fr. ed., 3: 8.

3.   In "Revoliutsiia poetokhronika" in *Sobranie sochineniia*, 1: 224-225, cited in Lincoln, 344.

4.   L. Bertie, *The Diary of Lord Bertie of Thame, 1914-1918* (New York: Doran, 1924), 2: 25.

5.   Rychlinski, 117.

6.   Sir Douglas Haig, *The Private Papers of Douglas Haig* (London: Eyre and Spottiswoode, 1952), 135.

7.   Ironside, *Tannenberg*, 25, cited in Lincoln, 62.

8.   Joffre, Fr. ed., 2: 175; Eng. ed., 2: 420.

9.   N. N. Golovin, *Iz istorii kampanii 1914 goda; nachalo voiny*, 1: 231 cited in Lincoln, 52: Knox, 1: 296; Nikolai N. Golovin, *The Russian Army in the World War* (New Haven, Conn.: Yale University Press, 1931), 20, 244; Hans Heilbronner, "Yakov Grigor'evich Zhilinskii," *The Modern Encyclopedia of Russian and Soviet History*, Joseph L. Wieczynski, ed. (Gulf Breeze, Miss.: Academic International Press, 1976-), 46: 50-52.

10.   "Perezhitoe, 1916-1918," 1-2, F. F. Palitsyn Papers, The Hoover Institution, Stanford, California.

11.   Ibid., 3-4, 9.

12.   Ibid., 13.

13.   Beliaev to Laguiche, 19 January 1916, 7N609, d. 2, folder "Organization," E-M de'A.

14.   Comp. de l'échelon des éléments russes partant pour la Russia, 5 August 1917, 7N610, d. 2, Etat-major de l'armée.

15.   Provision note attached to Order of the Day, 24 March/6 April, 1917, box 56, folder 225, Vrangel Archive.

16.   Annex 1 of Tableau no. 2, 22 June 1916, 7N390, d. Russie, Etat-major de l'armée.

17.   Valentinov, 12.

18.   Ibid.

19.   Poincaré, *Au Service*, 8: 238-239.

20.   Ibid., 8: 239-240.

21.   Valentinov quotes a report written on the brigades' activities in the early weeks but not dispatched until 31 January/13 February 1917, in Valentinov, 12.

22. Mements des consignes practiques destiné aux Troupes russes pour leur Entrée en Secteur, 22 June 1916, 17N649, d. 3, Missions militaires Françaises près des armées alliées, Bibliothèque des Armées, Château de Vincennes, Paris, France.

23. Instruction exigée des Troupes Françaises avant leur entrée dans les secteurs, 3 June 1916, 17N649, d. 3, Missions militaires Françaises.

24. Prikaz po 3oi osoboi pekhotnoi brigady, 26/8 Noiabria 1916, box 57, folder 230, Vrangel Archives; Rapport sur l'Instruction de la Brigade Russe, 1/14 May 1916, 17N649, d. 3; Pattyn, 61.

25. Noulens, 2: 137.

26. Marushevsky to Cmdt. I Army, 1 May 1917, 17N649, d. 4, E-M de 'A.

27. Gouraud to Cmdt. Brigade Russe, 13 June 1916, 17N649, d. 3, E-M de l'A.

28. *The Times* (London), January 19, 1917, 31.

29. Vavilov, 27. On July 7, 1916; this sector passed under the command of General J. B. Dumas.

30. Danilov, *Russkie otriady*, 71-73.

31. Pattyn, 64.

32. *Echo de Paris*, July 16, 1916, 2.

33. *Le Matin*, July 16, 1916, 1.

34. *Echo de Paris*, July 16, 1916, 2.

35. *The Times* (London), July 17, 1916, 7.

36. Ibid., 8c.

37. Vavilov, 28.

38. Lokhvitsky to Gen. Cmdt. Group Ouest, July 20, 1916, 17N650, d. 3, Missions Militaire Françaises.

39. Pattyn, 61-64.

40. Rychlinski, 122.

41. Ibid., 123.

42. Rodion Malinovsky, *Soldaty Rossii* (Moscow: Volnizdat, 1978), 229.

43. Danilov, *Russkie otriady*, 75.

44. Rychlinski, 122.

45. Danilov, *Russkie otriady*, 75-76.

46. Ibid., 76-77.

47. Vavilov, 29.

48. Ibid.

49. Danilov, 58.

50. See collection of papers, 5N394, d. "Journal militaire . . . russe," Cabinet de Ministre, Bibliothèque des armées, Château de Vincennes, Paris, France.

51. For a copy, see 17N651, d. russe 1; see copy of paper in Révolutionnaires russes, 1918, F' 12896, d. January 1918, Police Générale, Ministère de L'Interieur, Archives Nationales, Paris, France.

52. See folder "France--Relations with Russia," Box 16, Posol'stvo (France), Russia, The Hoover Institution, Stanford, California.

53. "Russkie soldaty," *K. A.*, 154.

54. Pellé to Gen. comdt. of the Army, 26 August 1916, 7N390, d. Brigade Russe, Etat-major de l'armée.

55. Ilya Ehrenburg, *People and Life, 1891-1921*, tr. by Anna Bostock and Yvonne Kapp (New York: Knopf, 1962), 226; Vavilov, 28-29.

56. *The Times* (London), January 19, 1917, 31.

57. Ehrenburg, *Life and People*, 227.

58. Poitevin, 18. All citations in this work are from his first book, *Une Bataille;* John Williams, *Mutiny 1917* (London: Heinemann, 1962), 14.
59. Note, 9 April 1917, G: R, 764: 198.
60. Malinovsky, 232; War to PM, 15 May 1917, 16N3018, d. 20, item 10.
61. Poitevin, 19.
62. Note to MFA, 25 April 1917, G: R, 764: 211-212.
63. Dokumenty . . . , 25ff., Box 3, Russian Expeditionary Force Papers, Bakhmetev Archive, Columbia University, New York City.
64. Ibid., 2.
65. Giraud to GHQ, 7 March 1917, 7N390, d. Service du personnel, Etat-major de l'armée.
66. Note to MFA, 25 April 1917, G: R, 764: 211-12.
67. Depenses . . . , n. d. dokumenty kratkoi . . . , item 5, box 3, REF Papers.
68. Ordre no. 187, 2/15 October 1916, 17N649, d. 2, Missions Militaires Françaises.
69. Ignat'ev, 705.
70. Danilov, *Russkie otriady,* 83-84.
71. Ibid., 85.
72. Ibid., 80-81.
73. Ibid., 89.
74. For an account of the trip, see Paul Miliukov, *Political Memoirs: 1905-1917* (Ann Arbor: University of Michigan Press, 1967), 340-360; "Russkaia parlamentskaia delegatsiia za granitsei 1916 g.," *K. A.,* 58 (1933), 3-23.
75. Poincaré, *Au Service,* 8: 233-34.
76. Translated from the *Stenograficheskie otchety,* IV Duma, 16 session, in Russia, Gosudarstvennaia duma. *Russia and Her Allies* (London: Burrup, Mathieson and Sprague, 1917), 10.
77. Trotsky, *History,* 1: 248.
78. La Colonie des politiques . . . , November 23, 1917, p. 9, F⁷12895, d. November (?), Révolutionnaires russes, 1917; Poitevin, 20.
79. F⁷12986, early dossiers, passim, Révoliutionnaires russes, 1918.
80. Memo, 7 April 1917, F⁷12895, d. "Avril," Révolutionnaires russes, 1917.
81. Isaac Deutscher, *The Prophet Armed: Trotsky, 1879-1921* (New York: Oxford University Press, 1954), 227-239.
82. Chicherin (Tschitcherine to Dridgo), 9 April 1917, d. "Avril," F⁷12895, Révolutionnaires russes, 1917.
83. List and biographical on Russian revolutionaries, untitled dossier, 2 April 1917, F⁷12895, Révolutionnaires russes, 1917.
84. A Russian library in Paris, *La Bibliothèque Slave de Paris,* founded in 1857 by Jesuits, operates to this day. It is possible that this library is the one to which the police report refers.
85. See F⁷12895, d. Janvier, passim, Révolutionnaires russes, 1917; Rapport, 21 March 1917, ibid.
86. La Colonie des politique russes à Paris, 4-5, in loose papers, apparently the November dossier, 23 November 1917, F⁷12895, Révolutionnaires russes 1917.
87. Ibid.
88. Untitled memo, 16 April 1917, ibid.
89. See ibid., unnamed dossiers and d. Mai.
90. Cambon, 3: 147.

91. Mikhail Rodzianko, *The Reign of Rasputin: An Empire's Collapse* (London: Philpot, 1927), 263.
92. "Perezhitoe," 26, Palitsyn papers.
93. Ibid.
94. *Russkie soldaty vo Frantsii* (Moscow: Gos. Izdat., 1919), 5.
95. Ioffe, 234; Kozlov, 14; Vavilov, 29-30.
96. Williams, 20; Poitevin, 24.
97. *New York Times Current History: The European War* (New York: The Times Co, 1914-1920), 11: 489.
98. Fournier to Gen. IV Army, 13 April 1917, 7N609, d. 2, Etat-major de l'armée.
99. Ibid.
100. Quoted in *Le Temps*, 13 April 1917, p. 2; Ioffe, 234.
101. Noulens, 2: 138.
102. Fournier to Gen. IV Army, 13 April 1917, 7N609, d. 2, Etat-major de l'armée.
103. Williams, 20.
104. Fournier to Gen. IV Army, 13 April 1917, 7N609, d. 2, Etat-major de l'armée.
105. Ordre au 1er regiment special, 18/31 March 1917, 21: 17, Europe, 1918-1940: Russie, Archives du Ministère des Affaires Etrangères, Paris, France.
106. See reports in G: R, 764: 201-203.
107. Ibid., 765: 218-219.
108. La Colonie des politiques russes, 23 November 1917, p. 5, F^{7}12895, d. Nov (?) loose papers; "Propagande pacifiste rev., 25 April 1916, d. not named, Révolutionnaires russes, 1917.
109. Fournier to Gen. IV Army, 12 May 1917, 7N609, d. 4.

Chapter 4

1. Bülow, 3: 195.
2. Ilya Ehrenburg, *Lik voiny* (Sofia: Rossiisko-bolgarskoe knigoizdatel'stvo, 1920), 75.
3. Sun Tzu, 20.
4. Ibid., 32.
5. Marshal Henri Philippe Pétain, *Une Crise morale de la nation en guerre, 16 avril-23 octobre 1917* (Paris: Nouvelles Editions latines, 1966), 9.
6. Gen. C-in-C to Gen. Micheler, 29 January 1917, carton 120, d. Inst. du GQG des Armées françaises, 16 November 1916-26 January 1917, Papiers Painlevé.
7. Danilov, *Russkie otriady*, 95-96.
8. Williams, 29.
9. Letter of Mazel attached to Micheler to Nivelle, 5 February 1917, carton 120, d. Inst. du GAR, 5-January-1 May 1917, Papiers Painlevé.
10. Poincaré, *Au Service*, 9: 98.
11. Barbara Tuchman, *A Distant Mirror* (New York: Knopf, 1978), 7, 13, 595-597.
12. Compte-rendu des Evenements du 31 mars (midi) au 1er avril (midi), 19 March/ 1 April 1917, 17N651, d. russe 1.
13. Ins. rel. au movement des V, VI, and X armées . . . vers la serre, 18 February 1917, carton 120, d. Inst. du GAR, 5 Jan-1 mai 1917, Papiers Painlevé; Danilov, 90.

14. Plan d'Engagement de la Brigade Russe Special, 27 (?) March, 1917, 7N390, no dossier.

15. Inst. particulière pour la 3e Brigade russe, 8 April 1917, 7N390, d. 3e brigade russe.

16. *Times History of the War*, 14: 57; A. Khazov, "Russkii ekspeditionnyi korpus vo Frantsii," *Kadetskaia pereklichka*, no. 46 (April 1989), 75.

17. Marushevsky to Cmdt. 37 D. I., 17 April 1917, 17N649, d. 4.

18. Lokhvitsky to Cmdt. 7e corps, V Army, 13/26 February 1917, 7N651, d. russe 1.

19. de Bazelaire to Lokhvitsky, 11 April 1917, 17N650, d. 2.

20. Dest. jour. du 12 Avril, 1917, 17N650, d. 2.

21. Col. Diakonov to Adm. 1st Special Brigade, 31 March-13 April, 1917, 17N650, d. 2.

22. Williams, 24-25; Paul Painlevé, *Comment j'ai nominé Foch et Pétain* (Paris: Alcan, 1924), 155-157, cited in Sinangoglou, 168.

23. *Voennaia gazeta*, no. 26, 6/19 May 1917, 5N394, d. "Journal militaire . . russe."

24. "Perezhitoe," 19, Palitsyn papers.

25. Alistair Horne, *Voices of the Great War* (New York: Dell, 1987), 166.

26. *Times History of the War*, 14: 49.

27. Untitled book ms, p. 119, carton 17, Papiers Mangin.

28. Williams, 33.

29. Later accounts refer to the 1st regiment as the 2nd is on the right of the 41st. Compte-rendu journalière, 16 April 1917, 17N651, d. russe 1.

30. *Oktiabr' za rubezhom, sbornik vospominanii*, ed. M. N. Pokrovsky (Moscow, 1924), 33, cited in Ioffe, 240.

31. French sources put the Russian losses on the 16th as 28 officers and about 50 percent of the effectives; it also reports 535 German prisoners taken. Khazov, 76, reports similar statistics.

32. Compte-rendu journalière, 16 April 1917, 17N651, d. russe 1.

33. Danilov, *Russkie otriady*, 105.

34. Williams, 45-46.

35. One report states that in the midst of this slaughter, the First Russian Brigade was relieved to give it some rest, but that is unlikely. Note sur Avril 1917, by Mazel, 22-23, 14 July 1917, 5N255, d. Pièces . . . Mazel.

36. Response . . . à une Question posée par le GQG, 16 Mai 1917, carton 120, d. Emploi de matériel, avril-mai 17, Papiers Painlevé; Note sur Avril, 1917, p. 26, 5N255, d. Pièce . . . Mazel.

37. Compte-rendu, 4/17 April 1917, 5/18 April 1917, 17N651, d. russe 1.

38. *Times History of the Great War*, 14: 59.

39. Ibid.

40. Poincaré, *Au Service*, 9: 119.

41. Ibid., 122.

42. Note sur Avril, 1917, by Mazel, p. 19, 14 July 1917, 5N255, d. Pièces . . . . Mazel.

43. Ibid., 20-21; Khazov, 77.

44. Micheler to C-in-C, 21 April 1917, 5N255, d. Offensive du 16 April 1917.

45. Khazov, 77-78.

46. Sir James Edmunds, *A Short History of World War I* (London: Oxford, 1951), 221; Falls, 279.

47. Note sur les Pertes (copy), 13 May 1917, carton 120, d. 1917 IV, V, etc., Papiers Painlevé.

48. Note no. 4., Rapport de la commission d'enquête, 14 July 1917, 5N255, d. A.
49. Danilov gives the 5,183 figure. Danilov, *Russkie otriady,* 123.
50. Voenno-istoricheskii sbornik, bam 4, p. 14, TSGVIA, f. 416/3, op. 1, d. 12, 1. 50, cited in Ioffe, 240-41; Khazov, 78.
51. Marushevsky to Médicin Inspecteur, 8 May 1917, 17N649, d. 4.
52. Gen. Marushevsky, Compte-rendu de l'attaque du Mont Spin, 19 April 1917, n.d., 7N390, d. 3e Brigade russe. On one of the casualty lists there appears the name of Pvt. 1st class Rodion Malinovsky, the man destined to become the defense minister of the Soviet Union under Khrushchev in the 1950s. He had been wounded on the first day of the offensive and appears as number 787 (ironically the last name) on a list of the First Brigade's wounded. List of wounded, box 64, file 255, Vrangel Archive.
53. Khazov, 77-78.
54. Ibid.
55. Orders 2252 and 27210, April 24, 1917, undated and untitled orders, 7N609, d. 1; *Voennaia gazeta,* no. 22, 8/21 April 1917, 5N394, d. Journal militaire pour les troupes russes en France.
56. Quoted in Valentinov, 13.
57. Ibid., 14.
58. *Novoe vremia,* 11/24 April 1917, cited in Ioffe, 241.
59. TsGVIA, f. 416/c, op. 1, d. 83, ll. 25-26, cited in Ioffe, 241.
60. Frankfurter to Lansing, August 7, 1917, 851.00/26 1/2a, Records of the Department of State relating to Internal Affairs of France, 1910-1929, National Archives, Washington, D. C.
61. Capt. B. H. Liddell Hart, *The Real War, 1914-1918* (Boston: Little, Brown, 1930), 301.
62. Falls, 279-81; for a detailed examination of the French mutinies, see Williams, and see Guy Pedroncini, *1917: Les Mutineries de l'armée française* (Paris: Juillard, 1968) and his *Les Mutineries de 1917* (Paris: Presses universitaires de France, 1967).
63. Note sur Avril, 1917, by Mazel, p. 16, 14 July 1917, 5N255, d. Pièces . . . Mazel.
64. Resumé de la Press Allemande (typescript), n. 62, le mois d'avril, p. 19, carton 186, only dossier, Papiers Painlevé.
65. Yuri Lissovsky, "Lager Lia-Kurtin," *Arkhiv russkoi revoliutsii,* 17 (1926): 263.
66. Ehrenburg, *Lik,* 78.
67. Lokhvitsky to Gen. Cmdt. 1ère Armée, 19 April/2 May 1917, 7N390, d. 1ère et 3eme Brigades russes.
68. Marushevsky to Gen. Cmdt. 1ère Armée, 1 May 1917, 7N390, d. 1ère et 3eme Brigades.
69. MW to Chef, 6 May 1917, 7N609, d. 3.
70. See Note pour directeur d'Artillery, 14 May 1917, carton 181, d. Armée russe, Papiers Thomas; see another memo in the same dossier dated 25 May 1917.
71. *Voenno-Istoricheskii sbornik,* 4 (1921): 13, cited in Ioffe, 237.
72. Institut Marksa-Engel'sa-Lenina pri TsKVKP (b)., V. I. Lenin, *Sochinenie* (Moscow: Gos. Izd. Polit. Lit), 23: 298.
73. Painlevé to C-in-C Armée Orient, 20 May 1917, G: R, 765: 9.
74. Ioffe, 239.
75. Ibid., 237-238.
76. Thomas to MFA, 24 May 1917, G: R, 765: 18.

77. Thomas to MFA, 25 May 1917, G: R, 765: 20.

78. J. Cambon (?) to MW, 27 May 1917, G: R, 765, 28. If Russian soldiers had docilely boarded ships, it is questionable whether they would have been transported by the Russian navy, which was, if anything, more rebellious than the army. Late in June, sailors of the Baltic fleet in Helsinki had voted unanimously, with only four abstentions, to protest against the dispatch of more Russian troops to France, a country that they felt had not adhered to the "principles of war proclaimed by Russia." Bulletin Périodique de la Press Russe, no. 50, 15 August 1917, p. 6, carton 182, d. Presse Russe, Papiers Painlevé.

79. "Perezhitoe," p. 25, Palitsyn papers.

80. Trotsky, *History*, 1: 259. Perhaps the Russians today are not so far removed from this understanding of "freedom." The day after the coup failed in the summer of 1991 and "democracy" had been victorious, 80 percent of those who gassed up their cars at the gas station on the road to the Pulkovo Airport in St. Petersburg, drove off without paying. Democracy, they thought, meant "free gasoline."

81. Trotsky, *History*, 1: 262.

Chapter 5

1. Rivet, 300.

2. Sun Tzu, 47.

3. "Voina i mir," *Sobranie sochinenii*, 1: 160, 164, 170, 173-175, cited in Lincoln, 272.

4. Lincoln, 177; Golovin, 240.

5. See Richard Watt, *Dare Call It Treason* (New York: Simon and Schuster, 1963).

6. One Russian émigré told this author in 1985 in an interview in his home in Meudon, France, that they were all "Jews from the United States." Interview with Mikhail Kolomitsev, November 1985.

7. Tr. article from *Sotsial demokrat*, 17/30 May 1917, in G: R, 765: 44-45.

8. Memo, 16 May 1917, Révolutionnaires russes, 1917, F^{7}12895, d. Mai.

9. Rapport du Commisariat Spécial, 9 July 1917, Révolutionnaires russes, 1917, F^{7}12895, d. Juillier (sic).

10. See Thomas R. Peake, "The Impact of the Russian Revolutions upon French Attitudes and Policies toward Russia," Unpublished Ph.D. dissertation, University of North Carolina, 1974, 70-71.

11. Resumé de la Presse allemande, no. 66 (3), Russie (juin-juillet, 1917), p. 22, carton 186, only dossier, Papiers Painlevé.

12. Pedroncini, *Les Mutineries*, 59.

13. Noulens, 2: 138.

14. Pedroncini, *Les Mutineries*, 77.

15. "Perezhitoe," 20, Palitsyn papers.

16. Ibid.

17. Ibid.

18. "Russkie soldaty," *K. A.*, 44: 156.

19. Ibid.

20. For the development of soldiers' committees, see Alan Wildman *The End of the Russian Imperial Army* (Princeton, N.J.: Princeton University Press, 1980), 246-

372, and "Army Committees," *The Modern Encyclopedia of Russian and Soviet History*, 2: 105-107.

21. Prikaz, date is 3/16 May 1917, but was doubtlessly issued earlier, folder 225, box 36, Vrangel Archive.
22. Note from Army HQ, 30 May 1917, G: R, 765: 31-32.
23. Prikazy po voennomu bedotstvu, 12 April 1917, p. 2, d. IX, Papiers General Nekrachewitch, AP65, Archives Nationales, Paris, France.
24. Kozlov, 14.
25. Vavilov, 31.
26. Note sur l'état morale . . . , 25 June 1917, 4-6, carton 181, d. Brigades russes, Papiers Thomas.
27. Note from army HQ, 30 May 1917, G: R, 765: 31-32.
28. Vavilov, 33.
29. Kozlov, 15.
30. Ibid., 15.
31. Ibid., 16.
32. Vavilov, 34.
33. Poitevin, *Une Bataille*, 31.
34. Lissovsky, 268.
35. Note sur l'état morale . . . , 25 June 1917, carton 181, d. Brigades russes, Papiers Thomas.
36. Kozlov, 17.
37. Poitevin, *Une Bataille*, 32; Kozlov, 17.
38. Ehrenburg, *People*, 227
39. Kozlov, 18.
40. De Castelnau to Gen. Com.-en-chief, 5 June 1917, Etat-major de l'Armee, 7N611, d. 2; Note au sujet . . . des Brigades russes, p. 3, 25 June 1917, carton 181, d. Brigades russes, Papiers Thomas.
41. Williams, 130.
42. Propagande pacifiste, etc., 14 December 1917, Révolutionnaires russes, 1917, F⁷12895, no dossier.
43. Prikaz 25 April/8 May 1917, box 64, folder, 255, Vrangel Archives.
44. "Vosstanie russkikh soldat vo Frantsii v 1917 g.," *K. A.*, 99 (1939-40): 56.
45. Memo, 16 May 1917, Révolutionnaires russes, 1917, F⁷12895, d. Mai.
46. Etat-major IIIe Brigade to Etat-major 1e Armée, 22 May 1917, Missions Militaire, 17N649, d. 4.
47. Chart on leaders, n. d., Missions Militaire, 17N687, d. 47.
48. Ibid.
49. Vavilov, 31-32.
50. Kozlov, 17.
51. Poitevin, *Une Bataille*, 30
52. Att. Mil. to War, 2 June 1917, Etat-major de l'Armée, 7N610, d. 3; see Ioffe, 236; untitled memo, 29 May 1917, Etat-major, 7N611, d. 1; Danilov, *Russkie otriady*, 132. The Third Brigade also sent a delegation of two men who spoke to the Petrograd Soviet on June 19 of the injustices confronting them. The sources are confusing and contradictory, and this delegation may have been one of those mentioned earlier.
53. See note, 29 May 1917, Etat-major de l'Armée, 7N610, d. 2.
54. Ibid.

Notes 353

55. Ioffe, 236.
56. Kerensky to Rapp, "Vosstannie," *K. A.*, 99: 56-57.
57. Commissaire Spécial de Nice, 7 May 1918, Révolutionnaires russes, 1918, F⁷12896, d. August 1918.
58. G: R, 765: 123 ff.
59. Lissovsky, 270.
60. Note . . . , G: R, 765: 52-56.
61. Pattyn, 78.
62. See Sinanoglou, 169.
63. Ehrenburg, *People*, 228.
64. "Au front," no date, carton 123, d. 2, Papiers Painlevé.
65. Foch to Cmdt.-en-chef Nord-nord-est, 20 May 1917, Grand Quartier Général, 16N3018, d. 20, item 29.
66. "Russkie soldaty," *K. A.*, 44: 156.
67. Ibid.
68. Prikaz, 14/27 May 1917, box 56, folder 225, Vrangel Archives.
69. Prikaz, 29 April/12 May 1917, box 64, folder 255, Vrangel Archives.
70. Prilozhenie k prikazu po polku no. 195, 18 May (o. s.) 1917, ibid.
71. Prikaz 8/21 May 1917, ibid.
72. *Istoricheskie zapiski*, 38: 78, cited in Ioffe, 242.
73. "Materialy k prebyvaniu russkikh voisk vo Frantsii v 1917 g.," *K. A.*, 101 (1940): 101: 231.
74. Lissovsky, 268.
75. Marushevsky to Cmdt. I Armée, 1 May 1917, Missions Militaire, 17N649, d. 4.
76. *Oktiabr' za rubezhom*, 29-30, cited in Ioffe, 243.
77. Estraits du . . . *Golos pravdy*, n. d., Cabinet du Ministre, 5N396, d. Journaux russes.
78. G: R, 765: 11.
79. Ibid.
80. *Oktiabr' za rubezhom*, 29-30, cited in Ioffe, 243.
81. Ioffe, 243.
82. Rapport entre les troupes russes et la population française, 26 May 1917, Etat-major, 7N609, d. 1.
83. Renseignments au sujet des troupes russes en France, n. d., but obviously written in June, Etat-major, 7N795, d. 3.
84. Bulletin Périodique de la Presse Russe, no. 50, 15 August 1917, p. 6, carton 182, d. Presse russe, Papiers Painlevé.
85. Alexandre Ribot, *Letters to a Friend: Recollections of My Political Life* (London: Hutchinson, 1926), 211; *Lettres à un Ami* (Paris: Bossard, 1924), 232.
86. Charles Chambrun, *Lettres à Marie, Pétersbourg-Petrograd* (Paris: Plon, 1941), 98.
87. De Robien quoted in Michael J. Carley, *Revolution and Intervention: The French Government and the Russian Civil War, 1917-1919* (Montreal: McGill University Press, 1983), 9.
88. *The Times* (London), 14 May 1917, p. 7.
89. Cambon, 3: letter of 19 June 1917.
90. Ibid., 180.
91. Jacques Sadoul, *Notes sur la Révolution Bolchévique* (Paris: Editions de la sirène, 1920), 234, cited in Carley, 23.

92. Gen. Cmdt.-en-chef to war, 28 May 1917, Fonds particuliers: Poincaré, Galliè-ni, Clemenceau, 6N285, d. September 1917 (sic).
93. Debeney to MW, 21 May 1917, Etat-major, 7N609, d. 1
94. La colonie, p. 13, [23] November 1917, F⁷12895, d. November.
95. "Perezhitoe," 35, Palitsyn papers.
96. Prikaz, 22 May/4 June 1917, box 64, folder, 255, Vrangel Archives.
97. Kozlov, 20.
98. Ibid., 21.
99. Note pour GHQ, 30 May 1917, G: R, 765: 32.
100. Ibid., 34-35.
101. Rapport de Castelnau, 5 June 1917, Etat-major, 7N390, d. Général-en-chef et Général Sarrail.
102. Williams, 130.
103. Misc. memo, untitled and undated in "Notes of Madame Contesse Busulhu, carton 123, d. 2, Papiers Painlevé.
104. Note sur l'état moral, 25 June 1917, piece no. 2, p. 1-4, carton 181, d. Brigades russes, Papiers Thomas.

Chapter 6

1. Trotsky, *History*, 2: 273.
2. Tikhomirov to Mlle. Chipov, 24 October 1917, in Extraits de [sic] lettres, 7N611, d. 2, E-M de l'A.
3. Poitevin, *Une Bataille*, 34.
4. Ibid., 36-37; Watt, 267.
5. Poitevin, *Une Bataille*, 39.
6. Cf. Poitevin, *Une Bataille*, 38; War to Cmdt.12th, 4 June 1917, 7N611, d. 2.
7. Ibid.
8. Ibid.
9. Poitevin, *Une Bataille*, 39.
10. Vidalon to War, 8 July 1917, 7N610, d. 2, E-M de l'A.
11. Ignatiev to War, 3/16 June 1917, 7N610, d. 3, E-M de l'A.
12. Poitevin, *Une Bataille*, 198-199.
13. Danilov, *Russkie otriady*, 134.
14. Poitevin, *Une Bataille*, 47-48.
15. Ibid., 37-42.
16. One account states June 17.
17. Poitevin, *Une Bataille*, 20.
18. "La situation est tendue." G: R, 765: 85.
19. Article by Stephen Valut, "Les Russes au camp," *L'Oeuvre*, 11 February 1918, carton 181, d. "Brigades Russes," Thomas Papers.
20. Ibid.
21. André Obey, "Comarades rouskii," *Revue de Paris*, 6 (November-December 1920), 533.
22. Poitevin, *Une Bataille*, 47.
23. See box 7, folder "Protokoly," REF papers.
24. Rapport, 8 July 1917, G: R, 765: 89.

25. G: R, 765: 77 ff.
26. Ibid., 77.
27. Ibid., 765: 114-116.
28. Obey, 533.
29. Ibid., 537.
30. Préfet de La Creuse to Min. Int., 11 July 1917, G: R, 765: 100.
31. Poitevin, *Une Bataille*, 50.
32. Lissovsky, 271.
33. Special Commissioner's report of 2 July 1917, G: R, 765: 85.
34. Vavilov, 40-42.
35. Kozlov, 25.
36. Lissovsky, 273.
37. Ibid.; Poitevin, *Une Bataille*, 55.
38. Ibid., 60.
39. Ibid., 61.
40. *Russkie soldaty vo Frantsii*, 8.
41. Poitevin, *Une Bataille*, 63.
42. Préfet de La Creuse to Min. Int., 11 July 1917, G: R, 765: 99-100.
43. Valot, "Les Russes," *L'Oeuvre*, 11 February 1918, carton 181, d. Brigades russes, Thomas Papers.
44. Ioffe, 249. The author does not give his source.
45. P. 2577 U, 25 March 1918, d. Rapp, $F^7$12896, 1918, d. March 1918, Rév. rus., 1918.
46. P. 2577. U. on Rapp, 25 March 1918, d. March 1918; Commissaire Spécial de Nice, 7 May 1918, $F^7$12896, d. August 1918 *(sic)*, Rév. rus. 1918.
47. Rapport du Commissionaire Spécial de Cannes, 28 June 1917, Révolutionnaires russes, $F^7$12896, d. June 1918 (document misplaced.
48. *Russkie soldaty vo Frantsii*, 8.
49. Poincaré, *Au Service*, 9: 271.
50. "Perezhitoe," 36, Palitsyn papers.
51. Kozlov, 23.
52. "Vosstanie russkikh soldat," *K. A.*, 99: 57.
53. Lissovsky, 272.
54. Min. Int. to PM, 1 and 4 July 1917, G: R, 765: 78-102.
55. Poitevin, *Une Bataille*, 53.
56. Préfet de La Creuse to Min. Int., 11 July 1917, G: R, 765: 100.
57. Poitevin, *Une Bataille*, 48-54.
58. Prikaz, 26 May/8 June 1917, box 64, file 255, Vrangel Archives.
59. R. A. Wade, "Argonauts of Peace: The Soviet Delegation to Western Europe in the Summer of 1917," *Slavic Review*, 27, no. 3 (1967): 455-456.
60. Poitevin, *Une Bataille*, 83-85.
61. Ibid., 66.
62. Ibid.
63. Ibid., 77.
64. Ibid., 78.
65. Ibid., 79.
66. Ibid., 79-80.
67. S to Russian Govt., no. 889, 23 August 1917, vol. 5 (January 1918), cited in Poitevin, *Une Bataille,*, 80.

68. Ribot to Fr. amb., 12 June 1917, G: R, 765: 61.
69. MW to attaché, 19 June 1917, G: R, 765: 67-68; Foch to Zankevich, 23 June 1917, G: R, 765: 70.
70. Telegram to Thomas, 26 June 1917, carton 181, 29 June 1917, d. Brigade Russe, Thomas papers.
71. Hallouin to War, 16 June 1917, 16N3018, d. 23, item 165, Grand Quartier Général.
72. Telegram no. 18 to Min. of Armaments, 28 June 1917, carton 181, d. Brigade russe, Thomas Papers; note by Thomas to cabinet, 30 June 1917.
73. Report of Min. Int., 8 July 1917, G: R, 765: 89.
74. Ibid.
75. Lissovsky, 274.
76. Report of Min. Int., 6 July 1917, G: R, 765: 85.
77. Lissovsky, 273.
78. Foch letter (Min. War) to PM, 10 July 1917, G: R, 765: 82-83.
79. Foch to Munitions, 9 July 1917, G: R, 765: 80-81.
80. Foch for MW to PM, 10 July 1917, G: R, 765: 82.
81. Ribot to Noulens, 13 July 1917, G: R, 765: 91-92.
82. Noulens to War, 13 July 1917, G: R, 765: 93.
83. Cambon to Amb. to Petrograd, 25 July 1917, G: R, 765: 111.
84. Ministerstvo inostrannykh del' SSSR, *Dokumenty vneshnei politiki SSSR* [hereafter cited as *D.V.P SSSR*] (Moscow: Gos. izdat., 1957), 1: 720, footnote.
85. Ribot to Noulens, 11 August 1917, G: R, 765: 154.
86. "Vosstanie russkikh soldat," *K. A.*, 99: 58.
87. For Vavilov's version, pp. see 43-45.
88. "Vosstanie russkikh soldat," *K. A.*, 99: 58.
89. Ibid., 59.
90. *Russkie soldaty vo Frantsii*, 8.
91. "Vosstanie," *K. A.*, 99: 59.
92. Ibid.
93. Poincaré, *Au Service*, 9: 218.
94. Poitevin, *Une Bataille*, 69-70.
95. Ibid., 70.
96. See the minutes in box 7 of the REF Papers.
97. Soldaty i ofitsery otriada, 30 June (o.s.) 1917, box 7, Protokoly otriadnogo komiteta, REF Papers.
98. Ibid., Protokol 23 July/5 August 1917.
99. Lissovsky, 272.
100. Vavilov, 39.
101. Kozlov, 25.
102. *Russkie soldaty vo Frantsii*, 9.
103. Lissovsky, 274.
104. Untitled memo dated 24 April 1918, 7N615, E-M de l'A; see also memo dated 27 July/August 9, 1917, spisok 1, box 57, REF Papers.
105. Trotsky, *History*, 2: 274.
106. Lissovsky, 278; Trotsky, *History*, 2: 274.
107. Poitevin, *Une Bataille*, 102.
108. Ibid., 103.
109. Vavilov, 39.

110. Poitevin, *Une Bataille*, 103.
111. Ioffe, 248.
112. Maurier (chef du 4e bureau), 24 July 1917, G: R, 765: 110.
113. Poitevin, *Une Bataille*, 86.
114. Painlevé to PM, 16 August 1917, G: R, 765: 158 ff.
115. Ibid.
116. Ibid.
117. Poitevin, *Une Bataille*, 106-107.
118. Note sur la discipline des Troupes Russes au Camp de Courneau, 14 September 1917, 7N611, d. 3, E-M de l'A.
119. Pattyn, 71.

Chapter 7

1. Gorky, "La Belle France," 7N642, d. Mikhailov, n.d.
2. Sun Tzu, 49.
3. Obey, 53.
4. G: R, 765: 107 ff.
5. "Ekaterinburgskaia tragediia," *Poslednaia novosti*, June 21, 1932, n. p.
6. Noulens, 2: 139.
7. Noulens to MFA (copy), 26 July 1917, carton 181, d. Brigades russes, Thomas Papers.
8. Dépêche télégraphique to Gen. Comby, n. d. 7N609, d. 1, E-M de l'A.
9. Noulens to MFA (copy), 27 July 1917, carton 181, d. Brigades russes, Thomas Papers.
10. Kerensky did decide to reestablish the death penalty in the army, but he had not announced it for fear of the Soviet's reaction.
11. Noulens to MFA (copy), 27 July 1917, carton 181, d. Brigades Russes, Thomas Papers.
12. Noulens to MFA, 8 august 1917, G: R, 765: 144.
13. Buchs to Fr. Govt., ibid., 145.
14. Foch to MW, 11 August 1917, G: R, 765: 148 ff.
15. "Vosstanie," *K. A.*, 99: 59-60.
16. Poitevin, *Une Bataille*, 112.
17. Telegram for the Préfet Maritime to Min. Marine, 11 July 1917, G: R, 765: 86.
18. Sevastopoulo to Fr. MFA forwarding Zankevich's letter, vol. 26, no. 7, p. 20, Doulcet Papers.
19. MFA to Kerensky, 13 August 1917, G: R, 765: 157-58.
20. Enclosed in Ignatiev to War, 31 July 1917, 7N610, d. 2, E-M de l'A.
21. Poitevin, *Une Bataille*, 108-109.
22. Ibid., 108-109.
23. "Vosstanie," *K. A.*, 99: 60.
24. Prikaz po 1-i osoboi pekhotnoi divisii, 27 August/9 September 1917, box 1, 20, REF Papers; Zankevich to MW, 10 September 1917, G: R, 765: 186.
25. MW to PM, 16 August 1917, G: R, 765: 158.
26. Williams, 226; Poitevin, *Une Bataille*, 91 ff.
27. Vavilov, 37-38.

28. Poitevin, *Une Bataille*, 91-92.
29. Ibid., 91-93.
30. Ibid., 94.
31. Ibid., 100.
32. Prikaze de la 1er division spécial no. 82, 24 July/6 August 1917, 17N649, d. 5, Missions militaires.
33. Poitevin, *Une Bataille*, 96.
34. "Vosstanie," *K. A.*, 99: 61.
35. Poitevin, *Une Bataille*, 105-106.
36. Noulens to MFA, 17 August 1917, G: R, 765: 164.
37. Poitevin, *Une Bataille*, 107.
38. Ribot to Noulens, 14 August 1917, G: R, 765: 162 ff.
39. Painlevé to Zankevich, 28 August 1917, G: R, 765: 174 ff.
40. Noulens to MFA, 1 September 1917, G: R, 765: 178.
41. Order no. 83 (from Felletin by Lokhvitsky), 24 July/6 August 1917, 17N649, d. 5, Missions Militaires.
42. Vavilov, 47.
43. Carnet de la Maréchal Foch, 4 August 1917, carton 5, no. 8, Foch Papers.
44. Poitevin, *Une Bataille*, 94-95.
45. Poincaré, *Au Service*, 9: 265.
46. Ioffe, 251.
47. War to Comby, 5 September 1917, 7N611, d. 2, E-M de l'A.
48. War (Vidalon) to Comby, 8 September 1917, 7N611, d. 2, E-M de l'A.
49. Poitevin, *Une Bataille*, 114.
50. Painlevé to PM, written in September, 1917, but for some reason hand-dated October 21, 1917, well after the revolt had been crushed. G: R, 765: 202; "Vosstanie," *K. A.*, 99: 61.
51. Lissovsky, 275.
52. Vidalon to War, 4 August 1917, 7N611, d. 3, E-M de l'A.
53. Poitevin, *Une Bataille*, 100.
54. Reed, 322-323.
55. Noulens to MFA, 1 September 1917, G: R, 765: 178.
56. "Vosstanie," *K. A.*, 99: 61-62.
57. Lissovsky, 275.
58. G. M. Derenkovsky, "Vosstanie russkikh soldat vo Frantsii v 1917 g.," *Istoricheskii zapiski*, 38 (1951): 91.
59. Poitevin, *Une Bataille*, 118.
60. Ibid., 132-133.
61. Ibid., 126-127.
62. Ibid., 103 and 119.
63. Ibid., 122.
64. Vavilov, 46.
65. Poitevin, *Une Bataille*, 119.
66. Ibid., 115-116.
67. Ibid., 130.
68. Gabriel Cluzeland, cited in ibid., 119-120.
69. "Vosstanie," *K. A.*, 99: 71.
70. Williams, 227; Poitevin, *Une Bataille*, 133.
71. "Vosstanie," *K. A.*, 99: 63-64; 67; Poitevin, *Une Bataille*, 124-125.

72. Poitevin, *Une Bataille*, 134-135; he does not give his source, but there is enough of a familiar ring that he may have paraphrased the other account.
73. "Vosstanie," *K. A.*, 99: 64-65.
74. Poitevin, *Une Bataille*, quoting Cluzeland, 138.
75. Ibid.
76. Ibid., 140.
77. "Vosstanie," *K. A.*, 99: 65-66.
78. *Izvestiia*, no. 249, 25/12 December 1917.
79. "Vosstanie," *K. A.*, 99: 66.
80. Poitevin, *Une Bataille*, 137, quoting Comby interview.
81. See REF Papers, box 1, 20.
82. Trotsky, 2: 274.
83. Poitevin, *Une Bataille*, 144.
84. Ibid., 142-143. Poitevin quotes Cluzeland.
85. Karev, 101 in Ioffe, 254. Once again Ioffe gives an incorrect page number.
86. Vavilov, 48.
87. Obey, 548.
88. Ibid., 548-549.
89. Reed, 323.
90. Watt, 274.
91. "Vosstanie," *K. A.*, 99: 67.
92. Ibid.
93. Ibid.
94. Vavilov, 49.
95. Poitevin, *Une Bataille*, 150, quoting Comby.
96. "Vosstanie," *K. A.*, 99: 68.
97. Ibid.
98. Ibid.
99. Vavilov, 48.
100. "Vosstanie," *K. A.*, 99: 71.
101. Poitevin, *Une Bataille*, 155.
102. Ibid., 151.
103. Lissovsky, 277.
104. "Vosstanie," *K. A.*, 99: 68.
105. Reed, 323.
106. Lissovsky, 277.
107. Foch to Cabinet, 23 September 1917, G: R, 764, 192 ff.
108. *Rabochii put'*, 4/17 October 1917, cited in Ioffe, 255.
109. Poitevin, *Une Bataille*, 156.
110. Robert Warth, *The Allies and the Russian Revolution* (Durham, N.C.: Duke University Press, 1954), 137.
111. Vavilov, 49-50.

Chapter 8

1. Question des troupes russes en France, n. d., 17N689, d. Brulard.

2. 11/24 October 1917, two in a packet entitled "Extraits des lettres, 8 November 1917," 7N611, E-Major de l'A.
3. 7N611, d. 2, E-M de l'A.
4. Rychlinski, 124.
5. *Russkie soldaty vo Frantsii,* 10.
6. Poitevin, *Une Bataille,* 161.
7. *Pravda,* May 29, 1924, no. 120, p. 8.
8. Note sur l'Emploi des troupes russes en France, 13 October 1917, 7N610, d. 1, E-M de l'A.
9. Poitevin, *Une Bataille,* 158.
10. Lissovsky, 277.
11. Ibid.; Obey, 551.
12. Lt. Col. Bureau Slav Cros, Note pour l'Etat-major de l'Armeé, 30 April 1918, 7N615, d. "Reseignments sur personnel russe, d. 1, E-M de l'A.; ibid., Bordereau d'Envoi, 4 April 1918.
13. Lissovsky, 278.
14. Poitevin, *Une Bataille,* 159.
15. PM to Com. 18e region, 29 December 1917, 7N611, d. 2, E-M de l'A.
16. Vavilov, 53.
17. Poitevin, *Une Bataille,* 165.
18. Comby to War, 8 November 1917, 7N611, d. 2, E-M de l'A.
19. General J. J. Pershing, *My Experiences in the World War* (New York: Stokes, 1931), 1: 211.
20. Major General James Harbord, *Leaves from a War Diary* (New York: Dodd, Mead, 1925), 191.
21. Quiquandon to PM, 3 November 1917, 7N611, d. 3, E-M de l'A.
22. Note, 27 November 1917, 7N603, d. 1, E-M de l'A.
23. Noulens to MFA, 27 September 1917, G: R, 765: 194.
24. Protokol, 19/1 October 1917, box 6, reel 6, REF Papers. I read some of these papers on microfilm, and it is not always clear where one box ended and another began. Therefore, when I am giving a source from my reading of filmed documents, I shall give the reel number.
25. Rapport au sujet de l'evacuation, etc., 20 October 1917, 7N611, d. 2, E-M de l'A.
26. Ibid.
27. Gen. Com. 18e region, 5 October 1917, 7N611, d. 3, E-M de l'A.
28. Pershing, 2: 207 and 211, respectively.
29. Rapport au sujet de la visite à l'Ile d'Aix du détachement russe, 5 October 1917, 7N611, d. 3, E-M de l'A.
30. Harbord, 192.
31. Gen. L'Espée to War, 8 December 1917, 7N610, d. 1, E-M de l'A.
32. From a pack of intercepted and translated Russian letters, c. October 1917, 7N611, d. 2, E-M de l'A; *Sotsial-Demokrat,* 11/24 October 1917.
33. There are two general sources for this "congress," two sets of minutes recorded that are contradictory in themselves and are somewhat incomplete. (1) 2e congress des Délégués des Troupes Russes en France (Résumé des Délibérations), 14N24, 12 November 1917, Fonds Joffre and Foch, Bibliothèque de l'Armée, Château de Vincennes, Paris, France, and Bordereau d'Envoi Etat-major de l'Armée, 1e bureau, Col. Cros, 10 October 1917, 7N611: 2.
34. Telegram 26/8 November 1917, box 7, reel 6, REF Papers.

35. Protokol, 13/26 October 1917, box 7, reel 6, REF Papers; 3/16 December 1917; 13/26 October 1917.

36. Protokol 7, 10/23 December 1917, ibid.

37. Protokol 45-57, 7 December 1917, box 58, reel 7, REF Papers.

38. Zankevich to Foch, 30 November 1917, 7N609, d. 1, E-M de l'A.

39. Prikaz po chastiam lia-Kurtinskago lagera, 26 November/9 December 1917, 7N611, d. 2, E-M de l'A.

40. Comby to War, 19 December 1917, 7N610, d. 1, E-M de l'A.

41. Note pour le Cabinet de Ministre, 12 Decembver 1917, 7N610, d. 1, E-M de l'A.

42. Révolutionnaires russes, December, n. d., 1917, F⁷12895, no dossier, Révolutionnaires russes, 1917.

43. Comby to War, 21 December 1917, 7N610, d. 1, E-M de l'A.

44. Note sur l'Emploi des troupes russes en France, 13 October 1917, 7N610, d. 1, E-M de l'A.

45. C-in-C to Chief of French Mission, 8 December 1917, 7N610, d. 1, E-M de l'A.

46. PM to Zankevich, 16 October 1917, 7N610, d. 1, E-M de l'A.

47. Sous-secrétaire d'Etat à la Marine des transports maritime de Marchande to PM, 6 October 1917, 7N610, d. 1, E-M de l'A; reply on 12 October 1917 attached.

48. Sous-secrétaire d'Etat pour Gen. Chef d'E.M.A., 23 December 1917, 7N611, d. 3, E-M de l'A.

49. Note relative aux conditions d'Emploi, 29 October 1917, 7N610, d. 1, and PM to Zankevich, 1 November 1917, 7N610, d. 1, E-M de l'A.

50. Debeney to Etat-major de l'Armée 1er bureau, 25 October 1917, 7N610, d. 1, E-M de l'A.

51. Zankevich to Foch, 20 October 1917, 7N610, d. 1, E-M de l'A.

52. Comby to Etat-major de l'Armée, 25 October 1917, 7N611, d. 3, E-M de l'A.

53. Fonssagrives to Cmd. 18e region, 25 October 1917, 7N610, d. 1, E-M de l'A.

54. Ibid.

55. Duboin to Vidalon, 11 December 1917, 7N610, d. 1, E-M de l'A.

56. Harbord, 191.

57. Tableau attached to PM to Zankevich , 1 November 1917, 7N610, d. 1, E-M de l'A.

58. Message Téléphone, 12 December 1917, 7N611, d. 2, E-M de l'A.

59. Note au sujet de l'Evacuation du Camp de la Courtine, 5 December 1917, 7N611, d. 2, E-M de l'A.

60. G: R, 765: 230-321.

61. Duboin to Vidalon, 14 December 1917, 7N610, d. 1, E-M de l'A.

62. Révolutionnaires russes, December, 1917, F⁷12895, no dossier, Révolutionnaires russes, 1917.

63. Foch to PM to Zankevich, 27 November 1917, 7N610, d. 1, E-M de l'A.

64. Cmdt. 13e région to War HQ Armée, 4e bureau, 25 October 1917, and conf. d'un Message Tél., 16 December 1917, both in 7N611, d. 2, E-M de l'A.

65. PM to Zankevich, 2 January 1918, ibid.

66. Alby for PM to Zankevich, 17 November 1917, 7N611, d. 1, E-M de l'A.

67. Questions soumises au Colonel . . . de son passage à l'Île d'Aix, 20 December 1918, 17N687, d. 47 irréductibles, Missions militaires.

68. Hallouin to Cmdt. 1st and 2nd subdivision, 30 December 1917, 7N611, d. 3, E-M de l'A.

69. Situation de l'Ile d'Aix, 1 January 1918, ibid.
70. PM (Vidalon) to Comby, 16 November 1917, ibid.
71. For examples, see Brulard to War, 7 February 1919, 17N656, d. 1, Missions militaires.
72. Kozlov, 57-60.
73. Ibid., 74
74. Ibid.
75. Ibid., 67-68.
76. Ibid., 76.
77. Ibid., 77-79.
78. Ibid., 81.
79. Ibid., 86.
80. Untitled list of rebel leaders, with their ranks, age, professions, etc., 15 June 1918, 17N687, Missions militaires.
81. See MFA to Noulens, 13 December 1917, 7N610, d. 1, E-M de l'A; Pattyn, 76.
82. Télégram, 4 December 1917, 7N611, d. 2, E-M de l'A; see also MW to Gen. Com.-in-chief Alger, 1 December 1917, 7N611.
83. Note au sujet de l'Evacuation du Camp de La Courtine, 5 December 1917, 7N611, d. 2, E-M de l'A.
84. Télégram chiffre, 17 December 1917, 7N610, d. 1, E-M de l'A.
85. Gen. Com 15e région [to?] Vice Adm Prefet Maritime Gov. Toulon, 18 December 1917, 7N610, d. 1, E-M de l'A.
86. Ligne républicaine russe, report, no date, 17N689, d. Brulard, Missions Militaires.
87. Bajolle to Gen. Cmdt. en chef des troupes françaises de l'Afrique de Nord, 5 February 1919, 7N636, d. 2, E-M de l'A.
88. Prefet du dept. de Constantine to Gov. Gen. Algeria, 123 August 1919, 7N636, d. 2, E-M de l'A.
89. American ambassador David Francis had purchased a Ford automobile to drive to the golf course, and it was indeed borrowed by the Russian government, but it only acted as an escort to the Pierce Arrow. It did, however, fly the American flag. Some distance outside the capital, however, it malfunctioned and had to be abandoned.
90. Poincaré, *Au Service*, 9: 357.
91. V. A. Maklakov to H. H. Fisher, 31 March 1934, box 2, Basil Maklakov Papers, The Hoover Institution, Stanford, California.
92. Vavilov, 54-55.
93. Zankevich's order of the day, 26 November 1917, no. 138, box 13, folder "Correspondence: General Zankevich, 1917," Russia. Posol'stvo (France).
94. Noulens report, 27 September 1917, G: R, 765: 194.
95. Noulens to MFA, 7 December 1917, 7N610, d. 1, E-M de l'A.
96. The French police maintained a close watch on these suspected Bolsheviks, keeping records on who had and had not returned to Russia during the year. See F⁷12895, Révolutionnaires russes, 1917, passim.
97. Mme Teoprieburg (?) to Min. Int., 12 October 1917, F⁷12895, d. Nov. 1917, Rév. russes, 1917.
98. Communiqué à Nice, etc., 27 November 1917, F⁷12895, d. November 1917, Rév. russes, 1917.

99. Letter with attachments, 20 October 1917, F⁷12895, d. October, Rév. rus., 1917.

100. See Commisserie (illigible) Spécial du Lerthus to le Directeur de la Sûreté Générale, 7-19 October 1917, F⁷12895, d. October, Rév. russes, 1917; Inf. no. 5905 R of 4 October 1918, transmitted from Madrid, 18 October 1918, F⁷12896, d. October 1918 and 02945u in d. Nov. 1918, Rév. russes, 1918.

101. Rapport mensuel, December 1917, F⁷12895, no dossier,

102. Rév. rus., 1917.

103. No title or date, F⁷12895, no dossier, Rév. russes, 1917.

104. Rapport Mensuel, December 1917, ibid.

105. La propagande pacifiste russe, 13 December 1917, ibid.

106. Message Téléphone, 2 December 1917, 7N611, d. 1, E-M de l'A; see also other reports in dossier 1.

107. Ben. Le Grand, Cmdt., 15e région to War, 28 November 1917, 7N611, d. 1, E-M de l'A.

108. 4 December 1917, ibid.

109. Note, 12 December 1917, 7N611, d. 2, E-M de l'A.

110. Noulens to MFA, 7 December 1917, G: R, 765: 225.

111. Albert Niessel, *Le Triomphe des Bolchéviques et la paix de Brest-Litovsk: Souvenirs, 1917-1918* (Paris: Plon, 1939), 160.

112. *Soldatskaia pravda*, no 45, 16/29 June 1917, cited in Ioffe, 242.

113. G: R, 765: 224.

114. Alby to War to Chef Mission Mil. Fr., 13 December 1917, 7N610, d. 1, E-M de l'A.

115. Ribot to Fr. Amb. London, 2 October 1917, G: R, 765: 195.

116. Sec. of War to F.O., under cover letter from O. Murry, 20 October 1917, 3016: 120, F. O. 371, General Correspondence, Public Record Office, London.

117. Cambon to MFA, 3 October 1917, G: R, 765: 201.

118. Cambon to Barthou, 30 October 1917, G: R, 765: 203-205.

119. MW to MFA, 19 November 1917, G: R, 765: 212-213.

120. Jusserand to MFA, 6 December 1917, G: R, 765: 228.

121. MFA to Fr. amb., 15 March 1918, 7N646, d. 1, E-M de l'A.

122. Tenley to Ct. 18e, 12 December 1917, 7N611, d. 3, E-M de l'A.

123. 124 Memo, G: R, 765: 230.

124. PM (Foch) to Zankevich, 15 December 1917, 7N610, d. 1, E-M de l'A.

125. Note pour le General, 15 December 1917, 7N610, d. 1, E-M de l'A; Note au sujet de l'Evacuation du camp de La Courtine, 5 December 1917, 7N611, d. 2.

126. Hallouin to PM-War, 26 December 1917, 7N611, d. 3, E-M de l'A.

127. Ibid.

128. 28 December 1917, ibid.

129. Cros to E. M. A. le bureau, 29 December 1917, 7N611, d. 3, E-M de l'A.

130. Order, 29 December 1917, 7N611, d. 3, E-M de l'A.

131. Rapport Mensuel, (January, 1918), F⁷12896, Rév. russes, 1918.

132. Tél. Mess. Cros to War, 1 January 1917 (sic but obviously 1918), 7N611, d. 3, E-M de l'A.

133. Ibid.

Chapter 9

1. Prince A. Lobanov-Rostovsky, *The Grinding Mill: Reminiscences of War and Revolution in Russia, 1913-1920* (New York: Macmillan, 1935), 381.

2. La Question des troupes russes en France, n. d., 17N689, d. Brulard, Missions Militaires.

3. Lissovsky to George Grigorevich [Kolykovsky], 3 August 1918, $F^7$12896, d. Août 1918, Révolutionnaires russes, 1918.

4. April report, n. d., $F^7$12896, d. April 1918, Rév. rus., 1918.

5. March report, ibid., d. Mars 1918.

6. Barjonet to off. regional 9th, 26 May 1918, 7N657, d. 2, E-M de l'A.

7. Rapport Mensuel, juin, n. d., $F^7$12786, d. Juin 1918, Rév. rus., 1918.

8. Memo, 30 December 1918, 5(1914-1918): 33-34, Stephen Pichon Papers, Archives du Ministère des Affaires Etrangères, Paris, France.

9. MFA to PM, 2 November 1918, 7N646, d. 1, E-M de l'A.

10. Rapport mensuel, October 1918, $F^7$12896, d. October 1918, Rév. rus., 1918.

11. Rapport mensuel, March, 1918, d. Mars 1918, ibid.

12. Min. Int. to MFA, 11 March 1918, G: R, 766: 127.

13. Lapidus to Russian embassy, 30 August 1918, box 32, d. Russian Army Abroad, Russia. Posol'stvo (France).

14. Memorandum, 24 July 1918, 7N633, d. 2, E-M de l'A.

15. Becker, 241-244.

16. Lapidus to embassy, 30 August 1918, box 32, d. Russian Army Abroad, Russia. Posol'stvo (France).

17. Lobanov-Rostovsky, 299.

18. PM (Alby) to Ignatiev, 16 February 1918, 7N623, d. 2, E-M de l'A.

19. D. A. Dans to War, 6 February 1918, 7N632, d. 2, E-M de l'A.

20. Barjonet to Cmdt. 18e région, 14 May 1918, 17N657, d. 2, Missions Militaires.

21. See 17N689, Missions Militaires, passim.

22. Rapport mensuel, May 1918, $F^7$12896, d. Mai 1918, Rév. rus., 1918.

23. *Pravda*, May 29, 1924, in an article entitled "In the Clutches of the Compassionate Frenchmen."

24. Relations avec l'Île d'Aix, n. d., ibid.

25. Barjonet of off. reg. 9e région, 18 June 1918, 17N657, d. 2, Missions Militaires.

26. Ibid.; Relations avec l'Île d'Aix, n. d., F712896, d. Août 1918, Rév. rus. 1918.

27. Message téléphone (Gen. 18th region to Col. Cros, 4 February 1918, 7N632, d. 2, E-M de l'A.

28. Baumgarten to War, 19 November 1917, 7N610, d. 1, E-M de l'A.

29. See numerous Rapports mensuels, n. d., $F^7$12896, d. Mai 1918, Rév. rus., 1918.

30. Carley, 33 ff.

31. Noulens to MFA, 27 April 1918, 7N646, d. 1, E-M de l'A; for the note in Russian see *D.V.P. SSSR*, 1: 253, footnote.

32. Pendries report, 18 May 1918, 7N646, d. 1, E-M de l'A.

33. Le Traitement . . . , 29 May 1918, ibid.

34. Rapport mensuel, July 1918, $F^7$12896, d. Juiller 1918, Rév. rus., 1918.

35. Pres. du Conseil, War to Gen. Cdt. des Armées du Nord et du Nord-Est et al., 29 August 1918, 7N633, d. 2, E-M de l'A.

36. Dutasta to MFA, War, 19 September 1918, 4N35, d. 3, Conseil Supérieur de Guerre.

37. MFA to PM, war, 19 October 1918, 7N646, d. 1.
38. Attaché Naval Londres to Marine, 29 November 1918, d. 1, no. 72, Eu. 1918-1940: Russie [hereafter cited as E: R].
39. PM to MFA, 31 January 1918, 7N646, d. 1, E-M de l'A.
40. G: R, 766: 46.
41. PM to Com. aux transports, maritimes, 15 February 1918, 7N646, d. 1, E-M de l'A.
42. Minute: procès-verbal de la Conference, 26 February 1918, ibid.
43. Attaché to War, 27 March 1918, ibid.
44. PM to Com. aux Transports Maritimes, 15 February 1918, ibid.
45. Rapport mensuel, Mai 1918, $F^7$12896, d. Mai 1918, Rév. rus., 1918.
46. See a list of officers to be repatriated, dated 27 April 1918, 7N646, d. 1, E-M de l'A.
47. Lokhvitsky to PM, 14 May 1918; Ren. sur Capt. Troitsky, 8 July 1918, ibid.
48. Jusserand to MFA, 7 March 1918, 7N646, d. 1, E-M de l'A.
49. Jusserand to MFA, 6 March 1918, G: R, 766: 119. Curiously the Russian "embassy" in Paris does not seem to have been informed of this hairbrained plan, probably because the French government felt that in any case, it did not concern it. There are no documents on this question in "Russia. Posol'stvo (U. S.), Box 1, correspondence, 1917-1918."
50. G: R, 766: 191.
51. Chef Mission to War, 23 April 1918, 7N646, d. 1, E-M de l'A.
52. Extrait du rapport du Capt. Terray, 20 May 1918, 7N646, d. 1, E-M de l'A.
53. Un nouveau journal russe, 3 December 1917, $F^7$12895, no dossier, Rév. rus., 1917.
54. Rapport mensuel, December, 1917, $F^7$12895, no dossier, Rév. rus., 1917.
55. *The Times* (London), 16 March 1918, p. 6.
56. Maklakov to H. H. Fisher, 31 March 1934, box 3, Maklakov Papers.
57. Ibid., 172.
58. Zankevich to Foch, 25 September 1917, and Clemenceau to Foch, 1 October 1917, 7N610, d. 1, E-M de l'A.
59. Zankevich to MW, 5 October 1917, 7N610, d. 1, E-M de l'A.
60. Fonssagrives to Cmdt. 18e région, 16 October 1917, 7N611, d. 3, E-M de l'A.
61. Harbord, 192.
62. Procès-Verbal, 10 December 1917, 7N632, d. 1, E-M de l'A.
63. V. Vasilev, "Russkii legion chesti," *Chasovoi*, no. 629 (January-February, 1981), 19-20.
64. Ibid., 20-24; see also M. A. Khasov's articled by the same title in *Kadetskaia pereklichka*, no. 46 (April, 1989), p. 87.
65. Ibid.
66. Khasov, "Russkii legion chesti," *Kadetskaia pereklichka*, p. 90.
67. See REF Papers, box 57, folder REF.
68. "Russkie soldaty," *K. A.*, 44: 158.
69. Vasiliev, "Russkii," *Chasovoi*, 21; see Khasoff article in *Kadetskaia pereklichka*, p. 91.
70. Note sur l'Etat-Major de l'Armée, 23 February 1918, 7N632, d. 2, E-M de l'A.
71. *L'Humanité*, 19 (?) December 1917, $F^7$12895, no dossier, Rév. rus., 1917; see also Appel de Gen. Lokhvitksy, 15 December 1917, 1256: 4, E: R.
72. Ibid.

73. Ioffe, 257 footnote.

74. G: R, 766: 211.

75. Gen. (name illigible) for Clemenceau to MFA, 11 March 1918, G: R, 766: 128.

76. Chef mission Française to War, 17 August 1918, 7N645, d. 2, E-M de l'A.

77. Barjonet to War, 20 March 1918, 7N612, d. Lég. Rus., 1.

78. Bouchez to Gen. Cdt. 1ère division Morocains, 1 November 1918, 7N612, d. Lég. rus., 2, E-M de l'A.

79. *The Times* (London), 4 April 1918, p. 7; Draft of call, n.d. n., F. O. 371, 3325: 464, General Correspondence.

80. See 7N612, d. Lég. rus. 1.

81. PM (Alby) to MFA, 18 February 1918, 7N632, d. 1, E-M de l'A.

82. 7N612, d. 2, E-M de l'A.

83. Rapport mensuel, Avril, 1918, F⁷12896, d. March 1918, Rév. rus., 1918.

84. Barjonet to War, 10 March 1918, 7N612, d. Lég. rus. 1; *The Times* (London), April 16, 1918, p. 5.

85. Vasiliev, "Russkii," *Chasovoi*, no. 629, p. 22.

86. Effectifs de la Légion russe, 21 April 1918, 7N614, d. Situation d'effectifs, E-M de l'A.

87. Danilov, 229-230.

88. Bouchez, 1 November 1918, 7N612, d. 2, E-M de l'A.

89. For organization, etc., see G: R, 765: 236 ff.

90. Instruction réglant l'organization et le commandment des contingents russes sur le territoire français, 21 December 1917 (date uncertain), 7N633, d. 1, E-M de l'A.

91. PM (Alby) to Zankevich, 6 January 1918, 7N637, d. 2, E-M de l'A; reply attached on January 7.

92. 17N655, d. 1, *passim*, Missions Militaires.

93. Lokhvitsky to PM and War, 18 February 1918, 7N632, d. 2, E-M de l'A.

94. Lobanov-Rostovsky, 290-291.

95. James Bunyan and H. H. Fisher, *The Bolshevik Revolution* (Stanford, Calif.: Stanford University Press, 1934), 523-24.

96. There follows after this statement a four-page legal defense of the question. Note pour l'Etat-Major de l'Armée, 4 March 1918, 7N612, d. Lég. rus., 1; See also MFA to PM, 26 March 1918, 7N612, d. Lég. rus. 1.

97. Barjonet to War, 6 March 1918, and Memo d'Etat-Major de l'Armée, 28 January 1918. 7N612, d. Lég. rus., 1, E-M de l'A.

98. *D.V.P. SSSR*, 1: 410, note 284.

99. Lokhvitsky to PM, 31 March 1918, G: R, 766, 183.

100. Danilov, *Russkie otriad*, 231.

101. Zankevich to PM and War, 10 January 1918, 7N632, d. 1, E-M de l'A.

102. Zankevich to PM, 30 January 1918, cover letter of Clemenceau to MFA, 4 February 1918, G: R, 766: 37-38.

103. Ibid.

104. Lokhvitsky to PM, War, 18 February 1918, 7N632, d. 2, E-M de l'A.

105. PM to Lokhvitsky, 7 March 1918, ibid.

106. Ibid.

107. Alexander Kerensky, *Russia and History's Turning Point* (New York: Duell, Sloan, and Pierce. 1967), 497.

108. Ibid., 498.

109. Ibid., 498-99.
110. Lokhvitsky to PM, 6 May 1918, 7N632, d. 3, E-M de l'A.
111. Daugan to Cmdt. chef, 3 June 1918, 7N612; *Chasovoi,* no. 629, p. 22.
112. Vasiliev, "Russkii," *Chasovoi,* 22.
113. Lokhvitsky to PM, 4 May 1918, 7N612, d. Lég. rus., 1, E-M de l'A.
114. Gerard to Pétain, 15 May 1918, 7N612, d. Lég. rus., 1, E-M de l'A.
115. Clemenceau to Lokhvitsky, 11 June 1918, 7N633, d. 1, E-M de l'A.
116. Barjonet to War, 5 June 1918, ibid.
117. Clemenceau to Lokhvitsky, 11 June 1918, ibid.
118. Ordre no. 112, 2/15 June 1918, 7N633, d. 1, E-M de l'A.
119. Brulard to War, 27 June 1918, 17N655, d. 2, Missions Militaires.
120. PM to Ignatiev, 1 July 1918, and Brulard to War, 27 June 1918, 7N633, d. 1, E-M de l'A.
121. Balbashevsky to Lokhvitsky, 3 July 1918, E: R, 1119: 66.
122. Lobanov-Rostovsky, 291.
123. Ibid.
124. Barjonet to War, 20 March 1918, 7N612, d. Lég. rus., 1, E-M de l'A.
125. Lobanov-Rostovsky, 293.
126. Télégram, 124 May 1918, 7N612, d. Lég. rus., 1, E-M de l'A.
127. Gen. ct. en Chef to War, 14 May, 1918, 6N285, d. Sept. 1918, Fonds particuliers.
128. Pétain to War, 20 May 1918, 7N612, d. Lég. rus., 2, E-M de l'A.
129. Extraits des Rapports mensuels, June 1918, and Bulletin confidential . . . , 15 June 1918, 7N614, d. Rapports mensuels, E-M de l'A.
130. Daugan to C-in-C, 24 June 1918, 17N668, d. 1, Missions Militaires.
131. Gen. C-in-C to Cmdt. GAE, 7 July 1918, 17N681, d. 43, Missions Militaires.
132. Gen. Brulard to War, 5 August 1918, 7N612, d. Lég. rus., 2, E-M de l'A.
133. For this account see P. 2531.U., 5 March 1918, F⁷12896, d. March 1918, Rév. rus., 1918.
134. Vos enfants de la Légion Russe to Brulard, 14 August 1918, 7N689, d. Brulard, E-M de l'A.

Chapter 10

1. Extraits des rapports mensuel, October, 1918, Contingents russes, 7N614, d. Lég. rus., 2, E-M de l'A.
2. La Question des troupes russes en France, n. d., 17N689, d. Brulard, Missions Militaires.
3. Carley, 163-164, citing "Review of the Political Situation in South Russia," 23 March 1919, F. O. 371, pp. 14-15.
4. *In Denikin's Russia* (New York: Arno, 1971), 32-33.
5. Ibid., 33.
6. Barjonet to War, 2 March 1918, 7N612, d. Lég. rus., 1, E-M de l'A.
7. Message Téléphon, 7 March 1918, ibid.
8. Vidalon to Gouv., 9 March 1918, ibid.
9. Télégram, 15 March 1918, ibid.
10. Barjonet to War, 10 April 1918, 7N655, d. 1, E-M de l'A.

11. Effectives de la Lég. rus., 10 April 1918, 7N612, d. Lég. rus. 1, E-M de l'A. Poitevin, as usual without giving his source, states a total of 1,625, with different numbers in the units.
12. Lobanov-Rostovsky, 293.
13. Khasov, "Russkii," *Kadetskaia pereklichka*, no. 46: 92-93.
14. Daugan to C-in-C, 1st Armée, 4 May 1918, 7N612, d. Lég. rus. 2, E-M de l'A.
15. Ordre général no. 96, 18 May 1918, 17N668, d. Lég. rus., Missions Militaires.
16. A la rédaction du journal *Le Soldat-Citoyen Russe*, n. d., 7N612, d. Lég. rus. 2, E-M de l'A.
17. Khasov, *Kadetskaia pereklichka*, no. 46: 97-98.
18. Ibid., 99-100.
19. See 17N668, d. 1, Missions Militaires.
20. REF Papers, 65-a, p. 43.
21. Execution de message téléphon, 30 May 1918, 17N655, d. 2, inter 175, Missions Militaires.
22. 17N668, d. 1, Missions Militaires, *passim*, Orders générals, no. 54R and 50R, 14 and 23 June 1918, 17N668, d. 1, Missions Militaires.
23. Poitevin, *Une Bataille*, 188.
24. Barjonet to War, 3 April 1918, 7N612, d. Lég. rus. 1, E-M d l'A.
25. Daugan to C-in-C, 4 May 1918, ibid.
26. *Le Temps*, 16 August 1918, cited in Serge Persky, *De Nicholas II à Lénine* (Paris: Payot, 1919), 131.
27. Khasov, *Kadetskaia pereklichka*, no. 43: 105.
28. Notice faisant ressortir . . . , 29 October 1918, 7N612, d. Lég. rus. 2, E-M de l'A.
29. Khasov, *Kadetskaia pereklichka*, no. 43: 106.
30. Ibid.
31. Ibid., 111.
32. Ibid., 112.
33. Ibid., 113.
34. Gen. C-in-C to War, 3 October 1918, 7N612, d. Lég. rus., 2, E-M de l'A.
35. Khasov, *Kadetskaia pereklichka*, no. 43: 111.
36. Matte to War, 17 September 1918, 4N46, d. 2, Conseil supérieur.
37. Donovan Webster, "The Soldiers Moved On. The War Moved On. The Bombs Stayed," *Smithsonian*, 24, no. 11 (February, 1994): 29.
38. *Voices*, 263.
39. Note au sujet de l'envoi éventuel au Maroc des contingents russes, 9 October 1918, 7N612, d. Lég. rus. 2, E-M de l'A.
40. War to Rabat, 15 November 1918, ibid.
41. Dissolution de la Base Russe de Laval, n. d., 7N636, d. 1, E-M de l'A; see also REF Papers, CW: Evacuation.
42. Contingents russes--situation actuelle, n.d. (Dec. 1918), 17N689, d. Brulard, Missions Militaires.
43. Note, 13 December 1918, 7N646, d. Rapatriement (Questions, etc.), E-M de l'A.
44. Lt. Lestideau to Brulard, 22 December 1918, 17N689, d. Brulard, Missions Militaires.
45. Lt. Delechesn to Cmdt. Base Russe, 11 January 1920, ibid.
46. Nadine Stchoupak to Capt. Cmdt. de la compagne russe, 4 February 1919, ibid.
47. Brulard to War, 15 March 1919, 17N656, d. 1, Missions Militaires.

48. Globa to Nachalnik russkoi basy, 22 February 1919, ibid.
49. Brulard to War, 15 March 1919, 17N656, d. 1, Missions Militaires.
50. A. Zitrone to J. Baltais, 11 February 1919, 17N687, d. 47 irréductibles.
51. Brulard to War, 12 April 1919, 17N656, d. 1, Missions Militaires; PM (Vidalon) to Pogouliaeff, 15 April 1919, 7N646, d. 2, E-M de l'A.
52. *D.V.P. SSSR,* 1: 720 (footnote).
53. Ibid., 1: 422, note 299.
54. Thiébaut to MFA, 13 August 1918, 168: 22, E: R.
55. *D.V.P. SSSR,* 1: 432-33, note 311. They had in the meantime approached both the Dutch and the Germans on the matter. See pages 427, 305, 661-662, note 328.
56. Thiébaut to MFA, 13 August 1918, 168: 24, E: R.
57. Ibid., p. 26-27.
58. Conty to MFA, 22 August 1918, 168: 34, E: R.
59. *The Times* (London), 7 September 1918, p. 6.
60. Conty to MFA, 29 August 1918, 168: 49, E: R.
61. Annexe de la Dépêche de l'Amb. de la France à Berne, 2 September 1918, 168: 111, E: R.
62. Ibid., various papers and 111-139.
63. Misc. letters between MFA and the missions in Stockholm, Christiana, Copenhagen, etc., 169: 166-181, E: R.
64. Thiébaut to MFA, 7 October 1918, 169: 186, E: R.
65. Ibid., 170: 28.
66. Ibid., 41.
67. Bapst to MFA, 18 October 1918, 170: 64, ibid.; unknown author to M. de Travaux Public, 25 October 1918, 170: 103, ibid.
68. Conty to MFA, 26 October 1918, 170: 76, ibid.
69. Note concernant M. Pierre Darcy, 1 September 1918, 168: 103-104, E: R.
70. Radio aux Maximalists, 10 November 1918, 170: 156, ibid.
71. MFA to Stockholm/Copenhagen, 5 December 1918, 171: 22, E: R.
72. Brig. Gen. E. L. Spears to Col. R. A., Steel, 9 December 1918, W. O 106/1251, no. 88, Directory of Military Operations and Intelligence.
73. See Beziehungen zwischen Russland und Frankreich, 31 December 1916-1 January 1920, Ausärtiges Amt, Berlin, Germany, *Passim.*
74. Radio à Envoyer, 9 December 1918, 171: 54, E: R.
75. Chicherin (Tchicherine) to Paris par radio, 11 December 1918, 171: 63-65, E: R.
76. Nouvel avertissement français au gouvernment des Soviets, 20 December 1918, 171: 141, E: R.
77. Commissaire aux Transports maritime to PM, 18 December 1918, 171: 165, E: R.
78. Copie, no. 1316 *(extreme urgence)*, 27 December 1918, 7N646, d. Rapatriement (divers), E-M de l'A.
79. Memo, 30 December 1918, 5: 33, Pichon Papers.
80. Ibid., 34.
81. MFA to Soviet Government, 27 December 1918, 172: 18-20, E: R.
82. *D.V.P. SSSR,* 1: 635, no. 459.
83. Radio no 1, 1 January 1919, 5: 35, Pichon Papers.
84. MFA to PM, War, 11 January 1919, 7N646, d. Rapatriement (divers), E-M de l'A.

85. Senders and receivers unclear, 7 January 1919, 172: 115, E: R.
86. Pichon to Copenhagen/Stockholm, 13 January 1919, 172: 166-67, E: R.
87. Delavaud to MFA, 16 January 1919, 173: 2, E: R.
88. Chicherin to MFA, 16 January 1919, 173: 11, E: R.
89. Chicherin to MFA, 21 January 1919, 173: 35, E: R.
90. Radio, 28 January 1919, 7N646, d. Rapatriement (divers), E-M de l'A.
91. Ibid.
92. Delavaud to MFA, 28 January 1919, 173: 90, E: R.
93. MFA to Peoples' Com. For. Aff., 5 February 1919, 173: 161, E: R.
94. Brugère to MFA, no. 75 (copie), 27 January 1919, 7N646, d. Rapatriement (divers), E-M de l'A.
95. Rapport, 17 April 1919, 1255: 129, E: R.
96. Lt. de Vaisseau *Vallée* to Vice-amiral chef-d'état major général, 25 February 1919, 174: 84, E: R.
97. Radio, 31 January 1919, 7N646, d. Rapatriement (divers), E-M de l'A.
98. Lt. de Vaisseau *Vallée* to le Vice-amiral Chef d'Etat-major général, 25 February 1919, 7N646, d Rapatriement (divers), E-M de l'A.
99. Ministers at Copenhagen and Stockholm, 31 January 1919, ibid.
100. MFA to PM, 17 February 1919, 174: 17; Russian embassy to MFA, 22 (?) February 1919, p. 37, E: R.
101. MFA to PM, 26 February 1919, 174: 64, E: R.
102. MFA to Min. Copenhagen, 1 March 1919, 174: 76, E: R.
103. *Le Petit Parisien,* p. 25
104. Projet de Réglementation, 15 April 1919, 175: 143-45, E: R.
105. MFA to Consulate Helsinki, 15 April 1919, 175: 154, E: R.
106. Delegation Française des Sections Ravitaillement to Transports maritime, 15 April 1919, 175: 182, E: R.
107. Sous-secrétaire (Revitaillement) to Adolf Torngren, 15 April 1919, ibid., p. 183.
108. L du Départe to Russian embassy, 15 April 1919, ibid., p. 184.
109. Radiogram to Paris, 16 April 1919, ibid., p. 186.
110. PM to Min. Int., 14 October 1920 (cover letter of memo to bring it up to date), 2: 1, E: R
111. Radio aux Commissaires du Peuple-Moscou, 6 April 1919, 175: 52-56, E: R.
112. 113 Projet de Radio, 11 April 1919, ibid., p. 7-8.
113. Projet d'enlèvement de la Délégation russe, 14 April 1919, ibid., p. 133.
114. Ibid., p. 134.
115. Ibid., p. 135.
116. Ibid., p. 137-38.
117. Declarations de Manouilsky, 15 April 1919, ibid., p. 174-75.
118. Radiogram, 16 April 1919, ibid., p. 176.
119. Pichon to Min. Copenhagen, 18 April 1919, 176: no page number, E: R.
120. See Rapatriement des Russes de France Mission Manouilsky, 22 February-18 April 1919, Rapports du Lieutenant Colonel Wehrlin, 18 April 1919. Also includes a report by Colonel Jacques Langlois, ibid., 131-150.
121. Radio de Moscou, no. 395, 9 May 1919, 7N646, d. Ra. (divers), E-M de l'A.
122. Radio de Moscou to MFA, 9 May 1919, 177: 158, E: R.
123. Conty to MFA, 15 May 1919, 177: 194, E: R.
124. MFA to Mins. Stockholm/Copenhagen, 16 May 1919, ibid., p. 205.
125. Conty to MFA, 20 May 1919, ibid., p. 227.

126. CPAE to Pichon, 29 May 1919, 178: 43, E: R.
127. Series of letters and memos, ibid., p. 45-54.
128. Note pour le ministre, 4 June 1919, 1255: 140, E: R.
129. Delavaud to MFA, 5 June 1919, ibid., 99.
130. Confidential memo of Delavaud, 8 July 1919, Z607-1 2: 22, E: R.
131. Delavaud to MFA, 7 June 1919, 178: 125, E: R.
132. CPAE to MFA, 7 June 1919, ibid., 128.
133. Radio, 7 June 1919, 7N646, d. Rap. (questions, etc.), E-M de l'A.
134. MFA to CPAE, 1 July 1919, 179: 3, E: R; Procès-verbal, 5 June 1919, 179: 14-16, E: R.
135. Radio pour les Com. du Peuple à Moscou, 1 July 1919, 7N647, d. 1, E-M de l'A.
136. Radio pour le Com. de Peuple, 10 July 1919, ibid.
137. PM to MFA, 18 July 1919, ibid.
138. Ibid., 81.
139. Chicherin to MFA, 22 July 1919, ibid., 90.
140. MFA to Fr. Amb. at London, 23 July 1919, ibid., p. 95.
141. MFA to CPAE, 4 August 1919, ibid., 158.
142. MFA to Min. Int., 6 October 1919, 180: 252, E: R.
143. Series of letters, 29 May 1919 ff., 180: 74-82; Defrance to FMA, 4 September 1919, 180: 96, E: R.
144. Amiral D. N. B. O. to Marine, 29 August 1919, ibid., 71.
145. Radio de Moscou, 29 November 1919, 181: 119, E: R.
146. Denikin to Fr. govt., 4 January 1920, 182: 2-3, E: R.
147. For a list of all Frenchmen still in Russia, see ibid., 128-43.
148. Ibid., 183: 64-137; for the full accord, see Duchesne to Litvinov, 21 April 1920, 7N647, d. 2.
149. Paléologue to French Min. Stockholm, 23 July 1920, 8: Personnel diplomatique et consulair, II.
150. War to Min. Int., n.d., (probably December 1918), 7N646, d. 1, E-M de l'A.
151. P.1663, 24 April 1919, F^{7}13488, d. Avril 1919, Russia, 1919.
152. Clemenceau to Cmdt. Base Russe, 4 February 1919, 7N646, d. Rap. (Questions, etc.), E-M de l'A.
153. Pagoulaev to PM, 29 April 1919, 7N634, d. Base russe, May 1919-August 1919, E-M de l'A.
154. Procès-verbal de la conference interministerielle, 13 June 1919, 7N646, d. Rap. (questions, etc.), E-M de l'A.
155. Clemenceau to Cmdt. Salonique and Berthelot, 30 January 1919, 7N646. d. Rap. (questions), E-M de l'A.
156. Rapport mensuel, Avril 1919, F^{7}13488, d. April 1919, Russia, 1919.
157. See Punition, 10 April 1919, 7N646, d. 2, E-M de l'A.
158. REF Papers, box 5, folder 1.
159. W. H. Bartholomew to Lt. Gen. N. Yermoloff, 10 October 1919, Box 59, folder 236, Vrangel Archives.
160. Note, 20 January 1920, 7N647, d. 1, Rap. (dépêches), E-M de l'A.
161. E: R, 185: 2.
162. Ibid., 249; 188: 33.
163. Ibid., 188: 87.
164. Ibid., 107 and 124.

Chapter 11

1. Sun Tzu, 35.
2. Brulard to MW, 20 November 1918, 7N612, d. Lég. rus. 2, E-M de l'A.
3. "In Defense of the body of Officers of Russia," by N. Shivotovsky, Paris. 21: 158, E: R.
4. Anton Denikine, *The White Army*, tr. by Catherine Zveginstvo, (Gulf Breeze, Miss.: Academic International Press, 1973), 238.
5. Eugene Reichardt, a Russian hussar in World War I, in a conversation with the author in the early 1980s.
6. Carley, 107.
7. Ibid., 122.
8. *Pravda*, February 17, 1918, cited in Noulens, *Mon Ambassade*, 1: 152, cited in Peake, 176.
9. Lobanov-Rostovsky, 320.
10. Denikine, *White Army*, 244-225.
11. George Brinkley, *The Volunteer Army and Allied Intervention in South Russia, 1917-1921* (Notre Dame, Ind.: University of Notre Dame Press, 1966), 216-217.
12. George Stewart, *The White Armies of Russia: A Chronicle of Counter-Revolution and Allied Intervention* (New York: Russell and Russell, 1933), 423.
13. Peter Kenez, *Civil War in South Russia, 1919-1920* (Berkeley, Calif.: University of California Press, 1977), 95.
14. Carley, 176 ff.
15. Denikin, *White Army*, 260; Kenez, 51, citing A. I. Egorov, *Razgrom Denikina* (Moscow, 1931), 71.
16. Carley, 114 ff.
17. Rapport fait au ministre, 5 July 1918, 21: 25-26, E: R.
18. Note sur la formation d'un Détachement Russe en France en vue de l'intervention des Alliés en France, n. d., c. August 1918, 7N612, E-M de l'A.
19. Documents remis par le Général Nechvolodov, 15 April 1918, 7N615, d. Cooperation Alliée en Russie, E-M de l'A.
20. Rapport et Memoir, 11 July 1918, 21: 1-26, E: R.
21. 21 PM to MFA, 26 July 1918, 21: 22-23, E: R.
22. Analyse: utilization du personnel russe de France, etc., 5 July 1918, 4N35, d. "Russe," Conseil supérieur de Guerre.
23. Poincaré, 10: 175.
24. Lokhvitsky to Pres. du Conseil and War, 22 May 1918, 7N633, d. 1, E-M de l'A.
25. Lokhvitsky note, 19 November 1918, 21: 17-18, E: R.
26. He suggested to Foch a scheme to form two companies of volunteers, adding that if it brought good results, the French government might consider creating others. Written by Gen. Sigillis for Clemenceau to Foch (?), 26 July 1918, 21: 23-24, E: R.
27. Clemenceau to MFA, 31 July 1918, 4N35, folder "Russe," Conseil supérieur de Guerre.
28. Note sur la formation d'un Détachement russe en France, etc., hand-dated 23 August 1918, 4N35, 3, folder "Russe," Conseil supérieur de Guerre.
29. Ibid.

30. Appel à tous les militaires russes et à tous les citoyens russes en France" (draft), hand-dated 23 August 1918, 4N35, 3, folder "Russe," Conseil supérieur de Guerre.

31. PM-War to Belin, 27 August 1918, ibid.

32. Col. Bouchez's evaluation report, 15 December 1918, ibid.

33. Prikaz, 18 December 1918, box 58, REF Papers.

34. See 17N689, d. 7, Missions Militaires.

35. PM to Shcherbachev, 27 January 1920, 7N636, d. 1, E-M de l'A.

36. Note, 14 June 1919, 7N646, d. Rap. (Questions, etc.), E-M de l'A.

37. Aublet to Brulard, 1 February 1919, 17N689, d. Brulard, E-M de l'A.

38. A/S du Mikhailov, 27 February 1919, F⁷13488, d. Mars 1919, Russia, 1919.

39. War office to Under-Sec. State for F. O., 30 August 1918, F. O. 371, 3288: 183, General Correspondence.

40. H. C. Roberts to Director of Mil. Int., 26 September 1918, F. O. 371, 3346: 537-38.

41. Résumé de mémoire du Général Miller, 15 November 1918, 7N633, d. 3, E-M de l'A.

42. Ibid.

43. Noulens to MFA, 19 November 1918, 21: 76, E: R.

44. Télégram chiffre, 21 January 1919, 7N645, d. 2, arc. Matushevsky, E-M de l'A.

45. Draft minutes of cabinet meeting, 27 June 1919, W. O. 106/5930: 7, Directory of Military Operations and Intelligence.

46. PM to Gen. Berthelot, 7N646, d. Rapatriement (Questions, etc.), E-M de l'A.

47. PM and War to Gen. Cdt. Base russe, 28 December 1918, 17N689, d. 8, Missions Militaires.

48. Gotua to Cmdt. Base russe, 6 January 1919, 17N657, d. 3, Missions Militaires.

49. See 7N645, d. 2, *passim*.

50. Denikine, *White Army*, 224.

51. Date not copied on this. Note sur rapat. des Russes, n. d., by Lt. Col. Cros, chef de Bureau Salve, 7N646, d. Rapt. (Questions, etc.), E-M de l'A.

52. Br.-Gen. E. L. Spears to Corvisart, 28 February 1919, W. O. 106/1252, Directory of Military Operations and Intelligence.

53. PM to Brulard, n. d., c. May 1919, 7N646, d. 2, "Buenos Aires," E-M de l'A.

54. Brulard to War, 21 February 1919, 17N689, d. Brulard, Missions Militaires.

55. Rapport mensuel, Mai 1919, n. d., F⁷13488, d. Mai 1919, Russia, 1919.

56. *Humanité*, 3 June 1919, F⁷13488, d. June 1919, Russia, 1919.

57. Copy of Saraikin letter, August 1919, 17N687, d. 47 irréductibles.

58. Note, 24 June 1919, 7N646, d. "Imperator," E-M de l'A.

59. Kenez, 23-24.

60. Dispatch untitled from Br. Amb. in Paris, 2 August 1919, 7N647, d. 1, E-M de l'A.

61. *Pravda*, 29 May 1924, p. 8.

62. Franchet d'Esperey to War, 31 October 1919, 7N647, d. 1, E-M de l'A.

63. Mangin to War, 25 November 1919, ibid.

64. Note au sujet du rapatriement des Russes, 12 November 1919, ibid.

65. Gassouin to Gen. Cmdt. Armées Alliés Orient, 27 January 1920, ibid.

66. Cmdt. Etievant to War, 7 August 1920, 7N647, d. 2, E-M de l'A.

67. *Urgent* [memo], 25 June 1918, 7N633, d. 1, E-M de l'A; Note sur Intervention Alliée 1 August 1918, 7N615, d. Cooperation Alliée en Russie, E-M de l'A.

68. Note sur la formation d'un Détachement Russe en France, 23 August 1918, 7N615, d. Cooperation Alliée en Russie, E-M de l'A.

69. 17N681, *passim*; Peter Fleming, *The Fate of Admiral Kolchak* (London: Rupert Hart-Davis, 1963), 197.

70. Pogulaev to PM, 14 August 1919, 7N646, d. 2, E-M de l'A.

71. Note pour l'Etat-major de l'Armée. 25 October 1918, 7N615, d. Cooperation Alliée en Russie, E-M de l'A.

72. Br. Gen. E. A. Spears note to Gen. Corvisart, 8 February 1919, W. O. 106/1252, Directory of Military Operation and Intelligence.

73. John Bradley, *Allied Intervention in Russia* (New York: Basic Books, 1968), 119.

74. Pierre Janin, *Ma Mission en Sibérie* (Paris: Payot, 1933), 149.

75. Stewart, 284.

76. Janin, 149.

77. Chef mission Français to War, no. 2328, 6 October 1919, 5N185, d. Sibérie, Omsk, etc., October 1919, Cabinet du Ministre.

78. Janin to War, 14 February 1920, 6N228, d. 1920, Fonds Particuliers.

79. See L. H. Grondis, *La Guerre en Russie et en Sibérie* (Paris, 1926) or his *Le Cas Koltchak*, cited in Fleming, 173.

80. Janin, 221.

81. Ibid., 220.

82. Bulletin de Presse, 4 January 1920 (?), 17N620, d. Aff. Irkutsk, Missions Militaires.

83. Stewart, 406.

84. Cmdt. Base Français in Vladivostok to War, 28 November 1919, 5N185, d. Sibérie et Russie méridionale, Cabinet du Ministre.

Epilogue

1. William Chapin Huntington, *The Homesick Million: Russia-out-of-Russia* (Boston: Stratford Co., 1933), 29.

2. Inscription on the monument to the dead at the Russian Cemetery at Mourmel-on-le-Grand.

3. Memoirs, 1: 265, dossier II in only carton, flier "L'URSS n'est pas la Russie," Nekrachevich Papers.

4. Frequently made remark to Vladimir Volkoff, a French writer of Russian descent, who was born in Paris and grew up in the Russian émigré community in France.

5. Extrait du Rap. no. 63 du Général de Boissoudy, 19 August 1920, 7N635, d. Base russe, 1920-23, E-M de l'A.

6. Situation d'effectifs états du personnel russe, 7N635, E-M de l'A.

7. Situation actuelle des contingents russes, n.d. (c. January-March 1920, 7N652, d. Dissolution, E-M de l'A.

8. PM to Col. Narboutt (sic), 19 September 1919, box 5, Civil War: Convoys . . . transport, REF Papers.

9. *D.V.P. SSSR,* 1: 720-21, footnote.

10. Perlier to War, 17 August 1922, 7N648, d. 2, E-M de l'A.

11. War to Cherbatochev, 17 June 1920, box 5, Civil War: Correspondence . . . , REF Papers.
12. Memo, 2 June 1922, 7N636, d. 1, E-M de l'A.
13. 7N636, d. 1 and 7N647, d. 2, russes repatriement.
14. Untitled and unsigned memo, 7 June 1924, carton 210, d. 4, Painlevé Papers.
15. Mikhailov to PM, 15 November 1919, 7N642, d. Mikhailov, E-M de l'A.
16. Russes ayant demandé à être rapatriés en Russie soviétique, n.d., apparently late 1921, 7N648, d. 1, E-M de l'A.
17. See box 4, untitled folder, REF Papers.
18. Rapport Mensuel, November 1919, $F^7$13488, d. November 1919, Russia, 1919.
19. Mikhailov to War, 28 May 1920, 7N642, d. Mikhailov, E-M de l'A.
20. Mikhailov to PM, 15 November 1919, ibid.
21. Huntington, 25-26.
22. Ibid., 22.
23. Huntington, 249.
24. Collection of letters on Razumov, c. 1923, 7N636, d. 1, E-M de l'A.
25. Fournier to Mme. Lejars, 27 April 1923, 7N636, d. 1, E-M de l'A.
26. War to General Miller, 28 September 1921, 7N644, d. 2, E-M de l'A.
27. Brulard to War, 3 May 1919, 17N656, d. 1, Missions Militaires.
28. Janin to War, 14 February 1920, 7N228, d. 1920, E-M de l'A.
29. P. 3357, u., 6 September 1919, $F^7$13488, d. September 1919, Russia, 1919.
30. Note sur Mr. (sic) Mikhailov, 25 November 1920, 7N642, d. Mikhailov, E-M de l'A.
31. Service de la Press Slave, no. 1391, 19 November 1920, ibid.
32. Anton Denikin, *Career of a Tsarist Officer: Memoirs, 1872-1916* (Minneapolis: University of Minnesota, 1975), 314.
33. War to Navy, 16 June 1920, 7N647, d. 2, II secret, E-M de l'A.
34. Kozlov, 91-131.
35. On her affair with Maslov, see Erika Ostrovsky, *Eye of Dawn: The Rise and Fall of Mata Hari* (New York: Dorset Press, 1978), 183-184.
36. Nikita Khrushchev, *Khrushchev Remembers*, tr. by Strobe Talbot (Boston: Little, Brown, 1970), 202.
37. This story was told me by Vladimir Volkoff.
38. Alexander Solzhenitsyn, *The Gulag Archipelago* (New York: Harper & Row, 1974), 1: 131.
39. Note sur le Général Marouchewsky, January 1922, 7N645, d. 1, E-M de l'A.
40. Popougaev to PM, War, 25 June 1919, box 58, reel 9, REF Papers.
41. Bordeau d'Envoi, 5 June 1918, 7N633, d. 1, E-M de l'A.
42. Unknown author to Palitsyn, 6 December 1918, box 9, folder "Palitsyn," Russia. Posol'stvo (France).
43. Zapiski Generala F. Palitsyna, part II, p. 631a, Palitsyn Papers.
44. Helene Izvolsky, *No Time to Grieve* (Philadelphia: Winchell Press, 1974), 115.
45. See also Teddy J. Uldricks, "Ignat'ev, Aleksei Alekseevich," *The Modern Encyclopedia of Russian and Soviet History* (Gulf Breeze, Miss. : Academic International Press, 1979), 14: 124-125.
46. Lokhvitsky Bordereau, 14 June 1923, 7N635, d. Divers, E-M de l'A.
47. *Figaro*, November 8, 1933, p. 3.
48. Khazov, *Kadetskaia pereklichka*, no. 46 (April, 1989), 66-67.

49. Michka, ourse mascotte russe, filleulede Paris, n. d., 1919, 17N668, d. 1, Missions Militaires.
50. Khasov, *Kadetskaia,* 116.
51. D. Varenov to the author, 30 December 1986.
52. Kolomitsev interview, November 1985.
53. Leonard V. Smith, *Between Mutiny and Obedience: The Case of the French Fifth Infantry Division during World War I* (Princeton: Princeton University Press, 1994).

Bibliography

ARCHIVES

Berlin. Auswärtiges Amt.
Russland 82, no. 3. Russische Generäle, Series I, 1 January 1912-1920
Russland 91. Beziehungen zwischen Russland und
Frankreich, 31 December 1916-1 January 1920

London. The Public Record Office.
CAB 23 Cabinet Minutes
CAB 37 Cabinet Papers (minutes before 1916)
F. O. 371 General Correspondence: Political
W. O. 95 War Diaries
W. O. 106 Directory of Military Operations and Intelligence
W. O. 158 Correspondence and Papers of the Military HQ
W. O. 161 Misc. and unregistered papers

New York. Columbia University. Bakhmetev Archive.
Col. Mikhail V. Karkhanin Papers
Petr V. Mironov Papers
Genera. Mikhail D. Nechvolodov Papers
Genera. Fedor F. Palitsyn Papers
Russian Expeditionary Force Papers
Vladimir N. Smirnov Papers

Paris. Archives de la Bibliothèque Nationale.
Papiers Raymond Poincaré

Paris. Archives du Ministère des Affaires Étrangères.
Europe, 1918-1940: Russie
Guerre, 1914-1918: Russie
Papiers Jules Cambon
Papiers Jean Doulcet
Papiers Maurice Paléologue
Papiers Stéphan Pichon

Paris. Archives Nationales.
Ministère de l'Intérieur. Police générale.

$F^7$12895 Révolutionnaires russes, 1917

$F^7$12896 Révolutionnaires russes, 1918

$F^7$12911 Propagande antimilitariste, 1912-1917

$F^7$13370 Propagande pacifiste, 1915-1919

F713487 Russie, 1914-1918

$F^7$13488 Russie, 1919

Papiers Aristide Briand 313 AP

Papiers Ferdinand Foch 414 AP

Papiers Paul Painlevé 313 AP

Papiers Alexandre Ribot

Papiers Charles Mangin 149 AP

Papiers Général Nekrachewitch 65 AP

Papiers Albert Thomas 94 AP

Paris. Chateau de Vincennes. Bibliothèque des Armées.

4N Conseil supérieur de Guerre, Section française

5N Cabinet du Ministre

6N Fonds particuliers: Poincaré, Gallièni, Clemenceau

7N État-major de l'armée

14N Fonds Joffre et Foch

16N Grand Quartier Général

17N Missions militaires françaises près des Armées Alliés

19N Les Armées

Stanford, California. The Hoover Institution.

V. A. Maklakov Papers

F. F. Palitsyn Papers

Russia. Posol'stvo (France)

Russia. Posol'stvo (U. S.)

General Peter Wrangel Military Papers

Washington. National Archives.

M-560 Records of the Department of State relating to Internal Affairs of France, 1910-1929

M-568 Records of the Department of State relating to Political Relations between the United States and France, 1910-1929

M-569 Records of the Department of State relating to Political Relations between France and other States, 1910-1929

ARTICLES AND BOOKS

Akademiia nauk SSSR. Institut istorii. *Pervaia mirovaia voina, 1914-1918 gg.* Moscow: Izdatel'stvo "Nauka," 1968.

Bathe, Rolf. *Frankreichs schweiste Stunde; die Meuterei der Armee 1917.* Pottsdam: Protte, 1937.

Becker, Jean-Jacques. *The Great War and the French People.* New York: St. Martin's, 1986.

Bertie. L. *The Diary of Lord Bertie of Thame, 1914-1918.* 2 vols. New York: Doran, 1924.

Blake, R., ed. *The Private Papers of Douglas Haig, 1914-1919.* London: Eyre and Spottiswoode, 1952.

Borisov, IU. V. *Sovetsko-frantsuzskie otnoshenie (1924-1945).* Moscow: Izd. "Mezhd. otnosh.," 1964.

Bradley, John. *Allied Intervention in Russia.* New York: Basic Books, 1968.

Brinkley, George. *The Volunteer Army and Allied Intervention in South Russia, 1917-1921.* South Bend, Ind.: University of Notre Dame Press, 1970.

Browder, Robert, and Kerensky, Alexander, eds. *The Russian Provisional Government.* 3 vols. Stanford, Calif.: Stanford University Press, 1961.

Brusilov, Aleksei A. *A Soldier's Notebook, 1914-1918.* Westport, Conn.: Greenwood Press, 1970.

Buchanan, Sir George. *My Mission to Russia and Other Diplomatic Memories.* 2 vols. Boston: Little, Brown, 1923.

Bülow, Prince Bernard von. *The Memoirs of Prince von Bülow.* 4 vols. Boston: Little, Brown, 1931.

Bunyan, James and H. H. Fisher. *The Bolshevik Revolution.* Stanford, Calif.: Stanford University Press, 1934.

Caillaux, J. M. A. *Mes Memoirs.* 3 vols. Paris: Plon: 1942-1947.

Cambon, Paul. *Correspondence, 1870-1924.* 3 vols. Paris: Crasset, 1946.

Carley, Michael J. *Revolution and Intervention: The French Government and the Russian Civil War, 1917-1919.* Kingston and Montreal: McGill-Queens, 1983.

Chambrun, Charles. *Lettres à Marie, Pétersbourg-Pétrograd.* Paris: Plon, 1941.

Churchill, Winston. *World Crisis.* 3 vols. New York: Scribner's, 1927.

————. *The Great War.* 3 vols. London: Newnes, Ltd., 1933-1934.

Clark, Rev. Andrew. *Echoes of the Great War: The Diary of the Reverend Andrew Clark, 1914-1919.* Oxford: Oxford University Press, 1985.

Clemenceau, Georges. *Grandeur and Misery of Victory.* New York: Harcourt, Brace, 1930.

Cockfield, Jamie H., "The Russian Expeditionary Force in France, 1916-1918," *The Modern Encyclopedia of Russian and Soviet History* (Gulf Breeze, Fla.: Academic International Press, 1983), 32: 193-194.

Crisp, Olga, "Some Problems of French Investment in Russian Joint Stock Companies, 1891-1914," *Slavonic and East European Review,* 35 (1956): 226 ff.

Danilov, Youri. *La Russie dans la Guerre Mondiale, 1914-1917.* Paris: Payot, 1927.

————. *Russkie otriady na frantsuzskom i makedon-skom frontakh, 1916-1918.* Paris: Soiuz ofitserov uchastnikov voiny no frantsuzskom fronte, 1933.

Davats, V. Kh., and L'vov, N. N. *Russkaia armiia na chuzhbine.* Belgrad: Russkoe izdatel'stvo, 1928.

Denikin (Denikine), Anton. *The Career of a Tsarist Officer: Memoirs, 1872-1916.* Minneapolis: University of Minnesota, 1975.

————. *The White Army.* Tr. Catherine Zvegintsov. Gulf Breeze, Fla.: Academic International Press, 1973.

Derenkovsky, G. M. "Vosstanie russkikh soldat vo Frantsii v 1917 g.," *Istoricheskie zapiski,* 38 (1951), 71-103.

Deutscher, Isaac. *The Prophet Armed: Trotsky, 1878-1921.* New York: Oxford University Press, 1954.

Dolgorouki, Princess Stephanie. *Russia Before the Crash.* Paris: Herbert Clarke, 1926.

Edmunds, Sir James. *A Short History of World War I.* London: Oxford, 1951.

Ehrenburg, Ilya. *Lik voiny.* Sofia: Rossiisko-bolgarskoe knigoizdatel'stvo, 1920.

———. *People and Life, 1891-1921.* Tr. by Anna Bostock and Yvonne Kapp. New York: Knopf, 1962.

Elliott, Mark R. *Pawns of Yalta.* Urbana: University of Illinois Press, 1982.

Emets, V. A. "O roli russkoi armii v pervyi period mirovoi voiny, 1914-1918 gg.," *Istoricheskie zapiski,* 77 (1965): 57-84.

———. "Petrogradskaia konferentsiia 1917 g. i Frantsiia," *Istoricheskie zapiski,* 83 (1969), 23-37.

Ezhegodnik gazety rech': 1915. Petrograd, 1916.

Falkenhayn, Erich von. *General Headquarters, 1914-1916, and its Critical Decisions.* London: Hutchinson, 1919.

Falls, Cyril B. *The Great War.* New York: Putnam, 1957.

Ferro, Marc. "Le Soldat russe en 1917," *Annales Économies Socités Civilisations* (Paris: Armand Colin, 1971), 14-39.

Ferry, A. *Carnets Secrets, 1914-1918.* Paris: Grasset, 1957.

Fischer, Fritz. *Germany's Aims in the First World War.* New York: Norton, 1967.

Fleming, Peter. *The Fate of Admiral Kolchak.* London: Rupert Hart-Davis, 1963.

Foch, Ferdinand. *The Memoirs of Marshal Foch.* Tr. Col. T. Bentley Mott. Garden City, N. Y.: Doubleday, Doran, 1931.

Gaponenko, L. S., ed. *Revoliutsionnoe dvizhenie v russkoi armii (27 fevral'-24 oktiabria 1917 goda).* Moscow: Izd. "Nauka," 1968.

Gilbert, Martin. *The First World War.* New York: Henry Holt, 1994.

Girault, Rene. *Emprunts russes et investments français en Russie, 1887-1914.* Paris: A. Colin, 1973.

Gleason, William. *Alexander Guchkov and the End of the Russian Empire.* Philadelphia: American Philosophical Society, 1983.

Golder, Frank, ed. *Documents of Russian History, 1914-1917.* Glouchester, Mass.: Peter Smith, 1964.

Golovin, Nikolai N. *The Russian Army in the World War.* New Haven, Conn.: Yale University Press, 1931.

Goulévich, Général de. *Le Rôle de la Russie dans la Guerre Mondiale.* Paris: Revue Hebdomadaire, 1934.

Grondis, L. H. *La Guerre en Russie et en Sibérie.* Paris, 1926.

Gukovskii, A. I. *Frantsuzskaia interventsiia na iuge Rossii, 1918-1919.* Moscow: Gos. Izd., 1925.

Gurko, Gen. V. *War and Revolution in Russia, 1914-1917.* New York: Macmillan, 1919.

Haig, Sir Douglas. *Sir Douglas Haig's Despatches (December 1915 - April 1919).* Ed. Lt. Col. J. H. Boraston. London: Dent, 1919.

Hanbury-Williams, Sir John. *Nicholas II as I Knew Him.* London: Humphries, 1922.

Harbord, Maj. Gen. James. *Leaves from a War Diary.* New York: Dodd, Mead, 1925.

Hardinge of Penhurst. *Old Diplomacy: The Reminiscences of Lord Hardinge of Penhurst.* London: J. Murray, 1947.

Herbillon, E. *Le Général Alfred Micheler. Souvenirs d'un officier de liaison pendant la guerre mondiale.* Paris: Tallandier, 1930.

Hindenburg, Paul. *Aus meinem Leben.* Leipzig: Herzel, 1920.

———. *Out of My Life.* New York: Cassell, 1920.

Hoffmann, Major-General Max. *War Diaries and Other Papers.* 2 vols. Tr. Eric Sutton. London: Martin Secker, 1929.

———. *The War of Lost Opportunities.* New York: International Publishers, 1925.

Hoover Institution. War Library Publications. *The Testimony of Kolchak and Other Siberian Materials.* Stanford, Calif.: Stanford University Press, 1935.

Horne, Alistair. *Voices of the Great War.* New York: Doubleday, 1986.

Huntington, William Chapin. *The Homesick Millions: Russia-out-of-Russia.* Boston: Stratford Co., 1933.

Ignat'ev, A. A. *A Subaltern in Old Russia.* Tr. Ivor Montagu. London: Hutchinson, 1944.

———. *50 let v stroiu.* Moscow: Gos. Izd. Khud. lit., 1948.

Institut Marksa-Engel'sa-Lenina pri TsK VKP(b). V. I. Lenin. *Polnoe Sobranie Sochineniia.* Moscow: Gos. Izd. Polit. Lit., 1941-1960.

Ioffe, A. E. *Russko-frantsuzskie otnoshenie v 1917 g.* Moscow: Gos. Izd. polit. lit., 1958.

Izvolsky, Helene. *No Time to Grieve.* Philadelphia: Winchell, 1974.

Janin, Pierre. *Ma Mission en Sibérie, 1918-1920.* Paris: Payot, 1933.

Joffe, Marshal Joseph Jacques. *Mémoires du Maréchal Joffre (1910-1917).* 2 vols. Paris: Plon, 1932.

———. *The Personal Memoirs of Joffre.* 2 vols. Tr. Col. T. Bentley Mott. New York and London: Harper Bros., 1932.

"K prebyvaniiu russkikh voisk vo Frantsii v 1917 g.," *Krasnyi arkhiv,* 101 (1940), 228-235.

Khazov, A. "Russkii ekspeditionnyi korpus vo Frantsii," *Kadetskaia pereklichka,* no. 46 (April 1989), 65-80.

Kenez, Peter. *Civil War in South Russia, 1919-1920.* Berkeley: University of California Press, 1977.

Kerensky, Alexander. *Russia and History's Turning Point.* New York: Duell, Sloan and Pearce, 1965.

Khrushchev, Nikita. *Khrushchev Remembers.* Ed. Strobe Talbot. Boston: Little, Brown, 1970.

Khasov, M. "Russkii legion chesti," no. 46, *Kadetskaia pereklichka,* no. 46 (April 1989), 79-96.

Knox, A. W. F. *With the Russian Army, 1914-1917.* 2 vols. London: Hutchinson, 1921.

Kohn, Stanislas, and Meyendorff, Baron Alexander. *The Cost of the War to Russia.* New Haven, Conn.: Yale University Press, 1932.

Kozlov, A. *Prodannye za snariady.* Leningrad: Gos. Izdat., 1931.

Lasies, Joseph. *La Tragédie sibérienne.* Paris: L'Édition Française illustrée, 1920.

Lazarevski, Vladimir, ed. *Archives Secrètes de l'empereur Nicholas II.* Paris: Payot, 1928.

Lenin, V. I. *Lenin o voine, armii i voennoi nauke: sbornik.* 2 vols. Moscow: Gos. Izdat., 1952.

Leuchtenberg, N. "La Débacle de l'armée russes en 1917," *Revue de Paris,* 28, pt. 3 (June 15, 1921), 697-710.

Liddell Hart, Capt. B. H. *The Real War, 1914-1918.* Boston: Little, Brown, 1930.

———. *Reputations Ten Years After.* Freeport, N. Y.: Books for Libraries Press, 1968.

Lincoln, W. Bruce. *Passage Through Armageddon.* New York: Simon and Schuster, 1986.

Lissovsky, Yuri. "Lager Lia-Kurtin," *Arkhiv russkoi revoliutsii,* 17 (1926), 256-279.

Lloyd George, David. *War Memoirs.* 6 vols. London: Nicholson, 1933-36

———. *The Truth About the Peace Treaties.* 2 vols. Boston: Little, Brown, 1938.

Lobanov-Rostovsky, Prince A. *The Grinding Mill: Reminiscences of War and Revolution in Russia, 1913-1920.* New York: Macmillan, 1935.

Ludendorff, Eric von. *Ludendorff's Own Story.* 2 vols. New York: Harper, 1919.

————. *Meine Kriegserinnerungen, 1914-1918.* Berlin: Mittler, 1919.

————. *Concise Ludendorff Memoirs, 1914-1918.* London: Hutchinson, 1933.

Lukomskii, Aleksandr. *Memoirs of the Russian Revolution.* 2 vols. London: Unwin, 1922.

————. *Vospominaniia.* Berlin: Kirkhner, 1922.

Lyton, Neville. *The Press and the General Staff.* London: Collins, 1921.

Malinovsky, Rodion. *Soldaty Rossii.* Moscow: Volnizdat, 1978.

Meriwether, Lee. *The War Diary of a Diplomat.* New York: Dodd, Mead, 1919.

Miliukov, Paul. *Political Memoirs, 1905-1917.* Ann Arbor: University of Michigan Press, 1967.

Ministerstvo inostrannykh del' SSSR. *Dokumenty vneshnei politiki SSSR.* Moscow: Gos. Izd. polit. lit., 1957.

The Modern Encyclopedia of Russian and Soviet History. Ed. by Joseph L. Wieczynski. Gulf Breeze, Fla.: Academic International Press, 1976- .

Moltke, Helmut von. *Erinnerungen, Briefe, Dokumente.* Stuttgart: Kommende Tag A.-G. Verlag, 1922.

Mordacq, J. J. H. *Le Ministère Clemenceau.* 4 vols. Paris: Plon, 1933.

Morris, L. P. "The Russians, the Allies, and the War, February-July, 1917," *Slavonic and East European Review*, 50, no. 118 (1972), 29-49.

Musgrave, George Clarke. *Under Four Flags for France.* New York: Appleton, 1918.

Na chuzhbin; sbornik proizvedenii russkikh voinov. 1928 (?): n.p.

Nabokov, Constantin. *The Ordeal of a Diplomat.* London: Duckworth, 1921.

Neilson, Keith. *Strategy and Supply; the Anglo-Russian Alliance, 1914-1917.* London: Allen and Unwin, 1984.

Neklyudov, Anatoli V. *Diplomatic Reminiscences before and During the World War, 1911-1917.* Tr. Alexandra Paget. London: Murray, 1920.

The New York Times Current History. The European War. 20 vols. New York: Times Co., 1914-1920.

The Nicky-Sunny Letters; Correspondence of the Tsar and Tsaritsa, 1914-1917. Hattiesburg, Miss.: Academic International Press, 1970.

Niessel, Albert. *Le Triomphe des Bolcheviques et la paix de Brest-Litovsk: Souvenirs, 1917-1918.* Paris: Plon, 1939.

Noulens, Joseph. *Mon Ambassade en Russie Soviétique.* 2 vols. Paris: Plon, 1933.

Obey, André. "Comrades Rouski," *Revue de Paris*, 6 (November-December,1920), 527-554.

Oktiabr' na fronte: vospominaniia. Moscow: Voennoe izd. Min. Oborony SSSR, 1967.

Oktiabria rubeyon. Moscow: Éditions d'État, 1929.

Oktiabr' za rubezhom; sbornik vospominaniia. Ed. M. N. Pokrovsky. Moscow, 1924.

Ostrovsky, Erika. *Eye of Dawn: The Rise and Fall of Mata Hari.* New York: Dorset Press, 1978.

Packard, Laurence. "Russia and the Dual Alliance," *American Historical Review*, 25 (1920), 391-410.

Painlevé, Paul. *Comment J'ai nommé Foch et Pétain.* Paris: Alcan, 1924.

————. *La Vérité sur l'offensive du 16 avril 1917.* Paris: Renaissance, 1919.

Paléologue, Maurice. *An Ambassador's Memoirs.* Tr. F. A. Holt. 3 vols. New York: Doran, 1924-1925.

————. *La Russie des tsars pendant la Grande Guerre.* 3 vols. Paris: Plon-Nourrit, 1921-1922.

Palmer, Alan. *The Gardeners of Salonika.* New York: Simon and Schuster, 1965.

Pares, Bernard. *The Fall of the Russian Monarchy.* London: Cape, 1939.

Pattyn, Frank. *La Russie en Guerre. Histories des unités russes sur le front occidental, 1914-1917*. Brussels: University of Brussels, 1979.

Peake, Thomas R. "The Impact of the Russian Revolutions upon French Attitudes and Policies toward Russia," Unpublished Ph.D. Dissertation, University of North Carolina, 1974.

Pedroncini, Guy. *Les Mutineries de 1917*. Paris: Presses universitaires de France, 1967.

———. *1917: Les Mutineries de l'armée française*. Paris: Julliard, 1968.

Pershing, J. J. *My Experiences in the World War*. 2 vols. New York: Stokes, 1931.

Persky, Serge. *De Nicholas II à Lenine*. Paris: Payot, 1919.

Pétain, Maréchal Henri. *Une Crise morale de la nation en guerre, 16 avril-23 octobre 1917*. Paris: Nouvelles Éditions latines, 1966.

de Pierrefeu, Jean. *French Headquarters, 1915-1918*. Tr. C. J. C. Street. London: Geoffrey Bles, 1924.

Pignaud, Albert. "La Mission de M. Paul Doumer en Russie," *Revue des deux mondes*, 9 (1932), 865-873.

Poincaré, Raymond. *Messages, Discours, Allocutions, Lettres et Télégrammes de M. Raymond Poincaré*. 2 vols. Paris: Blond and Gay, 1919.

———. *The Memoirs of Raymond Poincaré*. Tr. Sir George Arthur. London: Heinemann, 1926.

———. *Au Service de la France*. 11 vols. Paris: Plon-Nourrit, 1926-1974.

Poitevin, Pierre. *Une Bataille au centre de la France*. Limoges: Impr. Soc. des Journaux et Publ. du Centre, 1934.

———. *La Mutinerie de la Courtine*. Paris: Payot, 1938.

Ratinaud, Jean. *1917 ou la Tragédie d'avril*. Paris: Arthème Fayard, 1960.

Reed, John. *Ten Days that Shook the World*. New York: Modern Library, 1935.

Rémond, Adrien. "Quelques souvenirs de deux missions en Russie, 1916-1917," *Soc. Nivernaise des lettres, sciences et arts. Bull.*, 27 (1930), 525-575.

Renouvin, Pierre. "Opinion publique et la guerre en 1917," *Revue d'histoire moderne et contemporaine*, 15 (January-March, 1968), 4-23.

Ribot, Alexandre. *Lettres à un ami*. Paris: Bossard, 1924.

———. *Letters to a Friend: Recollections of my political life*. London: Hutchinson, 1926.

———. *Journal d'Alexandre Ribot et correspondances inédites, 1914-1922*. Paris: Plon, 1936.

Rivet, Charles. *The Last of the Romanofs*. New York: Dutton, 1918.

Roberts, Carl Eric Bechhofer. *In Denikin's Russia*. New York: Arno, 1971.

Robertson, William Robert. *Soldiers and Statesmen, 1914-1918*. London: Cassell, 1926.

Robien, Louis de. *The Diary of a Diplomat in Russia*. New York: Praeger, 1970.

Rodzianko, Mikhail. "Gosudarstvennaia duma," *Arkhiv russkoi revoliutsii*, 6 (1921), 5-80.

———. *The Reign of Rasputin: An Empire's Collapse*. London: Philpot, 1927.

Rodzianko, P. *Tattered Banners: An autobiography*. London: Seeley Service, 1939.

Rupprecht, Kronprinz von Bayern. *Mein Kriegstagebuch*. 3 vols. Munich: Deutscher National Verlag, 1919.

Russia. Gosudarstvennaia duma. *Russia and Her Allies*. London: Burrup, Mathieson and Sprague, 1917.

Russie. Ministerstvo inostrannykh del'. *Documents diplomatiques secrets russes, 1914-1917*. Tr. J. Polonsky. Paris: Payot, 1928.

"Russkaia parlamentskaia delegatsiia za granitsei v 1916 g.," *Krasnyi arkhiv*, 58 (1933), 3-23.

"Russkie soldaty na zapadnom fronte v mirovuiu voiny," *Krasnyi arkhiv*, 44 (1930-31), 152-161.

Russkie soldaty vo Frantsii. Moscow: Gos izd., 1919.

"Russians in France," *Literary Digest,* 52 (June 3, 1916), 1623-1624.

Rutherford, Ward. *The Ally: The Russian Army in World War I.* London: Gorden Cremonesi, 1977.

Rychlinski, Wladimir. "Souvenirs d'un officier du corps expéditionaire russe en France," *Revue historique de l'Armée,* no. 1 (1965), 110-125.

Sadoul, Jacques. *Notes sur la Révolution Bolchévique.* Paris: Éditions de la sirène, 1920.

Sazonov, Sergei. *Fateful Years, 1909-1916.* London: J. Cape, 1928.

Shliapnikov, A. C., ed. *Les Alliés contre la Russie, avant, pendant et après la guerre mondiale.* Paris: Delpeuct, 1926.

Schultz, Ernest. *La Vie des Soldats russes en France sur le front et à l'intérieur, 1916-1918.* Paris(?): 1918 (?).

Sharp, William Graves. *The War Memoirs of William Graves Sharp.* London: Constable, 1931.

Sidorov, A. L. "Otnosheniia Rossii s soiuznikami i inostrannye postavki vo vremia pervoi mirovoi voiny," *Istoricheskie Zapiski,* 15 (1945), 128-179.

———. *Finansovoe polozhenie Rossii v gody pervoi mirovoi voiny 1914-1917 gg.* Moscow: Nauka, 1960.

———. *Revoliutsionnoe dvizhenie v armii i na flote v gody pervoi mirovoi voiny; sbornik dokumentov.* Moscow: Nauka, 1966.

Sinanoglou, Ioannia. "France Looks Eastward: Perspectives and Policies in Russia, 1914-1918." Unpublished Ph.D. Diss., Columbia University, 1974.

Smith, C. J. *The Russian Struggle for Power, 1914-1917.* New York: American Philosophical Society, 1956.

Smith, Leonard V. *Between Mutiny and Obedience: The Case of the French Fifth Infantry Division during World War I.* Princeton, N. J.: Princeton University Press, 1994.

Solzhenitsyn, Alexander. *The Gulag Archipelago.* New York: Harper and Row, 1974.

Spirin, L. M., ed. *Razgrom Kolchaka: vospominaniia.* Moscow: Voen. Izd. Min. Obor. SSSR, 1969.

Steed, H. Wickham. *Through Thirty Years, 1892-1952.* Garden City, N. Y.: Doubleday, Page, 1925.

Stewart, George. *The White Armies of Russia: A Chronicle of Counter-revolution and Allied Intervention.* New York: Russell and Russell, 1933.

Stone, Norman. *The Eastern Front, 1914-1917.* New York: Scribner's, 1975.

Sun Tzu. *The Art of War.* New York: Delacorte Press, 1983.

Thompson, John M. *Russia, Bolshevism and the Versailles Peace.* Princeton: Princeton University Press, 1966.

The Times History of the War. 21 vols. London: The Times, 1914-1920.

Tolstoy, Leo. *Christianity and Patriotism.* London: J. Cape, 1922.

Trotsky, Leon. *My Life.* New York: Scribner's, 1930.

———. *The History of the Russian Revolution.* 3 vols. in one. New York: Simon and Schuster, 1937.

Tuchman, Barbara. *A Distant Mirror.* New York: Knopf, 1978.

Tyrkova-Williams, Ariadne. *Cheerful Giver: The Life of Harold Williams.* London: Peter Davies, 1935.

Valentinov, N. "Russkie voiska vo Frantsii i Salonikakh," *Voenno-istoricheskii Sbornik,* 4 (1920), 3-22.

Vasiliev, V., "Ruskii legion chesti," *Chasovoi,* no. 629 (January-February, 1981), 18-22.

Vavilov, Artur. *Zapiski soldata Vavilova.* Moscow: Gos. Izdat., 1927.

Viviani, René. *As We See It*. Tr. Thomas Ybarra. New York: Harper, 1923.

"Vosstanie russkikh soldat vo Frantsii," *Krasnyi arkhiv*, 99 (1939-1940), 52-71.

Vremennoe pravitel'stvo. Chrezvychainaia sledstvennaia komissia. *Padenie tsarskogo rezhima*. 7 vols. Leningrad and Moscow: Gosizdat, 1924-1927.

Wade, R. A. "Argonauts of Peace: The Soviet Delegation to Western Europe in the Summer of 1917," *Slavic Review*, 27, no. 3 (1967), 451-467.

Warth, Robert. *The Allies and the Russian Revolution*. Durham, N. C.: Duke University Press, 1954.

Watt, Richard. *Dare Call It Treason*. New York: Simon and Schuster, 1963.

Webster, Donovan, "The Soldiers Moved On. The War Moved On. The bombs Stayed," *Smithsonian*, 24, no. 11 (February, 1994), 26-37.

Weygand, Maxime. *Recall to Service: The Memoirs of General Maxime Weygand*. London: Heinemann, 1952.

Wheeler-Bennet, John. *Brest-Litovsk, the Forgotten Peace*. New York: MacMillan, 1938.

Wildman, Allen. *The End of the Russian Army*. Princeton, N. J.: Princeton University Press, 1980.

Williams, John. *Mutiny 1917*. London: Heinemann, 1962.

Wilton, Robert. *Russia's Agony*. New York: Dutton, 1919.

Wrangel, General Peter. *The Memoirs of General Wrangel*. London: Duffield, 1930.

————. *Always with Honor* New York: Speller, 1963.

Yakhontov, Victor. *Over the Divide*. New York: Coward-McCann, 1939.

Zaionchkovskii, A. M. *Kampaniia 1917 g.* Moscow: Gos. voen. izd., 1923.

Zeman, Z. A. B. *A Diplomatic History of the First World War*. London: Weidenfeld and Nicolsen, 1971.

NEWSPAPERS

Le Bonnet Rouge

Le Canard Enchaîné

Derevenskaia pravda

Echo de Paris

Figaro

L'Homme Enchaîné

Izvestiia

Journal de Pétrograd

Libre Parole

Le Matin

New York Times

Pravda

Le Temps

The Times (London)

Index